TRAVELER

florence
& tuscany

NATIONAL GEOGRAPHIC

TRAVELER

florence & tuscany

by Tim Jepson
photography by Tino Soriano

National Geographic
Washington, D.C.

CONTENTS

**Pages 2–3: The picture of young love is immortalized against the timeless
background of the Ponte Vecchio.
Opposite: A typical Tuscan farmhouse and cypress trees near Pienza in the Val d'Orcia**

TRAVELING WITH EYES OPEN

Alert travelers go with a purpose and leave with a benefit. If you travel responsibly, you can help support wildlife conservation, historic preservation, and cultural enrichment in the places you visit. You can enrich your own travel experience as well.

To be a geo-savvy traveler:

- Recognize that your presence has an impact on the places you visit.

- Spend your time and money in ways that sustain local character. (Besides, it's more interesting that way.)

- Value the destination's natural and cultural heritage.

- Respect the local customs and traditions.

- Express appreciation to local people about things you find interesting and unique to the place: its nature and scenery, music and food, historic villages and buildings.

- Vote with your wallet: Support the people who support the place, patronizing businesses that make an effort to celebrate and protect what's special there. Seek out local shops, restaurants, and inns. Use tour operators who love their home—who love taking care of it and showing it off. Avoid businesses that detract from the character of the place.

- Enrich yourself, taking home memories and stories to tell, knowing that you have contributed to the preservation and enhancement of the destination.

That is the type of travel now called geotourism, defined as "tourism that sustains or enhances the geographical character of a place—its environment, culture, aesthetics, heritage, and the well-being of its residents." To learn more, visit National Geographic's Center for Sustainable Destinations at *nationalgeographic.com/travel/sustainable.*

TRAVELER

florence
& tuscany

ABOUT THE AUTHOR & THE PHOTOGRAPHER

Tim Jepson has been a passionate and lifelong devotee of Italy, and of Florence and Tuscany in particular. Since graduating from Oxford, he has spent long periods of time living and traveling in city and region alike, including an idyllic summer in a vine-shaded house outside the little Tuscan town of Montalcino. Over the years he has written some 15 books on Italy, including several on various aspects of Tuscany, as well as numerous articles for the *Daily Telegraph, Vogue, Condé Nast Traveler,* and other publications. He wrote the following guides in the National Geographic Traveler series: Italy, Naples & Southern Italy, Piedmont & Northwest Italy, and Sicily. Jepson is a National Geographic Expeditions expert on Italy.

Now based in London, Jepson continues to visit Tuscany regularly, and as a keen hiker and outdoor enthusiast, he takes a particular interest in the region's sublime countryside. He also revels in Florence and Tuscany's more sedentary pleasures—the food, wine, art, and culture. Jepson has also worked on Italian programs for the BBC and commercial television.

Born and raised in Barcelona, Spain, **Tino Soriano** divides his work between photojournalism and travel photography. He has received a First Prize from the World Press Photo Foundation as well as awards from UNESCO, Fujifilm, and FotoPres. In addition to Italy, since 1988 Soriano has photographed in Spain (Catalonia, Andalucia, Galicia), France, Portugal, Scotland, and South Africa on assignments for *National Geographic* magazine. His work has also appeared in *Geo, Merian, Der Spiegel, Paris Match, La Vanguardia,* and *El País.* Soriano has also written *El Futuro Existe* (a story about children with cancer), *Travel Photography, Beats From a Hospital,* and *Dalí, 1904–2004.* He has also photographed for the following guides in the National Geographic Traveler series: Portugal, Sicily, and Madrid.

Charting Your Trip

No other region—and not too many countries—have Tuscany's perfect and immeasurably rich combination of culture, food, fashion, wine, medieval villages, historic towns, art-filled cities, and sublime pastoral countryside. A traveler could happily spend weeks in its main city of Florence. So planning your vacation is an essential part of your trip to Tuscany.

How to Visit & Get Around

Exploring Florence and Tuscany presents two distinct dilemmas: First, there is an enormous amount to see and do; second, a car offers the most freedom to explore Tuscany but is a liability in Florence and Siena, where vehicle access to the city centers is prohibited.

If you want to avoid renting a car, then the excellent rail network serves many key centers, notably Siena, Pisa, Lucca, Cortona, Arezzo, Volterra, and Pistoia, and also offers scenic journeys through some of the region's prettiest countryside. A combination of train and bus will take you to San Gimignano, Pienza, and Montepulciano, among other smaller towns. To see the best of the scenery, however, you will need a car, but perhaps only after you have visited the main cities.

Your choice of airport is a third consideration. Most European carriers and an increasing number of flights from North America serve Pisa's airport, an hour from Florence and well placed for seeing Lucca and Pisa at the beginning or end of a trip. However, Rome's Fiumicino (Leonardo da Vinci) airport has far more choice of intercontinental flights and is better placed, especially on a short trip, if you want to conclude a tour in the south of Tuscany, the most beautiful part of the region.

If You Have a Week

For a taste of the best of Florence and Tuscany in a single week, devote three days to Florence, a day each to Siena and San Gimignano, and two days to the south of the region, assuming your flight home is from Rome.

For ease of sightseeing in Florence, choose a hotel such as the Brunelleschi or Casci at the heart of the city—everything is within walking distance—and if you want to see the most famous works of art, then be certain to prebook

The Tower of Pisa leans into its battle against gravity and time.

timed tickets before you leave to avoid long lines: The Uffizi, Accademia (for Michelangelo's "David"), and Cappelle Medicee, among others, offer this service (see sidebar p. 98).

On **Day 1** see the Duomo and baptistery and climb the Campanile for an overview of the city. See the "David" and nearby Museo dell'Opera del Duomo. Walk past Orsanmichele to Piazza della Signoria, then take in the sights in the east of the city, notably the Bargello museum and Santa Croce.

Devote **Day 2** to the Uffizi and possibly the Palazzo Vecchio, then head west via the Cappelle Medicee to Mercato Centrale, San Lorenzo church and market, and, if time permits, Palazzo Medici-Riccardi. The churches of Santa Maria Novella and Santa Trìnita, the upscale stores on Via de' Tornabuoni, and the quaint streets off Via Porta Rossa are the main targets for the afternoon.

On **Day 3** cross the Ponte Vecchio to the Oltrarno district to see the Palazzo Pitti and Cappella Brancacci. Take a break from the art with a stroll in the Giardino di Boboli and/or by walking to San Miniato al Monte.

Rise early and catch a train on **Day 4** to Siena (90 min.). Take a taxi from the station to your hotel and stow your luggage. Then spend the day exploring the city.

On **Day 5** take a taxi to pick up a rental car and drive (or take a bus) the 25 miles (40 km) to San Gimignano, being sure to visit Monteriggioni and Colle di Val d'Elsa en route. Stay overnight in San Gimignano and drive south to Pienza (58 miles/93 km), devoting **Days 6 and 7** to exploring Pienza itself (your best base for the region), Montalcino (22 miles/35 km from Pienza), and Montepulciano (7.5 miles/12 km from Pienza). This will allow you plenty of time to fully appreciate the abbeys, small villages, and sublime countryside of this area of southern Tuscany.

NOT TO BE MISSED:

FLORENCE:

The Duomo (cathedral) of Santa Maria del Fiore and the Battistero (baptistery) 58–71

The view of the city from the Campanile (bell tower) 74–75

The Palazzo Vecchio 94–95

Visiting the ancient churches of Santa Croce and Santa Maria Novella 108–114, 150–155

The sculptures of Michelangelo in the Cappelle Medicee and Galleria dell'Accademia 128–131, 138–142

A walk across the magical Ponte Vecchio 162–163

TUSCANY:

Siena's Palio pageant 200–201

The medieval towers of San Gimignano 230

Wine tasting in Chianti 238

Pisa's Campo dei Miracoli 244–247, 250–251

A day trip to Lucca 252–260

Online Visitor Information

Start with the Italian State Tourist Board ENIT *(enit.it* or *italiantourism.com)* and the official regional Tuscan site *(turismo.into scana.it/en).* Florence's official tourism site is *firenzeturismo.it.* For Siena and its surroundings visit *terresiena.it.* Use search terms such as *"turismo," "ufficio informazioni," "pro loco"* (a small visitor center), and *"comune"* (city hall) plus a town name in researching smaller areas. For parks and reserves, visit *parks.it;* for museums, *musei online.info;* and for trains, *trenitalia.com.*

When to Visit

Weather-wise, the best periods are late April to early June and mid-September to the end of October. July and August are too hot to explore cities comfortably, but ideal for a sedentary villa holiday. Beach resorts are busiest in these months. Florence is busy with visitors year-round. The quietest periods are November (when it can be rainy) and January and February (often cold, but clear). In Tuscany, the countryside is at its most verdant in spring (late April and May). In September and early fall, the weather is more reliable, but the landscapes will have been burned brown by the summer sun.

If You Have More Time

Two weeks in Tuscany allow you to expand the Florentine component of your trip and explore different parts of the region depending on your interests—Chianti for wine, for example, the Alpi Apuane above Lucca for hiking, or the south around Sovana for Etruscan culture.

Days 1 to 5 can be spent in Florence adding walks and sights to the itinerary above such as the Museo di San Marco, Museo Galileo–Museo di Storia della Scienza, Palazzo Davanzati, and Museo Bardini, and allocating one day to a round-trip to Lucca by train. Alternatively stay overnight and rent a car in Lucca to see Pisa and Volterra and the generally less visited northwest of the region.

Otherwise spend **Days 6 and 7** in Siena, then rent a car to see San Gimignano and Colle di Val d'Elsa on **Day 8.** Drive east and spend **Day 9** touring Chianti. You might also spend **Day 10** here in a rural hotel such as the Badia a Coltibuono (25 miles/45 km from Siena) or Castello Di Gargonza (see Travelwise pp. 315 & 318) for a quiet day. Drive farther east to visit Arezzo, but spend the night of **Day 11** in or around nearby Cortona, a more amenable town. Visit Montepulciano en route to Pienza or Montalcino for **Days 12 and 13:** Either town makes a charming base for exploring the villages, abbeys, and landscapes of this part of southern Tuscany.

Allocate your remaining day depending on your interests: more time in Florence, say, or in Lucca, or a day by the sea or the pool of a peaceful rural hotel.

Daily Life: A Different Rhythm

Despite the inevitable inroads made by modernity and globalization, Tuscany continues to draw strength from, and retain its links to, the past. Your visit to small towns and the countryside is often an opportunity to leave modern life behind and adjust to a slower, more sensual rhythm.

Local Logistics

Most stores, banks, post offices, churches, visitor centers, and museums in Italy close for lunch (typically from 1 p.m. to 3 p.m.), opening again until 7:30 p.m. or 8 p.m. All-day opening *(orario continuato)* is much more common in Florence and Siena, though many museums and most churches continue to have closing periods.

Bars are more like cafés than their U.S. or U.K. counterparts—pay for what you want first at the cash desk *(cassa)* and take your chit *(scontrino)* to the bar to place your order. You pay more for waiter table service. Use café restrooms *(il bagno)* as public facilities are scarce. Tipping is less prevalent than in the United States—leave around 10–12 percent in restaurants, unless service *(servizio)* is included on the check *(il conto)*.

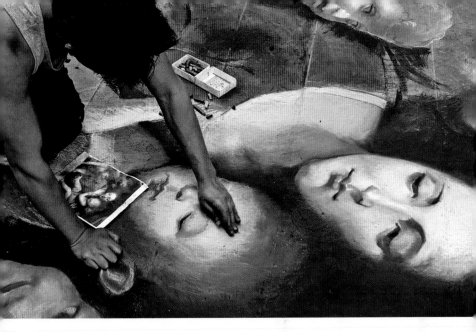

Artists commonly show off their talent on the streets around Florence's San Lorenzo.

However, this is far from being the case in Florence and, to a slightly lesser extent, in Siena, where visitors throng the streets and sights virtually year-round. Come between November and February and you may find fewer people, but at other times be prepared to share the city with multitudes of sightseers, especially in April and other supposedly "off-season" months, which are popular with large school parties.

As part of planning for your trip, therefore, you should make advance reservations whenever possible, to avoid disappointment and frustration. For example, city-center restaurants in all price brackets fill up quickly, so always try to reserve a table if you have a particular place in mind.

In rural areas of Tuscany, however, your experience is likely to be very different. City stores and businesses may now work through the day, but in the countryside and the smaller centers, the siesta, or post-lunch shutdown, is still a mainstay of the afternoon: Most churches, museums, and stores close (see sidebar opposite), with life returning to the drowsy, deserted streets about 4:30 in the afternoon. Soon after that it's time for another quintessential Italian ritual, the *passeggiata*, the early evening parade that sees a town's inhabitants, old and young, promenading along the main street, talking, flirting, courting, catching up, sipping an *aperitivo*, or simply enjoying cutting a *bella figura* (beautiful figure) for the admiration of onlookers. ■

Essential Etiquette

Florentines tend to dress well and to dress conservatively: Smart-casual (no need for jacket or tie) is the code for all but the finest restaurants. Cover your arms, shoulders, and knees when visiting churches and do not visit during services. Italians can be quite assertive in lines—do not necessarily expect "fairness." Most Tuscans speak some English, but "please" is *per favore*, "thank you" is *grazie* (GRATZ–E–AY), and *prego* means "you're welcome." Say *mi scusi* for "excuse me" or "I'm sorry" but *permesso* when you want to pass someone. Do not use the informal *ciao* as a greeting or farewell but *buon giorno* (good day) or *buona sera* (good afternoon or evening).

History & Culture

A young drummer at the Siena Palio

Bustling Piazza del Duomo, Florence

Florence & Tuscany Today

Florence and Tuscany have such powerful artistic and historical associations that it's easy to forget their significant role in the much changed world of modern Italy. Florence is a major central Italian city, a cosmopolitan and wealthy metropolis with considerable contemporary élan, while Tuscany is a region whose social and cultural traditions still find a powerful voice despite the changing face of its towns and countryside.

Locals practice the fine Italian art of conversation on a break from shopping on the streets around Piazza del Duomo, Florence.

Local Loyalties

Florence is the capital of Tuscany, but never confuse Florentines with Tuscans. In fact, never talk about Tuscans at all, except in the loosest sense, for most Tuscans are far more loyal to their local communities than to their region, never mind their regional capital. Italians generally retain prejudices that reflect their fractured history, and Tuscans are no exception. The Florentines and Sienese have been divided for centuries; so, too, the citizens of Lucca and Pisa, and the inhabitants of Arezzo and Cortona. This powerful sense of self-worth continues right down to the smallest village. The Italian word for it is *campanilismo*—the idea that your loyalties and worldly concerns extend no farther than the reach of your bell tower, or *campanile*. Modern mass media have produced a degree of cultural homogenization, but the weight of history and tradition still hangs heavy.

At first glance, these narrow loyalties might seem a force

for reaction, an inward-looking approach that perpetuates division and stifles social and other progress. Tuscany's modern roots go back to the era of independent city-states, or *comuni*, and countless towns still jealously preserve symbols, buildings, and civic structures that reflect and recall past glories—towers, piazzas, statues, palaces, and imposing medieval walls. Tuscans literally inhabit their history. Yet it is Tuscany's skill to have incorporated its attachment to the past into a distinctive modern outlook, retaining the sense of belonging created by small town loyalties and a pride in the past that sustains a confidence in the present.

> **Florence is the capital of Tuscany, but never confuse Florentines with Tuscans.**

The Economy

The apparent conservatism and strong civic ties within communities also belie the considerable changes that have taken place in Tuscany since the end of World War II. In 1945 the region's economy was still predominantly agricultural, with a majority of workers little more than landless laborers or small-scale peasant farmers. Between 1951 and 1971 some 375,000 workers left the land, about 72 percent of the original agricultural workforce. Most moved into the myriad small businesses that provided—and continue to provide—the motor of an economic miracle that transformed Italy in less than a generation into one of the world's leading industrial powers. Today, a little more than 4 percent of the workforce labor on the land, compared with about 20 percent in commerce, 37 percent in industry, and around 39 percent in service and other public or private businesses.

The Tuscan countryside is far from dead, however, for all the decline in numbers of agricultural workers. Some 52 percent of the region's available land is still given over to agricultural use. In some cases this means traditional crops—the great wheat fields of the rolling hills south of Siena or the sweeping vineyards swathing the slopes of Chianti and elsewhere. In others it reflects a willingness to turn the countryside into an arm of the tourist industry; *agriturismo* (staying and often working on farms), for example, is booming. Elsewhere, new crops and European Union subsidies have been embraced enthusiastically with sunflowers, rapeseed, and flax, among others, adding new seasonal colors to Tuscany's pastoral summer palette. At the same time, a revolution in old industries, notably viticulture (wine producing), has seen an expansion of old markets, with Brunello di Montalcino wines and the so-called super Tuscan vintages revitalizing an industry once linked solely with the thin, acidic staples of Chianti and its close cousins (see pp. 270–271).

Although there is increasing pressure to relax planning restraints, the Tuscan propensity for preservation and conservatism—a pride in what the people have and what they had—has ensured that the countryside, one or two exceptions allowing, has remained largely undesecrated by wanton development or industrial-scale agricultural practices. To a large extent, you can still gaze over Tuscany's vines, cypresses, olives, and terraced hillsides—all shaped by human hands for more than 3,000 years—and see the same landscapes used to such sublime effect in the backgrounds of Renaissance paintings.

Landscapes

In the same way that Tuscany's towns and people display extraordinary diversity and individuality, so the region as a whole is a patchwork of different landscapes and diverse character. To many visitors, the region may appear no more than the

Vineyards close to San Gimignano await the seasonal sunshine of another vintage year.

Vital Statistics & Fascinating Facts

- Population of Tuscany: 3.7 million
- Land area: 8,878 square miles (22,994 sq km)
- Population of Florence: 377,000
- Florence's highest recorded temperature: 109.5°F (43.1°C)
- Florence's lowest recorded temperature: minus 9.7°F (-23.2°C)
- Visitors to Florence: more than ten million annually
- Tuscany's highest point: Monte Prado (6,739 feet/2,054 m)
- The modern Italian sport of soccer is a derivative of the ancient intervillage battle called *calcio* (see p. 21). Calcio Storico Fiorentino was a 16th-century form of football that originated in Piazza Santa Croce in Florence.
- Tuscany has seven UNESCO World Heritage sites: the historic centers of Florence, Pienza, Siena, and San Gimignano; Piazza del Duomo in Pisa; the Val d'Orcia; and the Medici Villas and Gardens.
- Official estimates suggest 275,000 foreign-born immigrants live in Tuscany.
- Tuscany is divided into ten administrative provinces.
- Tuscany has Italy's third largest area given over to wine production after the Sicily and Puglia regions: Annual production, of which 80 percent is red wine, is almost 60 million gallons (272,765,400 L).

European artistic center par excellence: And no wonder, for in this regard it stands out even in Italy, the world's richest repository of Renaissance art. Tuscany boasts more than 270 individual museums and galleries, more than any other Italian region.

In Florence Tuscany has a capital whose artistic credentials need no emphasizing, while Siena is widely acknowledged as Europe's most perfect medieval metropolis. At the other end of the spectrum, virtually every village, however small, has some artistic treasure—a Romanesque church, a faded fresco, a carved Madonna—that would be the envy of many European cities.

Yet Tuscany is also a region of major industries, as you'll see if you visit or pass through Prato, one of the world's leading producers of high-quality textiles; the chances are your "Made in Italy" clothes were made nearby. It's also a region of small and highly specialized industries, many of them based on natural resources and local skills that date back centuries: marble extraction around Massa and Carrara, furniture-making in Poggibonsi and fine glassware in Colle di Val d'Elsa, alabaster-working in Volterra, the fashioning of gold and jewelry in Arezzo. It is a region of major ports—notably Livorno, Italy's second largest—and myriad islands such as Elba, Capraia, Giglio, and Cerboli. It is also a region of beach resorts, particularly along the Versilian coast north of Pisa; plains (the Maremma in the southwest); spectacular mountains (the Alpi Apuane north of Lucca); extinct volcanoes (Monte Amiata); immense, ancient forests (the Casentino); wild, little-visited uplands (the Mugello, Pratomagno, and Lunigiana); and the sublime and timeless landscapes—notably Chianti's woods and vineyards and southern Tuscany's villa-topped hills—with which the region is most closely associated. But, above all, of course, Tuscany is the region of Florence.

Florence

In many ways, Florence, the Tuscan capital, epitomizes the region's contrasts between the old and the new; here the traveler can feel the tensions and interplay between social and cultural traditionalism, the demands made on a modern region

Florence, where art, style, and design are as vital today as they were in the Renaissance

by its obligations to its heritage, and the pressures exerted by many millions of visitors. Then, of course, there are the Florentines. Social stereotyping is a dangerous game, but there's no escaping the fact that the average Florentine is a breed apart.

Dante (see pp. 49 & 78–79), the great medieval Florentine poet, was in no doubt about his fellow citizens. They were *"gente avara, invidiosa e superba*—mean, envious, and proud")*, and a Renaissance proverb described them as perpetual complainers, possessed of sharp eyes and bad tongues. Pride and arrogance are still charges leveled at Florentines by other Italians, a people who have well-rehearsed—and generally unflattering—stereotypes for inhabitants of all their major cities and regions. Walking around the city, you may indeed detect a rather haughty grandeur in the sleek, well-dressed Florentines parading their urbane streets with an obvious degree of self-satisfaction. But then who can blame them? After all, this is the city that nurtured the Renaissance; produced the likes of Dante, Michelangelo, Galileo, Machiavelli, and Leonardo da Vinci; invented French cuisine (see p. 22); rediscovered perspective; gave birth to many of Europe's greatest artists; created the Western world's first chair of Greek; invented Italian as a literary language; created the basis of banking and thus capitalism; and invented opera, the piano, eyeglasses, and much more.

The past sits easily with modern Florentines, who still bask in its glory, confident that the qualities that stood the city in good stead for 2,000 years—genius, diligence, verve, flair, hard work, vision—are qualities that still pertain. Florentines are generally dignified and decorous; you would never confuse a Florentine, for example, with a boisterous Neapolitan. They are often cultured and civilized—another legacy of their illustrious past.

Fashion: If you begin to suspect that the Florentines' sense of self-satisfaction is misplaced, then look no further than the city's continued strengths in such areas as fashion, design, and craft for proof that at least some of the traditional virtues still flourish. Young and old alike are testimony to the importance of fashion, displaying their finery as if on some giant public catwalk. The notion of *bella figura,* of cutting a beautiful figure and not making a fool of yourself, is an important one in Florence. Even the cynical statesman Niccolò Machiavelli (1469–1527) was moved to observe that the Florentines' main preoccupations were to always appear splendid in apparel and obtain a crafty shrewdness in discourse.

Young people may dress informally, but their sneakers are invariably immaculate, their jeans quite spotless, and their polo shirts and sunglasses sport the requisite designer labels. Older Florentines tend to prefer subtle and more sober clothes, blending a tweedy English classicism with dashes of designer and Renaissance ostentation.

Milan may now have the fashion shows and big names, but Florence is not without its own stars, not least Gucci, whose empire was founded in the city three generations ago, and Emilio Pucci, whose dramatically dyed silks caused a sensation in the 1950s and whose designs have recently found a new place in the hearts of fashion cognoscenti. Florence is also the headquarters of the company founded by one of the most famous shoemakers, Naples-born Salvatore Ferragamo (see sidebar p. 157), who emigrated to the United States at 15 and proceeded to design shoes for the likes of Greta Garbo, Vivien Leigh, and Gloria Swanson. Today, the company still makes clothes, shoes, and accessories at its Florentine base.

The Crafts Tradition: Such items find a natural home in Florence, not least because of its powerful traditions of art and crafts and its many artisans' workshops. Street names across the city bear witness to the countless trades once practiced in them—Via della Spadai (Street of the Swordmakers), Via dei Fibbiai (Street of the Bucklemakers), or Via degli Arrazzieri (Street of the Tapestrymakers). You may no longer be able to pick up a sword in downtown Florence, but other examples of the artisans' craft reveal themselves at every turn. Leather, for example, is everywhere, whether as chic Gucci loafers, fake designer handbags (fakes are everywhere on Florence's streets), or the countless belts, shoes, and jackets of the city's San Lorenzo market. Marbled paper is another specialty, as is jewelry, which you find in little stores across the city, but especially on the Ponte Vecchio, the jewelers' traditional Florentine home. Across the bridge, the old blue-collar Oltrarno district contains shops and workshops, from tiny ateliers jammed into backstreets to the grand antiques shops of Via Maggio. Similar workshops greet you in Via della Porcellana and in Santa Croce, where

> The notion of *bella figura,* of cutting a beautiful figure and not making a fool of yourself, is an important one in Florence.

Etiquette & Customs

Italians may have a reputation for being passionate and excitable, but they are also generally polite and considerate. On meeting people, or entering stores, bars, hotels and restaurants, use a simple *buon giorno* (good day) or *buona sera* (good afternoon/evening). Do not use the informal *ciao* (hi or goodbye) with strangers. "Please" is *per favore,* "thank you" *grazie,* and *prego* "you're welcome." Before a meal, say *buon appetito* (eat well), to which the reply is *grazie, altrettanto* (thank you, and the same to you). Before a drink, the toast is *salute* (good health) or *cin cin.* Say *permesso* when you wish to pass people, and *mi scusi* (excuse me) if you wish to apologize or ask for help. A woman is addressed as *signora,* a young woman *signorina,* and a man as *signore.* Kissing on both cheeks is a common greeting among men and women who know each other. Dress appropriately in churches and don't enter churches when services are in progress.

Italians are more assertive in lines, when they form them at all, and in stores, banks, and other offices you should not expect people to wait their turn.

doorways are a jumble of dismembered chairs and half-finished tables, and the air is heavy with the scent of varnish and wood glue.

Problem Areas: These images of past and present united in perfect harmony are not the full picture, of course, and no one would pretend that Florence is a city without problems. While family and social ties are stronger than in many places, drugs, homelessness, and unemployment are problems here as they are in any major metropolis. You would not want to spend time in the city's Cascine park after dark, for example, nor engage in conversation with many of the characters who hang around the railroad station in the small hours.

Other problems are more subtle but no less invidious. One of the most obvious is the sheer number of visitors to Florence. No one can quite agree on a precise annual figure—it certainly runs to many millions—but just a glimpse at the lines outside the Uffizi art gallery or at the battalions of backpackers slumped outside the city's cathedral, suggest that the number is often more than the city and its inhabitants can comfortably bear. Visitors create wear and tear on the city's infrastructure and on its fabric, and in a city like Florence, where the fabric is often the irreplaceable artistic legacy of several centuries, the impact is all the more damaging. The demands of visitors and the need to preserve buildings and works of art also impose a huge financial burden on the city council.

Florence often does not help itself. Pollution is a problem, though not as much of a problem as it is in Rome or Milan. Much of it is caused by the Florentines' passion for cars—there are 2.7 cars for every Florentine family—the majority of which, at least, have been banned from the city center since 1988 (but only after considerable controversy).

Other problems can be laid more squarely at the visitors' door and at the widening gates of globalization. Most notably, these include the replacement of neighborhood food stores by souvenir stores, the workshops long since edged out by high-rent boutiques, and the traditional trattoria (an informal restaurant or tavern serving simple Italian dishes) sacrificed to the modern mania for fast food.

Festivals

Tuscans are nothing if not sociable, something that is given full rein during the region's many festivals and historical pageants. These events combine the locals' love of drama and spectacle with yet another chance to relive and reevaluate their glorious past. A visit to at least one such festival is a must for a dramatic, sociable, and memorable insight into the way that the Tuscan psyche straddles both past and present with such ease.

At one extreme are the big set-piece pageants—of which Siena's Palio horse race is the most renowned—and at the other is a multitude of small village fiestas, or *sagre,* which you'll inevitably stumble upon if you travel through the region's more rural backwaters. Many events have a religious raison d'être—to celebrate Easter or a saint's day; others are held for gastronomic reasons—to toast the wine harvest or a local specialty; and others, such as Florence's Maggio Musicale (see sidebar p. 151), have obvious cultural associations. Virtually all involve an immense amount of pageantry, with processions, fireworks, medieval dress, and copious amounts of food and drink.

Don't make the mistake, however, of imagining that such events are either for the benefit of visitors or fossilized ceremonies perpetuated for reasons of sentiment and spectacle. As in most walks of Tuscan and Florentine life, history, in one guise or another, is never far from the surface. For the past, in this part of the world at least, is a vital part of both the present and the future. ■

Modern-day gladiators of Calcio Storico Fiorentino: The tournament, which is an early form of *calcio* (soccer), is held the third week of June at the Piazza Santa Croce in the center of Florence.

Food & Drink

One of the fruits of Tuscany's continued attachment to the land is the region's superb food and wine, a range of excellent ingredients contributing to a cuisine and variety of wines that are as good as any in Italy. Eating is a passion for Tuscans, and one that visitors can easily share. Lunch on a vine-covered terrace and dinner under a starry Mediterranean sky should be experiences as memorable as visits to the best museums and galleries.

Local cheeses, salami, prosciutto, and bread provide an informal lunch, accompanied by local red wine.

A Brief History of Tuscan Food & Dining

Much Tuscan food is based on peasant traditions—the so-called *cucina povera,* or cuisine of the poor—and dates from a time when poverty was the culinary mother of invention. Other Italians still call Tuscans *mangiafafioli*—bean-eaters—a somewhat unfair and derogatory appellation, but one that hints at the region's simpler staples.

Not all Tuscan cuisine, though, has humble roots. Florentines are quick to tell you, for example, that they invented many of the great dishes of French cuisine, a claim they trace back to the marriage in 1534 of

Caterina de' Medici to Henri de Valois, the future king Henry II of France. Caterina is said to have blanched at the idea of foreign food, and she made certain that she was accompanied to France by a retinue of Florentine chefs. Hence, according to the Florentines, the presence in France of such modern-day "French" staples as *canard à l'orange* (duck in orange sauce), a simple variation of the Tuscan *papero alla melarancia,* and the famous Gallic vol-au-vent, still found in Florentine pastry shops as *turbanate di sfoglia.* Catherine also introduced the French to two essentials of the modern table—the fork and the napkin.

Tuscan Food Today

Today's Tuscan food contains plenty of sophisticated dishes that wouldn't disgrace the tables of restaurants in London, Paris, or New York, but for the most part the region's cuisine is a rural one based on the area's simple staples: mouthwatering hams, cheeses, robust pulses, wild leaves, hearty soups, pastas, piquant salamis, grilled meats, fresh fish, seafood, and—of course—superb olive oil. Better still, most of this food is seasonal and locally produced, and it only appears at the time of the year it is grown. Visit during a few limited weeks in spring, for example, and you may be lucky enough to find tiny spears of wild asparagus on menus. Later, cherries will be in the shops, then apricots, and then peaches. In fall it is the turn of figs, field-fresh mushrooms, and of course, plump, gold-green grapes. Rarely in a Tuscan market or food store *(alimentari)* will you find the year-round supply of vegetables and imported fruits that is now routinely found in northern European and North American supermarkets.

But if seasonal produce changes, the course of Tuscan meals remains inviolate. Breakfast is a simple coffee and croissant *(una brioche* in Italian). Lunch and dinner begin with starters, or antipasti—literally "before the meal." These may include bruschetta, a rough slice of toasted bread rubbed with garlic and olive oil and topped with tomatoes or a simple grind of salt and pepper. Often they will include a variety of hams and salamis served with saltless bread, or tiny crusty toasts (crostini) topped with olive paste, chicken liver pâté, or other delightful savory garnishes.

You won't be expected to order every course, and at lunch most restaurants won't mind if you order just a first course and salad. First courses make less use of pasta than in many parts of Italy, tending instead toward soups such as minestrone (a rich ham and vegetable soup), *zuppa di fagioli* (bean soup), and the common *ribollita* (literally "reboiled"), a rich bean and cabbage soup that was traditionally reboiled and used to feed hungry workers on successive days.

EXPERIENCE: Cook Tuscan Cuisine

Several companies offer half- or one-day cooking courses in Florence that can easily be combined with sightseeing. Typically you will visit the city's Mercato Centrale with your instructor, choosing fresh ingredients amid the colorful bustle of the market for your Tuscan dishes. An excellent school is the **Food & Wine Academy** *(tel 055 0123 3994, florence cookingclasses.com, $$$$$)*, which offers a range of five-hour lessons.

Longer courses are available in countryside villas or farmhouses, where in-depth lessons can be combined with time by the pool, sightseeing, and visits to local producers. **Tuscookany** *(tel 703 9400 235, tuscookany.com, $$$$$)*, offers three-day and one-week residential courses in a choice of three attractive villas.

For one-day Tuscan cooking courses in Montalcino (see pp. 268–269), look no further than **Taste Tuscany** *(tel 338 921 6205, tastetuscany.co.uk)*. Here, you'll find one-day courses *(9:45 a.m.–3 p.m., including lunch with wine, pickups available from accommodations within 6 miles/10 km)* in Tuscan cuisine and cooking in the company of its English owner and local cooks. Groups are between two and six people, and the emphasis is on the practical, hands-on knowledge you will need to prepare a four-course Tuscan meal with dishes such as crostini, handmade *pici* pasta, *sugo di caccio e pepe* (cheese and pepper sauce), and *ribollita* soup. Noncooking friends are welcome for lunch and longer courses (to 5 p.m.), with a wine tasting also available.

Another common first course is *pappa al pomodoro,* bread or croutons cooked in an herby broth and mixed with sieved tomatoes. Classic pastas include *pappardelle alla lepre* (noodles with a hare sauce), while the undisputed king of Tuscan main dishes is *bifstecca alla fiorentina* (Florentine beefsteak). Among the myriad of cheeses in Tuscany, look out for Pecorino, regional sheep's milk cheese.

Desserts

Desserts include obvious Italian winners such as gelato (ice cream, see sidebar this page), but also be sure to try some of the regional specialties, especially the *panforte* of Siena, a rich cake of cocoa, walnuts, spices, and crystallized fruit, all deliciously baked to a 13th-century recipe.

Drinks of Tuscany

While you can eat like a king or queen morning, noon, and night in Tuscany, you can also drink well no matter the time of day or season. Good coffee is a given in almost every bar and café, from the breakfast cappuccino or caffe latte to the after-dinner espresso (Italians almost never drink cappuccino or other milky coffee after dinner). Freshly squeezed orange, lemon, or

INSIDER TIP:

Campari soda often comes ready mixed: For the real McCoy, ask for a Campari bitter.

—JUSTIN KAVANAGH
*National Geographic
Travel Books editor*

grapefruit juice *(una spremuta)* in season is another real treat in this region. Don't miss cooling novelties such as granita (crushed ice drenched with a coffee- or other flavored syrup) and frappé or *frullati* (shakes made with fresh fruit and milk or ice cream).

Closer to sundown try one of the classic Italian aperitifs such as Campari soda. Nonalcoholic *aperitivi* are also common; an Italian favorite is the slightly bitter Crodino. After dinner, brave one of many Italian digestifs: Grappa is a clear (sometimes flavored) spirit distilled from the skins left after grapes have been pressed for wine. *Amaro* (literally "bitter") is a fortified wine full of herbs and "secret ingredients" that Italians swear aids digestion; Averna is a good brand for the uninitiated.

EXPERIENCE: Make the Perfect Pizza & Gelato

Purists might insist that to learn how to make pizza properly you need to go to Naples. But Viator's **Florence Cooking Class** *(viator.com, see the "Florence/Cooking Classes" page)* offers expertise in making gelato and pizza—so let's treat the pizza element as a bonus.

You'll start with the first course—the pizza—learning a little of the history of the dish before moving on to making, rolling, tossing, garnishing, and baking your own dough—tasting different toppings as you go.

Then it's on to dessert and gelato. Again, you'll learn a little background—

how and why proper gelato is different to other ice cream around the world—as well as how to make it, tasting all the while, and gleaning plenty of insider tips and traditional Italian culinary methods from your Florentine chef.

Find details and make reservations through the Viator website. Groups consist of a maximum of 25 students, and courses last roughly three hours. Prices start at approximately $60 per person.

Viator also offers a three-hour Florence-based course in pastamaking and another two-hour class on how to create the perfect tiramisu.

Siena: Making hand-rolled *pici* pasta at Scuola di Cucina di Lella (Lella's Cooking School)

Wines of Tuscany

Tuscan wines enjoy a worldwide reputation, and with good reason. Chianti, the region's most famous red wine, comes in many guises and has been joined by some more ambitious reds, the "super Tuscans." Brunello di Montalcino and Vino Nobile di Montepulciano are the other big names (see pp. 270–271 for more on the wines of Tuscany). For lovers of food and fine wines, one of the delights of your stay in Tuscany will be a visit to a winery for lunch or dinner along with a wine tasting (see sidebar p. 238).

Delicacies: Truffles

Tuscany is a great place to try truffles. The Romans believed these mysterious subterranean ascomycete fungi—there are many varieties, of which six are commonly eaten—were created when lightning struck the earth. In the Middle Ages they were considered a manifestation of the devil. And no wonder, for they grow apparently without root, stem, leaf, plant, or flower.

In fact, the truffle has evolved over millions of years to grow underground as protection from the elements and from being eaten by animals. This precludes photosynthesis, so the truffle derives nutrients through a symbiotic relationship with the roots of certain trees, usually oak, hazel, birch, and lime.

But a truffle requires its spores to be spread for propagation, and this is where its famous perfume comes in, because while truffles mature over several months—reaching the size of anything between a pea and a soccer ball—they are only ripe, and give off their smell, for a window of a few days (thereafter they rot and become poisonous).

The smell attracts woodland animals, especially female wild boars, for among the volatile compounds truffles exude is one that resembles the musky pheromone of the male boar. These wild animals snuffle up the truffles, and the spores are released. Most truffles, except for the less desirable varieties of summer truffle, mature from November onward.

You can still experience all the fun of a truffle hunt with a local expert and a canine rather than porcine companion (see sidebar p. 279). Or try them in certain restaurants, or buy paste, oil, and truffles under oil to take home: Pienza (see Travelwise p. 325) is a particularly good place to shop.

History of Florence & Tuscany

The history of Florence and Tuscany stretches back almost 3,000 years, embracing the Etruscans, the mysterious forebears of the Romans; the rivalries of popes and emperors; the Medici, a family whose name echoes through many centuries of the region's past; and, in the Renaissance, one of the greatest periods of social, cultural, and intellectual change seen in the Western world.

The Etruscans

Tuscany's first significant inhabitants were the Etruscans, probably a mixture of indigenous peoples and settlers from Greece and Asia Minor, who inhabited much of central Italy from about the ninth century B.C. Tuscan towns with Etruscan roots include Arezzo, Cortona, and Volterra, but not Florence, whose present-day site the Etruscans overlooked in favor of Fiesole, a more easily defended redoubt in the hills nearby.

> Tuscan towns with Etruscan roots include Arezzo, Cortona, and Volterra, but not Florence, whose present-day site the Etruscans overlooked in favor of Fiesole, a more easily defended redoubt in the hills nearby.

Some of Fiesole's inhabitants may have frequented a market near the Arno, probably close to the present site of the Ponte Vecchio, the river's narrowest bridging point. Others may have formed a permanent community here in the fourth century B.C.

The Romans

Whatever the status of the site, it remained little altered until the rise of Rome, whose empire gradually encroached on Etruscan territory. Fiesole fell to the Romans in 283 B.C. but continued to enjoy relative independence until 60 B.C., when, according to myth, a Roman force under the general Fiorino was dispatched to confront Catiline, a renegade soldier who had assumed control of the town. Fiorino decided against attacking the well-defended citadel and instead starved the town into submission from a base on the Arno—the site of modern-day Florence. Fiorino was killed in the process, and Catiline, it is said, escaped to Pistoia before his eventual capture.

Only a sliver of this story has any grounding in fact. Catiline was a genuine figure and suffered defeat at Pistoia in 62 B.C. Fiorino was almost certainly mythical, however, as was the notion that he gave his name to the city that grew up around his camp. Equally unlikely is the idea that Rome's campaign against Fiesole was completed by Julius Caesar or that Caesar directly founded Florence—although many modern accounts record his involvement as fact. Myth, legend, and even historical hearsay go deep in Italian culture.

Caesar's actual role in the birth of the city was passive. He formulated the so-called Agrarian Law of 59 B.C., which made grants of land to retired army veterans. In doing so, he created the conditions that fostered the early development of a colony on the Arno. In time this colony acquired a name—Florentia—although just how is still a matter of much debate. Whatever the settlement's origins, the place soon prospered, the result of river trade and traffic on the Via Cassia, an important Roman road linking Rome to northern Italy.

Few memorials to the Roman colony survive today, save for its original gridiron plan, whose pattern can still be traced in the streets of the modern city: Piazza della

The Roman theater in Volterra is one of the finest and best preserved in Italy.

A 13th-century gold florin bears a fleur-de-lis, the symbol of Florence.

Repubblica was the old forum, Via degli Strozzi the main street, and Via de' Tornabuoni and Via del Proconsolo its western and eastern limits. The major physical mementos are a handful of ancient columns that were appropriated by later builders for use in the baptistery and San Miniato al Monte.

Popes & Emperors

In about A.D. 568, after the fall of Rome, Tuscany passed under the control of the Lombards, a Germanic tribe from northern Europe. The Lombards were defeated, in turn, after A.D. 774 by the Franks, yet another northern European tribe, under the command of Charlemagne, one of the most celebrated rulers of the age. Charlemagne was a Christian, and he awarded large areas of central Italy to the papacy, thus creating the germ of the Papal States, an enclave that would provide the basis of the papacy's temporal power for more than a thousand years. In return, the papacy crowned Charlemagne Holy Roman Emperor (R.800–814).

These events sowed the seeds of a fiercely divisive dispute between the papacy and the emperors that would reverberate through Tuscan and Italian history for centuries. Henceforth popes would claim they had sanctioned imperial rule, while emperors claimed they had created papal power. These claims to original, and thus ultimate, power oscillated between heaven and earth, as it were, with each side convinced of the righteousness of its stance. In later years supporters of the popes would become known as Guelphs; supporters of the emperors were called Ghibellines. Different towns and noble families often had different allegiances, although most were based on local rivalries rather than genuine allegiance to the empire or papacy. If your rival supported the pope, you would automatically side with the emperor. And if one or other superpower was in the ascendant, then you adapted your loyalties accordingly.

The empire and its rulers were based in northern Europe, however, and eventually allowed Tuscany to be ruled on their behalf by local Lucca-based princes known as margraves. As time went by, the physical distance between the margraves and the Holy Roman Emperors weakened links between the two. By 1077 the margrave Matilda (1046–1115), a devout Christian, had transferred her allegiance to the pope. At her death, she went further, bequeathing all her titles to the papacy with the important exceptions of Lucca, Florence, and Siena. It was at about this time that the region was referred to as Tuscany for the first time, its name derived from the Latin *Tuscia* (used after about the third century), in turn derived from Etruria, the name given to the land of the Etruscans, or Tusci.

New Wealth

As disputes between the papacy and the empire intensified, so the resulting power vacuum, coupled with an upsurge in trade, allowed for the growth of independent city-states across Tuscany. Some, such as Pisa, grew powerful on the back of maritime prowess. Others, notably Florence, owed their growth to textiles, which developed largely thanks to the water of the Arno, vital to an industry that required the washing and rinsing of both sorted and finished cloth. Innovative merchants also played their part, traveling as far afield as England in the search for wool and trawling the bazaars of the Orient for exotic dyestuffs. Dyeing would become one of Florence's major strengths, Florentine red emerging as a staple color across Europe. In the 12th century, just 100 years after the trade started in earnest, some 30,000 people—about a third of the city's population—were connected with textiles. Even in the 13th century, when trade had dropped by 90 percent from its peak, it is estimated the city was still providing the known world with a tenth of its textiles.

The relative decline of textiles proved of little consequence, for another more lucrative business had risen in its stead: banking. This business was to be of incalculable importance in the development of the city, and it is to Florentine bankers that we owe the pillars of modern commerce, including such fundamentals as checks, life insurance, credit, bills of exchange, and double entry bookkeeping. The Florentines also devised the world's first major international currency—the *fiorino,* or florin, a gold coin, whose rigorously enforced purity (and thus reliability) saw it adopted across Europe after its introduction in 1252.

On their own, such accomplishments might seem dull—if worthy—achievements. In the context of how bankers and a prosperous city might spend their profits, however, they were vital, not least because they provided the funding for many of the greatest Renaissance works of art. The city's most famous bankers were the Medici, a name that reverberated through Florentine history for centuries, but one that came relatively late to a clique of bankers that by 1250 already dominated Europe. Florence had no fewer than 24 major banking dynasties, most notably the Bardi and Peruzzi,

The Guilds of Florence

Florence's burgeoning power inevitably raised the question of who should govern the city. During the city's first stirrings of independence in the 11th century, its merchants had formed the Societas Mercatorum, a form of guild or confraternity, many of whose members served in a 100-man *comune,* or ruling council, established in 1115.

In time the Societas was replaced by the Arte di Calimala, a broad-based guild embracing most merchants. As trade diversified, this was superseded by seven powerful guilds known as the Arti Maggiori, among whom were the guilds of lawyers (Arte dei Giudici e Notai), bankers (Arte del Cambio), and wool merchants (Arte della Lana).

In 1289, 14 lesser guilds, the Arti Minori, were formed. These embraced middle-ranking merchants—anything from bakers and innkeepers to locksmiths and leatherworkers. Members of these guilds, and especially those of the Arti Maggiori, would effectively rule Florence for the next 400 years.

who were bankers to the kings of England, among others, and the Pazzi and Alberti (and later the Medici), who handled the enormous papal account. Other banking potentates are still remembered in palace and street names across the city: Antinori, Guardi, Strozzi, Davanzati, Tornabuoni, and many others.

The Signoria

In theory, Florence's system of government worked as follows: The names of selected guild members—the only people eligible for office— would be placed in eight leather bags, or *borse,* kept in Santa Croce. Nine names were then drawn at random: six from the Arti Maggiori, two from the Arti Minori, and one to act as a standard-bearer, or Gonfaloniere. These Priori, as they were known, formed a government known as the Signoria, which served for just two months, the short tenure designed to prevent corruption, favoritism, or the entrenchment of power.

The Signoria's authority was tempered by various committees, the number of which increased over the years. It also had to pay heed to the Podestà, an independent magistrate

brought in from an outside city to act as an objective arbitrator in disputes. In times of greater crisis, the Signoria called a Parlemento, or assembly, which consisted of all males over the age of 14. When a quorum of two-thirds was reached, the Parlemento was asked to approve a Balìa, or emergency committee, to deal with the crisis.

This was the theory. In practice, it was subverted in true Machiavellian fashion during all but a few short-lived periods of Florentine history. In this instance, the means of politics were used to justify the ends of the families of power. In the first place, powerful cliques or individuals ensured that only compliant candidates were put forward for office. Second, all the nobles and the lowly workers—the so-called Popolo Minuto—were excluded from the process. And third, controlling factions could engineer the calling of a Parlemento, often just a euphemism for the mob, if

> **The most powerful family of all, of course, was the Medici, which hailed from the Mugello, northeast of Florence. Its founding father was Giovanni di Bicci de' Medici (1360–1429).**

the Signoria failed to heed their wishes. Thus, it was in this way that powerful individuals or families could control Florence—and, by implication, most of Tuscany—while still paying lip service to its institutions.

The "Pianta della Catena" shows Florence as it was during the time of Lorenzo the Magnificent.

The Medici

The most powerful family of all, of course, was the Medici, which hailed from the Mugello, northeast of Florence. Its founding father was Giovanni di Bicci de' Medici (1360–1429). His banking acumen laid the foundations of the family fortune. Power was consolidated by his son, Cosimo de' Medici (1389–1464), also known as Cosimo il Vecchio, or Cosimo the Elder, to distinguish him from a later Medici, Grand Duke Cosimo I (see pp. 34–35).

Cosimo the Elder: Cosimo was a banker and politician of consummate skill, as well as an intellectual and enlightened thinker. When Cosimo first rose to prominence, however, Florence's dominant family was the Albizzi. His rise was due partly to public disenchantment with the autocratic Albizzi and partly to the support for Cosimo of the disenfranchised Popolo Minuto and lesser guilds, who saw the Medici as more democratically inclined. In 1431 the authorities (with Albizzi backing) imprisoned the rising star and then sent him into exile. He was gone just a year, invited to return after an emergency meeting of the Parlemento. In the words of Pope Pius II, he would "soon become master of the country and . . . King in all but name."

In Cosimo Renaissance Florence found the ruler it needed and deserved, although no formal title was ever granted. He bought off popular discontent with donations to charity; commissioned numerous buildings, including a magnificent public library; lavished patronage on artists and architects; sponsored humanist learning; founded an academy of learning based on Plato's Academy; and brought prestige to the city through the 1439 Council of Florence, a meeting of the Catholic and Eastern Orthodox churches. At the same time Cosimo wielded his power in a way that was always wary and discreet. "Do not appear to give advice," his father had warned him, "but put forward your views discreetly, never display any pride, . . . avoid litigation and political controversy, and always stay out of the public eye."

Cosimo's skill, and the period of prosperity that accompanied it, allowed Medici hegemony to survive through the short reign of his son, Piero de' Medici (1416–1469), also known as Piero il Gottoso, or Piero the Gouty, after the disease that crippled him. It also prepared the way for the most famous of the Medici, Lorenzo de' Medici (1449–1492), better known as Lorenzo il Magnifico, or Lorenzo the Magnificent.

Lorenzo the Magnificent: Where Cosimo had presided over the early and middle part of the Florentine Renaissance, Lorenzo ruled the city when Europe's

Gozzoli's "Adoration of the Magi" (1459–1461) shows Lorenzo the Magnificent as the youngest of the Magi.

greatest artistic flowering was at its zenith. Like his grandfather, Lorenzo was a man in tune with his times: An accomplished poet, he surrounded himself with scholars and thinkers, enjoyed the fine life of the country villa, and—while commissioning surprisingly few works of art—continued to foster the atmosphere in which artistic endeavor could flourish.

But while he retained the support of the Florentine public, his power, and that of his family, inevitably aroused jealousy among other leading families. None were more roused than the Pazzi, who were responsible for the most notorious of all anti-Medici uprisings—the 1478 Pazzi Conspiracy (see sidebar opposite).

Savonarola

Lorenzo's eventual death—by natural causes—in 1492 marked the end of an era. Pope Innocent VIII, hearing of his demise, remarked: "The peace of Italy is at an end." Sure enough, there followed one of the more tumultuous periods of Florentine (and Italian) history. Lorenzo's successor, his son Piero di Lorenzo (1471–1503), proved ineffectual, being ruthless and violent by turns; even his father had described

The Pazzi Conspiracy

The Pazzi Conspiracy was led by Pope Sixtus IV, angry at having been refused a loan by the Medici to buy Imola, a town near Bologna. With Sixtus was Francesco Salviati, whom the Medici had vetoed as archbishop of Pisa, an appointment made in breach of an agreement between the Medici and Sixtus. Finally came Jacopo de' Pazzi, the Pazzi "godfather," and Francesco de' Pazzi, head of the Pazzi bank in Rome. A mercenary soldier, Montesecco, was recruited to provide the military muscle, along with two priests, Maffei and Bagnone, and a violent sidekick, Bernardo Baroncelli.

The attack took place in Florence's cathedral on April 26, 1478. Giuliano, Lorenzo the Magnificent's brother, was stabbed 19 times by Francesco de' Pazzi. Lorenzo escaped, hiding behind the portals of the cathedral's Sagrestia Nuova.

Across the city, Salviati's attack on the Signoria failed when he was separated from his troops in the Palazzo Vecchio. Apprised of the coup, the mob gathered. Salviati and his troops were massacred, and Francesco was hanged next to Salviati. Maffei and Bagnone were castrated and hanged, and Montesecco was tortured and executed in the Bargello, as was Baroncelli. Jacopo de' Pazzi escaped, but he was captured, tortured, stripped naked, and hanged from the Palazzo Vecchio. After burial, his body was exhumed by the mob, dragged through the streets, and propped in front of the Palazzo Pitti, his decomposing head used as a door knocker. The rotted body was thrown into the Arno, recovered by children, flogged, hanged again, then hurled back into the river. Not everyone in Renaissance Florence was enlightened.

him as foolish. Within two years, in a panic-stricken funk, he had surrendered Florence to Charles VIII of France, who had entered Italy in 1494 to press his claim to the throne of Naples.

After Charles moved on, the power vacuum in Florence was filled by Girolamo Savonarola (1452–1498), one of the most extraordinary figures of the age. A monk of intense religious zeal, he was the prior of San Marco, a convent in northern Florence (see pp. 143–144), and even before Lorenzo's death had attracted immense crowds through the power of his preaching: Michelangelo would claim in old age that he could still hear the friar's speeches ringing in his ears. Savonarola saw Charles VIII as a figure of divine retribution, sent to punish the Florentines. The city's painters, he railed, made the Virgin "look like a harlot." Its prostitutes were "pieces of meat with eyes," and its "Sodomites . . . were to be burned alive." A torrent of decrees flowed from San Marco: Paintings were to be removed from churches; citizens would fast continually; children were to spy on their parents; and a vast bonfire of the vanities was to be built in Piazza della Signoria, piled with everything from wigs, mirrors, and false beards to books, paintings, and board games. A shell-shocked populace complied.

In Rome the corrupt Borgia pope, Alexander VI—denounced by Savonarola as an agent of Satan—at first cajoled and then pleaded with the charismatic monk, terrified at his hold over one of Italy's most powerful cities. Excommunication followed in 1497, coinciding in Florence with poor harvests, plague, and a war with Pisa, all of which—in the absence of real control in the city—contrived to turn the fickle Florentine mob against Savonarola. The monk was arrested, tortured, and burned for heresy in Piazza della Signoria in 1498.

Return of the Medici

Calm of sorts returned to the city after this remarkable interregnum, aided by a period in which Florence enjoyed a brief stretch of genuine republican rule under Piero Soderini, the city's chancellor, and his right-hand man, writer and diplomat Niccolò Machiavelli. In 1512, however, the republic sided with France against the combined armies of Spain and the papacy, and was duly defeated and dismembered. The papacy now held the upper hand, and the man who would shortly become pope was none other than Leo X, better known as Giovanni de' Medici (1475–1521), second son of Lorenzo the Magnificent. With his father pulling the strings, he had become a monk at the age of eight and Italy's youngest-ever cardinal at just 16. Assuming the Holy See, the high-living Giovanni de' Medici infamously remarked: "God has given us the papacy, so let us enjoy it."

Giovanni proceeded to rule Florence in all but name, at the same time packing the papacy with cardinals (31 in all) sympathetic to the Medici. This led to the election in 1524 of Pope Clement VII, better known as Giulio de' Medici (1478–1534), illegitimate son of Giuliano de' Medici, the Medici murdered in the Pazzi Conspiracy (see sidebar p. 33). Clement's control of Florence was cut short in 1527 when Emperor Charles V of Spain and Austria (R.1519–1556) sacked Rome, rendering the papacy impotent and allowing Florence to restore a republican administration. This again proved short-lived, and when Charles and Clement made peace in 1529—a peace cemented by the marriage of Charles's daughter to Alessandro de' Medici—the Medici were returned to power in Florence.

> Assuming the Holy See, the high-living Giovanni de' Medici famously remarked: "God has given us the papacy, so let us enjoy it."

This time, however, things were different. Neither Florence nor the Medici now had real influence. Rather, they were minor players in a game controlled by Europe's main imperial players, Austria and Spain. When Alessandro was murdered by a male lover (and distant cousin) in 1537, imperial advisers—with no direct Medici heirs—chose Cosimo de' Medici (1519–1574) from an obscure branch of the family, to act as a stooge. But Cosimo proved to be his own man and enjoyed a cunning and autocratic period in office (while being careful not to antagonize his imperial masters) that saw

History on the Streets

Dates from 19th- and 20th-century Italian history feature time and time again—always in Roman numerals—in street names in every town, city, and village in Tuscany and beyond.

Here's what some of them mean: **XXV Aprile** is the day that Italy was liberated from the Nazis during World War II; **XXIV Maggio,** the day in 1915 when Italy entered the World War I; **XX Settembre,** the day in 1870 that Italian troops entered Rome to complete Italian reunification; and **IV Novembre,** the day in 1918 that Italy's armistice with Austria took effect, marking the end of World War I in Italy.

The Nazis destroyed all of Florence's bridges except the Ponte Vecchio.

him take the title of Grand Duke of Tuscany in 1570. The small city-states in Tuscany that had remained free of Florentine control—Siena, in particular—now fell within the Medici and imperial orbit.

Cosimo's sons and successors, Francesco I (1541–1587) and Ferdinando I (1549–1609), were competent rulers, followed by Cosimo II (1590–1621), but they presided over a region in decline. Two ineffectual Medici followed, Ferdinando II (1610–1670) and Cosimo III (1642–1723), before the last in the family's male line, the hopeless Gian Gastone (1671–1737), bowed out without producing an heir. Some 300 years of almost continuous Medici rule ended when Gastone's sister, Anna Maria (died 1743), signed a treaty handing the Tuscan Grand Duchy to the Duke of Lorraine, later Emperor Francis I of Austria.

Unification & World Wars
Tuscany then enjoyed a modest resurgence under an administration that effected various economic and social reforms. These were interrupted by the arrival of Napoleon, who overwhelmed Austria in 1799; his troops remained in Tuscany until

EXPERIENCE: Cheering on Fiorentina Soccer Club

When in Florence, why not cheer on **ACF Fiorentina,** one of the most passionately supported teams in Italy's top league, Serie A. Your visit to **Stadio Artemio Franchi** *(Campo di Marte, it.violachannel.tv)* will be memorable for the singing, the roar of the crowd (47,000 capacity), and the fireworks and colorful banners. For tickets, try the Toto booth on Piazza della Repubblica on the Tuesday prior to a game, or visit the club's **official ticket office** *(Via dei Sette Santi Rosso 28, tel 055 553 2803, en.violachannel.tv/club-box -office).* Then don team colors of lilac with red and white trim and head to **Bar Maresi** on Via Manfredo Fantini, opposite the stadium, for a pregame drink with your newfound fraternity of Viola fans.

their leader's defeat in 1815. The Austrians then returned to power until ousted by a series of nationalist uprisings in the 1850s—an independence movement known as the Risorgimento. These culminated in Tuscany's joining a united Italy in 1860. From 1865 Florence served as the capital of the new state, Rome having remained under the control of French and papal troops. Victor Emanuel II (1820–1878), Italy's first king, moved into the Palazzo Pitti, and a parliament sat in the Palazzo Vecchio. In 1871, following France's defeat in the Franco-Prussian War, the capital was moved to Rome.

Foreign visitors made artistic pilgrimages to Florence and Tuscany—the 18th and 19th centuries were the era of the Grand Tour, a cultural round of Europe's great capitals—but neither city nor region would again feature prominently in Italy's political history, although events in Europe in the first half of the 20th century could not fail to touch them.

War memorials in every Tuscan village pay testament to the lives lost in two world wars, while the modern centers of cities such as Pisa and Livorno stand as memorials to strategic bombing by the Allies as they harried a retreating Nazi army in 1944. A handful of bombs also fell directly on Florence, but decisions made at the highest level on both sides largely spared the city's artistic heritage. Hitler himself, it is said, ordered the Ponte Vecchio to be saved when every other bridge across the Arno was mined.

The Modern Era

Since World War II, Florence and many other Tuscan towns and cities have shared in the miracle that has transformed Italy from an almost entirely agricultural country into one of the world's leading industrial nations. Rural poverty continued well into the 1950s, but even in the countryside, a revitalized wine industry and the advent of tourism have helped preserve a landscape shaped by human hand for almost 3,000 years. Nature has brought suffering to the region, nowhere more dramatically than in the catastrophic floods that ravaged Florence in 1966 (see pp. 160–161). The disaster proved a brief setback, however, and did little to interrupt the resurgence of fashion, design, and textiles as major moneymakers. In an era when many great artistic capitals are little more than fossils, Florence is an exception—a city neither living on nor overshadowed by its past glories. It may never again be, as it was during the Renaissance, Europe's artistic fulcrum, but as a living record of a time when it led the world, its future looks as assured as its past. ■

Living history: Fans of ACF Fiorentina, Florence's main soccer team, sport banners that include the fleur-de-lis and depictions of Calcio Storico Fiorentino contests.

The Arts

The arts in Florence and Tuscany are dominated by one magnificent period of change and individual genius—the Renaissance. This was an artistic flowering that had its roots in many diverse artistic and intellectual disciplines but which came to glorious fruition in the Florence of the 15th century. The obvious changes in the painting and sculpture of the time, however, should not obscure the advances made in architecture, nor the enormous contribution that Florence and Tuscany have made across the centuries in the fields of music, literature, and—more recently—cinema.

Painting & Sculpture

Early Influences: Most of Tuscany's earliest artistic creations belong to the Etruscans, whose civilization spread across much of central Italy—including Tuscany—from about the eighth century B.C. Over the centuries, the Etruscans traded extensively with Greece, adopting many Greek artistic and sculptural idioms in the process. Many of these Greek, or Hellenistic, influences can be seen in the urns and painted vases that adorn Tuscany's archaeological museums in Volterra, Cortona, and other cities and towns. At the same time, Etruscan art had its own distinctive style, often combining a vigorous and naturalistic approach with incredible delicacy, traits best seen in the exquisite jewelry in the museums of Cortona and Siena.

> The arts in Florence and Tuscany are dominated by one magnificent period of change and individual genius—the Renaissance.

The artistic legacy of the Romans, whose civilization replaced that of the Etruscans, is less obvious in Tuscany than in many other parts of Italy. Here there are few of the magnificent sculptures of Rome or Naples, merely a modest scattering of busts, coins, and minor artifacts around the rather dusty archaeological museums of Florence and elsewhere. Much the same can be said of the art of the five or so centuries that followed the decline of Rome in the sixth century, for Florence and Tuscany boast little in the way of Lombard or Byzantine works of art, although the influence of such works would later infuse the region's paintings and sculptures.

Road to Renaissance: You have to move to the 12th century to find Tuscany's first autonomous Christian-era works of art: A cross painted in 1138 by Tuscan artist Guglielmo is now in Sarzana cathedral, in the neighboring region of Liguria, and Lombard-influenced carvings adorn many of the tiny Romanesque churches of Pisa, Lucca, and Pistoia. More artists appeared a little later, about 1230, often in or around Pisa, then the richest and thus most artistically sophisticated city in Tuscany. Other minor centers included Arezzo, Siena, and Florence, where one of the most prominent early names was Coppo di Marcovaldo, an artist captured by the Sienese in battle and forced to complete paintings as part of the ransom for his return to Florence.

"Christ Pantocrator" from the cupola of the baptistery in Florence: Designers of this 24-foot (8 m) work included Cimabue and Giotto.

Pisa continued to be the motor of artistic development in Tuscany, particularly if you believe Giorgio Vasari (1511–1574), a Renaissance painter and critic whose writings have influenced art historians—some would say erroneously—almost to the present day. Vasari's premise, briefly put, was that the old artistic forms that dominated Italian art for centuries—those of the Byzantine world—first began to change in the realm of sculpture, notably in Pisa with the work of Nicola (circa 1220–1278) and Giovanni Pisano (1250–1314). Change came later in painting, where two key figures, Cimabue (1240–1302), whom Vasari called the father of Italian painting, and his pupil Giotto di Bondone (1267–1337), better known simply as Giotto, pioneered a move toward greater naturalism in art. Later, this pioneering work was developed further by a favored Vasarian triumvirate: Donatello (1386–1466) in sculpture, Brunelleschi in architecture (see sidebar p. 47), and Masaccio (see p. 176) in painting. The process culminated in the Renaissance, the 15th-century flowering of artistic endeavor that had Florence as its principal focus.

Most scholars now see this progression as too simplistic and view the long road to the Renaissance as a more complex affair, with numerous more subtle influences shaping artistic development in Italy and elsewhere. This said, Vasari's premise still makes a useful and persuasive basic model. To understand the background to events, however, and to appreciate the scale of artistic change, it is necessary to grasp the state in which Italian and other European art languished in the 13th century.

Art at the time was effectively the art of Byzantium, a hybrid of classical and Asian influences introduced by Justinian, emperor of the eastern half of the Roman Empire, when he invaded parts of Italy from his capital, Constantinople (now Istanbul), in the sixth century. Its distinguishing features were abstraction, gold backgrounds, and ornamental motifs, while its main images were almost exclusively portraits of saints, painted crucifixes, and the iconic figures of the Madonna and Child. It was reverential and stylized, especially in its beautiful but stilted paintings of the Madonna and Child, images conspicuously lacking in life, depth, movement, or naturalistic detail.

By the 13th century such art had begun to seem old-fashioned, its language

EXPERIENCE: Take Art Classes in Florence

It's hard to think of a better place to take lessons in art, architecture, or art history than Florence, where inspiration and good example gather on all sides.

You might have a morning class in theory or drawing in an historic building in the city and then visit any number of churches, palaces, or galleries to see the work of Renaissance and other artists and architects firsthand.

The challenge is to choose between the large numbers of courses available and—because art tuition courses invariably run over several weeks or months—to find a course suitable for the time you have available. Other factors to consider include the availability of English-language tuition, class sizes, and residential options. Summer is a popular time for short courses, but note that this is a busy and hot time to be in the city.

One of the oldest and most reputable organizations is the **British Institute** (britishinstitute.it), whose art history courses include "Art in the Renaissance" in July, when you can reserve up to 40 lessons or check in for just one session (from €45 per lesson).

outmoded in the face of new and wealthy city-states, greater learning, and a sophisticated population. Some new, or reinvented, artistic language was needed to match the
changes taking place in the social and economic domain. This language was first articu-
lated in sculpture by Nicola Pisano. His work in Pisa allowed him to borrow directly from
two of the richest artistic lexicons of all: the Roman and Greek forms that he found
woven into ancient classical sarcophagi recently brought to the city from the Holy Land.

A New Artistic Language: Such reworking of classical idioms was a
cornerstone of later Renaissance art, and it was adopted with alacrity by Nicola's
followers, Arnolfo di Cambio (see p. 47) and Giovanni Pisano, who produced
astounding sculptures in Pisa, Siena, Pistoia, and other towns. Painting lagged
only a short way behind, the first moves away
from Byzantium's hidebound strictures coming
with early fresco painters such as Pietro Cavallini
(circa 1250–1330) in Rome. He would come into
contact with the Florentine painter Cimabue
while working in the Basilica of St. Francis in Assisi,
Umbria. Cimabue, in turn, taught and worked with
Giotto, perhaps in Assisi's basilica, a major melting
pot of early Italian painting.

   Giotto was the innovator who turned Western
art on its head, laying some of the Renaissance's
principal foundations in the process. Although he
was not alone in effecting change, his individual
genius is indisputable, as is the profound shift in
artistic perception that his paintings represent.
Simply put, he attempted to introduce realism and
naturalism into his work, infusing his frescoes in
Florence's Santa Croce and other churches with
depth, detail, facial gestures, and human emotions.
He also made attempts—crude to modern eyes—
to master the notions of perspective, whose rules
were still not understood, and to look to the real
world for inspiration and subject.

   His example was taken up not only in Florence
by followers such as Maso di Banco (active circa
1335–1350) and Agnolo Gaddi (active 1369–1396)
but also in Siena, another increasingly prosperous city.
Siena's artists—most notably Duccio di Buoninsegna
(see p. 215)—had long fused a love of Byzantine

**Ceramics at Pienza's Galeria Piertine are part
of a tradition dating from Etruscan times.**

motifs with a distinctive passion for color, composition, and gold backgrounds. Artists
here included Simone Martini (see p. 215) and the brothers Ambrogio (circa 1290–1348)
and Pietro Lorenzetti (circa 1280–1348), who combined the lessons of Giotto with their
own artistic inheritance to produce courtly and exquisitely executed paintings.

   The gradual changes wrought by these and other painters dispel the notion of
the Renaissance springing suddenly from thin air. Rather, this rebirth, or *rinascimento*—

the Italian word for "renaissance"—was a serendipitous and long-maturing mixture of social, artistic, cultural, economic, and intellectual change. In scholarship the rediscovery and reevaluation of classical texts led to an upsurge in humanist thinking—the notion that the human and not the divine (or religious) was at the heart of existence. This freed art of its devotional obligations and reintroduced Greek and Roman ideas to intellectual debate. From there it was a short step to the reintroduction of the Greek and Roman classical ideal to art.

Florence's Golden Age: That Florence should become the epicenter of the Renaissance was no surprise. During the 15th century it was one of the wealthiest cities in the known world, a truly cosmopolitan melting pot whose free-thinking atmosphere provided a setting in which creativity could flourish. As its reputation rose, the city attracted more artists; as more artists arrived, so the fevered atmosphere of innovation intensified.

Three artists in three disciplines are often picked out as paramount in the early years of the Renaissance, which is often described (erroneously) as beginning in 1401, the year of a competition to design Florence's baptistery north doors (see p. 70). They are Brunelleschi in architecture (see sidebar p. 47), Donatello in sculpture, and Masaccio in painting. Donatello created work the like of which has not been seen before or since—notably in his statue of "Mary Magdalene" in Florence's Museo dell'Opera del Duomo (see pp. 76–77). He also reintroduced the nude, a mainstay of classical sculpture, to the mainstream of European art. Masaccio was equally groundbreaking, producing one of the first paintings to embrace the new laws of perspective—"The Trinity" in Florence's church of Santa Maria Novella (see p. 151)—and a fresco cycle in the nearby Cappella Brancacci whose innovations staggered contemporaries and became a point of reference for many major artists of the day (see pp. 176–179).

Other hallowed names soon joined this artistic trinity, among them Fra Angelico (see sidebar p. 142), a monk whose ethereal paintings, while still wedded to religious themes, combined an almost unequaled mastery of technique and color. Far less intense but more varied paintings were produced by Angelico's pupil Benozzo Gozzoli (1420–1497), known for his lyrical frescoes in Florence's Palazzo Medici-Riccardi (see pp. 133–135) and the church of Sant'Agostino in San Gimignano (see sidebar p. 215 & also p. 218). Paolo Uccello (1397–1475), by contrast, shared Masaccio's concern for perspective, becoming obsessed with its myriad possibilities and producing challenging, almost visionary work in the process.

The Medici & the Arts

The great art of the Renaissance period had to be paid for. Previous commissions had come almost exclusively from the Church, whose naturally cautious and conservative approach stifled innovation and invariably demanded entirely religious statements from artists and sculptors. Genius and creativity could flourish in this environment, but they could flourish more readily in the hands of wealthy lay patrons such as the Medici, whose largesse provided the financial wherewithal for artistic exploration, free from religious constraints.

Some idea of the sums involved can be gleaned from the Medici's own accounts, which for the years 1433 to 1471 show 663,755 florins spent on paintings, buildings, and charities. At that time 150 florins supported a Florentine family for a year, 1,000 florins would have bought an entire palazzo, and a Botticelli painting could be had for 100 florins.

Luca Signorelli's "Lamentation Over the Dead Christ" (1501–1502) at the Museo Diocesano in Cortona highlights the muscular figures that would influence Michelangelo.

Something of the links engendered by Florence's hothouse atmosphere can be seen in the many master-pupil relationships and in the cross-fertilization and dissemination of ideas these links produced. Masaccio, for example, had at least two prominent followers: One was Filippo Lippi (1406–1469), a wayward friar who habitually seduced his models but also produced poetic and often innovative paintings. The other was Andrea del Castagno (circa 1412–1457), whose bold frescoes can be seen in Florence's cathedral (see pp. 58–65) and in the church of Sant'Apollonia (see sidebar p. 146). Similar links existed between all manner of other Florentine artists.

Florence's orbit proved so powerful that few other Tuscan centers managed to produce or hold painters in the early 15th century. Only Siena produced significant artists during this era, and even then they tended to lag behind their Florentine rivals. Notable exceptions to this trend were painters such as Sassetta (see p. 216) and the sculptor Jacopo della Quercia (1374–1438), both innovative artists who could match their Florentine contemporaries.

Florence's hegemony began to crack as the Renaissance reached its zenith during the last quarter of the 15th century. Major painters from outside the Tuscan capital—there had always been minor ones—included Piero della Francesca (1416–1492), from the town of Sansepolcro, known for his precise but unsettling paintings, and his Cortona-born pupil Luca Signorelli (1441–1523), whose muscular figures would later influence the likes of Michelangelo. This said, Florence remained a hotbed of artistic activity, its annals filled with most of the great names of Renaissance art—including Sandro Botticelli (1445–1510), Leonardo da Vinci, Domenico Ghirlandaio (1448–1494), Luca della Robbia (1400–1482), and many more. Its painters also worked beyond Tuscany, a trait that would become more pronounced when the Renaissance reached its maturity, a period from about 1500 known as the High Renaissance.

High Renaissance: Three great painters dominated this artistic period, two of them Tuscan-born, one of them Tuscan-trained. The first was Leonardo da Vinci (1452–1519), born in a small village in the hills outside Florence, a consummate genius but one who left only three works in Florence, all of them in the Uffizi. The second was Michelangelo (1475–1564), born in eastern Tuscany, a painter, sculptor, architect, and poet who spent the early part of his career in Florence, where he completed the statue of "David" and the funerary monuments of the Cappelle Medicee (see pp. 128–131). His greatest works, however, the frescoes of the Sistine Chapel, were reserved for Rome. The third painter was Raphael (1483–1520), born in Urbino, in the Marche region of eastern Italy. He, too, was lured to Rome, but he left many masterpieces in Florence, works now found in the Uffizi and the Galleria Palatina of the Palazzo Pitti (see pp. 169–174).

> Tuscany's later artists excelled in a style Raphael had helped develop: mannerism, a genre in which style and artifice were important.

Tuscany's later artists excelled in a style Raphael had helped develop: mannerism, a genre in which style and artifice were important. This was also a style in which established conventions of color, scale, and composition were ignored or deliberately subverted. Its leading exponents were Rosso Fiorentino (1494–1540), Jacopo Pontormo (1494–1557), Agnolo Bronzino (1503–1572), and—to a lesser extent—Andrea del Sarto (1486–1530) and Domenico Beccafumi (1486–1551) in Siena. Sculptors, too, embraced the style, among them Florence-based artists such as Bartolommeo Bandinelli (1488–1560), Bartolommeo Ammannati (1511–1592), French-born Giambologna (1529–1608), and the swashbuckling Benvenuto Cellini (1500–1571).

These proved some of the last Tuscan names to burn brightly in Italy's artistic firmament. Artistic primacy moved to Rome, where the ornate baroque style flourished, thanks to papal patronage and the decline of Florence as a political and economic force. In later centuries only the so-called Macchiaioli group of painters (from the Italian *macchias*—spot or stain) rose above the humdrum, a movement whose style and outlook mirrored that of the French Impressionists. Paintings by the group's leading exponents, notably Giovanni Fattori (1825–1908), can be seen in the modern art gallery of the Palazzo Pitti. Tuscany's last well-known artist was Amedeo Modigliani (1884–1920), who was born in Livorno but spent most of his working life in Paris.

Architecture

The appeal of Florence's and Tuscany's architecture is almost as great as that of their art. From simple Etruscan tombs and superb Romanesque churches to the surfeit of Renaissance palaces and Gothic cathedrals, the area is a treasury of fascinating and beautiful buildings whose designs span almost 3,000 years.

Etruscan & Roman: Tuscany's earliest architectural forms are the Etruscan tombs found around Sovana and Pitigliano in the southern part of the region. Other Etruscan architecture is almost nonexistent, largely because the Etruscans constructed many of their buildings from wood, which perished over the centuries.

The use of striped marbles in Siena's Duomo was introduced by merchants returning from the Middle East.

The region's largest Etruscan structures are tracts of defensive walls found in Fiesole, most of which are believed to date from around the end of the fourth century B.C.

Fiesole also claims some of Tuscany's most important Roman monuments, namely a well-preserved Roman theater and the remains of a first-century Roman temple. Other similar remains survive at Volterra (see pp. 242–243), and in Lucca's Piazza dell'Anfiteatro you can still make out the shape—and occasional blocks of stone—from the city's Roman amphitheater. Elsewhere, little of Roman vintage survives, certainly not in Florence, where the only memorials are for the most part intangible—the Roman gridiron plan of the central streets, the occasional name such as Via delle Terme

(Street of the Baths), and the barely discernible outline of the old amphitheater in the streets west of Piazza Santa Croce.

Little remains, either, of the work of the Lombard (north Italian) and other masons who worked across Tuscany during the centuries following the fall of Rome, although their influence would survive in later buildings that incorporated their styles and techniques. Much the same can be said of Byzantine architecture, whose heavily decorated style, a blend of Greek, Roman, and Asian influences, was introduced to Italy from the East after the sixth century.

Romanesque & Gothic: Only in about the 11th century did Tuscan architecture begin to flourish, spurred on by the upsurge in church-building and the emergence of city-states. The new towns acquired palaces, towers, walls, piazzas, and churches, most of them built in the Romanesque manner, a style distinguished by simplicity, round arches, and—in churches—a plain basilican (rectangular) plan with a sunken crypt and raised choir (the area around the high altar). In time the style acquired various embellishments, in particular the tiny arches, myriad columns, and inlaid marbled patterning associated with Pisan-Romanesque architecture—refinements developed in the wake of Pisa's trading links with the East.

Perhaps the supreme expression of Tuscany's early Romanesque style is found in the Abbazia di Sant'Antimo (see pp. 272–273), while examples of Pisan-Romanesque are scattered across the region, particularly in Pisa (Piazza del Duomo) and Lucca (San Michele in Foro). In Florence the Romanesque is exemplified by the baptistery

The Abbazia di Sant'Antimo has weathered time and history to still stand in 21st-century Tuscany.

and San Miniato al Monte, two of the city's oldest and most beautiful buildings.

From about the 13th century, the Romanesque was enlivened and eventually replaced by Gothic architecture, a style largely introduced from France and identified by its pointed arch, vaulting, rose windows, airy interiors, and an emphasis on the vertical. Gothic designs infuse the medieval *palazzi pubblici,* civic palaces, of most Tuscan towns, whose power and wealth reached a zenith in this period, particularly those of Florence (Palazzo Vecchio) and Siena (Palazzo Pubblico). Gothic was also uppermost in the cathedrals of Florence, Siena, and other centers, and in the great Florentine churches of Santa Croce and Santa Maria Novella.

The late Romanesque and early Gothic periods also marked the emergence of the first architects whose names have come down to us, most notably Arnolfo di Cambio (1245–circa 1301), the architect responsible for Florence's cathedral, Santa Croce, and the Palazzo Vecchio. Arnolfo was followed by Giotto (see p. 40), better known as one of the great painters of the age but responsible for another of Florence's most prominent landmarks, the Campanile, or cathedral bell tower.

The New Wave: By the beginning of the 15th century, the forces that led to the Renaissance in painting and sculpture had also produced a revolution in architecture. Leading light of the new wave was the Florentine Filippo Brunelleschi, widely acknowledged as the first—and perhaps greatest—of all Renaissance architects (see sidebar this page).

Filippo Brunelleschi

Filippo Brunelleschi's (1377–1446) genius was to adapt the purity and simplicity of classical Roman and early Tuscan Romanesque buildings to his own concern for the practical problems of construction and management of space. He also played a major part in mastering the laws of linear perspective, combining his many talents for the first time in Florence with designs for the church of San Lorenzo (see pp. 122–127) in about 1418 and the arched loggia of the Ospedale degli Innocenti (see p. 72) a year later. His masterpiece was the construction of Florence's cathedral dome, one of the wonders of preindustrial engineering (see pp. 66–67). He also created several other Florentine gems, such as the Cappella dei Pazzi (see p. 114) and the church of Santo Spirito (see p. 187).

Florence's other major architect of the period, Michelozzo di Bartolommeo (1396–1472), lacked Brunelleschi's genius but had the singular advantage of being a favorite of Cosimo the Elder, one of the pillars of the Medici dynasty. He designed the Medici's first major Florentine home, the Palazzo Medici-Riccardi (see pp. 133–135), where he established a fashion for rustication—building with huge, rough-hewn blocks of stone—that can be seen across the city to this day. He also built or adapted several of the Medici's country villas, notably Careggi, as well as the tribune and sacristy of Santissima Annunziata and the cloister and library at San Marco, all projects dear to the Medici's hearts.

Santissima Annunziata's tribune was completed by the third of Florence's great architectural triumvirate, Leon Battista Alberti (1404–1472), a multitalented Renaissance man who was a playwright, painter, musician, scientist, athlete, and mathematician, as well as an architect. Alberti rarely concerned himself with the building of his works; he concentrated instead on design and theory, and in *De re aedificatoria* (1452) he produced the Renaissance's first major architectural treatise. He memorably defined beauty in architecture as "the harmony and concord of all parts achieved in such a manner that nothing could be added, or taken away, except for the worse." Alberti described decoration and ornament as "a kind of additional brightness and improvement of Beauty." He completed few buildings, but those he finished were all masterpieces. He also worked mostly outside Tuscany, his Florentine creations amounting to the facades of Santa Maria Novella and Palazzo Rucellai, both created for the textile baron Giovanni Rucellai.

Many of Brunelleschi's and Alberti's ideas were carried forward by lesser architects, notably Il Cronaca (1457–1508) and Giuliano da Sangallo (1445–1516). They worked not only in Florence but also in places like Pienza, where Pope Pius II employed Bernardo Rossellino (1409–1464), a disciple of Alberti (he oversaw construction of Alberti's Palazzo Rucellai), to create a model Renaissance city in his birthplace. None of these men, however, nor other jobbing Medici architects such as Vasari, Ammannati, and Buontalenti (see sidebar p. 173), approached the genius of Michelangelo. The great man completed only two Florentine projects, the cathedral's Sagrestia Nuova (see p. 65) and Medici Library and vestibule (see p. 127), but both were masterpieces that transcended genre and convention.

> Dante also formed part of a new wave of writers, a literary movement that he christened the *dolce stil nuovo* (gentle new style).

After the Renaissance: The next great architectural style, the baroque, largely passed Florence and Tuscany by in favor of Rome, as did mannerism, appearing only briefly in the facades of Ognissanti, Santa Trìnita, and a handful of lesser churches. Although many major buildings appeared across the region during and after the 16th century—notably the Uffizi, Palazzo Pitti, and numerous villas and palaces—none would approach the stature of earlier works by Brunelleschi and his followers. Indeed, worse was in store for Florence, namely the redevelopment of the city center in the middle of the 19th century, when countless old buildings were razed to make way for the Piazza della Repubblica. More areas were cleared in the 20th century around Santa Croce and Santa Maria Novella railroad station, while swathes of the old city were also destroyed by the Nazis in 1944 to delay the advancing British and U.S. armies. As a result, some of the architecture in Europe's most celebrated Renaissance city is—ironically—an ugly affront to its illustrious antecedents.

Literature

Tuscany's contribution to literature has been immense. Its principal role was to provide Italy with a literary language, a language that would eventually become Italian as it is spoken and written today. It also provided one of the greatest poets of any age or origin (Florentine Dante Alighieri) and several major writers—Petrarch, Boccaccio, and Machiavelli—whose works are still widely celebrated to the present day.

Early Tuscan literature, however, was long in thrall to the literature of the classical canon, notably ancient Roman poets such as Virgil and Ovid, and writers such as Pliny, Juvenal, and Suetonius. Almost all such literature was written in Latin, which continued to be Italy's literary and scholarly language until the 13th century, when Franciscan poets such as St. Francis of Assisi, borrowing from the troubadour traditions of Provence, began to write in the everyday, or vernacular, Italian dialects of the period.

In Tuscany the nascent literary landscape was dominated by Guittone d'Arezzo (1235–1294), whose lyrical verse adapted Provençal and Sicilian styles; Siena-born Cecco Angiolieri (1260–1312), whose deliciously bawdy sonnets celebrated the delights of wine, women, and song; and Brunetto Latini (1220–1295), whose writing tended toward the didactic and allegorical. Latini is also remembered as the teacher of the most famous of all Tuscan and Italian writers, Dante Alighieri (1265–1321; see pp. 78–79).

Dante & the New Style: Dante was the first to propose, in a treatise extolling the virtues of everyday Italian (by then a distant corruption of Latin), that Italian could be a literary language—although he presented his ideas, ironically, in a Latin text, *De vulgari eloquentia*. The importance of such literature was that it established Italian—or rather Tuscan Italian, the dialect in which Dante wrote—as a legitimate literary language. This made literature more widely disseminated: Poorly educated Italians could understand their own language but not Latin. It also established a linguistic pattern that would eventually become the model for a standard Italian across Italy (although Italy still retains a variety of strong regional dialects).

Dante wrote widely, with works on politics *(De Monarchia)*, philosophy *(Il Convivio)*, and love *(Vita Nuova)*. His masterpiece, however, *La Divina Commedia (The Divine Comedy)*, probably begun 1302, is a poem that transcended genre and today stands in the front rank of European literature. Dante also formed part of a new wave of writers, a literary movement that he christened the *dolce stil nuovo* (gentle new style). This pioneered the use of the vernacular and moved away from the poetry of spiritual and platonic ideals. The style was embraced by Tuscan authors such as Guinizzelli (1235–1276) and Cavalcanti (circa 1250–1300). Both were accomplished writers, but both were overshadowed by two other great literary figures who continued Dante's use of the vernacular: Arezzo-born Francesco Petrarca, better known as Petrarch (1304–1374), and Giovanni Boccaccio (see sidebar p. 154).

Petrarch was a traveler and a diplomat, and it was while in service to the papal court at Avignon in France that he more than likely met Laura de Noves, the amatory inspiration for

Tuscany's *Cinema Paradiso*

Tuscany has yielded no great directors but its landscapes have provided the setting for dozens of celebrated movies.

Giorgio Galliani, a location scout for almost 100 Tuscan-shot movies, explains: "Tuscany has a great attribute— if you plant a nail in the ground and extend a string for a radius of 30 miles you find everything."

Movies with Tuscan locations include James Ivory's *A Room With a View* (1986; shot in and around Florence), Anthony Minghella's *The English Patient* (1996; Pienza, Montepulciano, and the Val d'Orcia), and in this century *Gladiator* (2000; Val d'Orcia), *Hannibal* (2001; Florence), *Under the Tuscan Sun* (2003; Cortona), and *New Moon* (2009; Montepulciano), part of the *Twilight* series.

Tuscany has also produced one of Italy's best loved comic actors, Roberto Benigni, protagonist of the Oscar-winning *La Vita è Bella (Life Is Beautiful*, 1998).

The Tuscan Film Commission *(toscanafilmcommission.it)* offers information on all aspects of movies and movie life in Tuscany, including Florentine and other regional film festivals.

his *Canzoniere,* or *Songs,* some of the finest lyrical sonnets in the literary canon. Boccaccio is remembered for the narrative finesse of the *Il Decamerone,* or *The Decameron* (1348–1353), a series of 100 tales told by ten people over a period of ten days as the Black Death raged in Florence. Petrarch and Boccaccio were not entirely wedded to the vernacular, however, and joined attempts to revive Latin and Greek as literary languages, forming part of the humanistic and classical vanguard that paved the way for the Renaissance.

Classical ideals and a more human-centered cosmology found expression in the works of humanists such as Leonardo Bruni (1370–1444), buried in Florence's Santa Croce (see pp. 109–110), and the poet Angelo Poliziano (1454–1494; born in Montepulciano), a tendency encouraged by the patronage of men such as Lorenzo de' Medici. Artists such as Leonardo da Vinci, Michelangelo, Leon Battista Alberti, and Giorgio Vasari also wrote poetry and important artistic and architectural treatises.

Machiavelli & Other Greats

Florence's best remembered writer of the early 16th century is Niccolò Machiavelli (1469–1527), a noble, a diplomat, and the chancellor of the Florentine republic. His major work was *Il Principe (The Prince),* begun circa 1513 but only published posthumously in 1532, a masterpiece of political analysis that linked political science with a penetrating study of human nature. The book explored statecraft and the idea of historical cycles, basing itself on Machiavelli's clear-eyed notion that the world has always been inhabited by human beings who have always had the same passions. Today, Machiavelli's name is synonymous with devious political machinations, something not borne out by study of his writings—*Machiavellian* was originally a French term used to denigrate not Machiavelli, but all things Italian.

Machiavelli also wrote a Florentine history (*Istorie Fiorentine,* begun circa 1520), as did another major figure of the time, Francesco Guicciardini (1483–1540). A treatise of a different kind, *Galateo* by Giovanni della Casa (1503–1556), codified everyday aristocratic etiquette and became a handbook of good behavior in royal courts across Europe. Someone who could have benefited from the work was Benvenuto Cellini, a sculptor

EXPERIENCE: Speak Italian

Florence and Tuscany offer innumerable opportunities to learn or improve your Italian, from weekend courses in private homes to yearlong programs of regular, formal lessons. In Florence one of the longest established schools is the **British Institute of Florence** *(Piazza Strozzi 2, tel 055 267 781, britishinstitute.it).* Its range of courses includes one-, two-, and three-month semesters, at beginner, intermediate, and advanced levels. The **Dante Alighieri** school *(Via Tommaso Pendola, tel 0577 49 533, dantealighieri.com)* offers a similar range of courses in Siena.

Obvious tips include the need to be realistic about how much you can achieve in a short time and how much work you are prepared to put in. You should also be prepared to do some preparatory study prior to taking a course.

Accommodations are also a major consideration, as a homestay with a Tuscan family has obvious benefits for learning the language, as does access to a TV. A few hours watching news broadcasts, familiar films, or simple soap operas—foreign shows in Italy are all dubbed—provide a valuable aid to improving comprehension.

and goldsmith whose autobiography—widely available today in translation—is not only a gripping account of a wild and often violent life but also a graphic portrait of life in 16th-century Florence.

Machiavelli also turned his hand to comedy *(Mandragola)*, a little-explored genre in Renaissance Tuscany, but was overshadowed in this area by Arezzo-born Pietro Aretino (1492–1556), a writer of trenchant and hard-nosed satires. At the other literary extreme was Pisa-born Galileo Galilei (1564–1642), one of the first scientists to apply the modern concepts of his age—as opposed to hidebound theological- or philosophical-based approaches—to scientific research and treatises.

Later Tuscan literature produced fewer great names. One notable exception was the poet Giosué Carducci (1835–1907), Italy's first Nobel laureate, who spent his youth in Tuscany. Literary renown of a very different type was earned by Carlo Lorenzini (1826–1890), a man less well known than the character he created: Pinocchio.

Music

Composers and musicians have generally made little impact outside Tuscany. It was a Tuscan monk, however, Guido Monaco (995–1050),

The monument of Giacomo Puccini in his native Lucca

who devised the musical scale and forms of notation still used today.

The region may also have spawned Italy's greatest musical legacy—opera—whose origins many scholars trace to the *intermedii* of Florentine wedding ceremonies that involved a mix of singing, dancing, and static performance. Members of a Florentine academy known as the Camerata, inspired by these entertainments, began to combine elements of Greek drama with musical declamation. Two of the its members, Jacopo Peri and Ottavio Rinucci, produced the first opera—*Dafne*—in 1597, as well as the first opera to have survived in its complete form (*Euridice,* first performed at Florence's Palazzo Pitti for the marriage of Maria de' Medici to the French king Henry IV). One of the major figures of opera's golden age, Giacomo Puccini (1858–1924), was born in Lucca and embraced a prevailing trend in opera toward modern themes and *verismo* (realism) in operas such as *Tosca, Madama Butterfly,* and *La Bohème.* Today, a large number of musical festivals and concert cycles are held in towns across Tuscany. ■

Florence

The historic heart of Florence, home to the Duomo, its awe-inspiring dome, and the marble-clad baptistery

Piazza del Duomo

Pages 52–53: Florence's bridges span a golden Arno River.
Above: The Duomo, or cathedral, of Santa Maria del Fiore
Opposite: Detail of the east doors of the baptistery by Ghiberti

Piazza del Duomo

Piazza del Duomo is a stage for the sublimely beautiful baptistery, the soaring pinnacle of the Campanile, and the overwhelming grandeur of Florence's immense Duomo, or cathedral. This magnificent ensemble—together with the nearby cathedral museum—forms the first port of call for most visitors.

Florence's 700-year-old Duomo forms the centerpiece of the Piazza del Duomo.

Not all of Florence's roads lead to Piazza del Duomo, yet you find yourself drawn here by the looming presence of the cathedral dome, a masterpiece of medieval and Renaissance engineering that dominates the city's skyline. Up close, the dome is overshadowed by the eye-catching spectacle of the cathedral's exterior, a riot of red, green, and cream marble that makes the interior's more restrained appearance all the more surprising. Fewer artistic treasures lie concealed here than in other Florentine churches, but few works of art compare with the view that unfolds over the city from the top of the dome.

If you resist the lure of this panorama, temptation soon comes your way again,

for the vista from the nearby Campanile is perhaps even better, thanks to the fact that its bird's-eye view includes the cathedral and the distinctive octagon of Piazza del Duomo's third major component, the Battistero, or baptistery. The oldest building in Florence, the baptistery was used for centuries to baptize every Florentine child, thereby serving as a religious focus and a way of strengthening the allegiance of Florentines to their birthplace. Unlike the cathedral, this building is beautiful to look at both inside and out. The exterior's ornate marble decoration is complemented inside by a majestic mosaic ceiling, and a trio of doors decorated with some of the city's finest bronze sculpture.

The piazza's failings are the traffic, the school parties, and the tour groups crowding its environs. Unusually for an Italian square, there's next to no room for cafés from which to admire its human and architectural spectacle. You can escape the cars by walking to the rear of the cathedral, an area that is partly set aside for pedestrians. Here you find the Museo dell'Opera del Duomo, home to many works of art removed from the cathedral over the years. Most are statues and carvings—including masterpieces by Donatello, Michelangelo, and Ghiberti—making this the city's most important collection of sculpture after that of the nearby Museo Nazionale del Bargello. ■

NOT TO BE MISSED:

Climbing the cathedral dome
   for city views   59

The Duomo's frescoes   64–65

Studying the south and north doors
   of the Battistero   69–71

The Battistero's mosaic ceiling   71

Climbing the Campanile   75

Donatello's "Mary Magdalene"
   and Michelangelo's "Pietà"
   in the Museo dell'Opera del
   Duomo   77

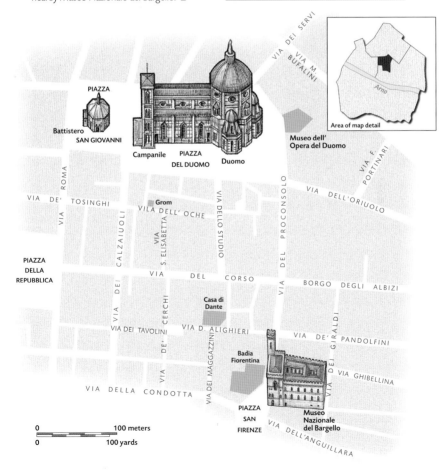

Duomo

The Duomo, or cathedral, of Santa Maria del Fiore is one of Italy's most distinctive landmarks, a lavishly decorated poem in stone whose magnificent dome soars in triumph above the cluster of Florence's central streets.

Worshippers light candles and offer prayers inside the Duomo, as they have for centuries.

Florence

Visitor Information

- ✉ Via Cavour 1r
- ☎ 055 290 832 or 055 290 833
- ✉ Piazza San Giovanni 1
- ☎ 055 288 496
- 🕐 Closed Sun. & p.m.

- ✉ Aeroporto Vespucci
- ☎ 055 315 874
- 🕐 Closed Sun. & p.m.
- ✉ Piazza della Stazione 4
- ☎ 055 212 245

firenzeturismo.it

Views from this breathtaking vantage point are one of the highlights of any Florentine sojourn, but the main body of the church also contains a wealth of artistic treasures.

Santa Maria del Fiore has not always been Florence's cathedral. Both the baptistery and church of San Lorenzo may once have fulfilled the role, while the cathedral on the present site was the cathedral of Santa Reparata, probably founded in the seventh century. Plans for a new Duomo were mooted toward the end of the 13th century, when Florence's burgeoning status as a wealthy and important

city had seen it outgrow its former cathedral. Other Italian cities had built or were building splendid new churches, not least Pisa and Siena, both major Florentine rivals.

Grandiloquent statements in stone were a vital part of any medieval city's sense of worth, hence the comment of Florence's ruling Priorate, or council, that Santa Reparata "was too crudely built and too small for such a city." In 1294 the council issued an edict demanding a cathedral of "the most exalted and most prodigal magnificence, in order that the industry and power of men may never create or undertake

INSIDER TIP:

The Biglietto Unico covers your visits to the Duomo, Santa Reparata, the Battistero, the Campanile, and the Museo dell'Opera del Duomo— all for €10 [about $14].

—NEIL SHEA
National Geographic writer

anything whatsoever more vast and more beautiful." It went on to say that the building was to be "so magnificent that it shall surpass anything . . . produced in the times of their greatest power by the Greeks and Romans."

Building the Duomo

For a while the Florentines had tried to patch up and enlarge Santa Reparata. In 1294, however, Arnolfo di Cambio (see p. 47) was asked to submit plans for an entirely new structure. The architect was then employed on a scheme designed to provide for the city's orderly enlargement, the fruits of which would include Florence's last and definitive set of city walls (1284–1333).

Arnolfo's plan for the new cathedral was for a vaulted basilica—one of the simplest architectural forms—a polygonal, or multisided, apse (the area around the high altar), and a gargantuan octagonal dome. How the last was to be built—it would be the largest dome raised since antiquity—he neglected to say.

The church's first stone was laid on September 8, 1296, and the building was given the name Santa Maria del Fiore, a title that deliberately linked the Virgin with Florence's flower (*fiore*) emblem. The stubborn citizens of Florence, however, insisted on calling the cathedral by its old name, Santa Reparata, until ordered to desist by a decree of 1401. Remnants of the earlier cathedral can still be seen below the present building.

Work on the mammoth project faltered after Arnolfo's death in 1302, but it received a new impetus when the body of St. Zenobius, Florence's first bishop, was moved to the site in 1331 (see p. 70). Construction was then entrusted to Giotto, better known as one of the most innovative artists of the age, but he devoted himself mainly to the Campanile, or bell tower

Duomo

- ▲ Map p. 57
- ✉ Piazza del Duomo
- ☎ 055 230 2885
- 🕐 Closed Sun., Jan. 1, Jan. 6, & Easter
- 💲 $$$ (Biglietto Unico covers the dome, Battistero, Campanile, Santa Reparata, and Museo dell'Opera del Duomo), church free
- 🚌 Bus: 1, 6, 14, 17, 23; C2 to Via de' Pecori or Via del Proconsolo

ilgrandemuseo
delduomo.it

Visiting the Dome

At some point during or after your visit to the interior you should consider joining the inevitable line for tickets to climb to the top of the dome (see pp. 66–67), both for the superb views and for the insights into the engineering skills that allowed it to be built. Note, however, that there are 463 steps, and that parts of the staircase are narrow. There is no elevator.

(see pp. 74–75). Thereafter, a series of lesser architects labored on the project, often working against a background of political and economic turmoil, not least the unrest caused by the Black Death, the plague that ravaged much of Europe in 1348.

Financing the project was a problem at the best of times. Some 10 percent of the initial cost was met by a tax on citizens' property, and as late as 1800 money was still being deducted from every deceased Florentine's estate to pay for the building. All fines from charges of drunkenness were also set aside toward construction costs.

Work on the nave was completed in 1378, on the ceiling in 1380, and on the tribunes (the three apses) and the dome's supporting drum in 1418. The construction of the dome, one of the greatest of all feats of medieval engineering, is a story in its own right (see pp. 66–67).

Touring the Duomo
The Facade: Today, the cathedral relies for its first, dazzling effect on its facade which, unknown to many visitors, is a comparatively recent creation. Arnolfo's original facade was pulled down in 1587 when still only a quarter finished, and plans were hatched to start again with a frontage more in line with the architectural taste of the late 16th century.

In any event, no new facade appeared on the cathedral for some 300 years. The present

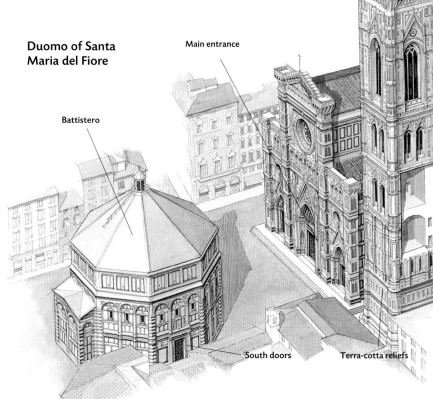

Duomo of Santa Maria del Fiore

Campanile

Main entrance

Battistero

South doors

Terra-cotta reliefs

front was built to a plan by the otherwise obscure architect Emilio de Fabris in 1887. His controversial scheme was selected after a total of 91 other plans had been rejected. The new facade was heavily criticized almost immediately after its completion, and even today—for all its gaudy impact and dramatic photo-opportunism—it is still belittled by most Florentine and other architectural purists.

The Interior: Moving to the cathedral's interior is something of a shock. Where the exterior is all ornament and color, the

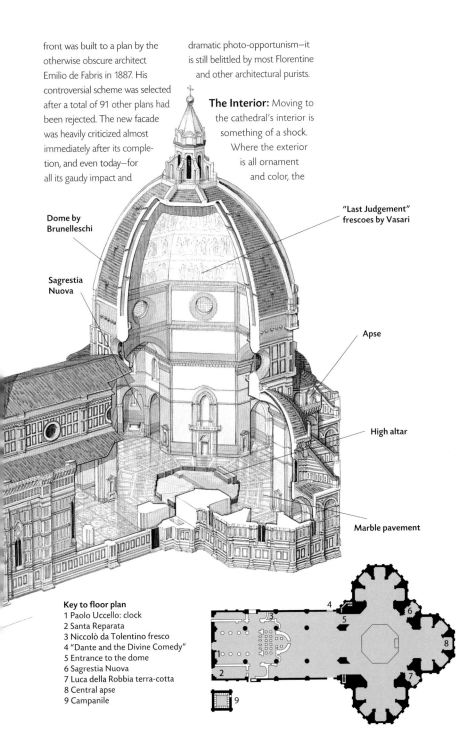

Dome by Brunelleschi

Sagrestia Nuova

"Last Judgement" frescoes by Vasari

Apse

High altar

Marble pavement

Key to floor plan
1 Paolo Uccello: clock
2 Santa Reparata
3 Niccolò da Tolentino fresco
4 "Dante and the Divine Comedy"
5 Entrance to the dome
6 Sagrestia Nuova
7 Luca della Robbia terra-cotta
8 Central apse
9 Campanile

INSIDER TIP:

The 463 steps of the dome shouldn't be attempted by anyone who is not reasonably fit or who suffers from claustrophobia.

—TOM O'NEILL
National Geographic writer

interior—at least at first glance—is all space and gloomy austerity. The Priorate's demand for a "vast building" was clearly taken to heart, as size for its own sake appears to be the interior's overwhelming concern; this is Europe's fourth largest church, after Milan's cathedral, St. Paul's in London, and St. Peter's in Rome. An edifice on such a grand scale was vital, both to outdo rival cities and to provide an indoor arena—the cathedral holds some 30,000 worshippers—that would offer a single point of focus for the city's inhabitants. For

example, the cleric and charismatic monk Girolamo Savonarola (see p. 33) regularly preached here to full houses, and the renowned Renaissance architect Leon Battista Alberti stressed that the cathedral dome should be "large enough to cover with its shadow all the Tuscan people" (*De re aedificatoria,* 1452).

The Dome, Crypt, & Other Attractions

The interior's austerity is deceptive, for it contains a number of artistic treasures, as well as two worthwhile side attractions. The first of these is the cathedral's **crypt,** where you can see ruins of the church of Santa Reparata; the second is the cathedral's **dome,** which offers an insight into the architectural acumen of its presiding genius, Filippo Brunelleschi. Better still, the dome offers a glorious panorama of Florence and its surrounding countryside.

Before your climb of the dome (see sidebar p. 59 & pp. 66–67), walk around the interior to enjoy its other highlights. Start by turning

Loggia del Bigallo

On the corner of Piazza del Duomo and Via del Calzaiuoli stands the Loggia del Bigallo, an arched structure dating from around 1353. It was built for the Compagnia della Misericordia, a confraternity and hospital charity.

In 1425 this charity united with the Compagnia del Bigallo, which cared for the poor, elderly, and orphans. The Compagnia used the loggia to display lost or abandoned children—with the hope they might be recognized—before

the organization took responsibility for them. The Misericordia headquarters is still opposite the loggia; you will recognize it by the ambulances parked outside the building.

Nearby, there is also a small museum *(Piazza del Duomo 20, open Mon. only)* with pictures and objects relating to the Misericordia's history. Another small museum, the **Museo del Bigallo,** *(Piazza San Giovanni, tel 055 288 946)* can be visited by appointment.

A statue of Filippo Brunelleschi, architect of the cathedral's dome. Critics thought his project could never be realized.

to face the main facade doors through which you've just entered. Above the main door you'll see a strange **clock** set to the so-called *hora italica,* an arrangement in which the 24th hour of the day ends at sunset. This system was designed chiefly to mark the religious divisions of the day, and it remained in widespread use across Italy until the 18th century. The heads of the prophets decorating the timepiece are the work of Paolo Uccello (see p. 42), an artist whose hand you'll see again elsewhere in the cathedral. The stained-glass windows on this wall were created to designs by Lorenzo Ghiberti (1378–1455), the sculptor responsible for the baptistery's east doors (see p. 71). To the right of the central door as you face it stands the tomb of Antonio d'Orso, Bishop of Florence (1323); it is the work of Tino di Camaino (1285–1337).

Moving to the south (right) wall, the first statue here portrays Brunelleschi, the dome's creator, and it was carved by Andrea Cavalcanti, his pupil and adopted son, in 1446. The figure by Benedetto da Maiano (1442–1497), to its left, shows "Giotto at Work."

By the nave's first right-hand pillar stands a pretty stoup, or holy water container, and the entrance to what remains of **Santa Reparata.** As far as the latter is concerned, however, it is barely worth paying the admission fee to see what amounts to little more than patchy ruins. The key point of interest is the tomb of Brunelleschi at the foot of the stairs, which you can glimpse

without paying. The fact the architect was buried in the cathedral underlines the esteem in which he was held by the city.

Now walk from the nave's right-hand side to look at the cathedral's three key paintings, all of which are on the left (north) wall opposite. From left to right, the first of these is the "Equestrian Portrait of Niccolò da Tolentino" by Andrea del Castagno (see p. 43), which shows a noted contemporary condottiere, or mercenary soldier, on horseback. The painting was clearly derived from the picture of the condottiere to its right, the "Equestrian Portrait of Sir John Hawkwood," painted 20 years earlier by Paolo Uccello. Notice how the latter painting's perspective is askew, the pedestal being painted as if seen from a completely different point

The mosaic above the main door of the Duomo and the facade was added between 1871 and 1887.

of view to the horse and rider above. Uccello was preoccupied with perspective—see his Uffizi and Santa Maria Novella paintings for further evidence of his fixation (see pp. 99 & 155). Here it seems he first painted the horse "correctly"—that is, from the point of view of an onlooker gazing at the pedestal—and as a result all that could be seen of the creature was a large portion of its belly. The cathedral authorities, understandably annoyed at the fresco's strange and disconcerting perspective, ordered the artist to repaint the offending section.

The third painting lies farther along, by the side door on the north of the nave, the Porta della Mandorla, and shows "Dante and the Divine Comedy" (1465). The work of Domenico di Michelino

(1417–1491), this picture portrays the eminent Florentine holding open a copy of *La Divina Commedia*, his most celebrated work, from which a ray of light shines on Florence. Note how Dante is shown outside the city walls, a symbol of his exile (see p. 79). If the nearby **Porta della Mandorla** is open, incidentally, be sure to step outside to admire its sculpture. The door takes its name from the almond-shaped frame (*mandorla* means "almond") that encloses a relief of "The Assumption of the Virgin" by Nanni di Banco (circa 1384–1421).

Returning to the church, walk to the crossing, the large open area under the dome. The three tribunes, or apses, are arranged around it. Look up to see Giorgio Vasari's dome frescoes of "The Last Judgment" (1572–1579).

In Florence, business addresses are suffixed with "r," *rosso* (red). Look for these numbers displayed in red on the street.

—MARINA CONTI
National Geographic Italy editor

The Sacristies: These showy pictures distract from the greater intrinsic merit of the sacristies, two enclosed areas to either side of the central apse. On the left as you face the high altar is the **Sagrestia Nuova,** or New Sacristy, decorated with 15th-century inlaid wood panelling and protected by bronze doors (1446–1467) designed by Michelozzo (1396–1472) and Luca della Robbia (1400–1482). Behind these doors Lorenzo the Magnificent sought refuge from would-be assassins during the Pazzi Conspiracy of 1478 (see sidebar p. 33). His brother, Giuliano, was hacked down on the steps of the high altar, his skull shattered and his body rent with 19 stab wounds. Portraits on the handles commemorate both brothers.

Above the door of the Sagrestia Nuova is a blue-white terra-cotta lunette of "The Annunciation" (1442) that would have looked down on the carnage. The work of della Robbia, it was the first of the glazed and colored ceramics with which his name would become synonymous. An almost identical lunette of "The Ascension" by the same artist graces the **Sagrestia Vecchia,** or Old Sacristy, on the other side of the church. Remember these sacristies when you visit the Museo dell'Opera del Duomo (see pp. 76–77), whose highlights include a pair of carved *cantorie,* or choir lofts, that once stood above each of their entrances.

Finally, take note of the magnificent bronze reliquary by Lorenzo Ghiberti above the altar of the central apse, crafted to contain the remains of St. Zenobius, Florence's first bishop.

Battistero

The Battistero di San Giovanni, or baptistery, is probably Florence's oldest building.

(continued on. p. 68)

Florence's Ice-Cream Wars

For years, there was no contest in the title for Florence's best gelato: Vivoli *(Via Isola delle Stinche 7r, tel 055 292 334, vivoli.it, closed Mon.),* founded near the church of Santa Croce in 1930, outshone all others. Now, however, there is a slick new challenger, Grom *(cnr. of Via del Campanile & Via delle Oche, tel 055 216 158, grom.it),* tucked away in a side alley off Piazza del Duomo. The upstart has been so successful that it has opened outlets not only in many other Italian cities but also farther afield in Manhattan, Malibu, Paris, Osaka, and Tokyo.

In these and other *gelaterie* (ice-cream parlors), the procedure is to choose a cup *(copa)* or cone *(cono)* and then specify the size, with increases usually in increments of 50 cents. The cheapest sizes usually allow you two flavors, larger ones three.

The Dome

Planning a dome for Florence's cathedral was one thing; building it was quite another. Earlier medieval domes had been constructed on wooden frames, raised to hold the structures' stones in place until the mortar set. A frame the size of the cathedral's dome, however, would have required most of the wood in Tuscany. Worse still, medieval masons had no experience of a dome this size and no notion of how to contain its estimated 25,000 tons (22,680 metric tons) of lateral thrust.

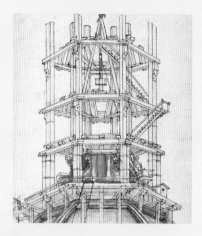

Construction of the lantern atop the dome began in 1446. A contemporary drawing shows the elaborate scaffolding.

All manner of ideas surfaced as to how the dome might be built. One suggested it could be made of pumice, a featherlight volcanic rock. In despairing mood, the city's elders mounted a competition in 1418 to devise a solution. Its winner was Filippo Brunelleschi, who narrowly beat Lorenzo Ghiberti, the victor over Brunelleschi in the competition to design the baptistery north doors in 1401 (see p. 70).

Brunelleschi had been a poor loser in 1401; this time it was Ghiberti who lost with bad grace, joining the chorus of doom-mongers who ridiculed Brunelleschi's plans as unworkable. An exasperated but canny Brunelleschi eventually feigned illness as an excuse to abandon the project, upon which Ghiberti took over, only to find himself out of his depth. By

1423 Brunelleschi had been reinstated as the dome's sole "inventor and chief director."

Brunelleschi's solutions to the dome's engineering problems were ingenious. Some are still not understood today, but in essence they boiled down to the construction of two shells: A light outer covering was about 3 feet (1 m) thick, and a more robust inner shell measured around 13 feet (4 m) thick. More importantly, the inner shell used a herringbone arrangement of bricks, whose cantilevered rings were immensely strong and allowed the dome to support itself as it rose.

INSIDER TIP:

Visit the Filippo Brunelleschi exhibit, devoted to the dome's construction, at the Museo dell'Opera del Duomo [see pp. 76–77].

—BILL McBEE
National Geographic
Marketing Services

No detail was too small for Brunelleschi, who provided on-site kitchens for his workers to save time, created a honeycomb of corridors to speed up movement around the dome, and provided scaffolding hooks to make cleaning and repairs easier for future generations. Other innovations included lightweight materials, fast-drying mortar, and special tools, some of which can be seen in the Museo dell'Opera del Duomo (see pp. 76–77).

Completion of the dome in 1436 allowed for the cathedral's consecration on March 25 that year. The present lantern, however—the very top of the cupola—was still not built, as many critics believed the dome would collapse under any more weight. Brunelleschi was again forced to suffer the indignity of a competition—which he won—and work on the missing lantern began a few months before his death in 1446. Only the exposed brickwork of a proposed gallery now remains unfinished, abandoned after criticism of the plan by one of the dome's most fervent admirers—Michelangelo.

Brunelleschi's solution to the problem of constructing the cathedral's huge dome was to design two shells, an inner one and an outer. A system of cantilevered rings and bricks enabled the structure to support itself as it rose.

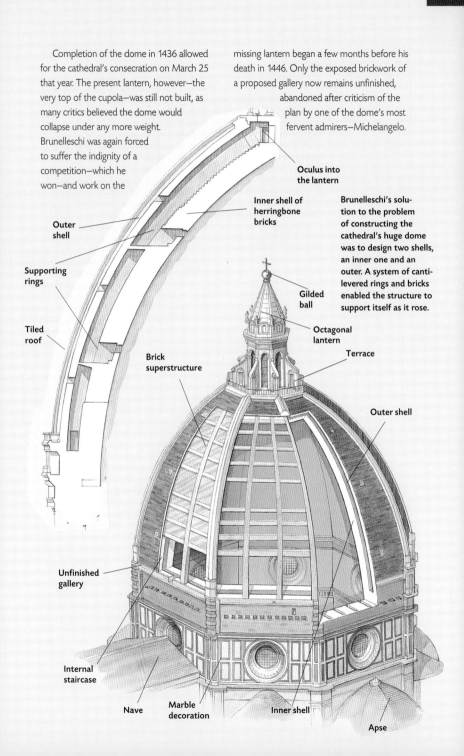

Oculus into the lantern

Inner shell of herringbone bricks

Outer shell

Supporting rings

Tiled roof

Gilded ball

Octagonal lantern

Terrace

Brick superstructure

Outer shell

Unfinished gallery

Internal staircase

Nave

Marble decoration

Inner shell

Apse

Battistero

-  Map p. 57
- Piazza San Giovanni-Piazza del Duomo
- 055 230 2885
- Closed daily until 11:15 a.m., Sun. p.m., 1st Sat. of each month, & religious holidays
- $$$ (Biglietto Unico covers the dome, Battistero, Campanile, & Museo dell'Opera del Duomo)
- Bus: 1, 6, 14, 17, 23; C2 to Via de' Pecori

ilgrandemuseo delduomo.it

For centuries, every Florentine child was baptized here, making it more precious to the city than the cathedral. Its octagonal interior is swathed with some of Europe's finest mosaics, but even these are eclipsed by the splendor of its three celebrated bronze doors.

In today's well-documented world, it's hard to believe that for much of the Middle Ages the Florentines forgot the origins of their baptistery. For years they thought it was a structure of Roman origin, a pagan temple to Mars, god of war, built to commemorate Florence's defeat of Fiesole and the creation of Florence in the first century A.D. (see pp. 26–27). It became a Christian building—or so they believed—in the fourth century, during the reign of Constantine, the first Christian emperor.

Today this theory is discounted, although scholars are still unsure of the baptistery's precise genesis. It is generally accepted that the present building occupies the site of a first-century Roman edifice—probably a grand *domus*, or house—although many of the interior's immense granite columns probably came from the Roman-era Capitol building in Florence, parts of which also found their way into San Miniato al Monte (see pp. 182–185).

The first documentary reference to a building here comes in 897, when it is mentioned as the city's cathedral. Much of the classically inspired decoration dates from about 1059 to 1128, perhaps later, a period of remodeling that saw the addition of the exterior's geometric medley of pillars, cornices, and colored marble friezes. This style of decoration would influence Tuscan architects and lead to the building of

The Battistero in Piazza del Duomo, viewed from the Campanile

Romanesque churches across the region for centuries.

The decoration's splendor was no accident. It was commissioned and paid for by the Merchants Guild, the Arte di Calimala (or Arte di Mercato), the most powerful of the city's guilds (see sidebar p. 29) and the body entrusted with the baptistery's upkeep. In caring for one of the city's most important buildings, it found itself in competition with a rival guild, the wealthy Arte della Lana (Wool Guild), which was responsible for the cathedral.

The Doors: Some idea of the baptistery's standing among Florentines can be gleaned from the fact that it was invariably the baptistery, not the cathedral—at least early on—that received the most lavish works of art. Nowhere is this more obvious than in the baptistery's three sets of doors, its most significant artistic features. The earliest of these are the **south doors,** designed by Andrea Pisano (1290–1348), a Pisan sculptor chosen partly because Pisa's recently completed cathedral was already celebrated for its magnificent bronze doors. Pisano completed wax models for the doors in just three months, their casting being entrusted to the Venetian Leonardo d'Avanzo. Casting took six long years, and the doors were installed in 1336, when they were placed at the baptistery's main entrance (facing the cathedral). They were moved to their present position in 1452 to make way for Lorenzo Ghiberti's east doors.

The 20 upper reliefs of the

doors' 28 panels portray episodes from the life of St. John the Baptist, Florence's patron and the saint to whom the baptistery is dedicated (Giovanni is Italian for John). The eight lower reliefs represent "Humility" and the "Cardinal and Theological Virtues." The doors' bronze frame is by Vittorio Ghiberti, son of Lorenzo Ghiberti, and was created when the doors were moved in 1452. The inscription at the top

---

Baptism: Rituals & Records

Baptism was important in medieval Tuscany, but not merely for religious reasons. In Siena children were baptized in the church of their *contrada*, or parish, while in Florence all children born in a single year were baptized communally in the Battistero on March 25, the Feast of the Annunciation. In both cities the idea was to pledge the child to his or her respective parish and city, as well as to God. In Florence, additionally, a black bean was dropped into an urn for a boy baby, a white one for a girl, allowing the birthrate to be calculated. During the 14th century there were roughly 6,000 births a year in a city with a population of around 90,000.

---

of the doors—"ANDREAS UGOLINI NINI DE PISIS ME FECIT A.D. M.CCC. XXX"—records that Andrea Pisano "*me fecit*—made me" in 1330.

Walk from the doors toward the apse, the area protruding from the building on the side away from the cathedral. Low down you'll see a panel with a relief of a naval battle, probably part of a fourth- or fifth-century **sarcophagus.** On the apse itself are two lions about to devour human heads, symbols of the castigation of sinners and common motifs on 12th- and 13th-century Romanesque churches. Continuing around the building you see the **Colonna di San Zanobi** (1384), a freestanding pillar that marks the spot where a miracle is supposed to have occurred as the body of St. Zenobius, Florence's first bishop, was being moved from San Lorenzo to Santa Reparata (then the cathedral) on January 26, 429. Richard Lassels, an early visitor

The east doors of the Battistero, crafted by Ghiberti

to Florence, describes the miracle in The Voyage of Italy (1603). He tells his readers "to take notice of a little round pillar with the figure of a tree in iron nayled to it, and old words engraven upon it, importing, that in this very place, stood anciently an Elm tree, which being touched by the hearse of St. Zenobious [sic] budded forth with green leaves though in the month of January."

The baptistery's second set of doors, the **north doors,** are now on your right, commissioned as a votive offering to spare Florence the ravages of another plague similar to the Black Death of 1348. A competition to select a suitable sculptor was arranged in 1401, a date often seen as marking the "beginning" of the Italian Renaissance. The judges were unable to decide between two panels—both representing "The Sacrifice of Isaac"—submitted by two young goldsmiths, Lorenzo Ghiberti and Filippo Brunelleschi. As a result, both were asked to work on the doors, at which point Brunelleschi appears to have stated that if he was not the outright winner, he was not interested in the commission. He then left Florence for Rome to study architecture, but he would later return to design Florence's cathedral dome, the churches of San Lorenzo and Santo Spirito, and the Cappella dei Pazzi alongside Santa Croce.

The victorious Ghiberti devoted much of the next 20 years to the north doors. The finished project was mostly traditional in outlook and retained the Gothic quatrefoil—the square that framed the reliefs—and 28-panel scheme of Pisano's earlier doors. At the same time, Ghiberti's reliefs are far more vivid and realistic than Pisano's. They also show the maturing of his style over 20 years, from the simple narrative of the early reliefs to the far more detailed and crowded scenes of later panels. The upper 20 reliefs describe "Stories from the New Testament," the eight lower panels the "Four Evangelists" and "Four Doctors of the Church."

So pleased was the Arte di

Calimala with Ghiberti's doors that it commissioned a second set in 1425. The **east doors** would be the artist's masterpiece and one of the supreme works of the Florentine Renaissance. Ghiberti worked on them for 27 years with, as he put it, "the greatest diligence and greatest love."

The doors on the baptistery today are copies—the originals are in the Museo dell'Opera del Duomo—but they still convey both Ghiberti's brilliance and the marked departure from what had gone before. He replaced the previous doors' 28-panel schemes, for example, with just ten reliefs; the traditional diamond quatrefoil was abandoned in favor of simple squared panels; several scenes in a story were often condensed into a single panel; the recently understood notions and rules of perspective were deftly employed; and the subtlety of expression, realism, narrative power, and fine composition embraced all facets of Renaissance artistic endeavor.

Entering the Battistero: Just before entering the baptistery, take in the two columns on either side of the east doors. They come with a little tale attached. In 1117, so the story goes, the Pisans set off on a voyage of conquest to Mallorca, an island off the Spanish coast. Fearful of an attack from Lucca in their absence, they asked the Florentines to guard their city, rewarding them on their return with two porphyry columns plundered from Mallorca. The columns' polished surfaces were said

to have magical powers, being able to predict acts of treason. The Pisans therefore spoiled the pillars' surfaces by baking them in embers before donating them. On arrival, the columns proved too weak for structural use and were relegated to the baptistery's exterior, where they have remained ever since.

Your first impression of the interior is of a bland shell. A glance upward, however, reveals a majestic **mosaic-covered ceiling,** a mostly 13th-century work begun by Venetian craftsmen using plans by local artists, the Florentines having had little or no grounding in mosaic technique. Its complex narrative embraces episodes from the lives of Christ, Joseph, the

INSIDER TIP:

Study the east doors, declared so beautiful by Michelangelo that they might serve as the gates of Paradise, hence their alternative name, the Porta del Paradiso.

—TOM O'NEILL
National Geographic writer

Virgin, and John the Baptist. To the right of the apse, stands Donatello and Michelozzo's tomb of the antipope John XXIII, an adviser to the Medici, who died in the city in 1419. Also worthy of note are the interior's band of granite columns, probably removed from the old Roman Capitol.

(continued on. p. 74)

A Walk From Santissima Annunziata to Santa Trìnita

This is a good walk to follow after visiting the Galleria dell'Accademia or Museo di San Marco, as both are close to its starting point in Piazza della Santissima Annunziata.

Start by admiring Giambologna's statue of Grand Duke Ferdinando I (1608) at the center of **Piazza della Santissima Annunziata,** a stately square laid out in 1420 by Brunelleschi. Your walk begins at the church of **Santissima Annunziata** ❶ *(closed 12:30 p.m.–4 p.m.)* on the square's northern flank. The church's vestibule, the Chiostrino dei Voti, features a fresco cycle on the "Life of the Virgin" and "Life of St. Filippo Benizzi" by Andrea del Sarto, Jacopo Pontormo, and Rosso Fiorentino. The chief interior attraction is Michelozzo's ornate tabernacle (1448–1461), commissioned by the Medici to enshrine a miraculous 13th-century image of the Virgin.

On the square's eastern margin stands the **Ospedale degli Innocenti** *(tel 055 203 7308, $$).* Created as an orphanage in 1445, it is known for Brunelleschi's delightful facade (1419–1426), with a nine-bay loggia decorated with terra-cotta roundels, two interior courtyards, and a modest Renaissance art museum.

Walk south on Via dei Servi to the **Piazza del Duomo.** Skirt the east end of the Duomo and exit the piazza by walking south on Via dello Studio. The poet Dante Alighieri (see pp. 78–79) was born in the tangle of streets here in 1265, though not in the so-called **Casa di Dante** ❷ *(Via Santa Margherita 1, tel 055 219 416, closed Mon. Oct.–March, $),* a mock medieval pastiche given over to a museum. Two nearby churches have Dante associations: Santa Margherita de' Cerchi was the parish church of the Portinari, the family of Dante's beloved Beatrice, while San Martino del Vescovo, opposite the Casa, was the Alighieri family church.

Walk east on Via Dante Alighieri and you pass the **Badia Fiorentina** ❸ (see p. 86), a tenth-century abbey church where Dante is said to have first glimpsed Beatrice. Highlights

NOT TO BE MISSED:

Piazza della Santissima Annunziata
• **Ospedale degli Innocenti** • **Museo Bardini** • **Palazzo Davanzati** • **Santa Trìnita**

are Filippino Lippi's painting of the "Apparition of the Virgin to St. Bernard" (1485) and the Chiostro degli Aranci, a cloister with a fresco cycle on the "Life of St. Benedict" (1436–1439). The campanile is from the 14th century.

Turn right, then left onto Via Ghibellina, stopping at the **Museo Nazionale del Bargello** ❹ (see pp. 80–85), before continuing to **Santa Croce** ❺ (see pp. 108–114). If time allows, make a detour to Vivoli *(Via Isola delle Stinche 7r),* makers of some of Florence's best gelato. Devotees of Michelangelo may wish to deviate north to the **Casa Buonarroti** *(Via Ghibellina 70, tel 055 241 752, casabuonarroti .it, $$),* a museum with some minor works and much miscellaneous ephemera connected with the sculptor.

South of Santa Croce is the **Museo Horne** *(Via de' Benci 6, tel 055 244 661, closed Sun. & p.m., $$),* a small art collection amassed by the English art historian Herbert Percy Horne (see pp. 117–118), housed in a 15th-century palazzo.

Now cross the Arno River via the Ponte alle Grazie to visit the similar **Museo Bardini** ❻ *(Via de' Renai 37, tel 055 234 2427, closed Tues.–Fri., $$),* the eclectic collection of famed art dealer Sergio Bardini (1836–1922).

From the museum, walk west on Via de' Bardi to the Ponte Vecchio (see pp. 162–163), then turn left to the church of **Santa Felicita** ❼ *(closed Sun. & 12 p.m.–3 p.m.),* worth a visit for

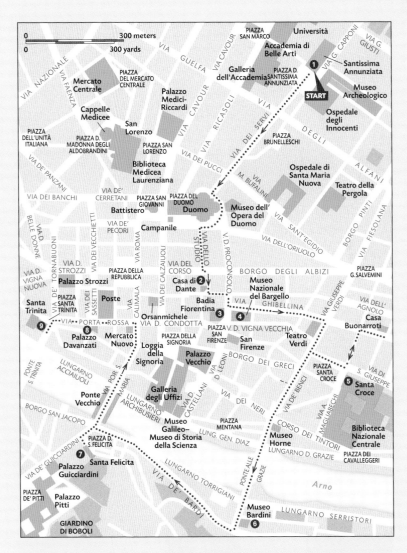

the Cappella Capponi, with Pontormo's strange painting of the "Deposition" (1525–1528). Return to the Ponte Vecchio and cross the river. Head north and, at the Mercato Nuovo, bear west on Via Porta Rossa. Midway down the street on the left is the museum of **Palazzo Davanzati** ❽ (*Via Porta Rossa 13, tel 055 238 8610, closed Mon., $*), whose interior preserves the decor of a medieval Florentine house. The piazza at the end of the street has the church of

- ⬔ See also area map p. 57
- ► Piazza della Santissima Annunziata
- ⏱ Allow at least half a day
- ⬌ 2 miles (3 km)
- ► Piazza Santa Trìnita

Santa Trìnita ❾ (*tel 055 216 912, closed Sun. a.m. & 12 p.m.–4 p.m.*), known for Ghirlandaio's fresco cycle (1483–1486) and altarpiece.

The Campanile

The Campanile is the cathedral's belfry. One of Italy's most beautiful medieval towers, it was designed by Giotto, the period's most accomplished painter, and adorned with reliefs and statues by Donatello, Luca della Robbia, and other leading Renaissance sculptors. Perhaps surpassing its artistic appeal are its breathtaking views of the cathedral and over Florence's rooftops to the hazy Tuscan hills beyond.

Construction: The tower was begun in 1334 under the guidance of Giotto, then employed as the city's *capo maestro,* or "master of works." He completed only the first of the tower's five stories before his death in 1337, but he probably left plans for the remaining levels that mirrored the multicolored decorative scheme devised by Arnolfo di Cambio for the exterior of the cathedral (then also under construction).

Work then proceeded in two phases, the first under Andrea Pisano, designer of the baptistery's south doors (see p. 69). He built the second story up to the level of the first pair of twin windows (1337–1342), and then Francesco Talenti completed the remaining three stories and their windows, the latter a motif borrowed from Sienese bell towers, from 1348 to 1359. Looking at the Campanile, the different work of the three architects is patently clear, suggesting that any plans by Giotto for a unified scheme were ignored.

The Campanile's 275-foot (84.7 m) height contravened a 1324 law designed to restrict privately built towers. Such laws were common—Italy's most notable towered village, San Gimignano (see pp. 230–239), had one—towers being an obvious means by which families could make their wealth and power conspicuous.

The Campanile as seen from the cathedral's dome

Sculptures & Views: The tower's present decorative sculptures are copies. The age-darkened originals now reside in the Museo dell'Opera del Duomo. The sculptures' arrangement and themes were carefully chosen, showing humanity's transition from a state of original sin (at the base) to a position of divine grace at the top. Christian and other philosophical thought of the day believed this transition was achieved through manual labor, the arts, and the sacraments and was guided by the influence of the planets and the cardinal and theological virtues.

The apparently disparate sculptural reliefs can therefore be behavior). About a century after these reliefs were made, Luca della Robbia added the "Five Liberal Arts" on the side of the tower facing the cathedral. These arts—Grammar, Music, Arithmetic, Philosophy, and Astrology—were believed to nourish and shape the spirit. Other works by Pisano in the second-story niches were later replaced by statues of the "Prophets, Sibyls, Patriarchs, and Kings" (1415–1436) by Donatello and Nanni di Bartolo. The originals of these works are also in the Museo dell'Opera del Duomo.

A climb to the top of the tower—there is no elevator—is rewarded with great vistas: The bird's-eye view of the baptistery

Campanile

- Map p. 57
- Piazza del Duomo
- 055 230 2885
- Closed Jan. 1, Easter, Sept. 8, Dec. 25, and p.m. on Jan. 6 & religious holidays
- $$$ (Biglietto Unico covers the dome, Battistero, Campanile, Santa Reparata, and Museo dell'Opera del Duomo)
- Bus: 1, 6, 14, 17, 23; C2 to Via de' Pecori

ilgrandemuseo
delduomo.it

The Bells of Florence

The Florentines lament the "Martinella," a bell that once accompanied them to war: It was lost in 1260 to Siena, where it resides to this day. San Marco's "Piagnona" was rung in 1498 to warn Savonarola of the approaching mob and "exiled" by the Florentines to a distant church in revenge. The Bargello's "Montanina" summoned the Florentines in times of siege or war and also tolled as condemned prisoners awaited execution. A local saying describes people as having a tongue like the "bell of the Bargello" when they speak only to condemn or abuse. The last times it tolled were after the recovery of the city from the Nazis in 1944, during the 1966 flood, and at the turn of the Millennium.

---

seen as a coherent philosophical whole. Thus the lowest register in hexagonal frames by Andrea Pisano and his pupils illustrates the "Creation, Art, and Works of Man." The upper register's diamond-shaped panels are allegories of the "Seven Planets" (whose movement was believed to influence human lives), the "Seven Sacraments" (which sanctify human life), and the "Seven Virtues" (which shape human and cathedral dome are especially memorable. There are 414 steps and an ominous first-aid post near the top. In a letter of 1861, English novelist George Eliot recorded her climb up "Giotto's tower, with its delicate pinkish marble, its delicate windows, . . . twisted columns, and its tall lightness." It was, she wrote, "very sublime getting upstairs indeed—and our muscles were much astonished at the unusual exercise." ■

Museo dell'Opera del Duomo

The Museo dell'Opera del Duomo contains many works of art removed for safekeeping from the Duomo, Battistero, and Campanile. It opened in 1891 in a building that since 1291 had been occupied by the Opera del Duomo, a body created to care for the cathedral. The museum is undergoing an extended period of renovation; while the location of the exhibits listed below will likely change, these remain the highlights and will be clearly signposted in any new layout.

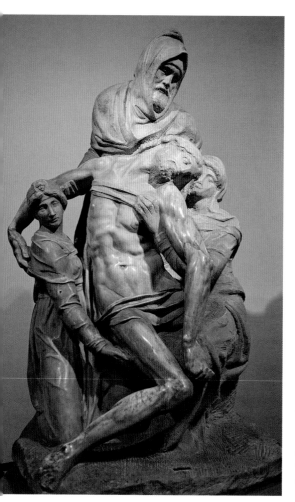

The damage inflicted by Michelangelo on his "Pietà" clearly shows on Christ's left arm.

Spend a moment in the museum courtyard, for it was here that Michelangelo sculptured much of his "David" before it was moved to Piazza della Signoria.

The museum's first major attraction is the **Sala dell'Antica Facciata del Duomo,** or Room of the Ancient Facade of the Cathedral. This collection consists of a host of statues, most of them rescued from Arnolfo di Cambio's quarter-finished cathedral facade, which was pulled down on the orders of Grand Duke Ferdinando I de' Medici in 1587. The most eye-catching works are both by Arnolfo di Cambio: The "Madonna of the Glass Eyes," and a statue of a seated "Boniface VIII," a vicious medieval pope. Also notice the three statues of the Evangelists: "St. Luke" by Nanni di Banco, Donatello's "St. John," and Bernardo Ciuffagni's "St. Matthew." All three were carved between 1408 and 1415, reputedly as part of a competition for the honor of creating a statue of St. Mark, the fourth Evangelist. Ciuffagni was accused of cheating by copying Donatello's "St. John." As a result, the contest was declared void and the job of carving Mark given to another sculptor, Niccolò Lamberti (1370–1451).

Also noteworthy is the **Ottagono delle Oreficerie** (1954), a modern octagonal chapel that features several precious reliquaries, ornate vessels used to house saintly and other relics (including the jaw of St. Jerome and a finger of St. John the Baptist). Over-shadowing these is an altarpiece painting of "St. Catherine and St. Zenobius" (1334) attributed to Bernardo Daddi.

Choir Lofts

The museum contains two stunning *cantorie*, or choir lofts, one by Donatello, the other by Luca della Robbia. Both were removed in 1688 from the entrances to the cathedral's two sacristies on the occasion of the marriage of Grand Duke Cosimo III de' Medici to Violante Beatrice of Bavaria. Both lofts are filled with depictions of dancing children playing instruments, but whereas Luca della Robbia's children are blithe, innocent creatures, those of Donatello have more the air of rowdy, free-spirited urchins. Donatello was also responsible for the room's bald-headed Old Testament prophet "Abacuc," or "Habbakuk" (1423–1425), one of 16 figures removed from the Campanile. The figure is a favorite of the Florentines, who have nicknamed him *lo zuccone*, or "marrow head."

Baptistery Artworks, the Alter, & "St. Sebastian"

Also worth a long look is a collection of items from the baptistery, including Donatello's celebrated

wooden baptistery statue of "Mary Magdalene" (1453–1455).

The centerpiece is a huge altar, a masterpiece of 14th-century Florentine gold and silver work, which once stood in the baptistery. Begun in 1366, it was not completed until 1480, but it fulfilled the demands of the Arte di Calimala, the baptistery's custodians, and the altar's commissioning agents that "no other similar work should be its equal."

Also look out for Giovanni di Bondo's triptych of "St. Sebastian"; an exquisite Byzantine mosaic; statuettes of "Christ in the Act of Blessing" and "Santa Reparata" by Andrea Pisano; a marble bust of a woman by Tino di Camaino; and 12 gold and silk altar panels (1466–1487) from the baptistery, which depict scenes from the life of St. John the Baptist. ∎

Michelangelo's "Pietà"

One real treasure of the Museo dell'Opera del Duomo is Michelangelo's "Pietà" (1550–1553), a late and unfinished work moved from the cathedral in 1981 and probably intended for the sculptor's own tomb; the figure of Nicodemus may well be a self-portrait. Michelangelo became disillusioned by the sculpture and the quality of the marble, and in frustration he smashed Christ's left arm and leg. The damage was later repaired by a pupil, but signs of Michelangelo's frenzy and the obvious discrepancy in styles are still clearly evident. This work is remarkable particularly for the extraordinary, limp body of Christ and what—without the small figure of Mary Magdalene on the left, added later by a pupil—would have been a curiously (but deliberately) lop-sided and "unfilled" composition.

Museo dell'Opera del Duomo
- Map p. 57
- Piazza del Duomo 9
- 055 230 2885
- Closed Sun. p.m.
- $$ or $$$ (Biglietto Unico covers the dome, Battistero, Campanile, Santa Reparata, and Museo dell'Opera del Duomo)
- Bus: 14, 23, C1 to Via dei Pucci; C1, C2 to Via dell' Oriuolo–Via del Proconsolo

operaduomo.firenze.it

Dante Alighieri

Dante Alighieri was one of the greatest poets of any age. His most celebrated work—*La Divina Commedia,* or *The Divine Comedy*—is a masterpiece of worldwide acclaim. He also served Florence as a diplomat and politician, but he was poorly treated by the city of his birth and spent his final years in bitter exile.

Dante was born in 1265 into a minor and impoverished aristocratic family. At the age of nine he met Beatrice Portinari, the girl who would blight much of his romantic life but inspire many of his literary endeavors. Then aged just eight, Beatrice was, in the words of fellow writer Giovanni Boccaccio (see sidebar p. 154), "so delicate and beautifully formed, and full, besides mere beauty, of so much candid loveliness that many thought her almost an angel" (*Life of Dante,* 1321). Dante, for his part, said that "she appeared to be born not of mortal man but of God."

A sculpture of Dante in the church of Santa Croce

Dante would never marry or even become close to Beatrice, however, for she had been promised by her family to Simone de' Bardi, whom she married at the age of 17. Such dynastic marriages were common. Dante himself was pledged to Gemma Donati at the age of 12. It may well be significant, however, that he married much later than Beatrice, at the age of 30. Beatrice's place in Dante's heart was cemented by her early death at the age of 24.

Early Career & Politics: Dante's early career was neither romantically nor poetically inclined; it leaned instead toward politics. He fought against the cities of Arezzo and Pisa, then enemies of Florence, and served on a number of civic committees after joining the Apothecaries Guild. In 1300, in his most

---

EXPERIENCE: Walking in Dante's Footsteps

It is one thing to visit the sites associated with Dante throughout Florence, quite another to join a guided walk that will add extra dimension to your knowledge and understanding of the writer and his place in the city of his birth.

    Context (*tel 215/393-0303 or 800-691-6036, contexttravel.com*) is a Philadelphia-based organization (which also has a New York office) that offers individual or small group tours it describes as "seminars" rather than "walks" in several historic cities. Groups are never larger than five people and leaders are highly qualified scholars or specialists. Its Italian seminars include a three-hour "Dante's Florence," which will take you from the Battistero to Dante's district, dipping into alleys and small piazzas that were home to many of Dante's enemies and confidantes. You'll also visit the Palazzo della Lana, home today to the Dante Library and a meeting place for the **Società Dantesca Italiana** (*dantesca.it /eng*). Here you will explore the tour's second theme, *The Divine Comedy,* as a work of fiction in which the city of Florence plays a central role.

"Dante Alighieri Reading *The Divine Comedy* in Guido Novello's Court," 1850, by Andrea Pierini (1798–1858)

notable diplomatic enterprise, he was sent to San Gimignano to talk the town into an alliance against Pope Boniface VIII, who was gathering his strength for an assault on Tuscany.

In the same year he attempted to heal the widening breach between the two factions of Florence's ruling Guelph party. One side, the Black Guelphs, were ranged against the imperial powers of the old Holy Roman Empire, while the Whites—to whom Dante belonged—were more conciliatory. The Blacks contained leading papal bankers—families such as the Pazzi, Bardi, and Donati—while the Whites included imperial bankers (Cerchi, Mozzi, and Frescobaldi).

Exile & Death: As the dispute intensified, Boniface VIII sided, predictably, with the Blacks, who eventually emerged triumphant. Dante's White sympathies condemned him, and he was exiled from Florence on trumped-up charges

for two years. While many of his fellow exiles later returned home, an embittered Dante forsook forever his city of "self-made men and fast-got gain." For years he wandered between Verona, Padua, Venice, and elsewhere, probably writing much of *The Divine Comedy* as he went.

This great epic takes as its narrative theme the passage of Dante in the guise of a pilgrim through Hell and Purgatory to God and Paradise. In doing so, it traces the redemption of both Dante and humanity, beginning in a dark wood, a symbol of the poet's state of moral and spiritual darkness after the death of Beatrice. Woven into the poem are many vitriolic references to contemporary and historical figures and events. The work was completed about 1321, just before Dante's death in Ravenna, where he is buried. Florence still sends a gift of oil to light the lamps on his tomb each September 14, the anniversary of his death.

Museo Nazionale del Bargello

The medieval building of the Museo Nazionale del Bargello has had a long and often troubled history. It began life as the Palazzo del Podestà in 1255, when it served as the headquarters of the Podestà, Florence's chief magistrate. It acquired its present name in 1574 when the Medici abolished the position of Podestà and gave the palace to the Bargello, or chief of police. Today it is home to Italy's greatest collection of Gothic and Renaissance sculpture.

The Bargello displays sculpture, such as this Michelangelo "Crucifix" (1495), in an enlightening way.

The museum was created in 1865, when it became Italy's first national museum (Museo Nazionale) outside the Vatican. Today, it is visited mainly for several rooms of sculpture, containing most of the finest works of the Tuscan Renaissance, including masterpieces from Michelangelo, Donatello, and others. At the same time, it is important to stress that the museum's many other rooms—often overlooked—contain a collection of ceramics, textiles, carpets, ivories, tapestries, silverware, and other beautifully crafted artifacts that could easily take up as much of your time as the famous sculptures themselves.

You enter the palace in the shadow of the **Torre Volognana,** a medieval tower that predated the palace and was incorporated into the first phase of its building (1255–1261). Traditionally its mighty bell is rung once every hundred years, at the turn of each century. From here you walk into the ticket office and then turn right into the first room, formerly the Bargello's armory, the core of the earliest palace.

Michelangelo's Work

In barely the blink of an eye you're confronted with the cream of Italy's greatest late Renaissance sculpture. Most people make straight for four works by Michelangelo. The most obvious is a lurching and very clearly drunk "Bacchus," carved when the sculptor was just 22. Rarely can inebriation have been portrayed so convincingly. This was the first major work in which Michelangelo was inspired by the sculpture of the classical world. It predated by about a year the work that secured his reputation—the more celebrated "Pietà" in St. Peter's in Rome. The statue of "David" was begun some five years later, in 1501. Compare Michelangelo's "Bacchus" with the nearby statue of the same figure by Jacopo Sansovino (1486–1570)—a work that shows its subject rather steadier on his feet.

The second Michelangelo in the room shows the sculptor in a subtler light: The unfinished "Pitti Tondo," or "Madonna and Child" (1504), is a beautifully delicate shallow relief that exemplifies a technique known as *sciacciato*. This stresses the subtlety of line above the depth of a sculpture, testing a sculptor's ability to create space and contrast in a shallow working area. Note the skill with which Michelangelo has carved

the figure of a young St. John the Baptist behind the Virgin's shoulder, a figure so insubstantial at first glance as to be almost invisible. Once seen, however, it lends the work an extraordinary impression of depth.

The room's third Michelangelo, a figure of "David-Apollo" (1530–1532), skips 30 years of the sculptor's life and artistic development, during which time, among other things, he had painted the ceiling of the Vatican's Sistine Chapel. Scholars are unsure of the work's precise theme. Renaissance painter and art critic Giorgio Vasari claimed it represented Apollo drawing an arrow from his quiver; others think the figure is the biblical hero David and suggest the object beneath his feet is the head of Goliath.

Museo Nazionale del Bargello

🅰 Map p. 57

✉ Via del Proconsolo 4

☎ 055 238 8606

🕐 Closed Mon., & Tues.–Sun. p.m., but open a.m. 1st, 3rd, & 5th Mon. of the month, and 2nd & 4th Sun. of the month. Check extended openings for special exhibitions.

💲 $ ($$ for special exhibitions)

🚌 Bus: C1 or C2 to Via del Proconsolo

firenzemusei.it

INSIDER TIP:

A good book to pack —or to download in Florence—is *The Agony and the Ecstasy*, the biographical novel of Michelangelo by Irving Stone.

—JUSTIN KAVANAGH
National Geographic Travel Books editor

No doubt surrounds the Bargello's fourth Michelangelo, a proud-faced head of "Brutus," the only bust completed by the artist. It was reportedly commissioned by an anti-Medici city council to celebrate the assassination of Alessandro de' Medici in 1537. Alessandro was probably the bastard son of Pope Clement VII, otherwise known as Giulio de' Medici, and proved to be one of the least appealing of all the many Medici (see sidebar p. 92). He is said to have been murdered by his lover and distant cousin, Lorenzaccio, whom Vasari claimed was the model for Michelangelo's statue.

Condemned to Immortality

Paintings of condemned criminals were commissioned from some of Florence's leading artists to decorate the Bargello's walls and courtyard. Andrea del Castagno (see p. 43) painted the members of the Albizzi family, hanged for subversion, producing a work described by one critic as a "perfect wonder," with the corpses portrayed in "the strangest attitudes . . . infinitely varied and perfectly fine." Botticelli (1445–1510) painted men executed after the Pazzi Conspiracy (at 40 florins a cadaver), as did Leonardo da Vinci, who noted one corpse's "turquoise blue jacket" and black satin vest as the body dangled lifelessly from a window of the Bargello.

Other Works

Scattered around the room are sculptures by Michelangelo's contemporaries. Chief of these are pieces by Benvenuto Cellini, a flamboyant character responsible here, among other things, for a "Bust of Cosimo I," his first foray into bronze, and several preparatory bronzes for his great statue of "Perseus" in the Loggia della Signoria (see p. 93). French-born Giambologna is represented by

his famous winged "Mercury," an image that has long since become the standard representation of the god. In any other company works by Bandinelli, Ammannati, and the other sculptors displayed would shine: Here they can't help but appear second-rate.

Cross the Bargello's courtyard, formerly the scene of executions, to take in the less arresting Gothic works by Arnolfo di Cambio and others in the ground floor's last two rooms. The crests around the courtyard walls belong to Podestà who occupied the palace through the centuries.

Elsewhere sculpture dots the courtyard, notably an ancient Roman sarcophagus adapted for use as a fountain (notice the dolphins), a 16th-century figure of Cosimo I de' Medici in the guise of a Roman emperor, and a group of late 15th-century figures by Benedetto da Maiano representing six musicians.

Donatello & Contemporaries

Climb the courtyard's external stairs to the second floor, where you're greeted by a wonderfully eccentric menagerie of bronze animals by Giambologna. Turn right and you come to the gallery's second major room, the **Salone del Consiglio Generale.**

The works here are generally earlier than those on the lower floor and represent the pinnacle of Renaissance sculpture. The preeminent role is here taken by Donatello, whose most famous sculpture is the androgynous "David" (1430–1440), a work described by American writer Mary McCarthy in *The Stones of Florence* (1959) as a "transvestite's and fetishist's dream of alluring ambiguity." Contrast the figure's raffish hat and sinuous lines with the sculptor's earlier marble "David" (1408–1409) nearby, a far more traditional treatment of a common theme. Compare it, too, with Donatello's heroic and more artistically adventurous "St. George," removed for safekeeping from its niche on the exterior of Orsanmichele (see pp. 104–105). It was commissioned by the Arte dei Corazzai e Spadai, or Armorers Guild, which took St. George as its patron saint and protector.

Other works in the room by Donatello attest to the sculptor's virtuosity and flexibility. The "Marzocco," Florence's heraldic lion, represents a simple piece of civic sculpture (a copy of this work sits in Piazza della Signoria), while the "Bust of Niccolò da Uzzano," a mercenary soldier, or condottiere, is a triumph of naturalistic portraiture. "Crucifixion" shows the sculptor working in a conventional Christian context, while the strange figure of the "Amor-Atys"—a prancing Cupid-like figure—shows he is also more than at home in the pagan world. Another work is the bronze of "San Giovannino" (the young St. John the Baptist), long attributed to the artist but now credited to a pupil of Donatello, Desiderio da Settignano (circa 1428–1464), an artist who adopted many of the low reliefs and portraiture techniques pioneered by his master.

Two other works of historical and artistic significance worth seeking out are a pair of reliefs depicting "The Sacrifice of Isaac" by Lorenzo Ghiberti and Filippo Brunelleschi. These were

This cast bronze of "David" by Donatello strikes an androgynous contrast with Michelangelo's masculine counterpart.

Useful Apps for Art Appreciation

The most immediately useful app to acquire for an insight into the finest art in Florence is the Uffizi's official paid-for app, **Uffizi** (Giunti Editore), which provides a room-by-room guide to the gallery, biographies of the artists, a catalog of works, notes on 100 key paintings, and an in-depth examination of 12 key masterpieces.

The more expensive, unofficial **Uffizi Touch** (Centrica) has a similar approach, and is distinguished, in particular, by its high-quality images.

The Galleria dell'Accademia also has an official, paid-for app, **Accademia** (Giunti Editore), with gallery plans, notes on

many of the key works, and plenty of information on the gallery's star turn, Michelangelo's "David."

You'll also find plenty of information on art, architecture, galleries, and museums on **Firenze: Infectious Beauty** (Magenta), the free app produced by Firenze Turismo, the city's official visitor organization. It has good images and mapping and also deals with sights and works of art outside the city.

A more general app is the paid-for **Instant Florence** (Donald Strachan), which features Art, Architecture, and Best Museums categories that deal with the most popular works and sights.

the joint winning entries of the famous competition held in 1401 to choose a sculptor for the baptistery doors (see p. 70). Also noteworthy are the distinctive polychrome glazed terra-cottas of Luca della Robbia, as well as works by Michelozzo, Vecchietta (1410–1480), Agostino di Duccio (1418–1481), Desiderio da Settignano, and other great names of Renaissance sculpture.

Decorative Arts

Most of the rest of the Bargello is given over to a ravishing collection of the decorative arts. Highlights on the second floor include the **Salone del Consiglio Generale,** the carpets and Islamic art in the **Sala Islamica** (Islamic Room), and the varied carpets, textiles, ceramics, and other treasures of the **Sala Carrand,** a room that houses a private collection bequeathed to Florence by the French antiquary Louis Carrand in 1888.

Just beyond the latter rooms lies the beautifully decorated **Cappella di Santa Maria di Maddalena.** This contains frescoes (1340) by the School of Giotto, discovered in 1840 when the chapel was being converted from a prison cell. The painting of "Paradiso" on the end wall features a depiction of Dante (in maroon in the right-hand group of the saved, fifth from the right). Many Renaissance critics believed the figure was painted by Giotto himself. The chapel's lovely pulpit, lectern, and stalls (all 1483–1488) were carved for the church of San Miniato al Monte (see pp. 182–185). A little beyond the chapel lies the **Sala degli Avori,** or Room of the Ivories, home to many intricately worked artifacts, some dating back as far as the fifth century.

On the third floor, watch for the enameled terra-cottas of the della Robbia family (Andrea, Luca, and Giovanni); bronzes and other sculptures by Antonio del Pollaiuolo (1432–1496) and Sienese artist Vecchietta; the Medagliere Mediceo, a collection of medals begun by Lorenzo de' Medici; the **Sala delle Armi,** a display of arms and armor; and the **Salone del Camino,** home to Italy's finest collection of miniature bronzes. The last has works by all the country's leading bronze-smiths, including many artists whose work on a larger scale you have already seen, notably Giam-bologna and Benvenuto Cellini.

Sala del Verrocchio

Retracing your steps, don't miss the Sala del Verrocchio, given over in part to works by Andrea del Verrocchio (1435–1488), an artist, sculptor, and head of a workshop that included the Umbrian master Perugino and Leonardo da Vinci among its pupils. He is also responsible for another "David," a bronze commissioned by the Medici in 1470 that makes an interesting comparison with Donatello's earlier statues of David. Also compelling is his bust of "Dama col Mazzolino," or "Noblewoman with a Nosegay," remarkable for the delicacy of the figure's hands and clothing.

The bust is one of many in the room. Such busts were once common in the homes of Florentine nobles, and the examples here in the final rooms of the museum are often overlooked. Anywhere but Florence they would be the pride of most collections. Works worthy of note include Verroc-chio's bust of "Piero di Lorenzo de Medici," a "Young Warrior" by Pol-laiuolo, the bust of "Battista Sforza" by Francesco Laurana, and works by other famous Tuscan names, such as Mino da Fiesole, Antonio Rossel-lino, and Benedetto da Maiano. ■

The courtyard of the Bargello was once used for executions.

More Places to Visit Near Piazza del Duomo

Badia Fiorentina

The Badia Fiorentina, or Florentine Abbey, lies opposite the Museo Nazionale del Bargello, its presence marked by a distinctive hexagonal bell tower (built 1310–1330), a prominent feature of the Florentine skyline. Founded in 978, the Badia was the creation of Willa, the widow of one of the margraves of Tuscany, erstwhile rulers of the region who had their headquarters in Lucca. In time it was further endowed by her son, Ugo.

In 1031 a hospital was opened in the complex, the city's first. The abbey bells tolled the divisions of the Florentine working day. During the 1280s it was rebuilt, probably by Arnolfo di Cambio, architect of the Duomo and Palazzo Vecchio. In 1307, however, part of the new building was demolished on the

Codex Trivulziano, 1080—an early manuscript of *The Divine Comedy* at the Casa di Dante

orders of the city, a punishment for the resident monks for the nonpayment of tax. The church was altered again in 1627, this time acquiring a heavy baroque gloss, though most of the interior's works of art escaped destruction. Opening times are variable, but the church's dark interior is well worth a few minutes if you find it open.

The main lure is Filippino Lippi's "Apparition of the Virgin to St. Bernard" (1485), the painting on the left when you enter the church. On the wall behind, to the right as you face the painting, is a tomb monument (1469–1481) to Willa's son, Ugo, the work of Mino da Fiesole. The same sculptor was responsible for the altar frontal of the "Madonna and Child with St. Leonard and St. Lawrence" (on the wall opposite the Lippi painting) and—around the corner to the left as you face the frontal—the tomb of Bernardo Giugni (1464–1470). The latter is accompanied by figures representing Justice and Faith, added because Giugni was a lawyer and diplomat. Don't leave without taking the door and stairs to the right of the high altar as you face it. They lead to the **Chiostro degli Aranci** (1432–1438), Cloister of the Oranges, named after the fruit trees that once grew here. Two sides of the cloister are covered in an anonymous fresco cycle (1436–1439) depicting scenes from the life of St. Benedict.
🅰 Map p. 57 ✉ Via Dante Alighieri–Via del Proconsolo ☎ 055 264 402 🕐 Closed Tues.– Sun. & Mon. a.m. 🚍 Bus: C1 or C2 to Via del Proconsolo

Casa di Dante

Don't be fooled by the Casa di Dante. The eponymous poet wasn't born here and never lived here. The house is actually a medieval pastiche built in 1910. This said, the building is right at the heart of a district with many Dantesque associations, and it's likely the poet was born close by, probably somewhere on the street that bears his name. The Casa di Dante serves as a modest museum devoted to the poet, its chief exhibits being editions of his major work, *La Divina Commedia*. Note the church of San Martino opposite the house, the Alighieri family's place of worship. *museocasadidante.it*
🅰 Map p. 57 ✉ Via Santa Margherita 1–Via Dante Alighieri ☎ 055 219 416 🕐 Closed Mon. Oct.–March 🆂 $ 🚍 Bus: C2 to Via Dante Alighieri

Piazza della Signoria, the Uffizi, Europe's finest art gallery, and a tangle medieval streets leading to the church of Santa Croce

Eastern Florence

Floor tomb of a knight inside the church of Santa Croce

Eastern Florence

Piazza della Signoria is somewhere you'll return to again and again, testimony to the role for which it was designed—to provide Florence with a meeting place and a setting for its civic (as opposed to religious) seat of power. To its east lies Santa Croce, one of Italy's most exalted churches, housing glorious works of art and the tombs of some of Florence's most illustrious individuals.

The Palazzo Vecchio, an early 14th-century building, provides the piazza's centerpiece, a castlelike monolith that served as the headquarters of the city's ruling bodies and many of its despots over the centuries. Inside, you can wander through a number of its beautifully decorated rooms, within which you encounter several artistic treasures including sculptural masterpieces by Donatello and Michelangelo.

Many visitors hurry past the palazzo, however, bewitched by the more tempting artistic allure of the adjacent Galleria degli Uffizi, home to the world's finest collection of Renaissance paintings. This is probably the one sight you should see in

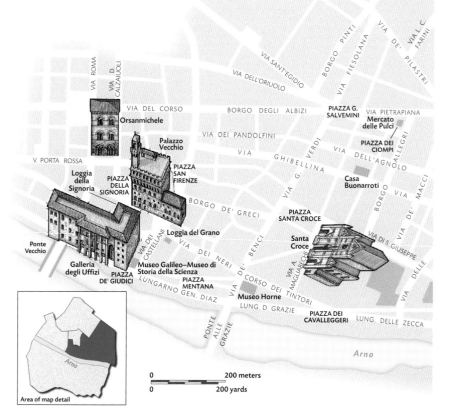

Area of map detail

0   200 meters

0   200 yards

Florence and Tuscany if you see no other, but it is besieged by hundreds of visitors virtually every day of the year. If you don't want to join the lines, it is possible to reserve a pre-timed ticket in advance (see sidebar p. 98).

Having sated yourself with paintings, turn back to Piazza della Signoria and give it the time it deserves. Ranged across its eastern flank is a row of eye-catching statues from a variety of eras. Opposite the Palazzo Vecchio is Rivoire, one of the more famous, and expensive, of

the city's cafés and a good place to indulge in a drink while you take in the square and its buzz of activity.

This activity is no accident, for the piazza has long been a meeting place. Political rallies and festivals were held here from earliest times—the city's Roman theater was close by—and in times of crisis the mob would be summoned to its precincts by the tolling of the Palazzo Vecchio's huge bell. The Loggia della Signoria, or Loggia dei Lanzi, on the Piazza della Signoria's southern side, is an open-air gallery of sculpture.

From the square you should walk briefly back toward Piazza del Duomo to see the lovely Orsanmichele, an easily missed church known for its fine exterior statues and its peaceful medieval interior, the latter home to a magnificent 14th-century tabernacle. From here walk eastward, winding through some of Florence's oldest and most fascinating streets to Santa Croce and its eponymous quarter, which—with the Sant'Ambrogio district to the north—contains some of the most interesting little stores, markets, bars, and restaurants in the city. ■

Piazza della Signoria

Piazza della Signoria is home to the Palazzo Vecchio, the seat of Florence's government for seven centuries. It houses notable sculptures and is a meeting place for visitors and Florentines alike. Close by is the entrance to the most exalted of all Florence's museums, the Uffizi.

Piazza della Signoria

- Map pp. 88–89
- Bus: C2 to Via della Condotta

Originally the area was close to the ancient heart of the Roman city: An old theater and *terme* (bath complex) were nearby, and on the piazza's southern (riverside) flank stood a *fullonica,* a colossal Roman building used to dye and manufacture textiles. All three structures, plus a church—San Romoloa—a loggia, and a huge fifth-century early Christian basilica, were lost, buried, or pilfered for stone over the centuries.

The origins of the piazza itself are encrusted with myth. The area is said to have belonged to the Uberti family, the leading lights of one of Florence's many opposing Guelph and Ghibelline factions (see p. 28). When the family was humbled in 1268, its land was confiscated and its property razed. In time much of the area was also paved, reputedly to prevent the Uberti from ever building on their former domain. This land was then considered tainted—one reason, supposedly, why it remained undeveloped and why the piazza today has such an unusual and asymmetrical shape.

In truth, the piazza's shape is probably a result of the piecemeal manner in which it evolved. Work on the square proper began in 1307, when the city set aside a small area for the Palazzo dei Priori, a civic council chamber that in time grew into the present Palazzo Vecchio. The choice of site—close to, and on a line with, Piazza del Duomo—was deliberate. Today, this original square corresponds to the open tract immediately north of the Palazzo Vecchio.

Work on the square was

The "Marzocco" guards the copy of Michelangelo's "David" that replaced the original (now in the Galleria dell'Accademia).

largely abandoned later in the 14th century, when the city's efforts were concentrated on the Palazzo dei Priori and Loggia della Signoria. Contemporary reports described the area as little more than a rubble-filled building site, and it was 1385 before the square received its first layer of protective paving. The piazza suffered further alterations after 1560, when Grand Duke Cosimo I made extravagant changes to the Uffizi, and again in 1871, when the medieval Loggia dei Pisani was demolished to open up the square to the west. Its indignities continued into the 1980s, when controversial archaeological excavations led to the removal of the original medieval paving stones. Many of the stones subsequently "disappeared," probably having been sold illegally to pave the drives of various villas in the Tuscan countryside.

The Statues

The square's most eye-catching features today—the Palazzo Vecchio aside—are its statues and the Loggia della Signoria. From left to right as you face the Palazzo Vecchio, the statues stand ranged across the piazza's eastern flank. The work on the far left is an equestrian monument (1594–1598) to the Medici duke Cosimo I by Giambologna. It was designed to recall the first-century A.D. Roman equestrian statue of the emperor Marcus Aurelius in Rome. In doing so, it drew parallels between Cosimo and the emperor, and aimed to link the glory of ancient Rome with that of 16th-century

Florence. The three reliefs at the statue's base commemorate key events in Cosimo's career: the Florentine senate's granting him the Florentine dukedom (in 1537); his entering the conquered city of Siena (1555); and the acquisition of the title of Grand Duke of Tuscany from Pope Pius V (1569).

INSIDER TIP:

The Palazzo Vecchio is among several museums offering new and innovative guided tours: Visit *musefirenze .it* for the latest details.

—CRAIG KISYLIA
National Geographic contributor

Cosimo appears again as the figure of Neptune in the next statue, the "Fontana del Nettuno," or "Neptune Fountain" (1563–1575). The work of Bartolommeo Ammannati and assistants (including Giambologna), it was ridiculed by Michelangelo, who wrote: "Ammannato, Ammannato, what a beautiful piece of marble you have ruined." Florentines call it "Il Biancone," or "The White Giant," and claim it wanders around the piazza when struck by the light of a full moon. Look for the stone inscription in front of the statue, the spot where Girolamo Savonarola and two fellow Dominican monks were burned for heresy on May 23, 1498 (see p. 33).

Next comes Donatello's "Marzocco" (1418–1420), a copy

of the statue now in the Bargello. The Marzocco, or lion, was Florence's traditional heraldic symbol and can be seen in many Tuscan towns conquered by the city after the 13th century. Captured prisoners were obliged to kiss its posterior. Its form may be based on a battered equestrian statue of Mars (Martocus) that stood by the Ponte Vecchio until a flood in 1333. Alternatively, it may derive from the lions kept in the dungeons behind the Palazzo Vecchio, whose behavior was watched for auguries in times of crisis (the street behind the palace is still called Via dei Leoni, or Street of the Lions). Donatello's statue was originally carved for a papal apartment in the church of Santa Maria Novella and moved to the piazza in 1812.

On the right side of the "Marzocco" is the electrifying "Judith and Holofernes" by Donatello, another copy of an original now in the Palazzo Vecchio's Sala dei Gigli (see p. 95). It was uprooted from the Palazzo Medici-Riccardi in 1495, after the Medici's temporary removal from power, and later erected in the piazza as a monument to the overthrow of tyranny. To its right rises "David," a copy of Michelangelo's sculpture in the Galleria dell'Accademia (see pp. 138–140). It stands on the spot occupied by the original statue until 1873.

Nearby are the figures of "Hercules and Cacus," carved by Bartolommeo Bandinelli as a companion piece for the "David." While the "David" was commissioned by Florence's republican council to celebrate the (brief) defeat of the Medici, Bandinelli's statue was commissioned by the Medici to mark the defeat of

Florence's Mighty Medici

Everywhere one goes in Florence, the traveler encounters great works of art and magnificent buildings commissioned by the Medici dynasty. The Medici were de facto rulers of Florence during much of the Italian Renaissance.

The Medici fortune was established by Giovanni de' Medici (1360–1429) a banker, and a great patron of learning, the arts, and architecture. The family's wealth and power were consolidated by Cosimo de' Medici, also known as Cosimo the Elder (1389–1464). The fruits of this success were enjoyed by Cosimo's heir, Lorenzo de' Medici, better known as Lorenzo the Magnificent (1449–1492). The enlightened patronage of the Medici and others, together with an upsurge

in classical and humanist scholarship, provided the spur for the Renaissance, a long-flowering artistic awakening that found fertile breeding ground in Florence, then Europe's most dynamic, cosmopolitan, and sophisticated city.

Medici power faltered in the 1490s with Lorenzo's death, leaving the way clear for Girolamo Savonarola (1452–1498), a charismatic monk eventually removed by the papacy in 1498. By 1512, the Medici were back in power, albeit a reduced form of power, only to be ousted again in 1527 by Emperor Charles V. Just two years later, the family had returned again, this time in the person of Cosimo I, who took control of Tuscany and assumed the title of grand duke.

their enemies; it was also a riposte to Michelangelo's "republican" masterpiece. For once the Medici were outclassed, for Bandinelli's work was ridiculed from the moment it was unveiled. The sculptor Benvenuto Cellini noted that the muscle-bound figures resembled "a sackful of melons."

Loggia della Signoria

You should now ignore the Palazzo Vecchio and Uffizi and stroll around the Loggia della Signoria on Piazza della Signoria's eastern side. The triple-arched space was begun in 1376, possibly with a design by artist Jacopo di Cione (active 1365–1398), to protect city officials from the weather during Florence's numerous public ceremonies. Craftsmen were called away from their work on the cathedral to build the loggia, hence the similarity between its arched interior and the cathedral's soaring vaults. In time the loggia was also used to greet visiting foreign dignitaries and as a shelter for the Swiss lancers (*lanzi*) of Cosimo I's guard; its alternative name is the Loggia dei Lanzi. Today it is a small outdoor museum for two major and several minor sculptures.

The most famous work is Benvenuto Cellini's distinguished bronze statue **"Perseus."** It shows the mythical Greek hero, the son of Zeus and Danaë, holding the severed, snake-covered head of Medusa, whose gaze turned humans to stone. The statue took almost ten years to complete (1545–1553). Cellini, a

"Hercules Beating the Centaur Nessus," (1599) by Giambologna in the Loggia della Signoria.

larger-than-life character, described in his 1554 *Autobiography* how the furnaces melting the bronze for the statue set fire to his house. As the inferno raged, Cellini and his assistants hurled all available metal in the house into the melt—including the cutlery and family pewter. When the bronze cooled, the statue was revealed as complete save for three toes on the right foot.

To Perseus's right stands Giambologna's **"Rape of the Sabine Women"** (1583), a virtuoso work carved from a single piece of flawed marble—the largest piece of stone ever brought to Florence. Despite the statue's title, it was originally intended as a study of old age, male strength, and female beauty.

Palazzo Vecchio

Palazzo Vecchio has dominated Piazza della Signoria for centuries, work having started on the building in 1299, probably to a design by the cathedral's architect, Arnolfo di Cambio. Initially it housed the Priori, or Signoria, the city's ruling council,

The battlements and tower of Palazzo Vecchio loom over Piazza della Signoria. A room in the tower was once a prison.

but in 1540 it became home to Cosimo I. Cosimo remained in residence just nine years before moving to the Palazzo Pitti, the point at which his "old" (*vecchio*) palace acquired its present name.

Today the palazzo once again houses the city's council, although much of its interior is also open to the public. You enter the complex via an inner **courtyard,** designed by Michelozzo in 1453 and delightfully decorated by Giorgio Vasari on the occasion of the marriage of Francesco de' Medici (firstborn son of Cosimo I) to Joanna of Austria in 1565. The bride's country of origin accounts for the paintings, which portray a series of towns and cities controlled by the Austro-Habsburg empire. The central **fountain** was added at the same time and features a putto (cherub) and dolphin by Andrea del Verrocchio, the teacher of Leonardo da Vinci. It was removed from the garden of the Medici villa at Careggi outside Florence. The present works are copies; the originals are inside the palace on the Terrazza di Giunone.

The precise route for visitors to reach the upper floors varies, but in an ideal world you should try to climb Vasari's magnificent main staircase to the **Salone dei Cinquecento,** or Room of the Five Hundred. This vast hall is the palace's centerpiece and was designed to accommodate the members of the Consiglio Maggiore, the republic's ruling assembly. Vasari was responsible for its 39 ceiling paintings, which depict the "Apotheosis of Cosimo I," and for the bombastic wall paintings, which illustrate various Florentine military triumphs.

Of greater artistic interest is Michelangelo's statue of "Victory" (1533–1534) on the wall almost opposite the room's entrance. Originally conceived as a female figure, it depicts the figure of

Genius slaying Reason. The sculptor's nephew gave it to the Medici, who had Vasari install it here in 1565 to commemorate Cosimo I's victory over Siena a decade earlier. On the opposite (entrance door) wall stands a model for Giambologna's "Virtue Overcoming Vice," commissioned as a companion piece for the "Victory." The room's other statues depict the "Labors of Hercules" and are masterpieces by an otherwise obscure sculptor, Vincenzo de' Rossi (1525–1587). Before leaving the Salone, don't miss the tiny **Studiolo di Francesco I,** a study created for Cosimo I's son. With your back to the Salone's entrance door, it lies off the end of the room to your right.

Other Areas of Note: Climb the stairs from the other side of the Salone and turn left and you come to a suite of rooms, the **Quartiere degli Elementi,** which leads to the **Terrazzo del Saturno,** a belvedere, for some fine city views. Turn right on the same staircase and you can look down on the Salone before coming to the **Quartiere di Eleonora,** the apartments of Cosimo I's wife. The highlight of these rooms is the tiny **Cappella di Eleonora,** a sumptuously decorated chapel by the mannerist artist Agnolo Bronzino (1503–1572).

Among the following rooms, the **Sala dell'Udienza** has good views over the Piazza della Signoria and a glorious ceiling by Giuliano da Maiano (1432–1490), who was also responsible, with his brother, for the carved doorway into the neighboring **Sala dei Gigli.** Named after its decorative lilies *(gigli),* this room features another fine Maiano ceiling, a fresco sequence depicting "Sts. Zenobius, Stephen, and Lawrence" by Domenico Ghirlandaio (1448–1494), and the original of Donatello's powerful statue of "Judith and Holofernes" from Piazza della Signoria. The next-door **Cancelleria** room was once Machiavelli's office, and the **Sala delle Carte** next door, now filled with lovely 16th-century maps, once housed Cosimo I's state costumes. The palace's **tower** can be climbed, though visits are suspended in poor weather, and those suffering from vertigo or claustrophobia are strongly advised against making the climb.

Galleria degli Uffizi

The Galleria degli Uffizi—more commonly known as the

Palazzo Vecchio

- Map pp. 88–89
- Piazza della Signoria
- 055 276 8325
- Palazzo & tower: Closed Thurs. p.m.
- $$ (palazzo), $$ (tower), $$$ (combined palazzo & tower)
- Bus: C2 to Via della Condotta or C1 to Via del Proconsolo

musefirenze.it

Palace Secrets

You can gain additional insights into the Palazzo Vecchio by joining the **Percorsi Segreti,** or Secret Itineraries, which are guided tours to parts of the palace that are normally off-limits or have restricted access. These include hidden chambers of the Studiolo di Francesco I, medieval passageways in the walls, and parts of the immense attic and superstructure of the Salone dei Cinquecento.

The tours last 90 minutes, cost €12, usually with at least one English tour daily. Find further information and make reservations at *musefirenze.it.* Other tours include the excavations of the Roman theater below the palace *(30 min., 2 p.m.– 4 p.m. Sat.–Mon., €12).*

Uffizi—is one of the world's greatest art galleries, home to a collection of Renaissance and other paintings that contains the most hallowed names in Italian and European art of the last 800 years. Its collection of Renaissance masterpieces is unequaled, but the huge city—on condition that it was never moved from Florence—by Anna Maria Luisa, sister of the last Grand Duke, Gian Gastone de' Medici (1671–1737). Sculpture from the collection was later moved to the Bargello, while Etruscan and other ancient art went to the Museo Archeologico. The paintings—which

Sandro Botticelli used classical rather than Christian imagery in his 1485 "The Birth of Venus."

gallery also features paintings from Italy's medieval, mannerist, and baroque heydays, as well as outstanding works of art from famous artists of Holland, Spain, and Germany.

Florence can thank the Medici for the Uffizi. The austere palace that contains the collection was built in 1560 as a rambling collection of offices (*uffizi*) for Grand Duke Cosimo I. The collection itself, gathered together by the family over the centuries, was left to the

in their day were considered less important than the sculpture—passed to the Uffizi and Palazzo Pitti.

At the time of publication, the Uffuzi is undergoing a major restoration, which entails an extension into vast areas beneath the present gallery, and a new exit. The locations of works, as listed below, will inevitably be altered, and you should check with the museum for the gallery layout at the time of your visit. The gallery currently has more than 45 rooms, and any brief account of its treasures can only touch on its highlights. Around 2,000 works can be admired at any one time, with another 1,800 kept in storage. Given the scale of the gallery, it can be a good idea to consider making two visits: one to take in the masterpieces of the Florentine Renaissance, and another to revel in the works of other Italian and foreign artists. Steel yourself for the possibility you will have to wait in line at almost any time of the day,

INSIDER TIP:

As restoration continues, check *polomuseale .firenze.it* for updated Uffizi layout plans.

—MARINA CONTI
National Geographic Italy editor

though note that tickets guaranteeing entry at an allotted time can generally be arranged in advance (see sidebar p. 98).

A medley of sculptures and frescoes of "Famous Men" (1450) by Andrea del Castagno make up the Uffizi's prelude: Only with three paintings of the "Maestà," or "Madonna Enthroned," in the **second major room** does the gallery hit its stride. Italy's three most eminent 13th-century artists—Giotto, Cimabue, and Duccio—were responsible for this trio of seminal paintings. Each artist orchestrated moves toward more realism in paintings and away from the stylization of Byzantine art, which had dominated Italian and other European art forms for centuries.

Altarpieces

Follow the evolution of altar paintings as you walk around the Uffizi, from the earliest small rectangles showing a series of saints to single panels (such as Duccio's "Maestà") that after 1300 grew larger so as to be visible as churches grew bigger. Then came diptychs, triptychs, and polyptychs—two-, three-, and multipanel paintings, usually in ornate Gothic frames with the Virgin and Child at the center and flanked by saints: Below might be a predella, a series of smaller panels depicting episodes from the life of Christ, the Virgin, or key saints. In the Renaissance, the popularity of a single panel, or *pala*, returned, often depicting saints, and now in simpler frames inspired by classical architecture.

This sense of transition can be seen in the manner in which the saints in Cimabue's painting of about 1275–1280 are ranged around the Virgin's throne. Cimabue's saints and angels stand in fixed and more realistic positions, while those of Duccio (painted about 1285), a painter more wedded to Byzantine tradition, seem to float haphazardly around the composition. And where Byzantine paintings were invariably "flat," Cimabue introduces hints of perspective to create a sense of space and depth.

At the same time, Cimabue's statuelike Virgin is still the aloof, detached Virgin of the Byzantine icon, while his Christ sports the harsh and unrealistic garb of a Roman general. Cimabue also uses gold to pick out the folds of the Virgin's cloak—very much a Byzantine device. Duccio's Virgin is equally aloof, but her throne

Galleria degli Uffizi

▲ Map pp. 88–89

✉ Loggiata degli Uffizi 6, off Piazza della Signoria

☎ 055 238 8651

🕐 Closed Mon.

💲 $$ ($$$ during special exhibits)

🚌 Bus: C1 to Via del Proconsolo; C2 to Via della Condotta; C3 or D to Lungaino Diazi

polomuseale .firenze.it firenzemusei.it

NOTE: Useful official apps to purchase: "Le vie degli Uffizi" & "Musei di Firenze"

is more realistically painted, as are the folds of her cloak, where light and shade are used to suggest the falling drapery. Duccio's painting also has a softer line and gentler and more realistic coloring.

But where Cimabue and Duccio struggled with half-realized innovation, Giotto's advances were marked and decisive. His "Maestà"—painted in 1310 for the church of Ognissanti (see p. 164)— retained some of the conventions of the Byzantine Madonna and Child. These included the gold background, Christ's hand raised in blessing, and the manner in which the Virgin points to the Child with her right hand. Giotto subtly subverted conventions, however, so that in the Virgin's gesture, for example, the pointed hand is turned into a hand resting on the Child's knee, a gesture of genuine human emotion missing from most earlier representations. In the same vein, the Virgin is portrayed for almost the first time as a real woman. There is, for example, the suggestion of breasts beneath her robes. Giotto's innovations also extend to the onlookers, who gaze with genuine eye contact and expression at the Holy Family. They also wear robes—as do the Madonna and Child—that are painted with a more realistic folding.

The painting's iconoclasm and realism also extend to its composition: The Madonna and her throne have solidity and depth; the surrounding saints and angels are standing on solid ground in a real three-dimensional space; and the pointed throne and three-point axis of angels and Madonna create a powerful pyramidal effect. This triangular compositional model would be emulated for centuries.

Rooms 3 to 6: That Giotto's lessons were not universally heeded

Beat the Lines With a Prepurchased Ticket

The lines at the Uffizi are extremely long year-round at any time of the day or week. Many private operators and several commercial websites offer advance tickets, but it's just as easy to go through the official ticketing agency, **Firenze Musei** (tel 055 294 883, firenzemusei.it).

You must choose a day and time, and pay a reservation fee (currently €4) on top of the standard entrance fee (extra charged for special exhibitions). Reservations must be made 24 hours in advance. On the day, collect your timed ticket from the galley across the piazza from the gallery entrance. If you miss your time slot, you will forfeit the right to skip the lines.

Tickets can also be reserved for the Galleria dell'Accademia (to see firsthand Michelangelo's "David"), the Museo Nazionale del Bargello, the Cappelle Medicee, and the Galleria Palatina and Appartamenti Reali in the Palazzo Pitti. These museums share a useful website (polomuseale.firenze.it), which offers additional information on tickets, plus details of how to purchase the **Firenzecard** (firenzecard.it). This costs €50 ($70) and is valid for entry (avoiding lines) to more than 60 museums, galleries, gardens, and villas in Florence, and also offers free Wi-Fi and use of public transit. It can be bought online or at nine points around the city and is valid for 72 hours. A Firenzecard app is also available.

is clear from the paintings of Italy's Gothic masters in Rooms 3 to 6, beginning with works from Siena, where painters continued to borrow heavily from the fading conventions of Byzantine art. Finest of all are Simone Martini's (see p. 215) exquisite "Annunciation" and the works by Pietro and Ambrogio Lorenzetti (see p. 41), two brothers who both probably died during the plague epidemic that swept Italy in 1348. Almost as beautiful are the exponents of the so-called International Gothic, a detailed and courtly style exemplified by the rapturous "Adoration of the Magi" by Gentile da Fabriano (1370–1427) and the lyrical "Coronation of the Virgin" by Lorenzo Monaco (1372–1424). These paintings have the detail of tapestry and also the escapist and ethereal beauty of fairy tales, with little of the realism that would be associated with Renaissance art.

"Maestà," or "Madonna Enthroned," by Duccio

Rooms 7 & 8: The first flowering of this style is seen in **Room 7,** which presents works by early Renaissance iconoclasts such as Masaccio, Masolino (1383–circa 1447), and Fra Angelico (see sidebar p. 142). One of the most eye-catching works is Paolo Uccello's "Battle of San Romano" (1435 or 1456), painted to recall the Florentines' victory over the combined armies of Milan and Siena in 1432. Uccello was concerned with the newly discovered rules of perspective to the point of obsession, a trait seen here in the almost surreal labyrinth of lances and horses disappearing to a single, central vanishing point.

The painting adorned the bedroom of Lorenzo the Magnificent, along with two sister panels now in the Louvre in Paris and London's National Gallery.

Room 7 also features a painting of the "Sacra Conversazione" or "Sacred Conversation" (1445), by one of the rarest of Italian painters, Venice-born Domenico Veneziano (died 1461), an artist with only 12 confidently attributed paintings to his name. Nearby hang two well-known works by one of Veneziano's pupils, Piero della Francesca (see p. 43)—portraits of Federico da Montefeltro, Duke of Urbino, and his wife, Battista Sforza. Federico was always portrayed in left profile, as here, after a jousting accident disfigured the right side of his face. Battista was depicted against a background that includes the town of Gubbio in Umbria, where she died after giving birth to her ninth child and first son. The portrait was completed two years after her death. Both pictures show the Renaissance in full flower, as becomes clear when you compare Piero's careful attention here to perspective, landscape, and detail—the jewelry, the wrinkles on the skin—with the paintings you've seen in earlier rooms. Battista's high, shaved forehead was a fashionable affectation of the time; in **Room 8,** it is shown on the Virgin in the painting by Filippo Lippi (see p. 43) of the "Madonna and Child with Two Angels." Lippi was the teacher of Sandro Botticelli (see below). He was also a monk by upbringing but something of a wanton man by nature: Seduced nuns were among his models.

Rooms 10 to 14: Rooms 10 to 14 are likely to be the Uffizi's most crowded, for these are the rooms given over to the gallery's most famous paintings: "La Primavera," or "Spring" (1478), and "La Nascita di Venere," or "The Birth of Venus" (1485), both by Botticelli (1445–1510). The latter, the "girl in a half shell," was the first pagan nude of the Renaissance and, like "La Primavera," drew heavily on classical myth and contemporary humanist scholarship. Significantly, neither of these paintings contains the religious content that had infused Western art for about a thousand years. According to the myth on which Botticelli drew, Venus was conceived by the ocean following the castration of Uranus and then rose from the sea, the tale suggesting beauty (Venus) was the result of a union between the physical and spiritual (Uranus). In the myth—and in the painting—the nymph Chloris and Zephyr, the god of wind, blow the risen Venus to the shore, where she is cloaked by the figure of Hora.

The theme of "La Primavera" is more uncertain. The name was

The Tribune Room

The octagonal Tribune Room (currently under major restoration) marks a transition between the pre-Renaissance and Renaissance painting you have already seen and the later and more widely sourced art that follows as you work your way through the Uffizi.

The room was specially built by the Medici family to house their most precious works of art, among which the "Medici Venus," a Roman statue, figured large. Widely celebrated as Europe's most erotic statue—the infamous English poet Lord Byron stood before it "dazzled and drunk with beauty"—the figure was the only Florentine statue removed to France by Napoleon after his invasion of Italy.

This room is also the only one in the gallery to retain the arrangement originally devised for all the Uffizi's rooms, which was to contrast the art of the ancient world—represented by Roman and Greek statues from the Medici collection—by placing it alongside the "modern" art of painting, seen in Italy's Renaissance masterpieces.

The Medici displayed their most treasured works of art in the Tribune Room.

actually chosen arbitrarily years later by the critic and painter Giorgio Vasari (see p. 40). Some critics suggest the work is an allegory of spring or all four seasons; others say it represents the Triumph of Venus, the attendant figures of the Graces in the painting representing her beauty, Flora her fecundity. What is certain is that the central figure is again Venus, goddess of spring and love, with her son, Cupid, depicted above her head. To the left, Mercury wards off the clouds of winter with his staff, while on the right you see the transformation of Chloris, after her rape by Zephyr, into the goddess Flora (shown scattering flowers). Other scholars have suggested the painting embodies the philosophy of the time as it related to love and beauty: Spring becomes the spur to awakening human emotions and desires, and Zephyr drives away the clouds of

melancholy so that these desires may evolve unimpeded. Zephyr, Chloris, and Flora may also symbolize lust, chastity, and beauty.

Whatever the paintings' precise meaning, the classical myth of their inspiration and their human-centered nature are unmistakable. As such, they contrast strongly with another famous painting in the room, the "Portinari Triptych" (1475–1480), commissioned by Tommaso Portinari, a manager of the Medici bank in Bruges, painted by the Flemish artist Hugo van der Goes (active 1467–1482). It created a sensation in Florence, where its use of light and background detail proved hugely influential. Although completed just before Botticelli's paintings, it was still almost entirely religious in inspiration and content. A nude such as the Venus on the half shell would have been unthinkable in northern Europe, a measure of the advances being made in Florentine art.

Rooms 15 to 29: The speed and development of these advances is borne out in the following rooms. **Room 15** contains two of only a handful of paintings existing in Florence attributed to Leonardo da Vinci: "Annunciation," painted when the artist was just 20, and the "Adoration of the Magi." Note how Leonardo omits many of the traditional elements of the "Adora-

Street Vendors

Around the Uffizi and other visitor attractions, notably the Galleria dell'Accademia, you will often come across street vendors selling "designer" watches, sunglasses, bags, and other goods. It is illegal to buy such goods, and police periodically swoop on both the sellers and buyers, who can be fined. Quality is low and, in making a purchase, you are supporting an iniquitous system of criminal middlemen that supplies and controls the vendors, who are often illegal immigrants from Senegal or Bangladesh. Don't buy.

tion" theme—the stable, Joseph, and the Three Kings—in order to focus attention on the Madonna and Child. As an 18-year-old, Leonardo also painted the angel on the left of Verrocchio's nearby "Baptism of Christ" (about 1475). Verrocchio, who was Leonardo's teacher, confessed that he could never hope to paint anything as beautiful. Looking at his own inferior angel—with its bony head and short hair—you can understand this lament of his own artistic limitations. Leonardo's paintings also overshadow pictures elsewhere in the room, notably those

of Luca Signorelli (1441–1523) from Tuscany and Pietro Perugino (circa 1446–1523), the greatest of Umbria's Renaissance artists.

The outstanding work in the six rooms devoted to Florentine, Venetian, German, and Flemish canvases is the "Sacred Allegory" in **Room 21** by Giovanni Bellini (1430/40–1516), arguably the finest of all Venetian painters.

In **Room 25,** well over halfway around the gallery, you come to the Uffizi's only painting by Michelangelo: the "Holy Family" or "Doni Tondo" (1504), painted on the occasion of the marriage of local aristocrats, Angelo Doni and Maddalena Strozzi (or possibly on the birth of their first child). It was painted around the time the artist was working on his statue of "David," a project with which he was far more enamored. Easel painting, as opposed to fresco or sculpture, he considered a chore, and this is the only such painting he brought close to completion. Little of the content is understood, but the pagan nudes to the rear of the painting and the wall—a symbol of exclusion—may be intended to suggest the exclusion of the pagan world from Christian salvation. Notice the unorthodox and original way Joseph is shown handing the Christ Child to the Virgin. The complex over-the-shoulder maneuver, among other things, allowed Michelangelo to indulge in twisted compositions and almost sculptural contortions that challenged his virtuosity.

The painting's deliberately obscure meaning, contorted composition, and often bright coloring profoundly influenced a style of painting known as mannerism, a genre whose leading lights are represented in the next four rooms. Look for "Supper at Emmaus" by Jacopo Pontormo (1494–1557) in **Room 27** and "Madonna and Child with Angels" by Parmigianino (1503–1540), the latter famous for the Virgin's elongated neck **(Room 29).**

Another late Renaissance painter who influenced the mannerists was Raphael (1483–1520), the cream of whose Uffizi paintings are found in **Room 26.** The most notable are the "Madonna of the Goldfinch" and unflinching portraits of the Medici pope Leo X, and cardinals Giulio de' Medici and Luigi de' Rossi. Raphael also influenced Titian (1487–1576), whose infamous "Venus of Urbino" (1538), one of the most explicit nudes in Western art, was described by Mark Twain as "the foulest, the vilest, the obscenest picture the world possesses."

Other Rooms: Rooms 30 to 35 deal largely in work by artists from northern Italy, notably Venice and Emilia-Romagna, but save your energy for the exceptional works in the gallery's final rooms. **Room 41** is dominated by Van Dyck (1599–1641) and Peter Paul Rubens (1577–1640), and in particular the paintings commissioned from Rubens following the marriage of King Henry IV of France (R.1589–1610) to Maria de' Medici (1573–1642). Caravaggio (1573–1610) flies the flag for Italy in **Room 43,** his bold drama in marked contrast to two introspective self-portraits by Rembrandt (1606–1669) in the next room. ■

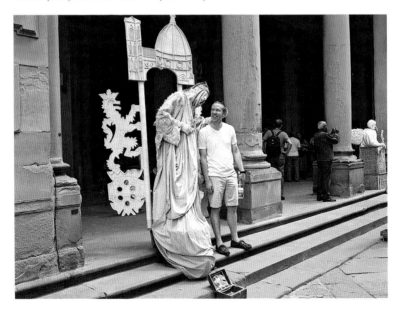

A Piazza degli Uffizi street performer entertains tourists.

Orsanmichele

Orsanmichele, a gaunt and fortresslike medieval church, stands incongruously amid the hurly-burly of Via dei Calzaiuoli. Its name comes from a corruption of San Michele ad Hortum, an oratory that once stood in the garden—Latin *hortum* or Italian *orto*—of a Benedictine abbey. Today, the church is celebrated for its tabernacle and remarkable collection of exterior sculptures.

Orsanmichele, a peaceful retreat from the crowds on Via dei Calzaiuoli

Orsanmichele
- Map pp. 88–89
- Via dell'Arte della Lana
- 055 210 305 (church), 055 284 944 (museum)
- Museum closed Tues.–Sun., church open daily
- Bus: C2 to Via della Condotta

A market for selling grain replaced the original abbey oratory around 1290. Despite the building's secular use, remnants of the site's religious past clung to it thanks to a revered image of the Virgin painted on one of its pillars, a picture believed to possess miraculous powers. Over the next hundred years the building was reshaped several times. By 1380 its lower half was once again a church—more or less the building you see today—while its upper portions were used as a granary.

The city's guilds (see sidebar p. 29) were entrusted with adorning the building in 1339. Each of its exterior niches was in the care of a particular guild, which in turn was responsible for commissioning artists to create a statue of the guild's patron saint for individual niches. However, the guilds obtained only one statue—a figure of the Arte della Lana's "St. Stephen."

With hindsight, it's easy to see how the 70-year hiatus worked to posterity's advantage. Instead of being produced at a time when Florentine sculpture was in a period of relative decline, the statues were actually created on the cusp of the Renaissance. As a result, some of the most distinguished artists of the period labored on the project, among them Donatello, Verrocchio, Michelozzo, and Ghiberti.

There are 14 statues in all, although some of the present works are copies, the originals having been moved for safety to the Bargello, Museo dell'Opera del Duomo, and elsewhere. Starting on Via dei Calzaiuoli, where there are three statues, the key works are those on the left and in the center as you face the church: The former portrays "John the Baptist" (1412–1416) and was produced by Lorenzo Ghiberti for the Arte di Calimala (Merchants Guild). The guild was convinced so large a bronze could not be cast and made Lorenzo responsible for the huge cost of the materials should he fail. He didn't—only one toe was missing when the casting was revealed. To the right stands Verrocchio's "St. Thomas" (1473–1483), created for the Mercatanzia (Merchants Tribunal). Its niche is the work of Donatello and Michelozzo. Donatello was also responsible for the figure of "St. George" (1416–1417) on the Via Orsanmichele flank of the church. The present statue is a copy, but the original is one of the stars of the Bargello.

Inside, patches of frescoes appear around the walls as your eyes become accustomed to the gloom, most of them images of the guilds' patron saints, pictorial equivalents of the statues outside. To the rear stands a magnificent **tabernacle** by Andrea Orcagna (1308–1368), built partly to house a painting of the "Madonna and Child" (1347) by Bernardo Daddi (circa 1290–1355), a work said to have inherited the miraculous powers of the Virgin on the pillar, which had been destroyed in a fire. The greatest work of its kind in Italy, the tabernacle was financed by votive offerings prompted by

The Quattro Coronati

Walk down Via Orsanmichele on the north side of Orsanmichele to admire the third niche down, devoted to the four statues of the Quattro Coronati (1409–15/17), the masterpiece of Florentine sculptor Nanni di Banco (circa 1384–1421). The Quattro Coronati were Christian stonemasons from present-day Hungary martyred in around A.D. 287 for refusing to carve pagan statues. As a result, medieval Florence's Maestri di Pietre e Legname, or masons and carpenters, adopted them as their patron saints and paid for this work. As the story goes, Nanni miscalculated the space available and the statues would not fit the niche until his friend, Donatello, suggested he simply make the figures slimmer.

the Black Death of 1348. Orcagna, for his part, has few surviving works, although he was perhaps the most important artist, sculptor, and architect to work in the era following Giotto's death.

The church's upper levels have rooms—reached by a small bridge from the **Palazzo dell'Arte della Lana**—that contain some of the original statues from the exterior of Orsanmichele. ■

A Walk From Piazza della Signoria to Sant'Ambrogio

This route provides an opportunity to see the many faces of Florence, from the grandeur of the medieval city to the sights and sounds of the markets and cafés around Sant'Ambrogio.

Some of the eclectic mix of offerings for sale at the Mercato delle Pulci

As you face the Palazzo Vecchio, take Via della Ninna to its right. At the end of the street you come to Via dei Leoni, named after the lions (*leoni*) once kept in dungeons at the rear of the Palazzo Vecchio. Continue on to Via dei Neri. Immediately on your right is the **Loggia del Grano ❶**, commissioned by Cosimo II (1590–1621) in 1619 and the last of a series of loggias designed to be used as markets; the others were the Loggia del Mercato and Loggia del Pesce.

Via dei Neri takes you into one of Florence's best preserved medieval quarters. Several houses and palaces here date from at least the 14th century, notably Palazzo Bagnesi (No. 25), Palazzo Grifoni (No. 6), and Palazzo Nori (No. 4). At the junction with Via della Mosca, turn left and you come to a square containing the 11th-century church of **San Remigio,** whose

NOT TO BE MISSED:

Loggia del Grano • Santa Croce • Sant'Ambrogio • Mercato delle Pulci

interior is tinged with traces of 14th-century frescoes. Then walk to the left of the church, turn left on Via de' Rustici, and bear left along Via dei Bentacordi to Borgo de'Greci. Turn right to Via de' Benci and walk south to Borgo Santa Croce, perhaps first visiting the nearby **Museo Horne ❷** (see pp. 117–118). Midway along Borgo Santa Croce you pass three notable build-ings on the right: the late 15th-century **Palazzo Antinori Corsini** (No. 6), which belonged to two noble families; the **Casa di Giorgio Vasari,** home of the 16th-century painter and art historian (No. 8; *guided visits Sat. at 10, 11, & noon*); and **Palazzo Spinelli** (No. 10), built in 1460 and notable for the painted "graffito" decoration of its facade and courtyard. Similar decoration adorns the **Palazzo Morelli** at No. 19.

At the end of Borgo Santa Croce you come to Piazza Santa Croce and the church of **Santa Croce** ❸ (see pp. 108–114). Note **Palazzo dell'Antella** halfway down the piazza on the south side (Nos. 20–22), notable for its exterior frescoes (1619) of the "Virtues and Divinities," completed by 12 artists in just 20 days. Follow Largo Piero Bargellini to the left of Santa Croce and take the first left, Via delle Pinzochere. From here you enter one of Florence's traditional blue-collar districts, best enjoyed in the **Mercato Sant'Ambrogio** ❹ (*Mon.–Sat. a.m.*), a food market reached by turning right off Via M. Buonarroti (the northern continuation of Via delle Pinzochere) onto Via dell'Agnolo. You may like to visit the **Casa Buonarroti** (see p. 116) on Via Ghibellina.

Turn right (north) on Via de' Macci and

you will reach the church of **Sant'Ambrogio** ❺ (see p. 118) at the junction of Borgo la Croce and Via Pietrapiana. Turn left on Via Pietrapiana and you come to Piazza dei Ciompi, site of the Loggia del Pesce (old fish market) and the **Mercato delle Pulci** ❻, Florence's flea market (*open Tues.–Sat. & 1st Sun. of the month*).

Return to Sant'Ambrogio and turn left on Via de' Pilastri in front of the church, and then take the second right on Via L. C. Farini. Here you'll find the **Tempio Israelitico** ❼, or Jewish Synagogue (*Via L. C. Farini 4, tel 055 234 6654, closed Fri. p.m. & all Sat.*), a Spanish-Moorish-style building built in 1882. Its small museum is worth a visit (*closed Fri. p.m. & Sat.*).

- 🅰 See also area map pp. 88–89
- ► Piazza della Signoria
- 🕐 2 hours
- ↔ 1.75 miles (2.8 km)
- ► Piazza Sant'Ambrogio. Walk or take bus C2 or C3 from the east end of Borgo la Croce back to the city center.

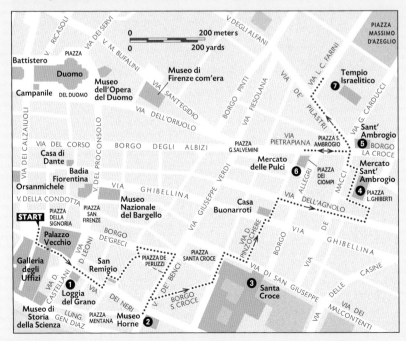

Santa Croce

Santa Croce is Florence's most majestic church. Its importance stems not only from its art—it contains sublime fresco cycles by Giotto and other medieval masters—but also from its status as the burial place of Galileo, Michelangelo, Machiavelli, and around 270 of the city's eminent citizens. In the Cappella dei Pazzi, it has one of the most perfect early Renaissance buildings.

Michelangelo was laid to rest in this tomb in Florence despite spending most of the last 25 years of his life in Rome.

Santa Croce

- ⬛ Map pp. 88–89
- ✉ Piazza Santa Croce
- ☎ 055 246 6105
- 🕐 Closed Sun. a.m. & religious holidays
- 💲 $$ (includes entry to Museo dell'Opera & Cappella dei Pazzi), $$$ (combined with Casa Buonarotti)
- 🚌 Bus: C1, C2, C3 to Piazza Santa Croce

santacroceopera.it

Santa Croce was built for the Franciscans. Its design has been attributed to Arnolfo di Cambio, the architect also largely responsible for Florence's cathedral and Palazzo Vecchio. It was started around 1294, partly to overshadow Santa Maria Novella—then being built across the city—the mother church of the city's Dominicans. Work was completed in 1385, but the church was consecrated only in 1443. Do not be fooled

by the facade; it is not original but was added in mock-Gothic style between 1853 and 1863. Its architect claimed to have discovered long-lost plans for an earlier medieval facade. In truth, he simply adapted his design from the tabernacle in Orsanmichele (see p. 105).

The Franciscans and others spent colossal sums on the church, despite the order's supposed vows of poverty. Much of the funding came from prosperous

Florentines, many of whom considered it an act of humility to associate themselves with, and be interred among, the humble Franciscans. Wealthy bankers also viewed sponsorship of churches as a means by which they might be freed from the stigma associated with usury, or lending money with interest, then still considered a sin.

The Tombs

The riches lavished on Santa Croce explain the considerable majesty of its countless chapels, most of which were named after the men that paid for their adornment. They also account for the splendor of its numerous tombs, the first of which—Giorgio Vasari's **monument to Michelangelo—** you find almost immediately on entering the church's soaring interior (opposite the first pillar on the south, or right, wall), placed close to the church's entrance at Michelangelo's personal request. The reason for its location, or so the story has been handed down through the ages, is that the artist wished to see the dome of Florence's cathedral as his first waking sight on rising from his tomb on the Day of Judgment.

To explore the interior of this densely detailed church, start by walking to the first pillar close to Michelangelo's tomb to admire the lovely relief by Antonio Rossellino (1427–1479) of the "Madonna del Latte," or "Madonna of the Milk." To the left of Michelangelo's tomb stands a **cenotaph to Dante.** This is not a tomb, as the poet is buried

in Ravenna on Italy's east coast, where he died in exile in 1321 (see pp. 78–79). Beyond this comes a noteworthy pulpit (1472–1476) by Benedetto da Maiano (third pillar of the nave), and then Antonio Canova's (1757–1822) "Monument to Alfieri," an 18th-century Italian poet known as much for his romantic liaisons as his literary achievements. To the left is the **tomb of Machiavelli,** crafted in 1787, some two centuries after the writer's death. It is unremarkable save for its famous inscription: *"Tanto nomini nullum par elogium—* No praise can be high enough for so great a name."

INSIDER TIP:

From Michelangelo's tomb, the best way to see Santa Croce is to follow the right (south) wall, study the frescoed chapels at the top, cross in front of the altar, and then work back down the left side of the nave.

—BILL McBEE
*National Geographic
Marketing Services*

Beyond these tombs, and past a recessed and gilded stone relief of the "Annunciation" (1435) by Donatello, lie the tombs of the opera composer Gioacchino Rossini (1792–1868) and—to its right—that of the 15th-century humanist scholar Leonardo Bruni (1370–1444). This tomb was the work of Bernardo Rossellino (see p. 48), and it became one of the most influential of all early Renaissance funerary monuments, mainly because it was the first time a non-religious figure—as opposed to the Madonna and Child—had dominated on a secular tomb. Among the works it influenced was the church's other great secular tomb, the 1453 monument by Desiderio da Settignano to Carlo Marsuppini

(1399–1453), another humanist scholar. It lies across the nave almost opposite the Bruni tomb.

The Chapels

Patches of faded fresco adorn many of Santa Croce's walls, sharpening the aesthetic appetite

Santa Croce

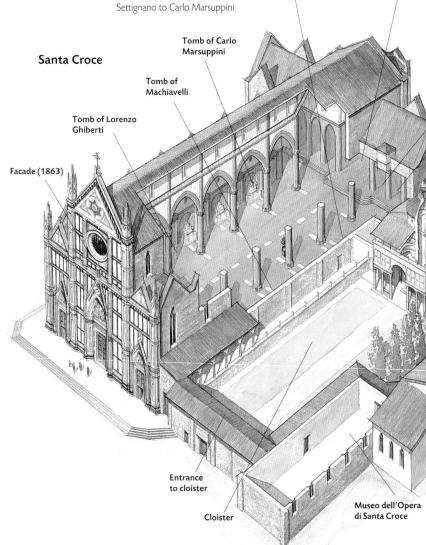

Tomb of Leonardo Bruni

Chancel

Tomb of Carlo Marsuppini

Tomb of Machiavelli

Tomb of Lorenzo Ghiberti

Facade (1863)

Entrance to cloister

Cloister

Museo dell'Opera di Santa Croce

for the church's pictorial highlights, most of which are contained in the chapels ranged across the apse and chancel, the area around the high altar. The first chapel, on the right beyond Rossini's tomb, is the **Cappella Castellani,** with paintings by Agnolo Gaddi (active 1369–1396)

and assistants. The right wall as you face the chapel contains scenes from the lives of St. John the Baptist and St. Nicholas of Bari. Nicholas is, among other things, the patron saint of children and the original Santa Claus. Here he is shown reviving three murdered boys and preventing girls without marriage dowries from falling into lives of prostitution. On the left wall are various scenes from the life of St. Antony Abbot, a theme often explored in Franciscan churches, as Antony gave away much of his wealth, making him a particularly popular figure with the

Neo-Gothic Campanile (1842)

Giotto frescoes

Cappella dei Pazzi

Key to floor plan
1 Tomb of Michelangelo
2 Cenotaph to Dante
3 Tomb of Machiavelli
4 Donatello "Annunciation"
5 Tomb of Leonardo Bruni
6 Tomb of Rossini
7 Cappella Castellani
8 Cappella Baroncelli
9 Sacristy
10 Cappella Rinuccini
11 Cappella Peruzzi
12 Cappella Bardi
13 Chancel
14 Tomb of Galileo
15 Museo dell'Opera di Santa Croce
16 Cappella dei Pazzi

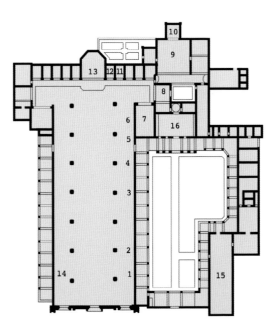

Scuola del Cuoio

The Leather School (*Via di San Giuseppe 5r, tel 055 244 533, scuoladelcuoio.com*) was started after World War II by the Franciscan friars of the Monastery of Santa Croce, with the help of the Gori and Casini families. Its aim was to teach war orphans a practical trade and thus give them a means to earn a living. Santa Croce, on the banks of the Arno, has long been a tanning district for leather goods, and the friars and families wished to keep alive the skills of Florence's master craftsmen, and to perpetuate fine Florentine craftsmanship.

poverty-conscious Franciscans.

The adjoining chapel, the **Cappella Baroncelli,** was painted by Agnolo's father, Taddeo (1300–1366), whose chosen theme was the "Life of the Virgin." Taddeo was a longtime pupil and assistant of Giotto, who was probably responsible for the chapel's altarpiece, the "Coronation of the Virgin." The corridor here leads to the **Cappella Medici** (usually closed) and a door that opens into the **sacristy,** a lovely room with a fine "Crucifixion" by Taddeo Gaddi and the small **Cappella Rinuccini** (behind a 1371 grille). The latter is smothered in frescoes on the life of the Virgin (on the left) and the life of St. Mary Magdalene (on the right) by Giovanni da Milano (active 1346–1369), an accomplished disciple of Giotto.

Giotto himself was responsible for the greatest of all Santa Croce's works of art: the **Cappella Bardi** and **Cappella Peruzzi** (both 1320–1325), two chapels in the main body of the church to the right of the high altar. In them, he

frescoed scenes from the life of St. John the Baptist and the life of St. John the Evangelist (in the Cappella Peruzzi) and episodes from the life of St. Francis (in the Cappella Bardi). Notice, in particular, the extraordinary composition of the "Funeral of St. Francis" in the latter, celebrated for its remarkable horizontal emphasis; virtually all the figures are prostrate, mirroring the stretched body of the saint and a deliberate echo of the lamentation over the body of Christ. Further parallels with the story of Christ are underlined by the Doubting Thomas figure, who pokes a finger into the wound in Francis's side, unable to believe the veracity of the saint's stigmata (the wounds of Christ, which Francis miraculously manifested). Michelangelo and Masaccio were just two of the later Renaissance artists who made a careful study of these frescoes.

Fresco cycles by artists influenced or taught by Giotto fill several nearby chapels. To the left of the Cappella Bardi, for example, the **chancel** area around the high altar is frescoed with the "Legend of the True Cross" (1380) by Agnolo Gaddi. The theme of the frescoes in this most important of positions (by the high altar) was determined by the name of the church—Santa Croce, or Holy Cross. The story they tell is the same one as Piero della Francesca's better known cycle in Arezzo (see pp. 284–287).

The **Cappella Bardi di Vernio,** the fifth chapel to the left of the high altar, has scenes from the life of St. Sylvester (1340) by Maso di Banco, one of Giotto's more innovative followers. Another

Cappella Bardi to its left contains a wooden "Crucifix" (1412) by Donatello, a much maligned work that was reputedly dismissed by Brunelleschi as resembling "a peasant on the Cross."

From here, turn your back on the high altar and walk toward the church's entrance. The first major monument on your right (to the right of the side door) is the tomb of Carlo Marsuppini (1453) by Desiderio da Settignano, a major work heavily influenced by the Bruni tomb opposite (see p. 109). Farther down, on the wall almost opposite the nave's fourth pillar, is a "Pietà" (1560) by Agnolo Bronzino, a leading mannerist painter. To its left lies a pavement slab marking the tomb of Lorenzo Ghiberti, the sculptor responsible for, among other things, the Battistero's hallowed east doors (see p. 71). Way down near the entrance, opposite the nave's first left-hand pillar, is the tomb of the noted scientist, Galileo Galilei (see p. 51).

Museo dell'Opera di Santa Croce

To the right of Santa Croce as you face the facade is the entrance to the church's cloister, now home to a small museum, the Museo dell'Opera di Santa Croce. Its highlights are Cimabue's late 13th-century "Crucifix," one of the principle artistic casualties of the 1966 flood (see pp. 160–161); Donatello's gilded statue of "St. Louis of Toulouse" (1424), created for the church of Orsanmichele; a detached mid-15th century fresco of "St. John the Baptist and St. Francis" by Domenico Veneziano; and Taddeo Gaddi's huge fresco of the "Last Supper," "Tree of Life" (1333), and other scenes.

Museo dell'Opera di Santa Croce & Cappella dei Pazzi

✉ Piazza Santa Croce 16

☎ 055 246 6105

🕐 Closed Sun. a.m. & some religious holidays

💲 $$ (includes entrance to Santa Croce)

🚌 Bus: C1, C2, C3 to Piazza Santa Croce

The former dormitory of the Franciscan friars now houses the Scuola del Cuoio (Leather School).

The Cappella dei Pazzi appears simple, but it hides a complex architectural and decorative scheme.

Cappella dei Pazzi

The church ticket also grants you entry to the Cappella dei Pazzi at the top of the cloister, commissioned from Brunelleschi in 1429 as a chapter house and family mausoleum by Andrea de' Pazzi, a leading light of the banking dynasty that tried to topple the Medici in the abortive Pazzi Conspiracy of 1478 (see sidebar p. 33). Brunelleschi labored on and off on the chapel until his death in 1446, but financial shortfalls meant the work was completed only in the 1470s. Completion coincided with the family's downfall, and no member of the Pazzi family was ever buried in their chapel.

To the modern eye the chapel can appear plain, even austere. But to earlier sensibilities the church represented one of the pinnacles of early Renaissance architecture. In particular, the Cappella dei Pazzi is admired for the manner in which its decoration so artfully complements the building's simple geometrical form.

The decoration begins with a frieze of medallions and angels' heads above the porch, the work of Desiderio da Settignano. Luca della Robbia was responsible for the tondo of "St. Andrew," above the beautiful main door by Giuliano da Maiano (1432–1490), and for the colored lining of the portico's dome and the garland of fruit clasped around the Pazzi coat of arms.

There are similarities to Brunelleschi's Sagrestia Vecchia in San Lorenzo (see p. 125) here: for example, the four similar tondi in the cupola, representing the Evangelists, the work of Luca della Robbia and his workshop. Luca also produced the 12 tondi of the Apostles around the walls. ∎

EXPERIENCE: Spend Extended Study Time in Florence

Of all the cities in Europe in which you might spend an extended period, few can be as tempting as Florence, especially if you are committed to furthering your interest or skill in an area of the arts and decorative arts for which the city has long been famous.

It is possible to spend short periods studying art history in Florence—you can sign up for as little as €45 per lesson (see sidebar p. 40)—but the many practical courses available in the city in painting, sculpture, and the decorative arts usually require a commitment of at least a week.

The beauty of such courses is that they allow you full immersion in a city where you are surrounded by some of the finest possible examples of the art or craft you are studying. Most courses are structured so that study can be combined with free time for exploring the city and beyond, and learning or improving your Italian (though teaching in the courses outlined below is in English).

Short Art Courses

Many would-be students are artists. **The Florence Art Studio** (tel 055 050 3628, theflorenceartstudio.com) is situated in the heart of the city and offers discrete and intensive one-, two-, three-, and four-week modules (usually all day, Monday through Friday) in drawing, painting, and still life. The modules can be pursued individually or combined to form a coherent, longer course. Thus you could devote a week's vacation one year to a module and then return another year to continue your studies.

Longer Art Courses

The **Accademia del Giglio** (tel 055 230 2467, adg.it) has been offering a larger range of courses in drawing, life drawing, fresco, trompe l'oeil, charcoal, watercolor, and more since 1995. It offers

INSIDER TIP:

Internships offer a deep immersion in Italian culture while completing college courses, especially if you are studying tourism or fashion [gooverseas.com/internships-abroad/italy].

—JUSTIN KAVANAGH
National Geographic
Travel Books editor

the option of spring, fall, and winter courses—many organizations only offer summer programs—in one-, two-, and three-week blocks or longer "units" of up to 36 weeks. A week's course involves 14 hours' tuition. The Accademia also offers Italian language courses.

Another Florentine organization, the **Accademia Riaci** (tel 055 289 831, accademiariaci.info), has a wide range of yearlong or semester-length programs as well as short-option ceramics and bagmaking courses (both a week), two-week programs in glass or shoe design, and four-week courses in restoration or painting and drawing (course lengths may vary year to year).

Fashion & Design Courses

Not surprisingly, the city that gave birth to Gucci and fostered the talent of Ferragamo also offers tuition in fashion—contact the **Accademia Italiana** (tel 055 284 616, accademiaitaliana .com) for monthlong and more extended courses. The Accademia also offers photography programs.

The **Florence Institute of Design** (tel 055 230 2481, florence-institute.com) has summer and yearlong courses in furniture, architecture, and graphic or interior design, while **Studiainitalia** (tel 347 558 3681 in Italy, 512/439-9665 in North America, studia initalia.com) has courses in casting, mosaic, enameling, engraving, 3-D computer design, design and technical drawing, wax, stone setting, and wood carving.

More Places to Visit in Eastern Florence

Casa Buonarroti

The Casa Buonarroti stands on the site of a property once owned by Michelangelo Buonarroti, the full name of the artist more commonly known simply as Michelangelo. Today it houses a sleek, modern museum with a handful of minor works by Michelangelo, as well as a wide range of artifacts connected with, or created in honor of, the great man. A variety of beautifully furnished and decorated rooms provides the setting for the exhibits.

Admission to the museum is relatively expensive for what you can see. The two most important sculptures are in a room on the upper floor: The "Madonna della Scala" (1490–1492) is Michelangelo's earliest known work, probably carved when he was little more than 16 years old. The accompanying "Battle of the Centaurs" was created a short time later, when the artist was apprenticed to the Medici household. In an adjacent room is a wooden model (1517) for Michelangelo's never completed facade of San Lorenzo (see pp. 122–127). Nearby is a strange-looking wax-and-wood torso of a "River God" (1524), probably the model for a sculpture destined for San Lorenzo's Medici chapels. Another room features a small crucifix by Michelangelo from the church of Santo Spirito (see p. 187) in the Oltrarno. A well-documented work, it was found only in 1963, having long been feared lost.

🅰 Map pp. 88–89 ✉ Via Ghibellina 70 ☎ 055 241 752 🕐 Closed Tues. & main pubic holidays 💲 $$ 🚌 Bus: C2, C3 to Via Ghibellina

Museo Galileo–Museo di Storia della Scienza

The renamed Galileo Museum–Museum of the History of Science is a fantastic museum for anyone with a passion for science or the beauty of old scientific and other instruments. Its sheer range and the intrinsic interest of its exhibits should also appeal to the nonspecialist, as well as to children. As a further recommendation, it's a modern and well-presented museum—not always the case in Florence.

The artifacts on display here help to underline Tuscany's contribution to scientific endeavor, an intellectual discipline often overshadowed by the region's better-documented achievements in the fields of painting and

---

Florence for Children

The **Museo Galileo** (see this page) should convince children that there's more to Florence than ice cream. Other fun sites include the **Museo dei Ragazzi** (Children's Museum) in the Palazzo Vecchio and the palazzo's "kit-tartarughe"–"tortoise" backpacks with a plan, binoculars, and notes *(musefirenze.it)*. Older children might enjoy the waxworks of the **Museo Zoologico–La Specola** (see p. 186); the **Galleria delle Costume** in the Palazzo Pitti (see p. 169); and the **Forte del Belvedere: The Palazzo Davanzati** (see pp. 158–159) and **Museo Horne** (see pp. 117–118) are among the museums that have special children's events. See the city's visitor center for more ideas *(firenzeturismo.it)*.

---

sculpture. One of the greatest of all scientists, Galileo, lived and worked in Florence, and in 1657 Grand Duke Ferdinando de' Medici and his brother Leopoldo founded one of the world's first scientific academies at the Palazzo Pitti, the Accademia del Cimento, or Academy of Experiment (motto: "Try and try again").

Individual rooms around the museum are devoted to a different branch of science or technology. Each is filled with the most beautiful old objects: astrolabes, armillary spheres, telescopes, ancient quadrants,

INSIDER TIP:

Be sure to visit the medieval pharmacy room at the Museo Galileo–Museo di Storia della Scienza. The potions on display include everything from Sangue del Drago (Dragon's Blood) to Confetti di Seme Santo (Confections of Blessed Seed).

–STEFANIA MARTORELLI
National Geographic Italy editor

fabulous antique globes and maps, beautiful clocks and timepieces, pneumatic pumps, prisms, and a host of other exquisitely fashioned scientific instruments.

Some of the most fascinating rooms lie at the end of the two-floor gallery, namely the medical section, which features some quite terrifying medical instruments and gruesomely detailed anatomical wax models. Another interesting exhibit is the room that has been transformed into a medieval pharmacy, where some of the potions displayed may be of dubious scientific efficacy.

🅰 Map pp. 88–89 ✉ Piazza de' Giudici 1 ☎ 055 265 311 🕐 Closed Tues. p.m., Jan. 1, & Dec. 25 💲 $$$ 🚌 Bus: C1, C3, D to Lungarno Gen. Diaz

Museo Horne

The art collection in this modest gallery may pale alongside most others in the city, but you still can't help but be envious of its former owner, Herbert Percy Horne (1864–1916), an English art historian who lived and worked in Florence.

Today, Horne is best known for his fine biography of Sandro Botticelli, a book that rescued the artist—today one of the most popular of all Italian painters—from almost complete obscurity. In his own time, Horne dabbled in the art market, accumulating a

collection of paintings, sculptures, ceramics, and objets d'art, as well as some exceptional furniture. Eventually he purchased the museum's present home, the **Palazzo Corsi-Alberti,** as a suitable setting for his collection. He left both the building and his collection to the city.

The palace, built by the Corsi family in 1489, is just as interesting as the exhibits. It represents a typical textile merchant's house of the period, complete with an open gallery for drying finished cloth and roomy cellars in which material would have been dyed. The collection itself has few genuine masterpieces, but it is both eclectic and interesting. It includes the occasional big name, notably Masaccio (a tiny panel of "St. Julian"); Giotto (a panel showing "St. Stephen," part of a larger painting); Benozzo Gozzoli ("Deposition,"

An armillary sphere ordered by Ferdinando de' Medici, made of gold and cypress wood

Fresh fare at the Mercato di Sant'Ambrogio

his last documented work); and Filippino Lippi (a small and timeworn "Crucifixion").

 Map pp. 88–89 ✉ Via de' Benci 6 ☎ 055 244 661 🕑 Closed p.m. & all Sun. 💲 $$
🚍 Bus: 23, C1 to Ponte alle Grazie

Sant'Ambrogio

Sant'Ambrogio is one of Florence's more outlying churches, but a visit can easily be combined with a trip to the Sant'Ambrogio market (see p. 107)—one of the city's most authentic general markets—and the pretty Cibreo café (see Travelwise p. 309). One of the city's older foundations, the church is mentioned in a document of 988, although restoration has left the present building a shadow of its former self.

Most of the church's treasures remain, however, most notably the **Cappella del Miracolo,** or Chapel of the Miracle, to the left of the high altar. This is dominated by a tabernacle by Mino da Fiesole, an accomplished sculptor born in nearby Fiesole (see pp. 226–227). He is buried in the church and commemorated by a pavement slab at the entrance to the chapel. Another artist, Andrea del Verrocchio (died 1488), the teacher of Leonardo da Vinci and Perugino, among others, is buried in the fourth chapel.

Alongside Mino's tabernacle is a fresco by Cosimo Rosselli (1439–1507), whose lovely narrative describes the miracle that gave the chapel its name. The story in question revolves around the discovery in 1230 of a chalice full of blood. This became precious to the Florentines, who believed it saved them from a virulent outbreak of plague in 1340 (although not, sadly, from the Black Death eight years later). The original chalice is enclosed within the tabernacle.

Other paintings worth hunting out around the church include a triptych that is attributed to Bicci di Lorenzo (in the chapel to the right of the high altar) and "The Madonna Enthroned with St. John the Baptist and St. Bartholomew," attributed to Andrea Orcagna or the school of Orcagna (second altar on the right).

 Map pp. 88–89 ✉ Piazza Sant'Ambrogio ☎ 055 240 104 🕑 Closed Sun. a.m.
🚍 Bus: C2, C3 to Borgo la Croce

EXPERIENCE: Live With Florentines

If you really want to get to know the Florentines and their way of life, become a **GeoVisions Conversation Corps** volunteer—it's a great experience. You teach members of a Florentine family English for 15 hours a week, Monday through Friday, and in return you get the chance to live with the family—making friends, learning Italian, and seeing firsthand how Italians really live and work

(minimum two-week stay). Alternatively, be a "Conversation Partner," helping Florentine English teachers improve their language skills, and receive accommodation and two meals a day in return for up to 20 hours of conversation a week (minimum one-month placement). Contact **GeoVisions** *(tel 203/453-5838 or toll-free 855/875-6837 in the U.S., geovisions.org)* for further information.

Michelangelo's "David," the Medici tombs, Florence's most colorful market, and the museum filled with Fra Angelico's sublime paintings

Northern Florence

Colorful leather handbags catch the eye in the San Lorenzo market.

Northern Florence

Northern Florence lies outside the old Roman city, whose limit was marked by the present-day Piazza del Duomo. The fact that the district was "beyond the pale" didn't stop its early development, which took place along the line of Via San Gallo, a northerly continuation of the *cardo maximus,* the name given to one of the main streets in a Roman colony.

During the Middle Ages, the area was known as the Quartiere di San Giovanni, or Quarter of St. John, one of four large parishes into which the medieval city was divided. Much of it comprised a closely packed—but now largely vanished—maze of residential streets. This labyrinth was particularly rich in convents, hospitals, and pilgrims' lodgings, the descendants of which survive to this day.

Change, when it came, was largely the result of Medici meddling. It was Florence's most powerful family, for example, who

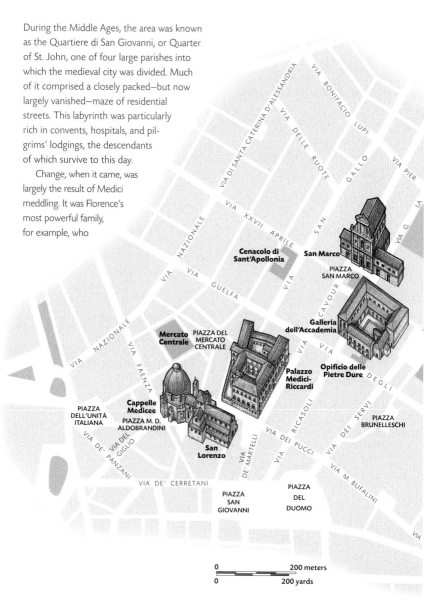

enlarged the old cathedral church of San Lorenzo, one of the district's pivotal points, now visited for a pair of pulpits by Donatello, the Medici library, and Brunelleschi's Old Sacristy. It was also the Medici who added the Cappelle Medicee to the rear of the church, later graced with several outstanding sculptures by Michelangelo. They also patronized the San Marco convent to the north, now the Museo di San Marco, a museum given over to the works of Fra Angelico, one of the most exalted of all Renaissance painters. And it was the Medici who built the Palazzo Medici-Riccardi near the cathedral, an enormous palace that remained the family's headquarters for about a hundred years. Its most enchanting sight is a fresco cycle by Benozzo Gozzoli, one of the most lyrical of all Italian painting cycles.

NOT TO BE MISSED:

Studying the pulpits of Bronzino's "St. Lawrence" and the Sagrestia Vecchia in San Lorenzo 122–127

Sampling delights at the food stalls of the Mercato Centrale 132

The quiet of Cappella dei Magi, Palazzo Medici-Riccardi 133–135

Marveling at Michelangelo's "David" and "Slaves," Galleria dell'Accademia 138–141

The "Annunciation" by Fra Angelico at the Museo di San Marco 144

Michelozzo's tabernacle, Santissima Annunziata 146

Strangely, the Medici had no hand in the district's most famous sight, Michelangelo's "David," which is housed in the Accademia, an art academy between the cathedral and San Marco. Michelangelo's statue is so compelling that visitors often overlook the Accademia's other exhibits, including several lesser sculptures by the same artist and a range of Italian Renaissance and other paintings that would shine elsewhere. There are often long lines here, so consider reserving a preestablished admittance time online (see sidebar p. 98).

No such measures are necessary for northern Florence's less prominent sights. Don't miss the San Lorenzo market, a busy labyrinth of stall-filled streets around the San Lorenzo church, nor the Mercato Centrale, Europe's largest covered food market. The latter is a cornucopia of sights, smells, and mouthwatering cheeses, hams, vegetables, fruit, and other seasonal gastronomic treats.

Finally, among the lesser sights, leave time for Piazza della Santissima Annunziata near the Museo di San Marco, a planned Renaissance square that provides a setting for the church of Santissima Annunziata and Europe's first orphans' hospital. ■

PIRA
ANTONIO MICHELI
GIARDINO DEI SEMPLICI
VIA GINO CAPPONI
Santissima Annunziata
VIA GIUSEPPE GIUSTI
GIARDINO DELLA GHERARDESCA
PIAZZA DELLA SANTISSIMA ANNUNZIATA
Museo Archeologico
Ospedale degli Innocenti
BORGO PINTI
ALFANI
BORGO PINTI
SANT'EGIDIO
Arno
Area of map detail

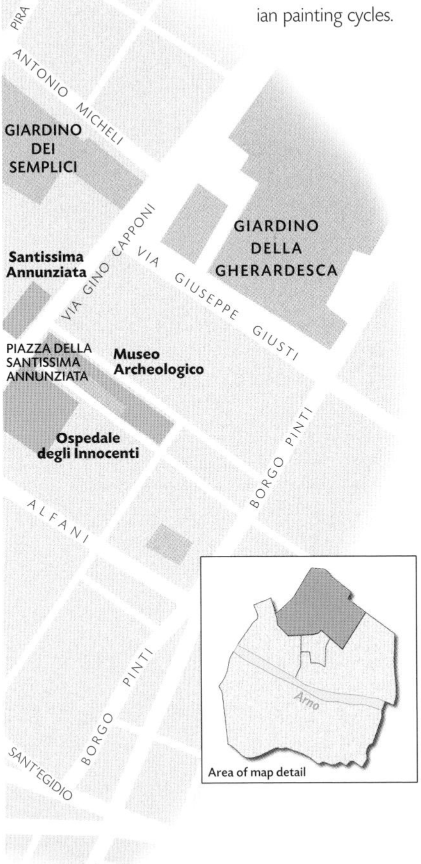

San Lorenzo

San Lorenzo is probably Florence's oldest church. For many years it served as the city's cathedral, and it was also the Medici's preferred place of worship. Several vast grants from the family helped transform the old church on the site into the present-day building, a restrained Renaissance masterpiece designed by Filippo Brunelleschi and scattered with works of art by Michelangelo, Donatello, and Filippino Lippi.

A great place to relax and enjoy the beautiful cloisters of San Lorenzo

San Lorenzo
- Map pp. 120–121
- Piazza San Lorenzo
- 055 214 042
- Closed Sun. a.m. & all day Sun. Nov.–Feb.
- $, $$ (combined with Biblioteca Medicea Laurenziana)
- Bus: C1 to Via de' Ginori, C2 to Via de' Cerretani

operamedicea laurenziana.it

There is more to San Lorenzo than first meets the eye. The church itself contains a variety of treasures, and annexed to the complex are two further architectural masterpieces—the Ricetto (Vestibule) and the Biblioteca Medicea Laurenziana (Medici Library)—both of which were wholly or partly designed by Michelangelo. Also part of the church, but with a separate entrance, are the Cappelle Medicee, or Medici Chapels (see pp. 128–129), the burial

place of many of the Medici's principal figures. Other prominent members of the family are buried in the main body of the church, and four of them are interred in the Sagrestia Vecchia, or Old Sacristy, San Lorenzo's architectural and decorative tour de force.

The original church here was reputedly founded in 393 and consecrated by St. Ambrose, the bishop and patron saint of Milan. At that time it stood outside the city's walls. The date of its consecration was significant, for it came only a few years after Christianity had been proclaimed the official religion of the Roman Empire. The church was dedicated to the martyred St. Lawrence (Lorenzo) and St. Zenobius, Florence's first bishop, who was buried here. It then served as the city's cathedral until the seventh century, when Zenobius's body was moved to the new Santa Reparata cathedral, later replaced by the present cathedral (see pp. 58–61).

In 1059 the first San Lorenzo was rebuilt as a Romanesque church. This structure survived until 1418, when nine wealthy parishioners, among them Giovanni di Bicci de' Medici, founding father of the Medici fortune, offered to finance a new church. Giovanni's motives were not entirely philanthropic, for his aim, among others, was that the new building would become a Medici mausoleum, thus further enhancing the family's already considerable standing. Three years later, the commission for the new church was awarded to Filippo Brunelleschi, then also busy working on the cathedral.

Construction of the church's Sagrestia Vecchia was completed before the death of Giovanni in 1429, but further progress was hampered by political and other upheavals, not least the death of Brunelleschi in 1446. Impetus was only regained in the wake of a 40,000-florin grant from Giovanni's son, Cosimo de' Medici, better known as Cosimo il Vecchio, or Cosimo the Elder see pp. 31–32). Some idea of the scale of Cosimo's generosity can be gauged from the fact that at the time 150 florins would support the average Florentine family for a year. Architect Antonio Manetti made full use of the Medici largesse, utilizing the funds in the years between 1447 and 1460 to bring the building to completion.

The Medici Emblem

The Medici's principal emblem—a group of balls—is seen across Tuscany. According to myth, the Medici descended from an eighth-century knight in Charlemagne's army, whose shield received six dents while he was fighting a giant. As a reward for the knight's bravery, Charlemagne allowed him to represent these marks on his coat of arms. Others say the balls represent medicinal pills, tokens of the Medici's origins as apothecaries or doctors, or that they are the traditional ball or coin symbol of pawnbrokers. Others claim they are bezants (Byzantine coins) connected to the arms of the Arte del Cambio, or Bankers Guild, of which the Medici were prominent early members. Although the emblem usually has six balls, in the 13th century there were twelve; San Lorenzo's Old Sacristy has eight, and Cosimo I's Cappella dei Principi (see sidebar p. 129) tomb has five.

Or not quite to completion, for the church's bare brick **facade** remains unfinished to this day. Pope Leo X (1475–1521), son of Lorenzo de' Medici, or Lorenzo the Magnificent (see p. 32), called upon Michelangelo to provide a suitably grand frontage in 1518. The artist's working models for the project can be seen in the Casa Buonarroti (see p. 116). Leo wanted stone for the church to be quarried from Pietrasanta on the Tuscan coast. The habitually difficult Michelangelo preferred the superior marble of Carrara in the Apuan mountains, to the north. After arguments as to where the marble was to be mined, work petered out, never to be resumed.

Inside, the church's simple, almost bland, **interior** marks a deliberate attempt by Brunelleschi to draw on his studies of the great classical buildings of Rome. The result was one of Italy's earliest Renaissance church interiors, and its harmonic proportions, lovely marble pavement, coffered ceiling, Corinthian pillars, and broad arches all profoundly influenced subsequent buildings in Florence and elsewhere. Its decorative coloring, for example, is something you'll see time and again around the city—a system of so-called *creste e vele* (waves and sails), with "sails" of creamy-colored walls and gray *pietra serena* stone.

The first artistic highlight is Rosso Fiorentino's painting of the "Marriage of the Virgin" in the second chapel on the south wall. The locally born Fiorentino—one

INSIDER TIP:

Whatever your faith, remember that churches like San Lorenzo are sacred places. Dress appropriately and turn off your cell phone.

—STEFANIA MARTORELLI
National Geographic Italy editor

The interior of San Lorenzo was designed by Brunelleschi, architect of the cathedral dome.

of Italy's finest mannerist painters (see p. 44)—would eventually despair of what he saw as the poor rewards of working in his native land. Within a few years of completing this painting he quit Florence for France "to raise himself . . . out of the wretchedness and poverty, which is the common lot of those who work in Tuscany." He may have had a point, for he achieved considerable renown in his adopted country, and among French critics Fiorentino is now considered one of the most influential artists of his day.

In the middle of the nave stand two raised **pulpits** whose superb bronze reliefs were among the last works of Donatello with the help of his assistants. The renowned sculptor is buried in the church; his memorial is on the right wall of a chapel in the left (north) transept. The raised pulpits make their sculptures rather difficult to decipher, but the episodes portrayed on the panels are the events before and after Christ's Crucifixion. Savonarola once thundered his sermons from the pulpits, but today their use—in honor of the Holy Week theme of their reliefs—is traditionally restricted to Easter.

To the pulpits' right as you face the altar is a tabernacle, the "Pala del Sacramento" by Desiderio da Settignano, while beneath the church's main dome an inscription on the floor—"Pater Patriae" (Father of the Fatherland)—and three grilles mark the tomb of Cosimo de' Medici (Cosimo the Elder), Donatello's chief patron and the church's main benefactor.

Further Medici tombs lie in the **Sagrestia Vecchia** (1421–1426; Old Sacristy), entered through doors to the left of the high altar. This tiny but exquisite space was commissioned as a private chapel by Cosimo the Elder's father, Giovanni di Bicci de' Medici. Its dedication was to St. John the Evangelist, Giovanni's namesake

The Medici Saints

San Lorenzo's sponsor, Giovanni di Bicci de' Medici, chose St. John the Evangelist as his patron saint, but the patron saints of the Medici family in general were Sts. Cosmas and Damian, or Cosma and Damiano in Italian. This was partly because they were doctors and the Medici were originally apothecaries, and partly because of a play on the word *medici,* which means "doctors" in Italian. The saints are particularly associated with works commissioned by Cosimo de' Medici, who, by remarkable coincidence, was reputedly born on September 27, the saints' feast day.

and patron saint. The sacristy was the only one of Brunelleschi's many architectural projects completed in his lifetime. Its apparently simple design—a combination of cube and hemispherical dome—disguises a masterpiece of spatial subtlety and decorative innovation.

On the left as you enter the sacristy stands an easily missed **tomb** (1472), the work of Verrocchio and the burial place of Giovanni and Piero de' Medici, the grandsons of Giovanni di Bicci de' Medici. Don't be fooled by its plainness: The people of Florence admiring the monument would have been aware that it was made

"The Martyrdom of St. Lawrence" by Bronzino depicts the saint being burned alive on a grill.

from three of the most precious materials of antiquity—bronze, marble, and porphyry. Giovanni di Bicci de' Medici himself is entombed with his wife, Piccarda Bueri, beneath the larger but far plainer, marble slab (1434) in the middle of the room.

Decoration in the sacristy was provided by Donatello between 1434 and 1443, some 20 years before his work on the pulpits in the main nave of the church. He crafted the eight colored tondi, or round reliefs, which depict the four Evangelists and four episodes from the life of John the Evangelist. Donatello was also responsible for the frieze of cherubim (in blue) and seraphim (in red), as well as the two large reliefs above the doors on the end wall, one of which (on the right) depicts Sts. Cosmas and Damian (see sidebar p. 125), the other Sts. Stephen

and Lawrence, twin protectors of Florence (on the left). The bust of St. Lawrence, nearby, also long attributed to Donatello, is now thought to be the work of Desiderio da Settignano.

Donatello is still credited with the **bronze doors** on the opposite end wall, their reliefs portraying several Christian martyrs on the left and the Apostles, John the Baptist, and the Fathers of the Church on the right. The left door opens onto a pretty marble lavabo, or wash basin, attributed to Verrocchio. Notice its various motifs; the falcon and lamb, for example, are heraldic symbols of Piero de' Medici, or Piero the Gouty, the man who commissioned the work. Finally, look up to the ceiling and its fine fresco of the constellations and path of the sun. Scholars are unsure whether it represents the position of the heavens on July 4, 1442; July 16, 1416, the birthday of Piero de' Medici; or July 6, 1439, when the union of Eastern and Western churches was feted in Florence.

Leave the church at the top of the north aisle, pausing to admire Filippino Lippi's altarpiece of the "Annunciation" (1450) and Bronzino's fresco of the "Martyrdom of St. Lawrence." Lawrence was martyred by being roasted to death on a gridiron, and he is reputed to have told his tormentors at one point that he was "done" on one side and could be turned over.

The Cloisters

From the church a corridor leads to the cloisters. A door to the right leads to the **Ricetto** (1559–1571), a small but bizarre vestibule designed by Michelangelo. The work has many odd touches, all doubtless intended to be provocative—pillars that carry no weight, columns sunk into walls, and brackets that support nothing but air. None, though, are as strange as the huge black staircase and rough rendering of the walls. This is one of the most unusual small architectural creations in the city, and it would influence later mannerist architects.

The staircase from the Ricetto leads to the main reading room of the **Biblioteca Medicea Laurenziana** (begun 1524), or Medici Library, commissioned by Pope Clement VII, formerly Giulio de' Medici, nephew of Lorenzo the Magnificent. Its purpose was to house the Medici's 100-year-old collection of 15,000 precious books and manuscripts. The Medici were not always cultured souls—an inventory of Giovanni di Bicci de' Medici's possessions in 1418 listed just three books. It was left to Cosimo de' Medici and his son and grandson, Piero de' Medici and Lorenzo de' Medici, to scour Europe in the quest to create the family library. The Medici also founded libraries in the convent of San Marco (see pp. 143–144) and the Badia Fiorentina (see p. 86).

Everything in the reading room, which was opened to the public in 1571, was designed by Michelangelo, even the desks. While it is not as eccentric as the Ricetto below, it has some interesting touches. Note, for example, the Medici crest incorporated into every window and the fact that all you can see of the room from the Ricetto is an entirely blank wall. The books and manuscripts from the collection on show vary, but the oldest work held, a fifth-century copy of works by Virgil, the Roman poet, is rarely brought out of safekeeping. ∎

Biblioteca Medicea Laurenziana

✉ San Lorenzo, Piazza San Lorenzo 9

☎ 055 210 760 or 055 264 5184

🕐 Closed Sat.–Sun.

💲 $$ (combined ticket with San Lorenzo)

EXPERIENCE: Enjoy Opera Up Close

Florence lacks a ravishing opera house, so while you won't revel in such splendor as Milan's La Scala, you can still enjoy great performances in the more intimate surroundings of the 19th-century **St. Mark's Anglican Church** *(Via Maggio 16, tel 055 294 764 or 340 811 9192 for tickets, stmarksitaly.com)*. Sitting close enough almost to touch the performers, you can watch full productions—with the odd adaptation to take account of the setting—of the classic operas of (usually) Verdi, Puccini, and Mozart or arias and other extracts presented in the popular two-performer "Love Duets" evenings. The church's season runs from March to July and October to September (with a reduced program in November and December), usually with performances every Wednesday and Friday at 9:15 p.m. While the emphasis is on opera, the program also includes other choral, solo, and orchestral performances, so that in season you can usually find music in the church most days of the month.

The church also has literary and other cultural programs. Further program and ticket information is available from the church and at *concertoclassico.blogspot .co.uk*. You'll also find information for other opera performances in Florence at *classictic.com*.

Cappelle Medicee

The Cappelle Medicee, or Medici Chapels, are celebrated for three major groups of sculpture by Michelangelo in the Sagrestia Nuova, one of three components of the rambling private mausoleum built for the Medici. The crypt contains many minor members of the dynasty, while the Cappella dei Principi is the last resting place of six Medici Grand Dukes.

The large sarcophagi in the Cappella dei Principi contain the remains of Grand Dukes Cosimo I and Ferdinando I.

You walk from the chapels' ticket office straight into the gloom of the **crypt,** home to the entombed bodies of 49 less notable scions of the Medici dynasty. Grand Duke Ferdinand III de' Medici placed many of them here in 1791, though according to one contemporary account the unfortunate corpses were thrown "together pell-mell . . . caring scarcely to distinguish one from the other." This jumbled assortment of bodies was exhumed in 1857—though only after much wrangling—and left to rest in a more permanent peace, one would hope, in their present arrangement.

Sagrestia Nuova

A corridor from the Cappella dei Principi (see sidebar opposite) leads to the Sagrestia Nuova, or New Sacristy, so-called to distinguish it from Brunelleschi's Sagrestia Vecchia (Old Sacristy) in nearby San Lorenzo (see pp. 125–126. The term *sacristy* is slightly misleading in this instance, for the Medici pope Leo X and his cousin, Cardinal Giulio de' Medici, commissioned the chapel in 1520 from Michelangelo to act as a mausoleum for two earlier Medici scions: Lorenzo the Magnificent and his brother Giuliano, the latter murdered during the infamous Pazzi Conspiracy of 1478 (see sidebar p. 33).

The chapel project was to be Michelangelo's first major architectural undertaking and, like most projects with which the artist was involved, it was hampered by multiple mishaps and false starts. Things went well until 1527 and the attack on Florence by the forces of Emperor Charles V (see p. 34), when Michelangelo was called away to assist with the siege defenses around San Miniato al Monte. After the successful restoration of the Medici dynasty to power in 1530, the artist worked halfheartedly on this and several other projects before eventually leaving Florence for Rome in 1534.

The result was a chapel based on the simple cube and half-sphere arrangement of Brunelleschi's Sagrestia Vecchia (Michelangelo probably inherited an existing floor plan). Here, however, in a striking departure from conventional practice, Michelangelo decided not to place the tombs and funerary statues at the center of the room, as was customary, but around the walls. Most of the statuary was completed when the sculptor abandoned the project, but its definitive arrangement was decided later (1554–1555) by Grand Duke Cosimo I and artists Giorgio Vasari and Bartolommeo Ammannati.

Michelangelo's Sculptures

With your back to the door after entering, the tomb on your left belongs to Lorenzo de' Medici, Duke of Urbino (1492–1519),

---

A Very Costly Crypt of Poor Taste?

Stepping out of the gloom of the crypt the visitor to the Cappelle Medicee enters the cavernous Cappella dei Principi, or Chapel of the Princes, the costliest single project the Medici ever commissioned. It was still a drain on the family's coffers in 1743 when the Medici line died out, almost 140 years after work on the chapel began. The immense interior contains the tombs of the six Medici Grand Dukes, Cosimo I having adopted the title "Grand Duke" in 1570. All six tombs are in highly questionable taste, matched in their gaudiness only by the vividly colored marbles gilding the walls. The most appealing things here are the stone coats of arms inlaid around the walls, which represent the 16 major Tuscan towns that came within the Medici orbit.

---

the grandson of Lorenzo the Magnificent; the tomb on the right is that of Giuliano de' Medici, Duke of Nemours (1479–1516), Lorenzo the Magnificent's third and youngest son. It is one of the chapel's enduring ironies that its grandest tombs belong to two of the Medici's most wretched offspring, whereas the tombs of the more worthy family members for whom it was designed—Lorenzo the Magnificent and his brother—remain unfinished. The Duke of Urbino combined arrogance with feeblemindedness and died young from tuberculosis and syphilis. The Duke of Nemours was more easygoing, but equally ineffectual, and ruled Florence after 1512 in name only, spending much of his short life in thrall to his elder

---

Cappelle Medicee

- Map pp. 120–121
- Piazza Madonna degli Aldobrandini 6
- 055 238 8602
- Closed p.m. daily & all day 1st, 2nd, & 4th Mon. & 2nd & 4th Sun. of every month
- $$
- Bus: 6, 11, 22, C2 to Via de' Cerretani, C1 to Via de' Ginori

firenzemusei.it

brother, Giovanni de' Medici, better known as Pope Leo X.

Here, therefore, is a case where the visitor is best advised to admire the sculpture and forget about the man within the tomb. The **tomb of Lorenzo de' Medici** aimed to represent its protagonist as a man of thought; hence, the main figure is seated with head on hand and the two allegorical statues below symbolize "Dawn" and "Dusk," the times deemed most appealing to the contemplative mind. "Dusk" is a male figure, portrayed exhausted and heavy with impending sleep; "Dawn" is the more animated female figure, sprightly with the vigor of a new day. Some have speculated that these figures may also represent the imbalance of Lorenzo's mind. Michelangelo was not unaware of the true character of his protagonists, and critics have suggested that Lorenzo's rather absurd hat may also be a subtle hint from the sculptor as to his subject's feeblemindedness.

INSIDER TIP:

The Cappelle Medicee is among the city's most popular sights, so avoid the long lines by booking a timed ticket [see sidebar p. 98].

—LARRY PORGES
National Geographic Travel Books editor

The **tomb of Giuliano de' Medici** depicts Giuliano as a decisive man of action—a Roman general, no less, complete with a commander's baton. Below him recline the allegorical figures of "Day"—the rough, unfinished male figure on the right—and "Night," the female form on the left, the latter portrayed with the moon, stars, and the symbols of sleep: the poppy, owl, and "mask of dreams."

Neither of the main tomb figures was taken from life. Here Michelangelo aimed to transcend

A Visit to the Hard Stone Workshop

To get some idea of the artisanship behind the art, a visit to the **Opificio delle Pietre Dure** *(Via degli Alfani 78, tel 055 218 709, closed Sun. & p.m. daily, $, bus C1 to junction of Via Cavour & Via degli Alfani or 14 & 23 to Via Cavour)*, or hard stone workshop, is recommended.

The Opificio is where many of the city's mosaics originated. *Pietre dure* means "hard stones" and refers to the craft of cutting and inlaying precious and semiprecious stones in mosaics and other works of art.

Of course, the possibilities of stone as a decorative medium can be witnessed

all over Florence, most notably in the Cappella dei Principi within the Cappelle Medicee, the building for which the Opificio delle Pietre Dure was first established by Grand Duke Ferdinando I de' Medici in 1588.

Since the devastating 1966 flood (see pp. 160–161), the Opificio has achieved an exceptional international reputation as a school and center of restoration. For the visitor, it's occasionally possible to witness restoration work in progress, but generally what's on view are the stones and the imitation painted marbles in the small adjoining museum.

simple portraiture and create instead timeless statues, hence his own preferred names for the two principal statues: "La Vigilanza" ("Vigilance") and "Il Pensiero" ("Thought"). When criticized for failing to create accurate portraits, the sculptor replied that in a thousand years no one would know—or care—what Lorenzo and Giuliano actually looked like. In this, as in other observations on the immortality of his art, he was right.

The chapel's third group of statues centers on an unfinished "Madonna and Child," flanked by "St. Cosmas" and "St. Damian," the Medici's patron saints (see sidebar p. 125). Only the Madonna is by Michelangelo, the saints having been completed by assistants to their master's original plan. Both saints gaze toward the Madonna, as do the figures of Lorenzo and Giuliano, imposing a subtle unity on the chapel, a device used here for the first time. The Madonna looks at the main altar wall, the altar serving as a symbol of Christ's death and Resurrection—and thus eternal life.

The notion of Resurrection should have been reinforced by a Michelangelo fresco of the subject on the sacristy's ceiling. Similarly, the tombs of Lorenzo the Magnificent and his brother should have faced one another in the same way as those of their feckless descendants (the pair are buried in a simple tomb near the "Madonna and Child").

Also missing from the chapel are statues representing heaven and earth, intended for the niches either side of the Duke

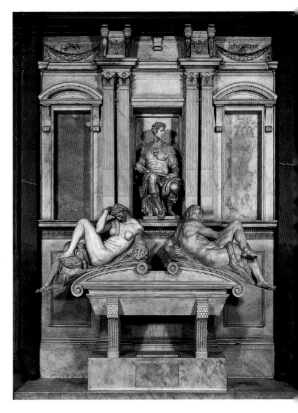

On the tomb of Giuliano de' Medici by Michelangelo, the lower statues are allegories of "Night" and "Day."

of Nemours, as well as statues of river gods representing the Tiber and Arno, symbols of Lazio and Tuscany, the regions ruled by the duke. These were all part of Michelangelo's grand design for the chapel that was to remain unfulfilled. His aim was to unite painting, architecture, and sculpture in a philosophical study of the progression from the material and temporal world (represented by the river gods) through humankind (the figures of Giuliano and Lorenzo) to eternal life represented by the Resurrection. ■

EXPERIENCE: Sampling Florence's Street Food

You'd have to be hard-hearted indeed not to warm to the Mercato Centrale, Florence's covered main food market, whose cornucopia of stalls sells mouthwatering cheeses, fish, pasta, meats, olive oil, and countless other gastronomic treats from Tuscany and beyond. At the Mercato and elsewhere, food lovers will find much to delight them on the streets of Florence.

Even if you have no intention of buying anything—and this is a good place for picnic provisions or treats to take home—then there's still plenty in the way of sights, smells, and sounds to satisfy the senses and pique your culinary curiosity. One of the busiest little stalls is **Ottavino** (open daily until 1:30 p.m. & Sat. p.m. in winter), a small traditional bar for authentic Florentine snacks that's popular with both shoppers and market workers.

Don't confuse the Mercato, Europe's largest covered food hall, with the San Lorenzo market of clothes and general goods that fills many of the surrounding streets. This market is a good place for gift-shopping, where you'll find a wide selection of inexpensive leather goods and woolens.

Dip a *Trippa*

Florence's favorite, and traditional, street food is *trippa*—tripe—eaten in a crusty roll and usually topped with either a *salsa verde* (green sauce) or a spicy red sauce (ask for *trippa alla fiorentina*). Often rolls are offered *bagnato*, or dipped in the tripe's cooking juices.

Trippa is available from *trippai*—traditional street corner kiosks and stands—and from venerable outlets such as **Nerbone** (tel 055 219 949, closed Sun.) in the Mercato Centrale. The trippai also sell other fillings, mostly variations on offal—such as *lampredotto*, made of the cow's fourth stomach—as well as robust red wine by the glass, often served from a flask.

Join the many Florentines standing in line at any of the numerous trippai to be found around town. One of the most convenient for Piazza del Duomo is in the **Piazza dei Cimatori,** at the corner of Via de' Cerchi and Via dei Tavolini (off Via dei Calzaiuoli). Other central outlets can be found at **Lupen e Margo** (cnr. of Via dell'Ariento & Via Sant'Antonio, closed Sun. April–Sept. & 2 weeks in Aug.), by the San Lorenzo market; **Orazio Nencioni** (Loggia del Porcellino, closed Sun. & Sat. June–July), at the Mercato Nuovo, a short distance from the Piazza della Signoria; and the venerable **Sergio Pollini** (cnr. of Via de' Macci & Piazza Sant'Ambrogio, closed Sun. & Aug.) near the Sant'Ambrogio market.

The Mercato Centrale offers a wealth of Tuscan tastes to sample.

Palazzo Medici-Riccardi

The Palazzo Medici-Riccardi was home to the Medici for almost a century, being their principal seat in the city from 1462—when it was completed for Cosimo de' Medici the Elder—to 1540, when Cosimo I moved the Medici court to the Palazzo Vecchio. Today, it is visited for one surviving jewel from the period, the Cappella dei Magi, a tiny chapel decorated with a three-panel fresco cycle (1460) by Benozzo Gozzoli (1420–1497).

Alas, little now remains of the palace's former splendor, restructuring over the years having turned the building into a brooding bureaucratic labyrinth. Nothing, though, detracts from Gozzoli's paintings, with their colorful narrative and minutely observed decorative detail. They are also among the most popular pictures in the city, so be prepared for lines.

The paintings' declared subject is the "Journey of the Magi," with one panel given over to each of the three kings from the story of the Nativity. Gozzoli, however, probably included aspects of the annual procession of the Compagnia dei Magi, the most important of Florence's medieval confraternities (semireligious and charitable organizations). Several Medici belonged to the organization, among them Piero de' Medici, who may have commissioned the frescoes. Gozzoli may also have been inspired by two other historical episodes: the council of bishops in Florence in 1439, which briefly led to the union of the Roman and Greek churches, and the visit to the city in 1459 (the year Gozzoli began the frescoes) by Aeneas Silvius Piccolomini, better known as Pope Pius II (1405–1464).

A detail from the "Journey of the Magi" cycle by Benozzo Gozzoli

The Medici knew of Gozzoli, having seen his work in the Convent of San Marco, where he painted a fresco in the monastic cell reserved for Cosimo de' Medici. This fresco also portrayed the Magi, underlining the Medici's affinity with the three kings and the feast of the Epiphany. American art critic Diane Cole Ahl suggests this was because "as temporal kings and the first Gentile witnesses to Christ, the magi were exemplars of worldly power humbled by faith. The portrayal of the Medici and their partisans in the magi's guise at once conveyed their authority and piety."

That the Medici had a chapel for Gozzoli to paint was testament

Palazzo Medici-Riccardi

- Map pp. 120–121
- Via Cavour 3
- 055 276 0340
- Closed Wed.
- $$
- Bus: C1, 14, 23 to Via Cavour

palazzo-medici.it

One of the Palazzo Medici-Riccardi's many stately, ornate rooms

to the family's standing. Only two other palaces in the city had chapels within their walls, a special dispensation having been issued personally in 1422 by Pope Martin V allowing Cosimo de' Medici and his wife the privilege of a portable altar for their devotions. Such dispensations were rare; this one was also granted in perpetuity, which allowed the altar to be transferred to the palace, thus facilitating the creation of the chapel.

No expense was spared. The gold leaf needed for the fresco cycle alone ran to 1,500 sheets and was imported through the rival city of Genoa. The frescoes' splendor was no matter of mere ostentation, for the chapel was intended as a reception chamber too. Visiting dignitaries awaited an audience with the Medici here, reflecting on the obvious wealth of their hosts as they did so.

Given the Medici's involvement with the chapel, it's no surprise that many of the family feature in the paintings, nor that they appear in the most splendid of the panels, which was placed on the east wall, an allusion to the Magi's origins in the Orient.

Putting definitive names to faces, however, has proved difficult. The obvious cloaked figure leading the procession on a white horse is often said to be a young Lorenzo the Magnificent, son of Piero de' Medici, the frescoes' probable sponsor. However, the figure's features and pictorial clues here are not specific, unlike the mounted riders just behind, where the nearer red-hatted figure in blue astride the light brown mule—a symbol of humility—is Cosimo de' Medici, while the red-hatted figure on his left in green and gold velvet is Piero de' Medici. Note the gold-embossed crimson livery on his white horse, which bears the Medici symbols of seven balls and three feathers (see sidebar p. 123). The word *semper,* meaning "always," refers to the supposedly eternal nature of the family's reign.

INSIDER TIP:

When confronted with a room or piazza awash with artwork, focus on a detail, or try an unusual angle or composition to make your photo memorable.

—CHRISTOPHER AUGER-
DOMÍNGUEZ
*National Geographic
International Editions photographer*

Gozzoli also included a self-portrait in the crowd behind the riders: He stands on the left, a couple of rows from the rear with the words *Opus Benotii*—the Work of Benozzo—picked out in gold on his red cap. The word *Benotii* was a deliberate pun, as *ben noti* means "well known" and *noti beni* means "take good note"; both meanings

were designed to underline Gozzoli's achievement.

The two young boys just below him in the east wall fresco, half-turned to one another, are probably Piero's sons, Giuliano (on the right), who would be murdered in the Pazzi Conspiracy (see sidebar p. 33), and Lorenzo the Magnificent (in half profile on the left with the distinctive upturned nose). The two young men on horseback in the far left foreground below are Galeazzo Maria Sforza and Sigismondo Malatesta. Both appear for political reasons: They were sons of two of Cosimo's main allies.

Gozzoli's self-satisfaction is further underlined by the fact that he painted himself in another fresco, the picture on the west wall with the white-bearded king. He stands on the right making a "V" with his fingers above the dismounting man. The sign is a visual pun, as it mirrors the horses' ears, suggests a farewell as he turns to join the procession, indicates his artistic dexterity (the hand is the right, or *dexter*), and stresses he has fulfilled his contractual obligation to paint the work by his own hand. ∎

EXPERIENCE: Make Beautiful Jewelry

Just as Renaissance Florence had artists and sculptors, so it had jewelers. And just as you can learn to paint and sculpt in Florence (see sidebars pp. 40 & 140), so too can you learn the art of jewelry-making. However, you need to commit more time than you would to art history classes. **Ken Scott** (*kenscott.lin34.host25.com*) offers 40-hour-plus bespoke courses, while **Alchimia** (*alchimia.it*), a school of contemporary jewelry, has two-week (more than 60 hours) courses. **Le Arti Orafe** (*artiorafe.it*) offers longer summer-school programs devoted to contemporary jewelry and flexible deals that let you attend classes for 3 to 10 hours a week.

The Art of Fresco

The wall paintings known as frescoes formed the most common mode of large-scale artistic expression in Italian art after the 14th century, when they largely superseded mosaics. They take their name from *fresco*, or fresh, because they were painted on wet (fresh) plaster, a procedure that resulted in the medium's particular strengths and weaknesses.

Fresco art: the "Crucifixion" by Andrea del Castagno in the convent of Sant'Apollonia

A fresco's main strength is its durability. Add paint to dry plaster, and any moisture or physical deterioration in a wall eventually lifts the paint off. But put paint on wet plaster—a mixture of lime, water, and fine sand—and, as the plaster dries, the lime (calcium hydroxide) combines with carbon dioxide in the air to create calcium carbonate. This then crystallizes around the sand particles, cementing them to the wall. If pigments are applied at the same time, then the process also fixes their particles, leaving them resistant to further action by moisture.

Much preparation was required, however, before an artist could proceed to the pigment stage. Base layers of plaster, known as the *arrichio*, were first applied to the wall. An artist or assistant would then scratch this with the painting's main outlines. A more detailed sketch was then drawn in red ocher—a study known as the sinopia for the red pigment used. This sketch often was made away from the painting's proposed site. *Sinopie* are often brought to light and preserved in Florence and elsewhere, notably in Sant'Apollonia (see sidebar p. 146). Preliminary sketches, or cartoons, were created as pictures became more complex, and chalk was dusted onto the wall through pinpricked outlines in the drawing.

Once a painting was under way, an artist could only work on an area small enough to be completed before the plaster dried. Assistants therefore divided the arrichio into *giornate*, or days, and then applied a thin layer of preparatory white finishing plaster, or *intonaco*. Yet another sketch—this time in a mixture of lime and black pigment *(verdacchio)*—then had to be drawn over the obscured portion of arrichio.

Painting was a race against the drying plaster. Once a wall was dry, a mistake could only be rectified by stripping off the dry plaster, creating another layer of arrichio, and starting again. The range of suitable pigments, and thus colors, was limited, and the pigments were hard to mix to create more depth of tone or more delicate shades. Skill, technique, and the use of subtle base layers were an artist's only recourse.

By contrast, painting on wood or canvas using tempera, a technique in which egg yolk was used to fix pigment, produced glorious colors, as many Sienese paintings testify. The introduction of oil-based paints toward the end of the 15th century also allowed for new subtlety. Neither, though, was suitable for large-scale frescoes, and when artists such as Leonardo da Vinci rebelled against the limitations of wet plaster, their frescoes were doomed.

The making of Piero della Francesca's fresco "Madonna del Parto" (1455)

1. Bare wall
The bare walls of churches or palaces had to be prepared with plaster (arrichio) before an artist could paint.

3. Coarse plaster
Base layers of plaster were applied to walls. An assistant then scratched or sketched the painting's main outline.

2. Artist's sketch
With complex compositions a "cartoon," or rough sketch, of the intended fresco was incised or drawn in chalk on the plaster.

4. Fresh coat of intonaco, or fine plaster
Frescoes can only be applied to wet plaster. Any unpainted dried plaster was hacked off and relaid the next day.

5. Final fresco
Artists had to work quickly before the plaster dried, and with a limited choice of color.

Galleria dell'Accademia

It would be hard to visit Florence without seeing Michelangelo's "David," the most celebrated—and arguably most overexposed—Renaissance image in Western art. Having stood for years in the Piazza della Signoria, the statue was moved to its present home in the 19th century, occupying pride of place in an academy created in 1784 by Grand Duke Pietro Leopoldo (1747–1792) to house a collection of Florentine paintings and sculpture.

Michelangelo enlarged the head and hands of "David" to create an added illusion of size.

On entering the Accademia you find yourself in a hallway. Beyond this stretches the so-called **Galleria del David,** where Michelangelo's looming statue is framed in its own domed space, the neoclassical Tribuna del David (1882). Walking along the gallery you pass other works by Michelangelo, but you'll probably want to see the "David" first and return to these later. Several rooms off the gallery and Tribuna can also wait, as can a quartet of salons on the first floor, which contain the Accademia's other paintings and sculptures.

Michelangelo's "David"

Michelangelo's celebrated statue was commissioned in 1501 by the Opera del Duomo, the body responsible for the care of the cathedral's fabric. At the time Michelangelo was just 26. The statue's subject—David, the Israelite shepherd boy, slayer of Goliath—was chosen because of parallels with Florence's recent history, in particular the city's (short-lived) liberation from Medici rule and its ability to withstand more powerful Italian and foreign foes. Once completed, the statue became a republican symbol of the city and

It's tempting to leave the Accademia after seeing the "David," but allow some time to see some of the gallery's other outstanding paintings and sculpture.

—MARINA CONTI
National Geographic Italy editor

Choosing the piazza was one thing; moving the statue there was another. One contemporary chronicler, Luca Landucci, recorded the transfer from the Opera del Duomo, where Michelangelo had worked on the statue, in his *Diario Fiorentino* (1504): "They had to break down the wall above the Opera door to allow it through," he wrote, adding that it was "moved along by 40 men" and that "beneath it were 14 greased beams,

Galleria dell'Accademia

- Map pp. 120–121
- Via Ricasoli 60
- 055 238 8609
- Closed Mon.
- $$
- Bus: C1 to the intersection of Via Ricasoli & Via degli Alfani

firenzemusei.it

of its passion for independence. It also firmly cemented Michelangelo's reputation, already heightened by his statue of the "Pietà" created for St. Peter's in Rome six years earlier.

Once the masterpiece was completed in 1504, where to put the statue immediately became a subject of controversy. During its gestation, the assumption had been that it would join a collection of statues outside the cathedral. This notion was quickly challenged. No fewer than 30 leading artists were asked to arbitrate in the ensuing dispute, some continuing to argue for the area in front of the Duomo, others—including such notables as Botticelli and Leonardo da Vinci— favoring the Loggia della Signoria in Piazza della Signoria. After a lengthy debate, it was decided to place the statue in front of the Palazzo Vecchio, then known as the Palazzo Pubblico, whose function as the seat of Florence's ruling council made it the obvious symbol and guardian of the city's civic and political freedoms.

The Making of "David"

Michelangelo's magnificent image of the nude boy warrior, at once alert and ready for battle, but also calm with the certainty of victory, is so familiar that it is easy to ignore its greatness.

The artist's achievement becomes still more remarkable when you learn that the statue was carved from a single block of marble more than 13 feet (4 m) high. Not only that, but the marble in question—an almost impossibly thin and fault-riddled block—was widely considered too damaged for artistic use. Several prominent artists, Leonardo da Vinci and Agostino di Duccio among them, had already failed to make anything of the stone. Indeed, until Michelangelo's arrival, the slab had lain unworked since being quarried from the Tuscan hills some 40 years earlier. Michelangelo confounded the doubters, completing the work in just three years.

which were changed from hand to hand . . . it took four days to reach the piazza." Another three weeks were then required to raise the statue on its plinth. Matters weren't helped by the fact the statue had to be protected night and day from stone-throwing supporters of the

EXPERIENCE: Sculpt Your Own Masterpiece

In the 15th century the great Lorenzo de' Medici lamented that while Florence had plenty of painters, it lacked sculptors. He duly directed Domenico Ghirlandaio to select any promising young sculptors from his workshop of young painters. A likely talent named Michelangelo would be one of the first chosen.

Much the same is true in Florence today. If you want to learn to draw or paint in the city, there are plenty of options (see sidebar p. 40). But for sculpture classes you have to look harder. One solution is the **Galleria Romanelli** (tel 055 239 6047, raffaelloromanelli.com), a wonderful studio and gallery space—the ceilings are 52 feet (16 m) high—crammed with sculptures, plaster models, historic tools, and works in progress. It was once a 15th-century church and later home to Lorenzo Bartolini (1777–1850), one of the city's leading 19th-century sculptors.

The studio has more recently been owned by five generations of the Romanelli family, all sculptors (the first was Bartolini's star pupil, Pasquale), including the latest scion, Raffaello Romanelli. There's no need to be an expert: Complete beginners can start modeling clay or plaster, and you can book lessons for a morning (from around €70) or for a number of days, weeks, or months. You can also learn to carve marble. If you prefer to sit rather than sculpt, you can also commission portrait busts and other works from Raffaello.

Medici. The family at the time had been removed from power, but it still had defenders. Ructions in 1527, again caused by the Medici's temporary absence, saw the statue's left arm smashed—the resulting scars are still clearly visible. Echoes of this vandalism resounded in 1991, when an onlooker smashed one of the statue's toes.

"David" remained in the square until 1873, where its long exposure to the elements resulted in the loss of the gold coloring that once tinted its hair and chest. Also now vanished is the original skirt of copper leaves designed to placate some of Florence's more prudish citizens.

Other Works

Away from the "David," the Galleria del David contains a variety of pleasing paintings and other works by Michelangelo, notably a statue of "St. Matthew" (1505–1506) and four "Slaves" or "Prisoners" (1521–1523 or circa 1530). The last were originally intended to form part of a colossal tomb for Pope Julius II (1443–1513) in Rome. But the tomb never materialized, and in 1564 Leonardo Buonarroti, Michelangelo's nephew, gave the unfinished statues to Cosimo I, the Medici Grand Duke. Cosimo in turn had them installed in Buontalenti's grotto near the entrance to the Giardino di Boboli (see pp. 174–175), where they remained until 1909, when they were moved to the Accademia. Two further "Slaves" from the group found their way to the Louvre in Paris.

The statues' rough and deliberately unfinished appearance exemplified Michelangelo's notion that sculpture was the liberation of an existing form "imprisoned" within unworked stone. The figure of "St. Matthew," by contrast, was one of 12 figures of the Apostles commissioned in 1503 for the exterior of the Duomo. The only one of the group that was even started, this work languished in the Opera del Duomo's workshop until 1831, when it was moved to its present home.

Two doors lead off right from the Galleria into the **Salone del Colosso** and the three-roomed Sale Fiorentine. At the heart of the first of these is a plaster model (1582) for Giambologna's "Rape of the Sabine Women" in the Loggia della Signoria (see p. 93). Also here are a variety of paintings, among which the highlight is "Deposition," begun by Filippino Lippi and completed after his death in 1504 by the Umbrian

The "Madonna del Mare," or "Madonna of the Sea," likely the work of the young Filippino Lippi, takes its name from the background landscape.

master Perugino, possibly with the help of Raphael, who was then his pupil. The picture was originally intended to form part of a four-picture altarpiece in the church of Santissima Annunziata (see p. 146). Another painting worthy of note is Fra Bartolommeo's (1472–1517) "Mystical Marriage of St. Catherine," originally painted for the church of San Marco.

The chief treasure in the first of the **Sale Fiorentine** is the Cassone Adimari, a 15th-century chest probably painted by Giovanni di Ser Giovanni, or Lo Scheggia, the half brother of Masaccio, who frescoed much of the Cappella Brancacci (see pp. 176–179). The paintings include a charming partial view of Florence as it appeared during a medieval festival.

Moving on, notice the tiny "Visitation" (1470), one of the first works completed by Perugino after his move to Florence from Umbria, and the large "Trinity with St. Benedict and St. Giovanni Gualberto," removed from the church of Santa Trìnita (see pp. 156–157). In the same room is a curious study known as "Tebaide," or "Solitude." The picture has been called one of Italy's most problematic 15th-century paintings, as neither its theme nor its artist are known—it is currently attributed to Paolo Uccello.

The last room features the fine "Three Saints" by Benozzo Gozzoli and a "Madonna and Child with St. Giovannino and Two Angels" by Botticelli. Other rooms leading off the left side of the Tribuna del David contain sculptures and busts, plus a variety of Byzantine and other paintings, among them some 22 small panels by Taddeo Gaddi removed from the church of Santa Croce. The upstairs rooms feature lesser works from the 14th and 15th centuries. ■

The Life of Fra Angelico

Pope John Paul II proclaimed the official beatification of Fra Angelico (circa 1395–1455) in 1982—the first step to sainthood—underlining the holiness of a life to which this artist gave full expression in some of the most sublime, reflective, and deeply spiritual works of the early Renaissance.

Fra Angelico—the "Angelic Friar"—was probably born in Vicchio, northeast of Florence, and joined the Dominican order of monks in nearby Fiesole at an early age. As a painter he would be summoned to work in Rome and Orvieto, in Umbria, but always remained a monk, also living and working in monasteries in

Cortona (see pp. 281–283) and Foligno, in Umbria.

Angelico lived in a time of artistic ferment. Despite the conservative strictures of much religious art of his day, he incorporated both the more traditional aspects of Sienese and International Gothic artists, such as the use of gold, decoration, and intense color—no artist before or since has matched his ethereal blues—and the more progressive traits of contemporaries such as Masaccio. Yet his works, and his influential altarpieces in particular, have a deceptive calm and simplicity, and an intensity of feeling, which mark him out as a timeless and singular genius.

Museo di San Marco

The Museo di San Marco makes a fitting home for the paintings of Fra Angelico, one of the most sublime of all Renaissance painters. The artist was both a monk and a prior of San Marco, the Dominican convent now given over to the world's finest collection of Angelico's work. The convent was also patronized by Cosimo de' Medici (the Elder), who helped create a library within its walls and paid for its enlargement in 1437.

The first area you come to is the **Chiostro di Sant'Antonino,** a cloister designed before 1440 by Michelozzo, an architect much favored by the Medici. It takes its name from Antonino Pierozzi (1389–1459), Archbishop of Florence, the convent's first prior and Fra Angelico's religious mentor. Admire the faded frescoes in the corners, all painted by Fra Angelico, then move to the **Ospizio dei Pellegrini** to see more majestic paintings by the same artist. The Ospizio was originally used to offer hospitality to pilgrims; it lies off the cloister on the right as you stand with your back to the museum entrance. The paintings here include two of the artist's greatest works: the "Madonna dei Linaiuoli" (1433) and the "San Marco Altarpiece" (1440), the latter commissioned by the Medici for San Marco, a church that you can visit to the west of the convent. The altarpiece also features Sts. Cosmas and Damian, who were almost certainly included by the artist because they were the Medici's patron saints (the pair were doctors, or *medici* in Italian).

A door off the top right-hand corner of the cloister opens into the **Sala del Lavabo,** which takes

The Museo di San Marco is devoted to Fra Angelico, a Dominican friar and leading Renaissance painter.

its name from *lavare,* meaning "to wash"; this was where the monks washed before eating. The entrance walls contain more frescoes by Angelico, while off to the right the large refectory—the monks' dining room—is dominated by the "Last Supper," the work of 16th-century artist Giovanni Sogliani. Depictions of the Last Supper, or Cenacolo

Fine frescoes and sculpture fill Chiostro di Sant'Antonino.

Museo di San Marco

▣ Map pp. 120–121

✉ Piazza San Marco 3

☎ 055 238 8608

🕐 Closed p.m. Mon.– Fri., & 1st, 3rd, & 5th Sun. & 2nd & 4th Mon. of month

💲 $

🚋 C1 & other services to San Marco

firenzemusei.it

in Italian, are often found in monastic refectories, and there are several versions around Florence, among them the version painted in 1480 by Domenico Ghirlandaio in San Marco's **Refettorio Piccolo** (Small Refectory). The painting is interesting for its symbols: Peacocks symbolize the Resurrection; ducks represent the heavens; oranges are symbols of fruits of heaven; and the cat represents evil—the reason it is painted close to the figure of Judas.

The **Chapter House** by the convent bell retains a fresco of the "Crucifixion" (1441) by Fra Angelico. Beyond the refectory a passage leads to the Foresteria, the former guest rooms.

Florence has many artistic surprises, but none as wonderful as the sudden sight of Fra Angelico's "Annunciation," an intensely moving painting at

the top of the stairs leading to San Marco's upper floor. Note the work's inscription, which reminded monks to say a Hail Mary as they passed. The next thing to catch the eye is a magnificent wooden ceiling, followed by a pair of corridors containing 44 **dormitory cells.** Most of the latter are painted with simple, pious frescoes by Fra Angelico and his assistants, each designed as an aid to devotion for the monk who occupied the cell. Cell numbers 1 to 11 of the corridor ahead of you on the left contain the frescoes in which Angelico's hand is most evident. Of these, numbers 1, 3, 6, and 9 are worthy of special attention and depict "Noli mi Tangere" (meaning "Do not touch me"), "Annunciation," "Transfiguration," and "Coronation of the Virgin," respectively. Also look at Cell 7, whose strange fresco illustrates the "Mockery of Christ" by isolating individual body parts of Christ's tormentors—a face spitting, a hand holding a scourge, and another hand holding a vinegar-soaked sponge.

Turn right at the end of this corridor and you come to a trio of rooms once occupied by Girolamo Savonarola (see p. 33). Turn right by the "Annunciation" along the nearer corridor and you come to the convent's Michelozzo-designed and Medici-donated **library** (1441–1444). Beyond the library, the last two cells on the right, both larger than their neighbors, were reserved for the use of Cosimo de' Medici. ∎

More Places to Visit in Northern Florence

Ospedale degli Innocenti

The Ospedale (or Spedale) degli Innocenti was Europe's first foundling hospital, or orphanage, a function most of the elegant Renaissance building on the eastern flank of Piazza della Santissima Annunziata (see below) fulfills to this day. Commissioned in 1419 as a charitable work by the Arte della Seta, or Silk Weavers Guild, it was designed mainly by Brunelleschi, who was also responsible for much of the piazza, hence the architectural harmony of both the square and Ospedale.

The building's exterior **loggia,** the first in Florence to be extended across the width of a building, was one of the city's first purely Renaissance creations. Notice its clever proportions: The width of the arches is the same as both the height of the columns and the depth of the portico behind. The loggia also artfully advertised the building's function using lovely glazed terra-cotta medallions of babies by Andrea della Robbia (1435–1525). Unwanted infants destined for the hospital would once have been left in a *rota,* or rotating door, the remains of which can still be seen at the left-hand side of the loggia as you face it. The device was abandoned in 1875.

Inside the Ospedale, you must pay to see two unexceptional cloisters: the main **Chiostro degli Uomini** (Men's Cloister) and narrower **Chiostro delle Donne** (Women's Cloister) to the right. You can also visit a small art gallery upstairs in the near left-hand corner of the main cloister. This boasts one significant work: Domenico Ghirlandaio's "Coronation of the Virgin" (1488). *www.institutodeglinnocenti.it*
🅐 Map pp. 120–121 ✉ Piazza della Santissima Annunziata 12 ☎ 055 203 7308 🕐 Closed p.m. 💲 $ 🚌 Bus: 14, 23 to Piazza della Santissima Annunziata

Piazza della Santissima Annunziata

This piazza just to the east of the Galleria dell'Accademia and Museo di San Marco is called one of the most beautiful in Florence, a claim rather undermined by its somewhat dilapidated appearance. It was laid out in the 1420s by Brunelleschi, taking its name from the Annunziata, or Annunciation—the moment the angel Gabriel appeared to the Virgin Mary. It was at this moment, too, that the Incarnation of Christ took place, for which reason the Feast of the Annunciation is celebrated on March 25, nine months before the Nativity. The Christian feast is of particular significance to Florence, whose old calendar began on this day.

INSIDER TIP:

If you're newly wed, you can observe a Florentine tradition by leaving your bridal bouquet at the shrine of Santissima Annunziata.

—BARBARA A. NOE
National Geographic Travel Books senior editor

The square contains two significant monuments—the church of Santissima Annunziata (see p. 146) and the Ospedale degli Innocenti (see above). At its heart is a statue of Grand Duke Ferdinando I on horseback (1608), the last work of French sculptor Giambologna. The statue was finished by one of Giambologna's pupils, Pietro Tacca (1577–1640), who cast the piece using metal from cannon captured from the Turks in the Battle of Lepanto in 1571. Tacca added the statue's water monkeys, bizarre additions that dribble water over two whiskered sea slugs.
🅐 Map pp. 120–121 🚌 Bus: 14, 23 to Piazza della Santissima Annunziata

Detail from the "Cenacolo," or "Last Supper" (1447), by Andrea del Castagno

Santissima Annunziata

The church of Santissima Annunziata (SS Annunziata) dominates the northern flank of Piazza della Santissima Annunziata. It is the mother church of the Servites, or Servi di Maria (Servants of Mary), a religious order founded in 1234 by Filippo Benizzi, a Florentine nobleman. The church grew in stature after 1252, the year a painting begun

by a Servite monk was miraculously completed by an angel. Pilgrims flocked to the image, and in 1444 a new Medici-financed church was commissioned from Michelozzo. Architect Leon Battista Alberti completed the project in 1481, also laying out the Via dei Servi, a link designed to unite SS Annunziata and the cathedral, both devoted to the Virgin Mary.

The church's covered entrance porch, or **Chiostrino dei Voti,** features an important fresco cycle commissioned in 1516 to celebrate the canonization of Filippo Benizzi. Three leading painters were involved—Andrea del Sarto, Jacopo Pontormo, and Rosso Fiorentino—and although time has faded some panels, the cycle's effect remains dazzling. Two walls are devoted to the life of the Virgin, two to episodes from the life of St. Filippo Benizzi. Note the marvelous **tabernacle** on your left as you enter, commissioned from Michelozzo by the Medici to house the church's original miraculous painting (now heavily overpainted). Map pp. 120–121 Piazza della Santissima Annunziata 055 266 181 Open 4 p.m.–5:15 p.m. Bus: 14, 23 to Piazza della Santissima Annunziata

In Search of Last Suppers

Cenacolo means "Last Supper" in Italian and refers to a painting often placed—for obvious reasons—in the refectories, or eating halls, of medieval convents and monasteries. Florence has five such paintings open to the public; you can see a version, for example, in the refectory of the Dominican convent of San Marco—better known these days as the Museo di San Marco (see pp. 143–144).

The "Cenacolo" of Sant'Apollonia is only a few minutes' walk away from San Marco, so view it after visiting the Museo di San Marco. The painting is the work of Andrea del Castagno, an early Renaissance painter, and is perhaps the most arresting and disturbing of all the Florentine "Last

Suppers." It is housed in a former Benedictine convent (*Via XXVII Aprile 1, tel 055 238 8607, closed 1st & 3rd Sun., 2nd & 4th Mon. of the month*), most of which is now private apartments. The painting's predominant color is blood red, and a sinister, black-bearded Judas—not Christ—is its principal figure. Note how Judas is placed on the viewer's side of the table, a traditional 14th-century arrangement in paintings of this subject that was abandoned by Leonardo da Vinci and other, later painters in favor of a seating plan that placed all the disciples with Christ. Notice, too, the *sinopie*, or sketches, for this and other frescoes around the walls (see pp. 136–137).

One of the city's finest churches, Santa Maria Novella, a fresco-filled gem; Santa Trìnita; and the incomparable Ponte Vecchio

Western Florence

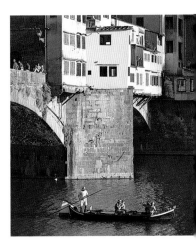

Boating on the Arno under the Ponte Vecchio

Western Florence

At first glance western Florence is not the city's prettiest or most coherent quarter. Most visitors give it short shrift, preferring the sights around Piazza del Duomo and Piazza della Signoria, or the districts of Santa Croce and the Oltrarno. The area, however, has one of Florence's key religious monuments in Santa Maria Novella, and there's a medley of other, unsung churches and medieval corners to be found by the adventurous traveler.

Players await their cue for the Calcio Historico Parade at the Santa Maria de Novella church.

One reason for the area's unfocused character is the fact that for centuries it lay outside the city limits. The western edge of the old Roman colony was marked by modern-day Via de' Tornabuoni, a border that remained unchanged when the city walls were constructed in 1078. Only with the second set of walls, raised in 1173, did the expanding city embrace some of the district's major sights—notably the church of Santa Trìnita and the Ponte Vecchio. The church of Santa Maria Novella, begun in 1246, was enclosed only by the city's third set of walls, built between 1284 and 1333.

Santa Maria is the key to the district, despite being near the unappealing area by the main railroad station. One of the most important Gothic buildings in Florence, it was built by

the Dominicans on the site of an 11th-century church. Just as the Franciscan church of Santa Croce dominates eastern Florence, so Santa Maria dominates the city's western fringes. Behind the church's glorious facade lie several outstanding fresco cycles, one of the greatest of all early Renaissance paintings, and a little-visited museum dominated by an array of huge wall paintings.

The church of Santa Trìnita is far more modest but worth a visit for its fresco cycles, sculptures, and fascinating assortment of architectural styles. It also lies conveniently close to some of the area's best shopping streets. To the north, Via de' Tornabuoni and Via della Vigna Nuova and the streets between them are the home of the city's major designer stores, not to mention the church of San Pancrazio and many of the Renaissance palaces—Palazzo Strozzio, Palazzo Rucellai, Palazzo Corsini, and Palazzo Ferroni.

The streets to the east, by contrast, offer fewer shopping opportunities but lots of interesting churches and secret corners. Here the best streets to stroll are Via Porta Rossa, Via delle Terme, and Borgo SS Apostoli, along with the countless *chiassi*, tiny alleys, that run between them. Follow any of these to the waterfront and you will come to the Ponte Vecchio, gateway to the Oltrarno district across the river. Streets to

NOT TO BE MISSED:

Masaccio's "The Trinity" and Santa Maria Novella's chapels   150–155

A visit to the Cappellone degli Spagnoli at the Museo di Santa Maria Novella   155

Marveling at Ghirlandaio's Cappella Sassetti frescoes in Santa Trìnita   156–157

Exploring the historic rooms of the Palazzo Davanzati   158–159

A walk across the unforgettable Ponte Vecchio   162–163

the west are less rewarding, but persevere with Borgo Ognissanti to see Ognissanti, a church that has links to Botticelli and Amerigo Vespucci (1454–1512), the Medici employee who gave his name to two continents. ■

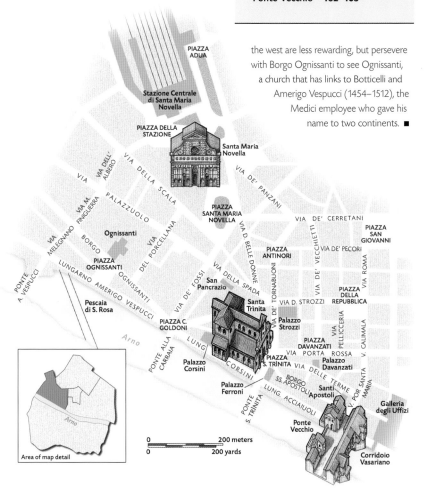

Santa Maria Novella

The mother church of Florence's Dominican order was begun in 1246. In time it would become the city's second most important church after Santa Croce. Both the facade and interior are exceptional, the latter housing a trio of captivating fresco cycles and one of the Renaissance's most influential paintings. Alongside the church lies Santa Maria's museum, visited chiefly for its painted cloister and a gloriously frescoed chapel.

Giorgio Vasari altered the Gothic interior of Santa Maria Novella in 1565, removing the screen and friars' stalls.

Before entering the church, take a look around **Piazza Santa Maria Novella,** not the loveliest of Florentine squares but of passing interest for its two large obelisks. Both are supported by amusing bronze turtles (1608), the work of sculptor Giambologna, and were raised in imitation of an ancient Roman *circo,* or circus, a chariot racetrack that used similar posts to mark the starting and finishing points of races. Cosimo I introduced his own chariot race to Florence in 1563, the Palio dei Cocchi, an event held annually in the piazza on June 23, the eve of the Feast of St. John, until the middle of the 19th century.

Having looked at the piazza, turn your attention to Santa Maria's **facade.** While the church's interior was largely completed by 1360, its Romanesque front remained half-finished until 1456, when Giovanni Rucellai, a local textile merchant, commissioned architect Leon Battisti Alberti to complete the facade in a more modern and classically influenced style. Rucellai's name in a latinized version—Iohanes Oricellarius—is stamped across the facade near the top, together with the year of the facade's dedication (MCCCCLXX, 1470). Also present are Rucellai's personal emblem, the billowing sail of Fortune, the Rucellai family emblem (feathers in a ring), and—in the topmost triangular pediment—a huge shining sun, the symbol of the Dominicans.

Inside, the church's overriding impressions are of size and sobriety. Note the trompe l'oeil effect that makes the church seem even larger than it is: The columns of the aisles become progressively closer, a trick designed to confuse your sense of perspective. Another triumph of perspective lies midway down the nave on the left as you face the high altar—Masaccio's groundbreaking fresco of the **"The Trinity"** (1427), one of the first Renaissance works in which the new ideas of mathematical proportion were employed. Florentines queued for days to share in the miracle of a picture that apparently created a three-dimensional space in a solid wall. Records suggest the painting took Masaccio a total of 24 days to complete. Note the kneeling figures at the painting's base—representing the judge and his wife who paid for the picture—and the skeleton with its chilling epigram: "I was that which you are, you will be that which I am." The painting's theme was suggested by the fact that the Dominicans' religious calendar began with the Feast of the Trinity.

Turn to your left as you face the painting, and alongside the second pillar in the nave is a **pulpit** (1443) paid for by Giovanni Rucellai, the sponsor of the church's facade, designed

by Brunelleschi, and executed by Andrea Cavalcanti, Brunelleschi's adopted son. It was from this pulpit, incidentally, that the Dominicans first denounced Galileo for espousing the Copernican view of the heavens—the idea that the Earth circled the sun, not vice versa. The Dominicans also ran the city's Inquisition, and the denouncement led eventually to the scientist's arrest and trial.

Frescoes & Other Works

Santa Maria is best known for its fresco cycles. The first of these lies in the **Cappella di Filippo Strozzi,** the chapel immediately to the right of the chancel, the area around the high altar. Sponsored

by banker Filippo Strozzi, the paintings (1489–1502) are the work of Filippino Lippi and deal with episodes from the life of Strozzi's namesake, St. Philip (San Filippo in Italian) the Apostle. At

Santa Maria Novella

- Map p. 149
- Piazza Santa Maria Novella
- 055 219 257 (church), 055 282 187 (museum)
- Closed Fri. a.m. & Sun. a.m.
- $$ (combined ticket for church & museum)
- Bus: 6, 11, 12 to Piazza Santa Maria Novella; C2 to Piazza dell'Unità Italiana

chiesasantamaria novella.it

EXPERIENCE: Enjoy the Maggio Musicale

If you're in Florence in May, try to attend one of the many concerts that make up the **Maggio Musicale** (tel 055 277 9350, operadifirenze.it), founded in 1933 and considered Italy's most prestigious classical music festival. If you can't make May, then other concerts are held much of the year in the festival's main venues, the **Teatro Comunale** and **Teatro Goldoni.** Consult the Florence visitor center (see p. 56) for details of organ and other recitals held in many of the city's churches.

the rear of the chapel stands the banker's tomb (1491–1495), an accomplished work by Benedetto da Maiano.

Long before the frescoes appeared, this chapel's predecessor was the fictional setting for the opening of *Il Decamerone,* or *The Decameron,* one of the foremost works of medieval literature. Written by Giovanni Boccaccio in the wake of the 1348 Black Death, this 100-tale epic is told by ten people over the course of ten days. For most scholars it marks the beginning of Italian prose, and it influenced many subsequent writers, among them Chaucer, Rabelais, and Shakespeare. Boccaccio found inspiration and reveled in a world turned upside down by the plague, a world where for a short while the normal moral, religious,

Santa Maria Novella

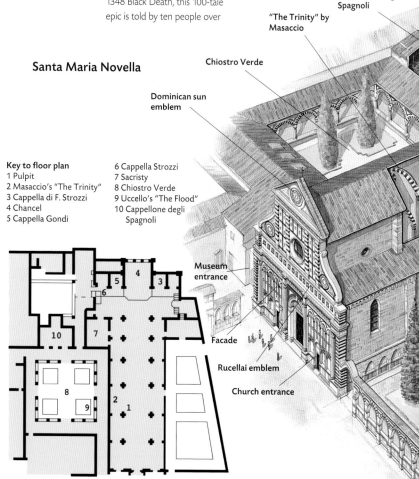

Cappellone degli Spagnoli

"The Trinity" by Masaccio

Chiostro Verde

Dominican sun emblem

Key to floor plan
1 Pulpit
2 Masaccio's "The Trinity"
3 Cappella di F. Strozzi
4 Chancel
5 Cappella Gondi

6 Cappella Strozzi
7 Sacristy
8 Chiostro Verde
9 Uccello's "The Flood"
10 Cappellone degli Spagnoli

Museum entrance

Facade

Rucellai emblem

Church entrance

and social constraints of life were suspended. Bawdy tales, courtly love, sexual high jinks, and high culture are mixed in a zestful and realistic narrative that starts when "seven ladies young and fair" meet in Santa Maria after Mass and decide to flee the pestilence-ridden city for the countryside.

Moving on, the church's second and most important cycle, a work by Domenico Ghirlandaio,

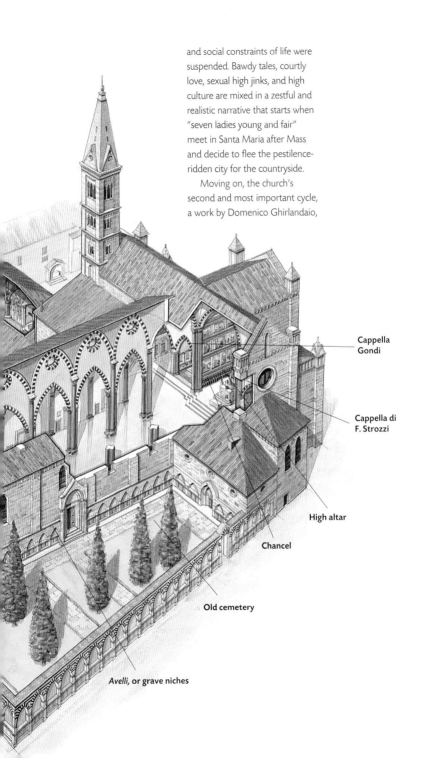

Cappella Gondi

Cappella di F. Strozzi

High altar

Chancel

Old cemetery

Avelli, or grave niches

Museo di Santa Maria Novella

✉ Piazza Santa Maria Novella (entrances in Piazza Santa Maria Novella & Piazza della Stazione 4)

☎ 055 282 187

🕐 Closed Fri. a.m. & Sun. a.m.

💲 $$ (combined ticket for church & museum)

museicivicifiorentini .comune.fi.it/

is arranged around the chancel, or **Cappella Tornabuoni,** to the left. It, too, was commissioned by a banker, Giovanni Tornabuoni. Here the themes are the life of St. John the Baptist (right wall) and the life of the Virgin. The cycle is crammed with numerous contemporary portraits—including members of the Tornabuoni family—and a wealth of fascinating insights into the daily life of 15th-century Florence. The chancel's previous fresco cycle, by Orcagna, was reputedly destroyed a century earlier after being struck by a bolt of lightning.

The chapel to the left of the chancel as you face the altar is the **Cappella Gondi,** known for Brunelleschi's wooden "Crucifix," the only such work by a man who scarcely returned to sculpture after failing to secure the commission for the baptistery doors in 1401 (see p. 70). Legend has it Brunelleschi executed the work because he was horrified by the uncouth nature of Donatello's similar "Crucifix" in the church of Santa Croce (see p. 113). The

(see p. 70)
(see p. 113)

INSIDER TIP:

Several fine hotels and restaurants grace the renovated Piazza Santa Maria Novella, where you can enjoy lunch or dinner with a view of the church.

—MARINA CONTI
National Geographic Italy editor

story goes that Donatello was so struck on seeing his rival's work that he dropped a basket of eggs.

Santa Maria's third fresco cycle lies in the **Cappella Strozzi,** the raised chapel in the north transept. Its paintings (1350–1357) were paid for by Tommaso Strozzi, a banking ancestor of Filippo Strozzi, and were commissioned to help expiate the sin of usury (lending money with interest), a practice then considered a sin by the Church. They are the work of Nardo di Cione (died 1366), brother of the more celebrated Orcagna (Andrea di Cione), who was responsible for the chapel's main altarpiece. The principal frescoes depict "Paradiso" (on the

Giovanni Boccaccio

Giovanni Boccaccio (1313–1375) was probably born in Paris, the illegitimate son of an Italian merchant. He grew up in Florence but fell in love with Naples in his 20s, having traveled there on business. He studied the classics and became part of the city's courtly circle before returning to Florence in 1340.

In Florence he met fellow writer Petrarch (see p. 50), with whom he shared

an interest in reviving Latin and Greek as literary languages. He also wrote his first major work, *Fiammetta* (1343), a romance based on a love affair at the Neapolitan court. He wrote his most famous work, *Il Decamerone,* or *The Decameron,* following the Black Death in 1348 (see pp. 152–153). He is also remembered for a life of Dante, *Vita di Dante,* written about 1360, and the *Teseide,* or *Knight's Tale.*

(see p. 50)
(see pp. 152–153)

left wall as you face the altar) and a pictorial version of Dante's "Inferno" (right wall). Dante has been painted as one of the saved in the "Last Judgment" fresco behind the chapel's altar; he is the figure third from the left, second row from the top. Tommaso is also present, being led to Paradise with his wife by St. Michael.

Moving back down to the main level of the church, you turn right through the transept door into the **sacristy,** whose highlights are a pretty glazed terra-cotta marble basin (1498) by Giovanni della Robbia (1469–1529) and a huge painted "Crucifix with the Madonna and St. John the Evangelist," an early work by Giotto (before 1312).

Museo di Santa Maria Novella

Alongside the church is the Museo di Santa Maria Novella. Inside lies the 14th-century **Chiostro Verde,** or Green Cloister, named after the predominant green *terra* pigment of its frescoes. The faded frescoes were painted in 1425–1430 by Paolo Uccello and depict stories from Genesis, of which the most famous panel is "The Flood" on the right (east) wall, with its images of Noah's ark before and after the Deluge.

Leading off the cloister is the **Cappellone degli Spagnoli,** or Spanish Chapel that was used by Eleonora of Toledo, the Spanish wife of Cosimo I. Most of its interior is adorned with magnificent frescoes, by the little-known

Ghirlandaio frescoes adorn the Cappella Tornabuoni in the church of Santa Maria Novella.

painter Andrea da Firenze (active 1343–1377). Those on the left wall depict "The Triumph of Divine Wisdom," those on the right wall "The Mission, Work and Triumph of the Dominican Order," all laced with much intricate symbolism. ■

Santa Trìnita

The church of Santa Trìnita is a fascinating hybrid of styles. Founded in 1092, it was rebuilt between 1300 and 1330, lending the interior a largely Gothic appearance that contrasts with the mannerist style of the replaced Gothic facade (1593) and fragments from the original 11th-century church. The building's main glory is artistic rather than architectural, however—a lovely Renaissance fresco cycle by Domenico Ghirlandaio.

Santa Trìnita's mannerist facade conceals an older Gothic interior filled with fine Renaissance art.

The church was founded by the Vallombrosans, a religious order established by Giovanni Gualberto, a nobleman turned Benedictine monk. One Good Friday, the story goes, Gualberto was scouring Florence seeking to avenge the murder of his brother. On finding the murderer, however, he spared his life—in honor of the holy day—and proceeded to the church of San Miniato al Monte to pray. There a crucifix miraculously bowed its head at Gualberto's act of mercy, a crucifix eventually installed in Santa Trìnita. A series of frescoes in the church portrays episodes from Gualberto's life.

Visiting the Church: The best way to visit the church is to work around the side chapels beginning on the south (right) wall. The fourth chapel is the **Cappella Bartolini-Salimbeni.** It contains a fresco cycle by Lorenzo Monaco (1372–1424) of the Virgin. These precede the church's pictorial highlight, a fresco cycle (1483–1486) by Domenico Ghirlandaio of episodes from the life of St. Francis in the **Cappella Sassetti** (the second chapel to the right of the high altar). The paintings were commissioned by

High Heels, High Art

The high heel, or stiletto—from the Italian for "little dagger"—is said to have been invented in Florence by Catherine de' Medici, who attempted to compensate for her diminutive stature by wearing 2-inch (5 cm) heels at her wedding in 1533 (aged 14) to the future King Henry II of France. How appropriate, then, that Florence should also be home to a temple to the shoemaker's art, the **Museo Salvatore Ferragamo** (Via dei Tornabuoni 2, tel 055 336 0846, closed Tues., $$), devoted to Salvatore Ferragamo (1898–1960).

Ferragamo was born in Naples. He emigrated to the United States at the age of 15, later making his name—and fortune—in Hollywood by creating shoes for Greta Garbo, Vivien Leigh, Rudolph Valentino, and Gloria Swanson, among others. On his eventual return to Italy he opened a store in Florence, still home to the headquarters of the company that bears his name. The company's museum is a shoe-lover's dream, featuring more than 16,000 pairs of shoes, exhibited in rotation.

Francesco Sassetti, a manager of the Medici bank and friend of Lorenzo the Magnificent, partly to outdo the frescoes of Sassetti's rival, Giovanni Tornabuoni, in Santa Maria Novella, also by Ghirlandaio (see pp. 150–155).

Piety & Politics: As in Santa Maria, Ghirlandaio uses a religious theme to portray 15th-century Florence. "St. Francis Receiving the Franciscan Rule" (in the lunette), for example, is set in Florence's Piazza della Signoria, complete with the Loggia della Signoria and a portrait of Sassetti between his son, Federigo, and Lorenzo the Magnificent (in the right foreground). Below Lorenzo stands the humanist teacher Angelo Poliziano (1454–1494) and three of his charges—Lorenzo's sons. The figure standing with his hand on his hip is Ghirlandaio.

Ghirlandaio also painted the chapel's altarpiece, "The Adoration of the Shepherds," a painting with a striking Renaissance fusion of Christian and classical iconography. Thus, Christ's manger is an old Roman sarcophagus and Mary and the shepherds are portrayed amid classical columns. The chapel's donors, or sponsors, Francesco Sassetti and his wife, Nera Corsi, are also portrayed.

In the next chapel to the left is the miraculous crucifix that bowed to Gualberto. Moving past the high altar, the second chapel on the left contains the church's other main treasure, Luca della Robbia's tomb of Benozzo Federighi, Bishop of Fiesole (1454–1456). Moving down the church's north wall toward the entrance, the first chapel contains a statue of Mary Magdalene (1455) by Desiderio da Settignano, a work influenced by Donatello's similar statue in the Museo dell'Opera del Duomo (see p. 77). The next chapel, the **Cappella Compagni,** has frescoes by Lorenzo di Bicci (circa 1373–1452) on the life of St. Giovanni Gualberto and Nero di Bicci's (1419–1491) painting (1455) of the same saint with members of the Vallombrosan order. ∎

Santa Trìnita

- 🅰 Map p. 149
- ✉ Piazza Santa Trìnita
- ☎ 055 216 912
- ⏱ Closed noon– 4 p.m. daily & Sun. 10:45 a.m.– 4 p.m.
- 🚌 C3, D to Ponte Santa Trìnita

Palazzo Davanzati

Posterity has done away with much of medieval Florence, building over its streets and houses, redesigning its churches and palaces, and consigning its paintings and sculptures to museums. This makes the Palazzo Davanzati all the more precious, for its beautiful interiors—complete with furniture and other period decoration—still perfectly capture the look and spirit of a Florentine medieval home.

The Sala dei Pavoni takes its name from its 14th-century frieze of peacocks (*pavoni* in Italian).

Palazzo Davanzati

- Map p. 149
- Via Porta Rossa 13
- 055 238 8610
- Closed 2 p.m. daily & 1st, 2nd, 3rd, & 5th Mon. of month; upper floors have guided tours at 10 a.m., 11 a.m., & noon.
- $
- Bus: C2 to intersection of Via della Condotta & Via Porta Rossa

firenzemusei.it

The palace was built about 1330 by the Davizzi, a family of wool merchants. In 1578 it passed to the Davanzati—whose coat of arms still adorns the facade—and remained with the family until 1838, when its last owner committed suicide by jumping from an upper-story window. It was then converted into apartments, before being restored in 1906 to something approaching its original state. Since 1956, it's been maintained as the Museo di Palazzo Davanzati.

Before entering the house, look up at its facade. It is crowned by a loggia and dotted with hooks

and rails once used for tying up animals, drying wool or clothes, or hanging banners during festivities. The courtyard provides a graphic glimpse of the realities of medieval life, where defense and survival in the event of attack were always paramount. The huge doors were designed to be siege-resistant, the storerooms could accommodate provisions for a year, and the well—a luxury at a time when much of Florence still relied on public fountains—ensured a constant water supply. Note the majestic wooden staircase, the only one of its kind to survive in Florence. Look, too, at the courtyard's rear right-hand pillar, whose carvings include portraits of the Davizzi family.

Inside the Palace: The emphasis on defense is maintained on the first floor, where in the main Sala Grande, or **Sala Madornale,** a room used for family gatherings, you can still make out four *piombatoi di difesa* (wooden hatches) used to pour molten lead onto attackers below. This sala's ornate ceiling and lovely decoration set the tone for many of the rooms that follow. Off to the left, for example, lies the **Sala dei Pappagalli,** named after the *pappagalli* (parrots) motifs of its frescoes. Once common, these paintings are some of the last of their kind in the city.

The most beautiful room of all is the nearby **Sala dei Pavoni,** or Camera Nuziale (Wedding Room), where another sublime ceiling is complemented by a wall frieze of trees, peacocks *(pavoni),* and the coats of arms of the families related to the Davizzi. Note the en suite bathroom, a rare luxury at the time. The more usual Florentine arrangement—as described in Giovanni Boccaccio's *Decamerone*—was a plank placed over a large communal pit. Drains in Florence were introduced at about the time the palace was built, and it was only in 1325 that a law had been passed forbidding the tipping of sewage onto the streets. Before that, the law required only that you utter three warning shouts to passersby.

As you explore the palace's rooms and move up through its four stories, you come across all manner of decorative touches and pieces of period furniture, not to mention numerous incidental antiques, tapestries, sculptures, ceramics, and textiles. One of the most fascinating rooms, however, is also one of the most austere— the medieval **kitchen.** This room was on the top floor as a precaution against fire. The women and servants spent most of their time here; in winter it would have been the warmest part of the house. The kitchen utensils on display are of note, especially the unwieldy *girapolenta,* used for stirring polenta, and the *impastatori,* used for mixing pasta and bread dough.

Take a look at the views from the kitchen windows, but don't be fooled by the leaded windows. For much of the Middle Ages, the best windows most people could hope for were rags soaked in turpentine (for waterproofing) and stretched across rickety frames. ∎

Lovely, Little Santi Apostoli

Why, you may ask, would you want to visit Santi Apostoli, close to the Palazzo Davanzati *(Piazza del Limbo)* between Via Porta Rossa and the Arno, when Florence has so many larger and more famous churches? The answer is principally because the building is probably at least 1,000 years old and retains an austere Romanesque beauty, largely unadorned with later additions, that is unique in the city center: Only San Miniato above the Arno is comparable (see pp. 182–185). The 16th-century artist and writer Giorgio Vasari claimed that Brunelleschi used this "small and most beautiful" building as his main model for the churches of Santo Spirito and San Lorenzo.

The Floods

Of all the episodes in Florence's recent history, none has captured attention as forcibly as the events of a November dawn in 1966 when a flood of staggering intensity hit the still slumbering city. Many people were killed and innumerable works of art were either lost or damaged beyond repair. And yet the catastrophe was not without precedent, for this was simply the latest episode in a history of flooding.

Books dry out after the inundation of 1966.

Visit Florence in summer and gaze down at the benign, slowly flowing waters of the Arno, and you may wonder how such an innocuous-looking river could ever threaten the city. Mark Twain, writing of the river in *Innocents Abroad* in 1869, was unimpressed: "This great historical creek," he wrote, "with four feet in the channel . . . would be a very plausible river if they would pump some water into it." Compare this with the account of K. K. Taylor, another American writer, who described a very different scene in her 1966 *Diary of Florence in Flood:* "A tumultuous mass of water stretches from bank to bank," she wrote, "a snarling brown torrent of terrific velocity, spiraling in whirlpools and countercurrents . . . this

tremendous water carries mats of debris . . . in a swelling turbulence."

Florentine chronicles over the years tend more to Taylor's view than Twain's. "A great part of the city became a lake," lamented one writer in 1269, when floods carried away the Carraia and Trìnita bridges. In 1333 a four-day storm unleashed floods so violent that church bells were tolled to drive out the devils blamed for the watery disaster. With the increasing extremes in Europe's recent weather systems, Florence can expect more floods such as those that affected the city as recently as 2012.

But why is Florence prey to such disasters? The main culprits are the surging meltwaters of the Apennine Mountains and Florence's own position—ringed by hills and just downstream of the Sieve, a major tributary of the Arno.

November 4, 1966

In 1966 the potential for disaster had been magnified by almost 40 days of rain. The final straw came on the night of November 4, when sluice gates above Florence were opened to prevent the collapse of a dam.

Almost the only people made aware of the dangers were the Ponte Vecchio jewelers, summoned by a night watchman as the bridge began to shake. At dawn, water crashed through the city, moving with such ferocity that commuters in the railroad station subway were drowned where they stood. Thirty-five Florentines perished in all, and many hundreds were made homeless. Great damage was done to the city's buildings and works of art. In places water reached 20 feet (6 m) above street level. Damage was exacerbated by heating oil,

Cars and debris were tossed like corks as floodwater coursed through Florence in 1966.

recently delivered for the winter and flushed out of basements by the water. Such was the power of the torrent that five of Lorenzo Ghiberti's bronze panels were torn from the baptistery doors. Slurry slopped around paintings in the Uffizi's cellars and damaged books and manuscripts in the Biblioteca Nazionale.

Donations and volunteers flowed into the city to help with the cleanup. Many advances were made in restoration techniques, but even today only about 70 percent of the stricken paintings are on show; two laboratories—one for sculptures, one for paintings—still operate to repair the damage of a single night.

Ponte Vecchio

The magnificent Ponte Vecchio is among Florence's most famous sights, but the fact that this bridge has survived for almost seven centuries is something of a miracle. It easily could have been destroyed in one of the many floods to have ravaged the city or have fallen victim to the Nazis in 1944: It was the only bridge spared—apparently on Hitler's orders—as Field Marshal Kesselring attempted to slow the advance of the United States Fifth Army.

The arched spaces near the center of the Ponte Vecchio were originally designed to allow garbage to be tipped directly into the Arno.

Ponte Vecchio

🗺 Map p. 149

🚌 Bus: C3, D

A bridge has probably existed on the site of the Ponte Vecchio—at the Arno's narrowest point—since the Etruscan era. In Roman times it carried the Via Cassia, a vital highway that linked Rome to northern Italy, although some historians suggest the Roman-era bridge was located farther upstream. For centuries the crossing remained the city's only trans-Arno link, but its wooden superstructure was replaced on several occasions, usually in the wake of floods.

The reorganization of Florence's defenses in 1172 brought large areas south of the river within the city's orbit, a move that made the crossing still more important as a pivotal point in the urban fabric. When floods swept away the wooden bridge in 1117, the city fathers commissioned what was probably the first stone bridge on the site, albeit one that still had a wooden roadbed. When floods destroyed this structure in 1333, the city commissioned the present stone bridge in 1345.

At this point the crossing took its present name—which means the "old bridge"—coined by the Florentines to distinguish it from the Ponte alla Carraia (1218) upstream, then known as the Ponte Nuovo, "new bridge." At the same time the bridge was made the fulcrum of the city's riverside defenses. All adjoining facades on the Arno deemed a threat in the event of attack were altered so as to be "blind," or without windows.

The Shops & Other Uses

The Ponte Vecchio's shops had appeared on previous incarnations of the bridge during the 13th century. Most belonged to butchers and fishmongers, who used the river as a convenient dumping ground for their waste. Next came the tanners, who used the river to soak their hides before tanning them in horse urine.

The bridge received a major face-lift in 1565, when Grand Duke Cosimo I built the **Corridoio Vasariano,** a covered passageway from the Uffizi, then the Medici's offices, to the Palazzo Pitti, a newly acquired Medici palace across the river. The passageway was built to celebrate the marriage of Cosimo's son, Francesco, to Joanna of Austria. Construction was trusted to Giorgio Vasari, a painter and writer best known for his biographies of great Italian painters. Vasari made much of the fact the project took only five months to complete.

Today, the corridor runs in an obvious line across the top of the bridge's shops. Once across the Arno it skirts above Santa Felicita, passing over the church's main portico in order—so it's said—that Cosimo could attend services without having to mix with the congregation. Inside, the corridor is lined with self-portraits but is open only intermittently.

EXPERIENCE: Take a Lazy Trip Down the Arno

See Florence from a different perspective on an intimate tour aboard a vintage *barchetto,* a small, traditional flat-bottomed boat propelled by a pole. The boats were used for centuries during floods and as ferries. Today they offer peaceful vistas of the city as you drift past the Uffizi and under the Ponte Vecchio, then past the churches of Santa Trinita and San Jacopo. The hour-long tour (*$$$$$*) departs at 5:45 p.m., Monday, Thursday, and Saturday, May through September. Book through **Florence and Tuscany Tours** (*Via Condotta 12, tel 055 210 301, florenceandtuscanytours.com*).

A future Medici Grand Duke, Ferdinando I, was irked by the smells and noises emanating from the shops. In 1593 he banished the practitioners of what he called these "vile arts." In their place—at double the rent—he installed some 50 jewelers and goldsmiths, many of whose descendants still trade from the pretty *madielle,* or hatches, of their wood-shuttered shops. A bust (1900) of one of Florence's most famous goldsmiths, Benvenuto Cellini, stands at the middle of the bridge. ■

More Places to Visit in Western Florence

Cenacolo di Ghirlandaio

This painting of the Cenacolo (Last Supper) is one of several in Florence (see sidebar p. 146); it was painted in 1480 by Domenico Ghirlandaio for the refectory of the convent next to the church of Ognissanti (see below). Like many of his paintings, notably the frescoes in the churches of Santa Trìnita and Santa Maria Novella, this work is placid and lyrical, and filled with narrative detail. *firenzemusei.it* Map p. 149 ✉ Ognissanti, Borgo Ognissanti 42 ☎ 055 238 8720 or 348 645 0390 (cell) ◷ Closed p.m., Sun., & Wed.–Fri. 🚌 Bus: 36, 37, C3 to Piazza Ognissanti

Ognissanti

For much of Florence's medieval history, the core of its thriving textile industry was located in a western district close to the river. At this area's heart lay the church of Ognissanti, or All Saints, founded around 1251 by the Umiliati, a religious order from Lombardy renowned for expertise in weaving woolen cloth.

Inside the church, on the second altar on the south (right) wall, is a painting of the "Madonna della Misericordia" (1473) by Domenico Ghirlandaio (the lower of two paintings here). Look for the face squeezed

All shapes and sizes at Museo Marino Marini

between the Madonna and the dark-cloaked figure. It belongs to Amerigo Vespucci, a Medici agent in Seville, Spain, whose voyages to the New World in 1499 and 1501 would see the Americas named in his honor.

The altar was paid for by his family, prominent local silk merchants. Other family members feature in the painting, not least Simonetta Vespucci (at the Virgin's left hand), considered the most alluring woman of her day. She was the mistress of Giulio de' Medici, as well as the model for Venus in Botticelli's famous painting now in the Uffizi (see p. 100). Botticelli came from a family—the Filipepi—who lived locally. The artist is buried in the church beneath a round tomb marker in the south (right) transept. He also painted "St. Augustine's Vision of St. Jerome" (1480) between the third and fourth altars on the wall opposite Ghirlandaio's "Madonna." *chiesaognissanti.it* Map p. 149 ✉ Borgo Ognissanti ☎ 055 239 8700 ◷ Closed 12:30 p.m.–4 p.m. & Fri. a.m. 🚌 Bus: 36, 37, C3 to Piazza Ognissanti

San Pancrazio

San Pancrazio's long life as a church ended when it was deconsecrated in 1808. Today, it houses the **Museo Marino Marini,** devoted to the works of the noted Pistoia-born painter and sculptor Marino Marini (1901–1980). Also worth seeing is the **Cappella Rucellai,** once part of the church but now entered from Via della Spada. Remodeled for Giovanni Rucellai (see p. 150), it preserves its original design and the Tempietto del Santo Sepolcro (1467), a copy of Jerusalem's Holy Sepulcher. The design and the temple were the work of artist and architectural theorist Leon Battista Alberti. *museomarinomarini.it* Map p. 149 ✉ Piazza San Pancrazio ☎ 055 219 432 ◷ Closed Sun., Tues., & Aug. 💲 $ 🚌 Bus: 6, 11 to Via della Vigna Nuovo

A district on the river's southern bank with its own name and its own identity—the Oltrarno, or "beyond the Arno"

Oltrarno

Ancient cypress trees and statues flank the Viottolone in the Giardino di Boboli.

Oltrarno

The Oltrarno is the southern part of Florence. The city's original Roman colony developed on the Arno's northern bank at the narrowest bridging point across the river. But while there was a bridge to the southern shore, not to mention an important Roman road that traversed the area to the south, Florence remained a city confined to its northern bank for many centuries after its foundation.

This state of affairs continued until at least 1218, the year a second bridge was forced across the river—the Ponte alla Carraia. The new link was prompted in part by the

Oltrarno's growing importance as a commercial center, and in particular as one of the city's main areas of textile production. Textile businesses were attracted primarily by

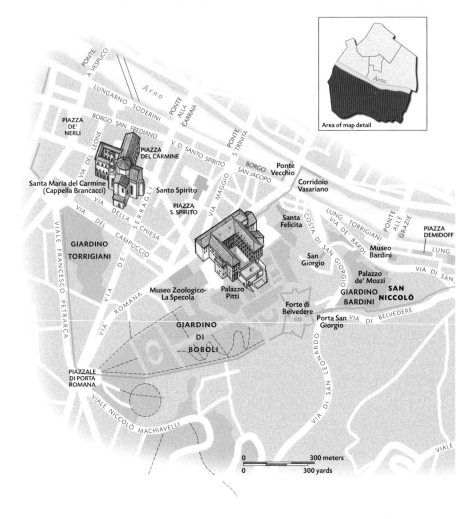

Area of map detail

0   300 meters
0   300 yards

the river, whose water was vital for washing, dyeing, and other processes involved in the manufacture of wool and other cloth.

The area maintained a reputation as a blue-collar district for centuries afterward, and although this has changed a little in recent years, one of the Oltrarno's charms is still the large number of artisans' workshops, the existence of villagelike neighborhoods, and the earthier and more traditional atmosphere of its streets and squares.

Further impetus to the district's growth came in the 13th century with the building of two major churches—Santo Spirito and Santa Maria del Carmine. So marked was Santo Spirito's effect that, when the city was divided into four areas in the 14th century, the whole Oltrarno area was given its name. Another strong spur to the area's development came in the 15th century with the construction of the Palazzo Pitti, a vast palace that became the Medici's principal home and court.

The palace is one of the Oltrarno's key sights, one whose colossal and rambling structure dominates—and seems out of place

> ## NOT TO BE MISSED:
>
> **Admiring the art in the Galleria Palatina, Palazzo Pitti 169–174**
>
> **A visit to the Museo degli Argenti, Palazzo Pitti 170**
>
> **Strolling in the Boboli and Bardini Gardens 174–175 & 187**
>
> **The beautiful frescoes of the Cappella Brancacci 176–179**
>
> **Enjoying the views from Piazzale Michelangelo 181**
>
> **The Romanesque church of San Miniato al Monte 182–185**
>
> **Pontormo's "Deposition," on the Santa Felicita Estate 186–187**

in—what is otherwise a modest and intimate district. Today, the palace serves as a vast museum complex, although only two or three of its museums are of interest to most visitors. The main one is the Galleria Palatina, whose beautiful salons provide a splendid setting for part of the Medici's extensive collection of paintings. With numerous works of art by Raphael, Titian, and others, this gallery is second only to the Uffizi in terms of the quality and quantity of its paintings.

Despite the importance of the Palazzo Pitti, the Oltrarno continued to be somewhat marginalized, and there is a relative shortage of major monuments compared to the area north of the river. This said, those that do exist are some of the most exquisite in the city. The fresco cycle in the Cappella Brancacci is one of the most important in Western art; the hilltop church of San Miniato al Monte is among Tuscany's most beautiful Romanesque buildings; and the Giardino di Boboli, or Boboli Garden, behind the Palazzo Pitti, is the loveliest open space in the city. Last, but not least, the *coste,* or old lanes, leading to San Miniato, provide walks through an almost rural city enclave, with fine views to the Tuscan hills. ■

Palazzo Pitti

The Palazzo Pitti may not bear the Medici name, but members of Florence's first family were the owners of this monolithic palace for many centuries. Its countless rambling rooms house several museums, the most important of which is the Galleria Palatina, whose beautiful salons are filled from floor to ceiling with paintings from the Medici's private collection.

The Sala dell'Educazione di Giove in the Galleria Palatina

Palazzo Pitti

 Map pp. 166–167

 Piazza de' Pitti

Bus: C3, D to Piazza di Santa Felicita

The palace was begun about 1458 by Luca Pitti, a merchant and banker. Part of his intention in conceiving so grandiose a building was to challenge the might of the Medici, his despised business rivals. The original design may have been the work of Brunelleschi, who is said to have taken the plan to Pitti after Cosimo de' Medici (the Elder) rejected it as too ostentatious. Cosimo's taste was notoriously sober, as is clear from the plain-faced Palazzo Medici-Riccardi, begun

for him by Michelozzo 14 years earlier (see pp. 133–135). The wily Medici godfather was not necessarily modest, however; he simply realized that too conspicuous a show of wealth and power would alienate many everyday Florentines.

The project rejected by Cosimo eventually crippled the Pitti financially, forcing them—ironically—to sell out to the Medici in 1549. The palace was bought by Grand Duke Cosimo I, partly on the prompting of his Spanish wife, Eleonora di Toledo, who had little time for Cosimo's previous lodging, the Palazzo Vecchio. Eleonora immediately set about expanding the palace, which at the time was only a single room deep, being hemmed in by the hills of the Boboli Garden to the rear. Cosimo, for his part, linked his new home with the old Medici offices, or Uffizi, now the gallery of the same name. To do so, he commissioned the artist and critic Giorgio Vasari to construct the Corridoio Vasariano (see p. 163), a raised and enclosed passageway that still runs across the top of the Ponte Vecchio.

INSIDER TIP:

Combined tickets allow you to see the galleries, museums, apartments, and gardens at your ease. Always check in advance for weekly and seasonal closings.

—NEIL SHEA
National Geographic writer

The palace remained the seat of the Medici court and that of the family's successors, the Lorraine dynasty, for some three centuries. Following Italian Unification in 1860, it was also used as the seat of the Savoy kings during Florence's brief spell as the Italian capital between 1865 and 1870. (Rome at the time was still occupied by French and papal troops.) By this time it had expanded to its present enormous size, the

facade alone being three times the width planned for the Pitti some four centuries earlier.

The spacious palace interior and parts of the Boboli Garden to the rear are given over to a series of museums that, at first sight, present an intimidating sightseeing prospect. In fact, only two of the galleries are essential viewing—the **Galleria Palatina,** which holds much of the Medici's private art collection, and the **Museo degli Argenti** (see sidebar p. 170), a collection of the family's silver, antiques, and other precious objets d'art.

Whether you see the other galleries will depend on your time and tastes. The **Appartamenti Reali** are a suite of richly decorated royal apartments; the **Galleria delle Porcellane** is a collection of Medici and Lorraine porcelain housed in the Casino del Cavaliere in the Boboli Garden; the **Museo delle Carrozze** is a collection of Medici and Lorraine state carriages (currently closed); the **Galleria delle Costume** features an impressive array of sumptuous 18th- and 19th-century clothing (housed in the Palazzina della Meridiana, entered from the Boboli Garden). The **Galleria d'Arte Moderna** is a 30-room collection of mostly uninspiring paintings and sculptures from the early 18th century onward.

Galleria Palatina

Whichever of these you decide to see, make sure that your first visit is to the Galleria Palatina, laid out in its present guise toward the end of the 18th century. It houses

Galleria Palatina, Appartamentali Reali, & Galleria d'Arte Moderna

- ✉ Palazzo Pitti, Piazza de' Pitti
- ☎ 055 238 8614
- 🕐 All closed Mon.; Appartamentali Reali closed Jan.
- 💲 $$$ (combined ticket), $$$$ (combined ticket during special exhibitions)
- 🚍 Bus: C3, D to Piazza di Santa Felicita

firenzemusei.it

Museo degli Argenti, Galleria delle Porcellane, & Galleria delle Costume

- ✉ Palazzo Pitti, Piazza de' Pitti
- ☎ 055 238 8713
- 🕐 All closed 1st & last Mon. of month
- 💲 $$ (combined ticket, including Giardino di Boboli & Giardino Bardini), $$$ (combined ticket during special exhibitions)
- 🚍 Bus: C3, D to Piazza di Santa Felicita

firenzemusei.it

the parts of the Medici's immense art collection that couldn't be fitted into the Uffizi. But, don't come here with the idea that the works on display are second-rate leftovers. The collection has no fewer than 11 works by Raphael and 14 by Titian, plus paintings by all the other great names of the Florentine canon, many works by Venetian masters, and paintings by Caravaggio, Peter Paul Rubens, Anthony Van Dyck, and others.

A Silver Lining Museum

No matter how long you decide to spend at the Palazzo Pitti, be sure to visit the Museo degli Argenti, which you enter from the palace's main courtyard. Its beautifully decorated rooms are attractions in their own right, almost overshadowing the exhibits, which consist of precious artifacts from the Medici's private collection. These include glorious pieces of goldware and silverware (*argento* is Italian for "silver"), stunning *pietre dure* (inlaid stone) vases, precious stones, caskets, fabrics, carpets, furniture, and a host of other extravagant (and sometimes gaudy) precious objects.

The Galleria, like the palace, can be disorienting. Having bought your ticket, walk to the rear right-hand corner of the huge inner courtyard and climb the imposing staircase to the Palatina's entrance. You then pass under a magnificent chandelier—all of the palace is gloriously decorated—and walk through two rooms with lovely views over the Boboli Garden. In the third room you come to the start of the gallery's set itinerary, a route that takes you through seven art-filled rooms and then back through five similar but still more spectacular rooms, with several masterpieces by Raphael.

A glorious "Madonna and Child" (1450) by Filippo Lippi dominates the first major room, the **Sala di Prometeo** (Hall of Prometheus), off which opens a warren of rooms to the right crammed with minor paintings. Then comes the **Sala di Ulisse** (Hall of Ulysses), which contains Raphael's "Madonna dell'Impannata" (1514) and a work by Filippino Lippi—the son of Filippo Lippi—the "Death of Lucretia," painted when the artist was still studying in the workshop of Botticelli. Moving on, you come to the **Bagno di Napoleone,** converted in 1813 into a bathroom for Napoleon, and then to the beautifully tiled **Sala della Stufa,** or Room of the Stove, so-called because it provided the heating for the palace's other principal rooms.

Allori's Bloodless Gore: From here you enter the **Sala dell'Educazione di Giove** (Room of Jove's Education), the last of the first line of principal parallel rooms. Its main attraction is Caravaggio's "Sleeping Cupid" (1608), painted in Malta for a Florentine nobleman. The room also contains Cristofano Allori's (1577–1621) "Judith and Holofernes," one of 17th-century Florence's most popular paintings. It is a curiously bloodless picture, given the theme—Judith clutching Holofernes's severed head—and is notable for the fact that the main models were the artist, his mother, and his mistress.

Other Highlights: Raphael is the star of the **Sala dell'Iliade** (Hall of the Iliad), the first of the six rooms on the return side of the palace, with "La Gravida," or "The Expectant Mother" (1506), an unusual theme for the time. In the next room, the **Sala di Saturno** (Hall of Saturn), you can trace Raphael's development in a series of paintings that span almost his whole career. One of the earliest is the "Madonna del Granduca" (1506), which shows the soft-toned influence of Leonardo da Vinci and Raphael's teacher, Perugino. Its name comes from the fact that its owner, Grand Duke (Granduca) Ferdinand III of Lorraine, is said to have taken the painting with him wherever he went. A year or so later Raphael painted "Agnolo and Maddalena Doni" (1506–1507), whose style would influence portraiture for years. Maddalena's pose, you may notice, deliberately copies that of Leonardo's famous "Mona Lisa." The pictures were painted to celebrate the couple's marriage, an event also commemorated by Michelangelo's "Doni Tondo," the Uffizi's only painting by the artist (see p. 102).

Also here are the "Madonna del Baldacchino," left unfinished when Raphael went to Rome in 1508, a "Portrait of Tommaso Inghirami" (1510), and perhaps the gallery's finest work, the "Madonna della Seggiola" (1513–1514), whose tondo, the round panel on which it is painted, is said to have come from the bottom of a wine barrel. Tondo paintings were common in Florence, and Raphael was keen to

"Judith and Holofernes" by Cristofano Allori. The model for the main female figure was the artist's mistress.

excel in the discipline their particular form imposed. He succeeded, and for centuries this was the most popular image of the Madonna in Italian art.

The **Sala di Giove** (Hall of Jove) was once the palace's main throne room. Today, it contains some of Florence's most precious paintings, including the "Three Ages of Man" (1500)—attributed to Giorgione (1478–1510), a painter whose known works are one signed painting and a fresco, though others are attributed to him—and several of a total of

17 works by Andrea del Sarto (see p. 44) in the gallery. Andrea was perhaps the major artist working in Florence from about 1510 onward, when his most notable contemporaries, Raphael and Michelangelo, were dominant in Rome. Ironically, the works of the first of these, Raphael, provide the cornerstone of this room, much as they have in the preceding rooms. Here you can see his "Donna Velata," or "Veiled Woman" (1516), an idealized portrait of a Roman baker's daughter turned model who was reputedly the painter's mistress.

Sala di Marte & Beyond:

The next room, the **Sala di Marte** (Hall of Mars), is dominated by an immense painting by Rubens called "The Consequences of War" (1638), an allegory of the Thirty Years' War, a conflict that ravaged much of Europe between 1618 and 1648. Describing the painting, the artist explained that the central figure of a "grief-stricken woman is the unfortunate Europe, who, for so many years now, has suffered plunder, outrage and misery." Don't miss the Medici's six-ball symbol emblazoned across the ceiling (see sidebar p. 123), nor the room's trio of fine portraits: Van Dyck's "Cardinal Bentivoglio," a Bolognese prelate who was papal ambassador to the Low Countries (present-day Luxembourg, the Netherlands, and Belgium); the almost modern-looking "Portrait of a Man," by the Venice-based painter Veronese (1528–1588); and Titian's "Ippolito de Medici," a Medici scion made a cardinal at 18 and poisoned at 24. Here he is shown setting off to lead an

A 16th-century silver and crystal casket by Renaissance artist Valero Belli, on view in the Museo degli Argenti

expedition against the Turks in defense of Vienna.

Titian (1487–1576) also features in the next room, the **Sala di Apollo** (Hall of Apollo), most notably with a sensuous "Mary Magdalene," and "A Portrait of an Englishman," one of his best known and most penetrating portraits (the sitter's identity is unknown). The room's most eye-catching picture is an altarpiece of

The beautiful **Sala di Venere** (Hall of Venus) is as fine as the previous rooms. Its ceiling—like those of the preceding four rooms—is covered in frescoes by Pietro da Cortona (1596–1669), a program of mostly mythological scenes intended to glorify the Medici by associating them with the legends of the classical world. Below, the walls are smothered in painting, their apparently

A Bastion of Buried Art & Fine Views

The Forte di Belvedere (access from Via di Belvedere and Costa di San Giorgio) is the large fortress looming over the Boboli Garden (see pp. 174–175). Its main attractions are its ramparts, with broad views of the city, the Arno Valley, and the distant silhouettes of the Tuscan hills. Commissioned by Grand Duke Ferdinando I to defend the city and discourage insurrection, architect

Bernardo Buontalenti (circa 1536–1608) sank its foundations in 1590, burying with them some 20 bronze portraits of Ferdinando and a picture of how he hoped the fort would look on completion. Most of the building was finished the following year. The castle's bastions are grouped around the Palazzina di Belvedere, an earlier building now used for temporary exhibitions.

the "Madonna and Saints" (1522) by Rosso Fiorentino (1494–1540), a disillusioned mannerist artist who eventually left Florence for France. Also interesting is a double portrait of King Charles I of England (R. 1625–1649) and his wife, Henrietta Maria (1609–1669), a picture long attributed to the Flemish master Van Dyck. Its date and actual artist are unknown, but Henrietta was a scion of the Medici family, who at one time tried to assemble a portrait collection of all the crowned heads of Europe. This project explains why you will find a rather out of place portrait of Queen Elizabeth I of England (R. 1558–1603) in the Sala dell'Iliade.

haphazard arrangement the one preferred by the Medici. Here, as elsewhere, you can only pick out the absolute highlights, so wander until you find something that catches your eye.

The Sala di Venere takes its name from the "Venere Italica," or "Italian Venus," by Antonio Canova, a statue commissioned in 1812 to replace the famous "Medici Venus" removed to Paris from the Uffizi by Napoleon. Canova's work was moved here when the stolen statue was returned to the Uffizi after Napoleon's defeat. The key paintings are all by the Venetian artist Titian and include "Portrait of Pietro Aretino," a lecherous poet

Giardino di Boboli

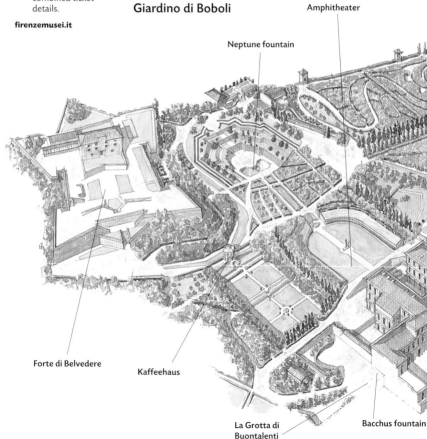

- **Map pp. 166–167**
- **Entrances: Palazzo Pitti courtyard, Via Romana, Porta Romana**
- **055 238 8713**
- **Closed first & last Mon. of month**
- **$$ (combined ticket), $$$ (combined ticket during special exhibitions); see p. 169 for combined ticket details.**

firenzemusei.it

and friend of the artist; "Portrait of Pope Julius II," copied from a portrait by Raphael; and "The Concert," an early work purchased by Leopoldo de' Medici in the mistaken belief he was buying a picture by the celebrated Venetian artist Giorgione. Don't miss two fine marine paintings in this room by the Neapolitan painter Salvator Rosa (1615–1673) and two gargantuan landscapes by Rubens.

Giardino di Boboli

The Giardino di Boboli (Boboli Garden), Florence's main park, lies behind the Palazzo Pitti. One of the largest gardens in Italy, it was begun by Grand Duke Cosimo I in 1549 and opened in 1766. In high summer, parts can be dust-dry and a little dog-eared, but during the rest of the year this makes a great place to stroll and take a break.

Giardino di Boboli

Amphitheater

Neptune fountain

Forte di Belvedere

Kaffeehaus

La Grotta di Buontalenti

Bacchus fountain

Moving from west to east, the garden's main sights are the **Forte di Belvedere** (see sidebar p. 173) on the hill and one of three grottoes in the garden, **La Grotta di Buontalenti,** a folly that contains casts of Michelangelo's "Slaves" (see p. 140) and lascivious 16th-century statues of "Venus Bathing" and "Paris Abducting Helen of Troy" by Giambologna and Vincenzo de' Rossi.

You can purchase refreshments in summer at the 1776 rococo-style **Kaffeehaus,** or Coffee House. One of the garden's most bizarre sights is the **Bacchus fountain,** a copy of a 1560 statue of Cosimo I's court dwarf, shown naked in the guise of Bacchus astride a tortoise. The **Neptune Fountain** stands in a small lake amid terracing dotted with Roman statues.

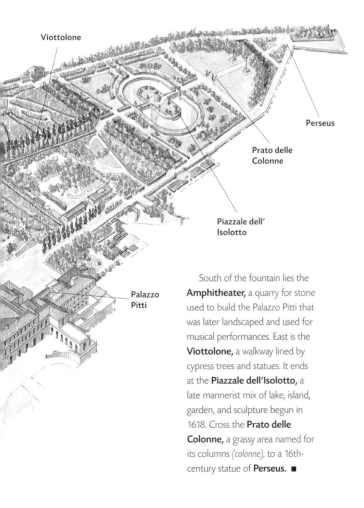

Viottolone

Perseus

Prato delle Colonne

Piazzale dell' Isolotto

Palazzo Pitti

South of the fountain lies the **Amphitheater,** a quarry for stone used to build the Palazzo Pitti that was later landscaped and used for musical performances. East is the **Viottolone,** a walkway lined by cypress trees and statues. It ends at the **Piazzale dell'Isolotto,** a late mannerist mix of lake, island, garden, and sculpture begun in 1618. Cross the **Prato delle Colonne,** a grassy area named for its columns (*colonne*), to a 16th-century statue of **Perseus.** ∎

Cappella Brancacci

Florence has many majestic and important works of art, but few are held in such high esteem by art historians as the frescoes by Masaccio, Filippino Lippi, and Masolino da Panicale in the Cappella Brancacci, a chapel adjoining the church of Santa Maria del Carmine. Begun when the Renaissance was close to its peak, the innovation and invention of the paintings would influence Florentine and other painters for generations to come.

The chapel and its paintings were paid for by Filippo Brancacci, a silk merchant and diplomat, who commissioned them in 1423 on his return from a posting to Egypt as the Florentine ambassador. Work on the frescoes probably began a year later and was initially undertaken by Masolino (1383–circa 1447) and his promising young assistant, Tommaso di Ser Giovanni di Mone Cassai (1401–1428), better known as Masaccio, a nickname that meant "Mad Tom." Masaccio's talents were given room to blossom in 1426 when Masolino, who held the post of official painter to the Hungarian court, was called to Budapest. When he returned to Florence in 1427 he found himself in the shadow of his former assistant.

The Frescoes

The pair's frescoes embraced a new sense of realism, dramatic narrative, and handling of perspective that surpassed anything seen in Italy, dazzling other artists of the time. In the words of Giorgio Vasari, the 16th-century artist and art historian, "the most celebrated sculptors and painters . . . became excellent and illustrious in studying their art." The pictures, he added, were nothing less than a *"scuola del mondo,"* or a "school for the whole world." Even the great Michelangelo came here to sketch Masaccio's paintings.

Masaccio died when he was just 28, and in 1428 Masolino was called to Rome, never to return. Work on the chapel ceased completely in 1436 when Brancacci

In Masaccio's "St. Peter Healing the Sick," the figure in the red hat is a portrait of the artist Masolino.

EXPERIENCE: Explore Florence's Gardens

The Oltrarno contains Florence's finest gardens, the **Giardino Boboli** (see pp. 174–175) and the newly reopened **Giardino Bardini** (see sidebar p. 187). These are great to explore at your own speed, or simply as peaceful places of retreat from sightseeing. But those with a passion for Italian gardens should consider a tour with an expert for more historical and horticultural background.

As well as these two key gardens, tours often visit some of the city's dozen or so other parks and gardens, as well as private villas and other gardens around the city not normally open to the public.

Half- or full-day individual tours of one or both of the Boboli and Bardini Gardens are available with **Grifo Tours** (tel 050 760 388, grifotour.com). **Guided Tours of Florence,** with local guides Alessia and Tatiana (tel 347 938 1292, guidedtoursof florence.com), offers tailor-made individual tours to a variety of gardens, and **Tuscany Tours** (tel 347 657 2611, florencetour.com) has a full-day small group tour of the key Medici villas and gardens in the hills around the city. Garden aficionados could join the five-day "Spring Gardens of Florence and Fiesole" trip run by U.K.-based **Susan Worner Tours** (tel 01423 326 300, susanwornertours.com) or **Martin Randall Travel's** "Gardens of Tuscany" tour (tel 800/988-6168 in the U.S., martinrandall.com) in the company of an expert lecturer.

was exiled by the Medici, his crime having been to marry the daughter of Palla Strozzi, leader of the city's defeated anti-Medici faction. The cycle was completed some 50 years later by Filippino Lippi, whose copying skills proved so consummate that his part in the chapel was only recognized as recently as 1838.

That the paintings have survived is a miracle. When Brancacci was exiled, the Carmelite monks in charge of the chapel, anxious to placate the Medici, removed all portraits of their disgraced patron. And by 1680, when artistic tastes had changed, the chapel's new sponsor, Francesco Ferroni, argued that "these ridiculous men in their cassocks and old-fashioned outfits" should be scrubbed out. In 1771 a fire ruined the pictures' frames and added to the wear and tear caused by centuries of candle grease and varnish. Proper restoration took place between 1983 and 1990.

Masaccio was responsible for the cycle's most famous image, the stark, emotionally charged panel portraying **"The Expulsion of Adam and Eve From Paradise"** (upper register, far left, on the entrance arch as you look at the frescoes). Compare Eve's open-mouthed cry of pain and Adam's head-in-hands despair with Masolino's more anodyne rendering of **"Adam and Eve"** in the fresco in the same position on the opposite wall. The contrast between the two interpretations is striking: No other scene better illustrates the psychological depth and emotional intensity Masaccio brought to Florentine painting.

All other panels in the cycle deal with episodes from the life of St. Peter, who is picked out in every scene by his orange cloak. The most striking panels, all by Masaccio, are **"Christ and the Tribute Money," "St. Peter Healing the**

Cappella Brancacci

- Map pp. 166–167
- Santa Maria del Carmine, Piazza del Carmine. The entrance is to the right as you face the church.
- 055 276 8558 or 055 276 8224 (reservations obligatory)
- Closed Sun. a.m. & Tues. Groups of 30 admitted for 15 min.
- $$, $$$ (combined ticket with Palazzo Vecchio)
- Bus: D

museicivicifiorentini .comune.fi.it

The frescoes in the Cappella Brancacci (see numbered position diagrams)
1 "The Expulsion of Adam and Eve From Paradise"
2 "Christ and the Tribute Money"
3 "St. Peter Preaching"
4 "St. Peter Visited by Paul"
5 "Raising of Theophilus's Son"; "St. Peter Enthroned"
6 "St. Peter Healing the Sick"

1	2	3
4	5	6

Sick," and the combined **"Raising of Theophilus's Son"** and **"St. Peter Enthroned."** The first is one of the most complicated and accomplished compositions of the early Renaissance, its single panel embracing no fewer than three separate episodes. At the center, Masaccio paints Christ at the gates of Capernaum being asked to pay a tribute owed to the city (the figure at the extreme right of the group may be a self-portrait of the artist). On the left, St. Peter picks coins from the mouth of fish to pay the tribute (Christ can be seen in the central scene clearly indicating where the money will be

found), and in the right-hand scene St. Peter hands over the tribute money to an official.

In **"St. Peter Healing the Sick"** (lower register, left of the altar), the sick are shown being healed as the saint's shadow passes over them; depicting beggars and the infirm with such graphic realism was revolutionary at the time. The fresco on the same lower level to the right of the altar shows Sts. Peter and Paul giving alms, a reference to the customs of the early church, where part of one's wealth was given in charity. Also shown is the fate of Ananias, who withheld some of his wealth with the knowledge of his wife, Sapphira, and died with her after being castigated by Peter.

In the "Raising of Theophilus's Son" and "St. Peter Enthroned" (completed by Lippi), Masaccio depicts the episode of St. Peter raising the dead son of Theophilus,

7	8	9
10	11	12

the Prefect of Antioch. In return, the grateful citizens build a throne from which the saint can preach, a scene portrayed to the right. The figures in the doorway to the right of the throne are widely thought to be Masaccio, Brunelleschi, and Renaissance architectural theorist Leon Battista Alberti. Masaccio originally painted himself touching Peter's cloak, a reference to the statue in St. Peter's, Rome, which pilgrims touch for luck. When he completed the panel, Lippi thought this inappropriate and painted out the arm. Look closely for signs of the alteration.

There are more portraits in the fresco on the facing (right) wall,

which combines the episodes of **St. Peter's crucifixion** (left) and **Peter being sentenced to death by the emperor Nero.** The figure looking out at the spectator in the group to the left of the cross is Botticelli, Filippino Lippi's teacher, and the figure in a beret at the right of the Nero scene is a self-portrait of Lippi.

It is thought that Masaccio was responsible for panels 1, 2, 6, 7, and 10 (see plan), while Masolino worked on panels 3 and 9. Filippino Lippi was responsible for panels 11 and 12. Note the panels on which two artists worked. Masaccio began work on panel 5 but it was completed by Lippi. The other clear collaboration is panel 8, where Masaccio worked on the left-hand section and Masolino on the right. Masolino, in general, had a more decorative style than Masaccio's simpler and more realistic approach. ∎

7 "St. Peter Baptizing the Converts"
8 "St. Peter Healing the Cripple"; "Raising Tabitha"
9 "Temptation of Adam and Eve"
10 "St. Peter and St. John Giving Alms"
11 "St. Peter's Crucifixion"; "Before the Proconsul"
12 "The Release of St. Peter"

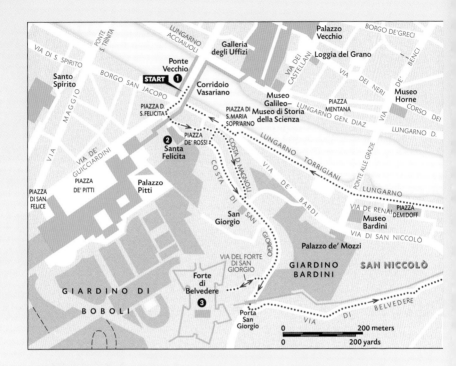

A Walk Through the Oltrarno to San Miniato al Monte

This attractive walk takes you from the Ponte Vecchio to the hilly slopes above the Arno and the glorious Romanesque church of San Miniato al Monte.

It's often said that Florence's main failing is its shortage of gardens and open space. This walk corrects that notion, taking you into an almost rural part of the city just minutes away from its center. It's not a long walk, but it is uphill, so you may want to take a bus to San Miniato and follow the itinerary in reverse (downhill). Or, return by bus. Be sure to time your walk to see inside San Miniato; the church is closed daily from 1 p.m. to 3:30 p.m. from November through March.

Start on the southern side of the **Ponte Vecchio ❶** (see pp. 162–163) and walk across Borgo San Jacopo, the street running along the river to your right as you face away from the

NOT TO BE MISSED:

Ponte Vecchio • Santa Felicita
• View from Piazzale Michelangelo
• San Miniato al Monte

bridge. You step almost immediately into Piazza di Santa Felicita, where you should stop to see the church of **Santa Felicita ❷** (see pp. 186–187) and its strange mannerist paintings. Then take the small lane to the left of the church, which brings you to Piazza de' Rossi, from whose eastern edge you can proceed up either Costa

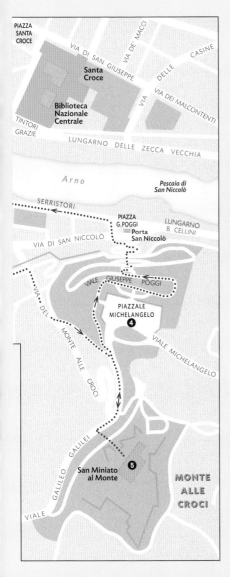

- See also area map pp. 166–167
- ▶ Ponte Vecchio
- ⏱ Allow half a day
- ↔ 1.5 miles (2.4 km)
- ▶ San Miniato al Monte
- 🚌 Bus: 12, 13 to/from Piazzale Michelangelo; C3, D to Ponte Vecchio

home to the scientist Galileo Galilei, and again at the church of San Giorgio, whose plain facade contrasts with its richly decorated interior.

Near the top of the street watch for Via del Forte di San Giorgio, where you should turn right if you want to make a short detour to the **Forte di Belvedere ❸** (see sidebar p. 173). Otherwise continue to Porta San Giorgio, a gateway that still contains a fresco of the "Madonna Enthroned with St. Leonard and St. George" (1430) by Bicci di Lorenzo (1373–1452).

Through the Porta turn left on Via di Belvedere (the "street of the beautiful view"), which follows the line of the old city walls and, as its name suggests, has a fine panorama over olive groves and pastoral countryside to the south. You have to climb once more when you reach the first major turning on the right, Via del Monte alle Croci. Turn right here and then left on the lane ahead lined with trees and crosses. This emerges at Viale Galileo Galilei, where a left turn brings you quickly to **Piazzale Michelangelo ❹**, a busy and often visitor-choked viewpoint. Return to Viale Galileo Galilei and this time turn right; then climb the steps leading off the left side of the road to **San Miniato al Monte ❺** (see pp. 182–185).

To walk back via a different route, follow the steps and road back to Piazzale Michelangelo. Then take the path leading off the extreme left side of the piazza, and bear right to follow a series of winding paths and steps steeply down to Porta San Niccolò. From here you can walk west on Lungarno Serristori along the river to the Ponte alle Grazie or Ponte Vecchio. Alternatively, walk via the Museo Bardini (see p. 186) and Giardino Bardini, which has a second entrance at Via de' Bardi.

de' Magnoli or Costa di San Giorgio. Ultimately you want to follow the picturesque Costa di San Giorgio—Costa de' Magnoli meets it after a short time—for its entire length to the Porta San Giorgio. This is a steep climb, so pause to catch your breath occasionally, especially for a visit to the Giardino Bardini (see sidebar p. 187), or at Porta San Giorgio No. 2, or at No. 19, once

San Miniato al Monte

Tuscany's most beautiful Romanesque church can be seen from across the city atop its hill on the Oltrarno's leafy fringes. It sits over the site of an earlier chapel dedicated to San Miniato, a saint martyred and buried on the spot in A.D. 250. Initially run by the Benedictines, the church passed in 1373 to the Olivetans, a minor Benedictine order, which lives there to this day.

The facade of San Miniato al Monte has the white and green marble decoration typical of Tuscan Romanesque churches.

St. Minias, or San Miniato, was probably Florence's first martyr. Whether he was a Greek merchant or Armenian prince, no one is quite sure, but it is known that he originally came to Italy on a pilgrimage to Rome and settled in Florence about A.D. 250. He was martyred during the Christian persecutions by the emperor Decius (R.249–251). Christian lore posits that after being beheaded near the present-day Piazza della Signoria, he picked up his severed head and carried it across the Arno and up the hill to the site of San Miniato al Monte. The saint had already lived nearby as a hermit, and the hill—then known as Mon Fiorentius—was scattered with pagan temples.

History & Exterior: Documentary evidence records the presence here of a chapel to the saint in the eighth century. Construction of the present church began in 1018 on the orders of Bishop Ildebrando, who in turn was acting on the instructions of Henry II, the Holy Roman Emperor (R.1002–1024). Henry endowed the church, according to one chronicler, "for the good of his soul." Building progressed in phases and was completed only in 1207, a date you can see inscribed on the marble pavement inside. Before entering the church, admire the sweeping panorama over the city and the church's magnificent exterior (see sidebar below).

The Interior: If the exterior dazzles, then the interior is beyond compare. The beautiful **pavement** dates from 1207 and is covered in symbolic and other figures, although no one is quite sure what they mean. Some obviously depict the zodiac, but others may be taken from precious Sicilian fabrics or derive from Byzantine models introduced to Italy either through trade or during the crusades. Much of the interior, of course, has been restored and added to, but it still appears much as it must have almost a thousand years ago. Its three distinct levels— the nave, sunken crypt, and raised presbytery (the area by the high altar)—are unchanged, as are most of the pillars and capitals, many of which were salvaged from Roman and Byzantine buildings.

The center of the nave is dominated by Michelozzo's **Cappella del Crocefisso** (1448), or Chapel of the Crucifix, created to house a miraculous crucifix that bowed its head to St. Giovanni Gualberto; the shape made for the now missing cross is still clear. (See pages 156–157 for a description of Santa Trìnita and the story of Gualberto and the crucifix's fate after 1671.) The space left by the cross is bordered by painted panels (1394–1396) attributed to Agnolo Gaddi and depicting the "Annunciation," stories of the Passion, and scenes from the lives of Sts. Gualberto and Miniato.

The chapel was commissioned by Piero de' Medici, or Piero il

San Miniato al Monte

- 🗺 Map pp. 166–167
- ✉ Cnr. of Via del Monte alle Croci & Viale Galileo Galilei
- 🕐 Closed 1 p.m. – 3:30 p.m. Nov.– March
- 🚌 Bus: 12, 13 from city center to Piazzale Michelangelo then 5-min. walk

sanminiatoalmonte.it

San Miniato al Monte's Facade

Among Florentine Romanesque buildings, only the baptistery, on which San Miniato's appearance was modeled, comes close to matching the beautiful facade. It is perhaps no coincidence both structures were mistaken during the Middle Ages as buildings of Roman origin. No similar facade would be built in the city until that of Santa Maria Novella (see pp. 150–155), completed in the 15th century—and even that copied San Miniato.

The frontage was probably built in several stages, the simple five-arched lower register dating from the 11th century, the upper order being added a century later. From 1288, the church's upkeep was the responsibility of the Arte di Calimala, or Merchants Guild, which is why its

emblem crowns the facade's summit—an eagle clutching a *torsello*, or 12 lengths of cloth. The mosaic below portrays "Christ Between the Virgin and St. Minias" (1260). It is noteworthy for Christ's unusual blue Oriental bolster.

The unfinished bell tower (begun in 1523) replaced the original, which toppled in 1499; this new tower, in turn, was threatened with destruction in 1530 during the siege of Florence by the troops of Emperor Charles V. During the conflict the tower was used as an artillery post, and thus it attracted the attention of enemy gunners. Michelangelo, enlisted to advise on the city's defenses, wrapped the tower in mattresses to protect it from cannonballs.

High in the hills, the grounds of San Miniato al Monte provide heavenly views of the city.

Gottoso (Piero the Gouty), the father of Lorenzo the Magnificent. It was one of only a handful of commissions he made in his brief period as head of the Medici clan. Parts of the frieze and the marble medallion to the rear are adorned with Piero's personal symbols and motifs, namely the eagle with three feathers, an uncut diamond, and the motto *Semper,* meaning "always." The last two motifs are references to the toughness and durability of Medici power. Note, also, the two eagles, symbols of the Arte di Calimala. They are designed to remind onlookers that while Piero de' Medici may have commissioned the chapel, the guild was responsible for organizing its actual creation. The glazed terra-cotta in the chapel is the work of Luca della Robbia.

Steps to the side of the chapel lead down to the **crypt,** the oldest part of the church, housing the tomb of San Miniato and 36 ancient and mismatched columns.

Bishop Ildebrando confirmed the bones interred here in the 11th century as those of Miniato, conveniently overlooking a well-documented account of how the "real" bones had earlier been removed to Metz in Germany.

Back in the main body of the church, steps lead up to the raised choir, where you're greeted by a superlative Romanesque **pulpit, screen,** and glittering apse **mosaic** of 1297. The last—as on the facade—portrays Christ between the Virgin and San Miniato. It's believed the same artist may have been responsible for both works. The crucifix above the high altar is attributed to Luca della Robbia, while the fine panel (1320) to the right of the altar, adorned with episodes from the life of San Miniato, is by an obscure Tuscan artist, Jacopo del Casentino. The corresponding panels (1354) left of the altar contain scenes from the life of St. Giovanni Gualberto. The artist

INSIDER TIP:

Travelers who like the quieter life should consider staying in the calm, shady Oltrarno neighborhood. It's away from the crowds yet close to the sights.

—PAT DANIELS
National Geographic contributor

is not known. Off to the right of the raised presbytery stands the sacristy, whose walls are covered in a memorable fresco cycle by Spinello Aretino (1345–1410) portraying episodes from the life of St. Benedict (1387).

In the lower part of the church, off the north aisle, is the **Cappella del Cardinale del Portogallo** (1473), which features the tomb of Iacopo di Lusitania, a young Portuguese scholar, cleric, and diplomat who died in Florence in 1459. Iacopo was the nephew of King Alfonso V of Portugal (*R.*1438–1481) and had been sent to Perugia, in central Italy, to study law. Later he became Archbishop of Lincoln, a cardinal, and ultimately ambassador to Florence. On his death in the city, his aunt and humanist friends in Florence united to pay for the chapel, making the cardinal the only person, San Miniato aside, buried in the church. This is an extraordinarily low number of tombs for a Florentine church; Santa Croce, by comparison, has well over 250.

The chapel is one of Italy's great Renaissance ensembles, a carefully unified composite of sculptures and paintings by Antonio Rossellino (1427–1479), Alesso Baldovinetti (1426–1499), and Luca della Robbia. Della Robbia's ceiling and the four glazed terracotta sculptures of the "Cardinal Virtues" (1461) are especially fine, and many of the individual details are worthy of special attention. Notice the grille behind the cardinal's effigy, a metaphor for the Gates of Paradise, and the empty judge's throne, an allusion to the Last Judgment. The angel holding the Virgin's crown symbolizes the cardinal's chastity, as do the unicorns, a reference to the belief that the mythical single-horned horse could only be captured by a virgin.

The chapel's main altarpiece painting is a copy of a work by Antonio and Piero del Pollaiuolo now in the Uffizi. Among other figures it includes a depiction of St. James, featured because he was the young cardinal's patron saint. ∎

The Tombs of Florence

Rich patrons or their family or followers often commissioned ornate tombs and chapels from the leading artists of their day, for the purpose of self-glorification, and also to ensure a safe passage to heaven. San Miniato, for example, has the tomb of Iacopo di Lusitania (see this page); Santa Trìnita (see pp. 156–157) and Santa Maria Novella (see pp. 150–155) have tombs and accompanying chapels frescoed by Ghirlandaio, among others, and paid for by bankers. In Santa Croce (see pp. 108–113), where you'll find the city's finest funerary art, the bankers' memorials—such as the ill-fated Cappella de' Pazzi—sit alongside monuments to scholars, artists, and scientists.

More Places to Visit in the Oltrarno

Marine wonders at Museo Zoologico-La Specola

Museo Bardini

The newly restored Museo Bardini takes its name from Stefano Bardini (1836–1922), the foremost art dealer of his day. Bardini sold major Italian works to many of the great galleries of Western Europe and North America. He also collected on his own behalf and built the museum for his hugely eclectic collection, which was bequeathed to Florence on his death. Bardini's methods were often questionable. An old church on the site was pulled down on his wishes, and much of the gallery's interior detailing was "salvaged" from medieval buildings around Tuscany.

The haphazard museum entices with a wealth of beautiful objects—paintings, ceramics, musical instruments, swords, armor, carpets, and more. Many of the artifacts packed into its 20 or more rooms are unlabeled and randomly displayed, allowing you to spend time wandering, inspecting, and admiring at will. Don't forget to visit the recently restored Bardini Gardens too (see sidebar p. 187).

🗺 Map pp. 166–167 ✉ Via de' Renai ☎ 055 234 2427 🕐 Closed Tues.–Thurs. (call for details) 💲 $$ 🚌 Bus: 23, D

Museo Zoologico-La Specola

The Zoological Museum, which forms part of the natural history museum of the University of Florence, was founded by Grand Duke Pietro Leopoldo in 1775. It occupies the third floor of a former astronomical observatory (*la specola* means "telescope," hence the museum's colloquial name). Most people come here not for the mounted animals but for its remarkable and often ghoulish collection of medical and other waxworks. They include about 1,400 beautifully crafted models of arms, legs, organs, and other body parts, an eye-opening obstetrics section, and a series of entire corpses in which every muscle, sinew, vein, and capillary has been splayed and displayed in loving detail. The collection was created as a teaching aid between 1775 and 1814.

Tucked away in one of the museum's side rooms, a four-piece wax tableau by a Sicilian cleric, Zumbo, shows vignettes of Florence during the plague. The tiny three-dimensional scenes show piles of variously rotted corpses, along with such details as rats gnawing on spilling intestines and mushrooms growing from putrefying flesh.

🗺 Map pp. 166–167 ✉ Via Romana 17 ☎ 055 228 8251 🕐 Closed Mon. 💲 $$ 🚌 Bus: 11, 36, 37, D

Santa Felicita

Santa Felicita is one of Florence's oldest churches. It was probably founded on the site of an early Christian cemetery and fourth-century basilica dedicated to Felicita, an early Christian martyr beheaded or thrown into boiling oil for refusing to renounce her faith. Archaeological evidence suggests the church lay close to the Via Cassia, an important Roman road to the south, and may have been the work of Greek and Syrian merchants responsible for introducing Christianity to the city. Rebuilding over the centuries culminated in the creation of the present church in 1739, and nothing remains to suggest the site's antiquity.

The church contains one of Florence's strangest paintings, Jacopo Pontormo's **"Deposition"** (1525–1528), which lies behind railings in the Brunelleschi-designed Cappella Capponi, or Cappella Barbardori, immediately on your right as you enter. Normally a painting on this theme—Christ being taken from the Cross—would contain the Cross itself, Roman soldiers, and the thieves crucified with Christ. Here all you see are an ethereal background cloud and an unrelated and vaguely androgynous group of figures (the brown-cloaked figure on the group's extreme right is believed to be a self-portrait of the artist). Many of the figures owe something to the sculptural forms of Michelangelo, but their extraordinary range of colors was unique at the time. Only Christ is painted with any attempt at verisimilitude; the rest of the painting is a bizarre palate of acid pink, electric blue, and puce green.

Pontormo's more restrained two-part **"Annunciation"** hangs on opposite sides of the window on the right-hand wall as you look at the chapel. Three of the four ceiling tondi (round paintings) of **"The Evangelists"** are also by Pontormo. The fourth, of St. Mark, is a copy of a work by Agnolo Bronzino, a painter who shared Pontormo's strange mannerist concerns (see p. 44). A Map pp. 166–167 ⊠ Piazza di Santa Felicita ☎ 055 213 018 🕒 Closed Sun. & daily 12:30 p.m.–3:30 p.m. 🚌 Bus: D

Santo Spirito

In its day, Santo Spirito was the most important church in the Oltrarno, giving its name to a quarter of the city. Architectural purists revel in the building, which is considered one of Filippo Brunelleschi's masterpieces; its interior, however, may seem rather too gloomy for modern tastes. Brunelleschi designed the church in 1434,

but construction started only in 1444, two years before his death. Work was more or less completed in 1487, obliterating virtually all traces of the 13th-century Augustinian church on the site.

Giardino Bardini

If Italian gardens are your passion, be sure to visit the recently restored Bardini Gardens in the Oltrarno (Museo Bardini, Via de' Renai, bardinipeyron.it; see p. 186).

The Bardini Gardens, located close to the eponymous museum and villa, have had a long and checkered history. They date back to at least the 13th century and passed through many hands before Stefano Bardini acquired them at the start of the 19th century. A long legal dispute following the death of Bardini's son in 1965 was only resolved in 2000, followed by five years of painstaking restoration that saw the garden and its fountains, parterres, "English" wood, and other areas transformed into a beautiful green enclave at the heart of the city.

Amid the welter of chapels and works of art, just two paintings stand out. The first is Filippo Lippi's "Madonna and Child with Saints" (1493–1494) in the south, or right, transept—second chapel from the left of the four chapels on its south, or back, wall. The other, in the left transept opposite, is the strange and unmistakable **"St. Monica and Augustinian Nuns,"** attributed to the little-known artist Francesco Botticini (1446–1497)—second chapel on the right wall as you stand with your back to the main body of the church. basilicasantospirito.it A Map pp. 166–167 ⊠ Piazza Santo Spirito 30 ☎ 055 210 030 🕒 Closed Wed. & daily 12:30 p.m.–4 p.m. 🚌 Bus: 36, 37, D

Tuscany

Europe's most perfect medieval city, whose myriad medieval charms
make it an ideal antidote to Florence's crowds and Renaissance finery

Siena

Enjoying *gelato classico* on Siena's
Via dei Rossi
Opposite: The Palazzo Pubblico and
Torre del Mangia dominate Il Campo.
Previous pages: The village of San
Gimignano in the heart of Tuscany

Siena

Siena is a medieval jewel. Intimate and manageable, the city is an immediately likeable place, crammed with art, culture, and outstanding churches and museums, and laced with countless quiet streets and hidden corners.

Myth claims that Siena was founded by Senius and Acius, sons of Remus—hence the statues around the city of the she-wolf who suckled Rome's mythical founders, Romulus and Remus. In fact, Siena—like Florence—began as an Etruscan settlement, evolving into a Roman colony, Saena Julia, at the beginning of the first century A.D. Flourishing banking and textile concerns in the Middle Ages then made it one of Europe's great medieval cities.

Its stature inevitably drew it into conflict with Florence. Siena's greatest triumph over its rival came in 1260 at the Battle of Montaperti, a contest fought a few miles east of the city. In 1348 the scales tipped the other way, when the Black Death wiped out 70,000 of Siena's 100,000-strong population (today's population is 56,000). Mortally wounded, the city struggled to retain its independence until 1554, when Montalcino, the last bastion of the Sienese Republic, surrendered to Florence and the Medici Grand Duke Cosimo I. Thereafter, Florence deliberately suppressed the city, whose decline is one of the reasons for its remarkably unsullied appearance today.

Nowhere is this unspoiled appearance more striking than in the Campo, or Piazza del Campo, the enthralling medieval square. The stage for Siena's centuries-old, twice-yearly horse race, the

NOT TO BE MISSED:

Exploring the Campo and taking a drink in the piazza 194–199

A visit to the Palazzo Pubblico's Museo Civico 195–199

Climbing the Torre del Mangia 198

Experiencing Siena's Palio 200–201

Duccio's "Maestà" at the Museo dell'Opera del Duomo 212–213

A leisurely Campo walk 218–219

Campo is enjoyable year-round for the Palazzo Pubblico, with its museum and panoramic tower.

After the Campo, the next natural target is another piazza, Piazza del Duomo. This is the setting for the city's ravishingly decorated cathedral and the Museo dell'Opera del Duomo (or Cathedral Museum), which in Duccio's painting of the "Maestà" has one of Europe's medieval masterpieces. More treasures await in the Pinacoteca Nazionale, a leading gallery and the

best place to see the changing styles of painting produced by Sienese artists over five centuries.

Take two or three days and you'll have time to visit Siena's major churches—San Domenico, San Francesco, and Santa Maria dei Servi—and to duck into smaller galleries such as the archaeological museum. You'll also have the chance to explore the secretive delights of its old streets and alleys. If you're staying in Siena, aim to be in the city center and book hotels well in advance. ∎

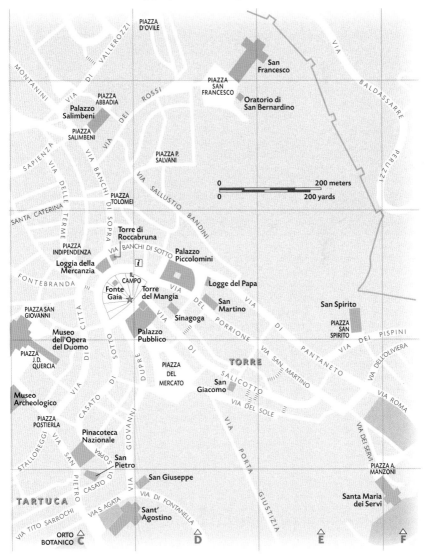

Il Campo

The Campo is a magnificent scallop-shaped square at the heart of Siena, a sweeping piazza ringed by soaring towers, huge palaces, and countless other medieval buildings. As well as being a natural meeting place, it is also the seat of the Palazzo Pubblico, housing one of Tuscany's foremost art galleries, and the setting for the city's famous twice-yearly Palio horse race.

The paving of the Piazza del Campo is divided into nine sections to symbolize the cloak of the Madonna and the Council of Nine, Siena's medieval rulers.

Siena

 192–193

Visitor Information

✉ Piazza del Campo 56

☎ 0577 280 551

🕐 Closed 1 p.m.–3 p.m. daily, Sat. p.m., Sun., & holidays

terresiena.it

Few Tuscan experiences are as memorable as the moment you first see the Campo. The huge, sloping space of its broad arena comes as a wonderful surprise after the city's narrow medieval streets. Today, the piazza's site appears naturally ordained, for it sits at the convergence of the city's three hilly spurs, at the meeting point of its three *terzi*, or traditional districts (literally, "thirds"). In truth, its emergence as the city's natural focus was a result of circumstance. When Siena's 13th-century ruling body,

the Council of Nine, began acquiring land in 1294 to create the square, this was the only central area that belonged to none of the terzi or *contrade* (parishes) and thus remained free of the rivalries that divide the city to this day.

The square was paved in brick and marble between 1327 and 1349, when the fan-shaped area of paving was divided into nine distinct portions, an arrangement that becomes clearer when seen from the vantage point of the Torre del Mangia, the piazza's colossal tower (see sidebar p. 198). The layout was designed both to recall the Council of Nine and to suggest the layers of the Madonna's cloak symbolically sheltering the city beneath its protective embrace. In this it evoked a type of medieval painting known as the "Madonna della Misericordia," a genre in which the Madonna is shown holding her open cloak over the members of a religious order or a town's inhabitants.

The Campo is incomparable as a general ensemble but lacks specific sights. The best thing to do is to enjoy its spectacle from one of the square's many cafés; be prepared for high prices. As you sip your drink, notice the **Fonte Gaia,** the fountain near the square's highest point, a 19th-century copy of a work by Jacopo della Quercia (see p. 43), one of Siena's greatest Renaissance sculptors (the original, removed to protect it from the elements, is in the Palazzo Pubblico's Museo Civico). Take in the largely Gothic **Cappella di Piazza,** the distinctive arched structure that juts from the foot of the Torre del Mangia. This was begun by the city's council in 1352 to mark the passing of the Black Death four years earlier. The upper level was added more than a century later, between 1463 and 1468, hence its distinctly different appearance.

Palazzo Pubblico

A door to the right of the Cappella di Piazza ushers you into the courtyard of the Palazzo Pubblico, the huge building beneath the **Torre del Mangia,** where you have a choice of climbing the tower (entrance on your left; see sidebar p. 198) or seeing the **Museo Civico,** which occupies the palace's upper floors (the ticket office is to your right).

Sala del Risorgimento: The Museo Civico starts in rather disappointing fashion with a lackluster five-room gallery of undistinguished paintings. Then comes the Sala del Risorgimento, a room decorated in the 19th century with pictures celebrating the exploits of Italy's first king, Vittorio Emanuele (R. 1861–1878), and his part in the Risorgimento, the 19th-century unification of Italy.

INSIDER TIP:

Climbing the Torre del Mangia's 503 steps might not leave you in the mood for viewing art, so see the Museo Civico first.

—TOM O'NEILL
National Geographic writer

Sala di Balia: With the next room, however, the Sala di Balia (or Sala dei Priori), the gallery quickly finds its feet. The Sala's walls are covered in paintings by Spinello Aretino (1345–1410) and his son, Parri, of the life of Alexander III, a pope born in Siena. Many of the pictures portray episodes from Alexander's long-running conflict with

Il Campo

⛰ 193 C3–D3

Museo Civico

✉ Piazza del Campo

☎ 0577 226 230

💲 $$, $$$ (combined ticket with Torre del Mangia)

museisenesi.org

Frederick Barbarossa, the Holy Roman Emperor. Note, in particular, the scene of the naval battle, which shows the Venetians—then allies of the pope—capturing the emperor's son and the efforts of the imperial forces to rescue him.

Anticamera del Concistoro:
The next room you come to is the Anticamera del Concistoro, or Sala dei Cardinali, noted chiefly for Ambrogio Lorenzetti's 14th-century detached fresco of "Three Saints and Donor" (by the entrance door). The donor was the person who commissioned a painting and was often depicted kneeling at the feet of the Virgin. The missing Madonna suggests this work was once part of a larger painting.

Sala del Concistoro: From here you move to the Sala del Concistoro, passing through a beautifully ornate marble doorway designed by Bernardo Rossellino

(1409–1464), an artist whose work you will see again if you visit the southern Tuscan town of Pienza (see pp. 274–276). The room's ceiling frescoes are the work of Domenico Beccafumi (1486–1551), Siena's most accomplished mannerist painter. The paintings portray episodes from Greek and Roman myth and history, but they were intended to symbolize or evoke parallels with the history and triumphs of Siena—as were virtually all the other works of art commissioned for the palace.

Vestibolo, Anticappella, & Cappella del Consiglio:
Turn back into the Anticamera and take the first door on your right into the Vestibolo to see, among other things, a gilded bronze statue by an unknown artist of the "She-Wolf Suckling the Twins Romulus and Remus" (1429). You'll see several similar

The Martini Mystery

For centuries, the large equestrian portrait of "Guidoriccio da Fogliano" in the Palazzo Pubblico's Sala del Mappamundo was attributed to Simone Martini. In recent years, however, it has become the subject of one of the bitterest disputes in Italian art history circles. The pro-Martini camp includes most of Siena and many Italian scholars. The anti-Martini group numbers several prominent foreign scholars, most notably American Gordon Moran, who for a time was banned from the palazzo and accused of being in the pay of the C.I.A.

The intricacies of the debate are complicated, but in essence boil down

to a question of timing: The picture was probably painted about 1328, which begs the question of why it is painted over (not under) a fresco to the right by Lippo Vanni, executed in 1364.

The controversy is still not settled, despite the arbitration of independent experts, but you'll probably find the debate irrelevant. The painting is a compelling work, whatever its authorship. It offers a strange but striking image of medieval chivalric endeavor, with Guidoriccio, a mercenary leader, portrayed setting forth to lay siege to a small walled village (probably present-day Montemassa, southwest of Siena).

statues around Siena, as ancient chroniclers believed Siena was founded by Senius and Acius, sons of Remus. The small room to the left of the Vestibolo is the Anticappella, which is adorned with frescoes by Taddeo di Bartolo (1362–1422) depicting "St. Christopher" and further scenes intended to glorify Siena by association with episodes from the past. Beyond the Anticappella lies the Cappella del Consiglio, with more frescoes by Taddeo—on the life of the Virgin—a fine set of inlaid wooden choir stalls, and a redoubtable wrought-iron screen, probably forged to a design by Jacopo della Quercia, both from the 15th century.

Sala del Mappamundo: From either the Vestibolo or Anticamera you walk into the Sala del Mappamundo, the museum's centerpiece, where you find two of the greatest—and most controversial—of all Sienese paintings. On the left wall as you enter the room is Simone Martini's sensational "Maestà" (1315), or "Madonna Enthroned," the first major work commissioned for the Palazzo and the first major work by a painter who would become—along with Duccio—Siena's most renowned artist (see p. 215). The work firmly links Siena with Christ and the Madonna: The Christ Child is shown holding a parchment that records the city's motto of Justice, and the steps below the Virgin's throne are emblazoned with two stanzas from Dante reminding onlookers that the Virgin will not protect those who betray

Watching the world pass by in Piazza del Campo

her or oppress the poor. The opposite (right) wall contains the controversial equestrian portrait of "Guidoriccio da Fogliano" (see sidebar opposite).

Other paintings in the room are less contentious, such as the pair of saints (1529) below the fresco by Giovanni Antonio Bazzi, or Sodoma (see p. 216), and two large scenes by Lippo Vanni and Cristofori Ghini, painted in 1364 and 1480 respectively, depicting Sienese military triumphs in the Val di Chiana and Poggio Imperiale (both in Tuscany). On the pillars below the latter are paintings by a

The Torre del Mangia

From the courtyard of the Palazzo Pubblico you can get your daily workout in by climbing the 503 steps of the 330-foot (102 m) Torre del Mangia (constructed 1338–1348; *Piazza del Campo, tel 0577 226 230, $$ or $$$ combined ticket with Museo Civico*), designed by a leading Sienese painter, Lippo Memmi (active 1317–1347). But remember, it's a challenging 503 steps to the top . . . and another 503 steps back down.

The bell tower was reputedly named after its first watchman and bell ringer, Giovanni da Balduccio, a notable *mangiaguadagni*, literally an "eater of profits," or profligate. Your climb will be well rewarded, as the views are magnificent.

The Torre del Mangia's sonorous bell was originally used to mark the end of the working day in Siena, as well as the opening and closing of the city gates in the morning and the evening.

trio of notable artists. From left to right these are Sodoma's "Blessed Tolomei," a portrait of the founder of the abbey at Monte Oliveto Maggiore (see pp. 266–267), "St. Bernardino" by Sano di Pietro (1406–1481), and "St. Catherine of Siena" by Vecchietta (1410–1480).

Sala della Pace: Most palace-museums would be content with the two masterpieces of the Sala del Mappamundo: not, however, the Palazzo Pubblico, whose last major room, the Sala della Pace, features one of Europe's great secular (non-religious) fresco cycles—Ambrogio Lorenzetti's "Allegories of Good and Bad Government" (1338). The two large frescoes show the effects of good and bad civic rule on a city clearly intended to represent Siena, graphically illustrating these effects with fascinating contemporary details and activities—dancing, farming, building, and many more. The paintings work wonderfully well on the level of simple narrative; note, for example, the executed bandits in the countryside, hanged by Good Government. But they also contain more complicated meanings, which would have been clearly understood by Siena's more educated citizens. In the fresco of Good Government, for example, the throned figure represents Siena's Comune, or council, and is garbed in the city's colors to make the point more strongly.

The Virtues are portrayed as figures to his side and include the reclining white-robed figure of Peace (*pace* in Italian), from whom the room takes its name; Faith, Hope, and Charity circle the throned figure's head. To the left, you see the seated figure of Justice (with Wisdom shown above) dispensing punishment and reward; Harmony is below, advising politicians of their civic responsibilities. In Bad Government, by contrast, the central figure is Fear (or the devil) surrounded by the Vices, the effects of his reign made abundantly clear in the painting's ravaged crops, scenes of robbery, garbage-strewn streets, and tumbledown buildings.

Sala dei Pilastri/Sala delle Colonne: One more room remains to be discovered beyond the Sala della Pace. This is the Sala dei Pilastri, which is also known as the Sala delle Colonne. Here, the works worth seeking out are "Massacre of the Innocents" by Matteo di Giovanni (1435–1490), a most graphic and violent depiction of the slaughter of the first-born children as ordered by King Herod of Judea; Guido da Siena's "Maestà" (probably created circa 1261), in which the face of the Madonna is believed to have been painted by Duccio

di Buoninsegna; and Neroccio di Bartolomeo's (1447–1500) "St. Bernardino Preaching in the Campo," which is interesting for the detail that shows Bernardino's listeners chastely separated by a sheet into groups of men and women. ∎

INSIDER TIP:

Siena's Campo is certainly where the action is, but be sure to wander the medieval alleys beyond to get a sense of the city's quieter side.

—BARBARA A. NOE
*National Geographic
Travel Books senior editor*

The Fonte Gaia (Fountain of Joy) provides avian refreshment in the Piazza del Campo.

Palio

The twice-yearly Palio is Italy's most dramatic pageant. A spectacular bareback horse race, it involves just three laps of the Campo, but the excitement, processions, drumming, flag-waving, and colorful spectacle associated with the event can go on for months. This makes it far more than an exhibition created for the sake of visitors, for the race is a living embodiment of rivalries and traditions that have been played out for more than 700 years.

Riders make three circuits of the Campo in the Siena Palio. The race lasts just 90 seconds.

The Palio has been run in some form since the 13th century. In its infancy it was run around the city streets; the three-lap circuit of the Campo was only instigated in 1656. The prize, though, has always been the embroidered banner, or *pallium,* from which the race takes its name. The dedication, to the Virgin, has remained inviolate and this is why the races are run on July 2 and August 16, feast days devoted to the Madonna. The race is a vivid expression of the rivalries between Siena's *contrade,* the parishlike

districts into which the city has long been divided. Today there are 17 contrade, fewer than in times past, when Siena has had as many as 42. Each *contrada* has its own church, social club, heraldic device, museum, flag, and symbolic animal that often lends the contrada its name. Allegiance to a contrada is absolute: Baptism of a contrada baby, for example, is held in the contrada church and is followed by baptism in the child's contrada fountain. Each contrada also holds its own yearly procession and supports a band of drummers *(tamborini)* and flag-throwers *(alfieri)*; you'll often see drummers going through their drills on the streets.

Preparations & Race Day: The ten contrade that can take part in the Palio are drawn by lot. Riders from the other contrade get to accompany the Carroccio, or chariot, that parades the pallium in the prerace procession. This procession is just one area in which skulduggery can bear fruit. All the contrade are fiercely independent, but each also has its own special rival, and much planning goes into ensuring a rival's humiliation. Alliances are forged and bribes arranged. Horses may be doped, and it's even been known for men and animals to be kidnapped. Riders and animals are therefore watched day and night. Religion also plays its part, namely in the blessing of horses and riders in the contrada churches: *"Va' e torna vincitore,"* intones the priest—"Go, and return the winner."

On race day, all but one of the horses and its rider gather for the 90-second dash at

Members of the Contrada dell'Onda celebrate triumph in the twice-yearly Palio.

around 7 p.m. The race begins when the lone rider charges his rivals. The only rule is that jockeys can't interfere with another rider's reins. The race is hectic, fast, violent, and dangerous, both for riders and horses: Sand and mattresses are laid out to help prevent serious injury. Defeat is acrimonious, and rumors and memories of dark doings can fester for years.

EXPERIENCE: Revel in the Frenzy of the Palio

Siena reaches fever pitch in the three days before the Palio, when the prerace rituals begin in earnest. Spectacle, noise, and color fill the streets and squares. The different **contrade** (parishes) deck the streets with their flags and banners. Parades of drummers in medieval costume march through the streets, and parties go on long into the night. Horses are chosen in public and then blessed in **contrada** churches.

On race day, you can sit in reserved seating around the Campo or file into the Campo. For the Campo, arrive early and be prepared to spend many hours on your feet, with no shade and little likelihood of being able to escape the hyperactive throng. The race does not run on a timetable—despite an official "starting time"—as part of the strategy of the race is

for some riders to false-start deliberately, thus spooking and tiring rival horses that are known to be skittish. Preliminaries to the race, even with the horses and riders in the Campo, can therefore go on for hours.

After the race, the atmosphere in the Campo becomes even more frenzied. People rush to try to touch the winning horse (for good luck in matters sexual), and losing contrade vent their disappointment on their jockeys. As the evening wears on, the winning contrada celebrates with an enormous outdoor street banquet.

Seats in the reserved seating (like the city's hotels) are booked months in advance and are very expensive. The visitor center (see p. 194) offers leads on how to secure these seats, but it is often easier to go through a ticket agency such as **Liaisons Abroad** *(liaisonsabroad.com)*.

Duomo

Siena's Duomo is one of Italy's most beautiful cathedrals. Superior to that of Florence in all respects—artistic and architectural—save for Brunelleschi's dome, it contains statues by Michelangelo, a sublime pulpit, gorgeous frescoes, and countless other outstanding paintings and sculptures.

Much of Siena's cathedral is built in the Gothic style, such as the facade; the marble-striped bell tower is Romanesque.

The building rises at one of the city's highest points, the site's exalted position having long made it a place of special significance. One of the city's most important Roman shrines, a temple to Minerva, was probably built here, and a Christian church existed nearby in the ninth century, possibly earlier. The present cathedral is traditionally said to have been consecrated in 1179 by the Siena-born pope, Alexander III, although the bulk of the construction work was completed in 1215. The cupola was added between 1259 and 1264, and the lower part of the extraordinary **facade** was created by the eminent Pisan sculptor Giovanni Pisano (see p. 40) in the years up to 1296. Many of Pisano's statues and other sculptures have been replaced with copies, the originals having been moved to the nearby Museo dell'Opera del Duomo (see pp. 211–213).

Save for the odd additional flourish, 1296 might have marked the end of the building's history. By 1339, however, the growth in Siena's population and wealth, and the desire to emulate the cathedral of the city's hated Florentine rivals, prompted the start of the so-called Duomo Nuovo, or New Cathedral. If realized, this would have been the largest church of its day.

But the scheme was defeated by political upheavals and the chaotic and impoverished aftermath of the Black Death of 1348. A hint of what might have been can be seen to the right of the cathedral as you look at it: The outline and partly finished stone frame of the proposed nave are still visible.

Thwarted in their ambitions, the Sienese decided to make do with the original building, adding

INSIDER TIP:

Don't miss the annual Cinghiale ("wild boar") Festival held in June in Vescovado di Murlo, a few miles south of Siena—a feast of many boar-based foods.

—MEREDITH WILCOX
National Geographic Books, director of administration & rights clearance

finishing touches to the apse (the area behind the high altar) and completing the upper part of the facade (1376) in the ornate style of the cathedral in Orvieto, a town a few miles away in the neighboring region of Umbria. The three upper mosaics were added in the 19th century by Venetian mosaicists.

A Wealth of Artworks: Unlike Florence's cathedral, whose interior is relatively unadorned, Siena's cathedral dazzles with its wealth of interior works of art. Almost the first thing you notice are the countless sculptured heads around the upper walls. These are 15th- and 16th-century works that represent 172 different popes and—at intervals below—36 assorted Holy Roman Emperors. Less immediately eye-catching, but infinitely more precious, is the cathedral's **pavement,** or floor, which is covered in a series of 56 *graffito* (incised) marble panels. Many—sadly—are kept covered to protect them from wear and tear. The first were created about 1369

Duomo

- 192 B2
- Piazza del Duomo
- 0577 286 300
- Closed Sun. a.m. & during services
- $$$ (when the Duomo sidewalk is uncovered), $$$$ (combined ticket with baptistery, Museo dell'Opera del Duomo, and crypt)

operaduomo.siena.it

NOTE: Tickets for the Duomo must be bought at the Museo dell'Opera del Duomo ticket office (see pp. 211–213).

EXPERIENCE: Discover the Secrets of Sienese Food

Siena is a singular city, with its own food and wine specialties. You can learn more with the Siena-based **Tuscan Wine School** (*Via Stalloreggi 26, tel 0577 221 704, tuscanwineschool.com*). On its two-hour, no-need-for-lunch "Savor Siena Walk" (*Mon.–Sat., noon–2 p.m., €40*) you'll drop into tucked-away stores and meet artisanal makers to sample oil, saffron, wine, chocolate, cheeses, and salami, along with coffee from the city's best

barista. You'll learn about truffles and how they're found, how balsamic vinegar is made, why Tuscan bread is saltless, why the Cinta Senese pig is so celebrated, the stories behind Siena's *panforte* and *ricciarelli* desserts, and the intricacies of Italian coffee culture.

You should note that this is a food tour and not a guided historical and cultural walk of the city. Two-hour wine classes are also available.

and feature simple geometric patterns. The last one, dated 1547, is far more ornate. In all, some 40 artists, including most of the leading Sienese painters of their day, provided designs for the panels' complex biblical, allegorical, and secular narratives.

Several key works stand out among the plethora of other paintings and sculptures around the walls. The first is the staggering **pulpit** toward the end of the nave on the left, with its celebrated bas-reliefs of the life of Christ. It was the work of Nicola Pisano (see p. 41), father of Giovanni Pisano, the sculptor responsible for much of the facade. Giovanni assisted his father on the project, along with Arnolfo di Cambio, the architect of Florence's cathedral, and in doing so helped to create one of the supreme masterpieces of Italian medieval sculpture.

The second notable work of art is another piece of sculpture, the so-called **Piccolomini Altarpiece,** on the north (left) side of the church to the left of the entrance to the Libreria Piccolomini (see opposite). Much of its elegant sculpture is by Andrea Bregno (1421–1506), an accomplished, if second-rank, sculptor. What lends the piece a special importance is the fact that

The dramatic frescoes in the Libreria Piccolomini by Umbrian artist Pinturicchio

four of the statues in the lower niches—Sts. Gregory and Paul on the right, Peter and Pius on the left—are the work of the young Michelangelo.

The Frescoes: The interior's third and most lavish work of art is the **Libreria Piccolomini,** or Piccolomini Library, which is decorated with a fresco cycle by the Umbrian artist Pinturicchio (1454–1513). The area was originally set aside in 1495 by Cardinal Francesco Piccolomini, later Pope Pius III (whose reign lasted just ten days), to house the library of his Tuscan-born uncle, Enea Silvio Piccolomini, better known as Pope Pius II (1405–1464).

The frescoes, which are remarkably well preserved, retaining their vibrant colors, depict ten episodes from the life of Pope Pius II and may owe something to the hand of Raphael, who is believed to have assisted Pinturicchio with their initial design. Raphael lived and worked in neighboring Umbria for several years, where he was the pupil of Pinturicchio's fellow Umbrian master, Perugino.

The paintings trace Pius's secular and religious careers and are typical of Pinturicchio's delightful narrative style, being full of detail, color, and incident. The cycle starts to the right of the window with Pius's diplomatic career, beginning in panel 1 with his attendance at the Council of Basle as secretary to an Italian bishop; the storm scene here is one of the first in Western art. Panel 2 depicts Pius

presenting himself as an envoy to King James II of Scotland (*R.*1437–1460); panel 3, his coronation as a poet laureate in 1442 by the Holy Roman Emperor, Frederick III (*R.*1440–1493); and panel 4, his representing Frederick on a mission to Pope Eugenius IV (*R.*1431–1437).

INSIDER TIP:

A fraction of those visiting Siena's Duomo also go to see the baptistery, but its frescoes and sculpture make it essential viewing.

—MARINA CONTI
National Geographic Italy editor

Panel 5 shows Pius—by now Bishop of Siena—at a meeting between Frederick III and his prospective bride, Eleanora of Portugal, held by Siena's Porta Camollia. Panels 6 and 7 detail Pius's promotion to cardinal in 1456 and pope in 1458, followed in panel 8 by his proclamation in 1459 in the northern Italian city of Mantua of an ultimately unsuccessful crusade to retake Constantinople (now Istanbul) from the Turks. Panel 9 shows his canonization of St. Catherine of Siena in 1461, and panel 10 his arrival and death in Ancona on Italy's eastern coast, a town he visited to encourage the troops about to depart for his crusade. His death in 1464, it is said, may have been brought on by

Libreria Piccolomini

✉ Piazza del Duomo

☎ 0577 283 048

🕐 Closed Sun. a.m. Nov.–March

💲 $, or $$ with Biglietto Cumulativo, which covers Libreria Piccolomini, baptistery, & Museo dell'Opera del Duomo

Hot-air ballooning over the bare clay hills of the Sienese Crete

poison administered by soldiers disenchanted with their mission.

Other Highlights: At the center of the room stands a famous statue of the "Three Graces," a Roman copy of a Greek original that inspired artists such as Raphael and the neoclassical sculptor Antonio Canova (1757–1822), who sculptured his own version of the Three Graces, now in London's Victoria and Albert Museum. Also exhibited in the room are several illustrated 15th-century miniatures and choir books from the Duomo and Ospedale di Santa Maria della Scala (see pp. 208–210).

Turn left out of the library and move down the north (left) wall and you turn into the left transept, where the circular chapel in the corner, the **Cappella di San Giovanni,** contains more frescoes (1504) by Pinturicchio, a lovely 15th-century font, and a statue of St. John the Baptist by Donatello. Donatello was also responsible for a bronze pavement tomb of Bishop Giovanni Pecci, positioned just past the transept in the angle on the right beyond Pisano's pulpit. On the wall above is Tino di Camaino's (1285–1337) tomb of Cardinal Riccardo Petroni, a work that had a great influence on funerary sculpture during much of the 14th century.

Next walk across the church to

the high altar, which is topped by a large bronze altarpiece (1476) by Vecchietta, one of the finest of Siena's Renaissance artists and sculptors. The work was originally housed in the nearby Ospedale di Santa Maria della Scala but was brought to the cathedral in 1506, when it replaced Duccio's "Maestà" as the altar's centerpiece.

Continue to the right transept to see the circular **Cappella della Madonna del Voto,** or Cappella Chigi, a highly ornate work designed by the Roman baroque master Gian Lorenzo Bernini (1598–1680). Bernini also created the gilded bronze angels and the figures of St. Giralomo and Mary Magdalene by the chapel entrance. *Voto* means "votive," hence the many votive offerings—thanks or pleas for intercession by the Virgin—that cover the walls.

The Baptistery

Outside the cathedral lies the **Battistero di San Giovanni,** the Baptistery of St. John. Unlike Florence, Siena did not build a separate baptistery. It is part of the cathedral and is reached by walking along the right side of the building as you face the facade and down the steps straight ahead of you. The entrance lies on your left in Piazza San Giovanni at the foot of the steps.

The small admission charge is well worth paying, for inside stands an unexpected artistic bonus: the 15th-century baptistery font, with bronze reliefs by three of the leading sculptors of their day—Sienese Jacopo della Quercia ("The Announcement of the Baptist's Birth"), Florentine Lorenzo Ghiberti ("The Baptism of Christ" and "St. John in Prison"), and Donatello (the panel of "Herod's Feast" and the tabernacle's sculptured angels). Also well worth the price of admission are the many 15th-century frescoes including the Apostles and an "Assumption," most of which are by Vecchietta. ∎

Battistero di San Giovanni

✉ Piazza San Giovanni

☎ $ or $$$ with Opasi Pass, which covers the Duomo, baptistery, crypt, & Museo dell'Opera del Duomo

EXPERIENCE: Take a Hot-Air Balloon Trip Over Siena

Balloon trips are more than magical in Tuscany, for you can get a bird's-eye view of the beauty of a city such as Siena, peering down on sights like the Duomo. You can also view wonderful hill towns, seeing their medieval plans and buildings from a different perspective, and enjoy huge panoramas of some of the most beautiful landscapes in Europe.

Balloon in Tuscany (*tel 055 807 7940, balloonintuscany.com*) has some 20 years of experience ballooning in the region. Among its newest flight routes are trips over Florence and flights that can accommodate wheelchair users. Its most popular long-running flights are over Siena and parts of Chianti; the latter is the one to choose if you want to experience the best Tuscan landscapes. The British-owned-and-run **Ballooning in Tuscany** (*tel 338 146 2994, ballooningtuscany.com*) offers takeoffs from close to Siena; it also flies from Montisi, which allows for flights over the sublime scenery of the Crete, Pienza, the Val d'Orcia, and other parts of southern Tuscany. A third option, in the Val di Chiana, allows for flights if you're based in or around Cortona.

Santa Maria della Scala

Until the 1990s, Santa Maria della Scala had served as Siena's principal hospital for almost a thousand years. Today, it is being converted into the city's main art and cultural center, providing a home for exhibitions and a unique setting for some of the superb works of art—notably an outstanding fresco cycle—commissioned for the hospital over the centuries.

A fresco shows Mary and Jesus attended by St. John the Baptist and St. Zeno.

Santa Maria della Scala

🅼 192 B2
✉ Piazza del Duomo 1
☎ 0577 534 571
💲 $$

santamariadellascala .com

Legend claims Santa Maria was founded by Beato Sorere, a ninth-century cobbler and monk renowned for his work among orphans and abandoned children. Sorere was actually a mythical figure, his name probably a corruption of the Italian word *suore* (nuns), a reference to the members of religious orders who tended the sick and orphaned as part of their religious vocation.

The first written reference to the institution comes in 1090, when its development was prompted by the huge numbers of pilgrims traveling the Via Francigena, a major medieval pilgrimage route between Rome and northern Europe. The road ran beneath Siena's walls, its presence one reason for the city's early growth. All manner of inns and resting places *(ospedali)* grew up along the route to provide "hospitality" to pilgrims, with 40 in Sienese territory alone. Hospital work in the modern sense—caring for the sick—came later.

Bequests of money to what for centuries was known as the Ospedale di Santa Maria della Scala turned it into one of the city's wealthiest and most important institutions. Part of its income was diverted to artistic and other ends, including the purchase of saints' relics—of which Santa Maria has a bewildering collection—and the construction of the long stone bench outside the building, which was used to provide shade for the hospital's dignitaries during long civic and other ceremonies. More significant commissions included the major paintings inside the hospital, the main reason for a visit today.

The Madonna & Her Cloak

Domenico di Bartolo's "Madonna della Misericordia" in Santa Maria della Scala's Sagrestia Vecchia portrays a theme—the Virgin casting a protective cloak over people and places—that is common across central Tuscany: In Siena you can see examples by Simone Martini and Giovanni di Paolo in the Pinacoteca Nazionale (see pp. 214–217) and Santa Maria dei Servi (see p. 222), respectively. It derives from a vision of the Virgin experienced by a ninth-century Cistercian monk, and at first only members of religious orders were depicted: monks to one side, nuns to the other. Later, religious confraternities were included, and eventually townspeople, though always segregated. Bartolo's version, where the population is mixed, is unusual.

Sala del Pellegrinaio: The most important of these art works are found in the Sala del Pellegrinaio, covered in an outstanding fresco cycle (1440–1443) by Domenico di Bartolo and several other artists. Each of the cycle's eight major panels portrays aspects of the hospital's history and work. The secular content is extraordinary for a painting of this period—at the height of the Renaissance—a time when most works of art had a predominantly religious slant.

Beginning at the far wall on the left, the first panel—the work of Sienese artist Vecchietta—describes "The Dream of the Mother of Beato Sorere." This depicts the vision in which Sorere's mother sees her son's future work with Santa Maria's abandoned children, who are shown climbing a ladder (scala) to Paradise and the arms of the Madonna. A ladder, or step, provided the hospital with its name and symbol, perhaps for the proximity of the cathedral's steps or because a three-rung ladder, seen as a symbol of the Trinity (Father, Son, and Holy Ghost), was found during its construction. Stages of this construction are shown in the ward's second fresco. The third fresco depicts the "Investiture of the Hospital Rector," while the fourth shows Pope Celestine III (R.1191–1198) awarding Santa Maria the right to elect this rector, a vital point in the hospital's history, for it transferred control of the institution from the city's religious guardians to its lay authorities. The paintings on the end wall are later 16th-century works, but they portray a fascinating aspect of the hospital's work, the employment of wet nurses to suckle the huge numbers of orphans cared for by the hospital. The nurses are being paid in cash on the right and grain on the left.

Moving to the ward's other long wall, you come to the cycle's fifth and most celebrated panel, "The Tending of the Sick"; notice the monk on the right hearing the confession of a patient before surgery. To the right of this panel, the sixth fresco shows "The Distribution of Charity"—bread being given to the poor—and the next panel illustrates how the hospital provided for the reception of young girls from an early age, along with their subsequent education and marriage. You can see wet nurses

A Magical Musical Week

Siena's first Settimana Musicale, or Musical Week, was organized in 1939 and similar weeks have been a feature of the city's cultural life ever since. They take place in July and are organized by the Accademia Musicale Chigiana (tel 0577 22 091, chigiana .it) from its palazzo headquarters at Via di Città 89: Most concerts are held in the palazzo or its courtyard. If you can't be in the city in July, the Accademia organizes **Micat in Vertice,** a series of chamber, small ensemble, and solo recitals (usually mid-Nov.– mid-April) and the **Estate Musicale Chigiana,** a far-ranging classical music festival throughout much of July and August.

in action on the left, along with other scenes to suggest weaning, learning, and play. The eighth and final painting shows the feeding of the poor and elderly, but it is less convincing than other scenes, largely because of the unfortunately sited window. It's said this was built by a lazy 19th-century supervisor so he could watch over his patients

without going down to the ward.

Close to the Sala del Pellegrinaio is a tiny vestibule, or **Cappella del Manto,** beyond the ticket office, which contains a lovely fresco of "St. Anne and St. Joachim" (1512), the parents of the Virgin Mary, by Sienese mannerist artist Domenico Beccafumi. The pair are shown kissing, a moment that symbolizes the Immaculate Conception of the Virgin.

Also beyond the sala on the left is the **Sagrestia Vecchia,** or Old Sacristy, which has a fresco cycle by Vecchietta illustrating the "Articles of the Creed." This is less impressive than the cycle you've just seen and rather more difficult to understand without a sound biblical knowledge. Each panel shows an Apostle holding one of the Articles, while the accompanying fresco contains a story from the Old Testament that illustrates the text. Domenico di Bartolo's fine altarpiece here of the "Madonna della Misericordia" (1444; see sidebar p. 209) shows the Virgin casting a protective cloak over Siena's citizens.

Vecchietta features again in Santa Maria's church, **Santissima Annunziata,** where he was responsible for the high altar's bronze statue of the "Risen Christ" (1476). Down in the depths of the building, be sure to see the **Oratorio di Santa Caterina della Notte,** a gloomy but atmospheric oratory whose highlight is Taddeo di Bartolo's glorious triptych (three-paneled painting) of the "Madonna and Child with St. Andrew and St. John the Baptist" (1400). ■

Museo dell'Opera del Duomo

The Museo dell'Opera del Duomo houses works of art removed for safekeeping from Siena's cathedral over the centuries. Among these are a wide variety of sculptures, some lovely pictures, and one of the greatest of all early European medieval paintings, Duccio di Buoninsegna's "Maestà." The museum also offers magnificent views over the city.

The Sala delle Statue contains works removed from the facade of the Duomo for safekeeping.

The museum, to the right and rear of the cathedral as you face it, is housed in a building that occupies what would have been part of the nave of the 14th-century Duomo Nuovo (see pp. 202–203). The first room you come to on the ground floor is the **Sala delle Statue,** or Hall of the Statues. At its center, ahead of you, are two sculptural masterpieces. The first is a delicate honey-colored relief of the "Madonna and Child" by Florentine sculptor Donatello (removed from one of the cathedral's doorways); the second is a relief of the "Madonna and Child with St. Girolamo" by Jacopo della Quercia, Siena's leading Renaissance sculptor (1374–1438). Around the walls stand sculptured prophets and other figures (1284–1296) by Giovanni Pisano; removed from the cathedral facade, the group ranks among Europe's most significant Gothic sculptural ensembles. If the figures seem oddly distorted, remember they were designed to be viewed from below and at a distance—hence the irregularities. Similar considerations accounted for the physical distortions in Michelangelo's "David" in Florence.

Museo dell'Opera del Duomo

🅰 193 C2

✉ Piazza del Duomo 8

☎ 0577 283 048

💲 $$ or $$$$ with Opasi Pass, which covers the Duomo, baptistery, crypt, & Museo dell'Opera del Duomo

operaduomo.siena.it

The "Maestà" by Duccio di Buoninsegna in the Museo dell'Opera del Duomo

The "Maestà": Stairs from the museum's lower level then lead you to the **Sala di Duccio,** whose low, almost reverential light is designed to protect one of Italy's most marvelous paintings, the "Maestà" by Duccio di Buoninsegna (see p. 215). Painted on two sides, and with no fewer than 45 accompanying panels, this was, as far as scholars can tell, the most expensive painting ever commissioned at the time. Duccio was an unruly character, if his many fines for various misdemeanors are anything to go by, and it took him some four years to finish the work. On completion, it was accounted a masterpiece and paraded around the Campo en route for the cathedral, where it was inaugurated with a special Mass.

The painting's main subject is the "Madonna Enthroned," or "Maestà" (Italian for "majesty"), a form of painting in which the Virgin is depicted as the Queen of Heaven surrounded by a heavenly court of saints and angels. The genre was a Sienese invention. You can see similar paintings—to name but two examples—by Simone Martini in Siena's Palazzo Pubblico (see p. 197) and the Museo Civico in San Gimignano (see pp. 235–239), a village that once formed part of Sienese territory. The preoccupation with the Virgin was no accident, for she had been declared the patroness and protector of the city on the eve of a famous Sienese victory over the Florentines at Montaperti in 1260.

Every Italian town and village had a patron. Some covered themselves by appointing several protectors, hence Siena's quartet of "secondary" patrons—Sts. Ansano, Savino, Crescenzio, and Vittore—who stand in the front rank of characters before Duccio's Virgin. The picture's abundance of detached panels, each a tiny masterpiece of narrative and detail, describe 19 episodes from the lives of Christ and the Virgin, and 26 scenes from the Passion, the events leading up to Christ's Crucifixion. Unfortunately, the entire painting was dismembered in 1771 and its panels dispersed before the picture was moved to the museum in 1887.

Most have since been recovered, with only a handful still in foreign hands. These overseas owners—to understandable Sienese indignation—refuse to release them to restore one of the world's masterpieces. The guilty parties include London's National Gallery (three panels), the National Gallery of Art in Washington, D.C. (two), and the Frick and Rockefeller collections in New York (three).

Other Highlights: The "Maestà" rather overshadows the room's other highlights, which include a "Madonna and Child," an early work by Duccio; the "Nativity of the Virgin," a late endeavor by Pietro Lorenzetti; and a series of sculptures in side rooms that feature works by Jacopo della Quercia. Another room has 19th-century drawings of the designs on the pavement of the cathedral.

Steps then lead you to the **Sala del Tesoro,** where the most captivating works are the 13th-century "Reliquary of San Galgano," one of many religious artifacts here, and Giovanni's tiny wooden statue of the "Crucifixion" (1280). The latter shows Christ on a strange Y-shaped tree growing from the skull of Adam. This alludes to the Tree of Life, or Tree of Knowledge, which in the apocryphal biblical story grew from a shoot planted in the dead Adam's mouth and was eventually used to make the cross of Christ's Crucifixion. The story is the same one told in Piero della Francesca's famous fresco cycle in Arezzo (see pp. 284–287).

Moving on, you enter the **Sala della Madonna dagli Occhi Grossi,** or Hall of the Madonna of the Large Eyes, named after a striking work here by an unknown 13th-century painter; it occupied the cathedral's high altar before being ousted by Duccio's "Maestà." Before the Battle of Montaperti in 1260, Siena's entire population came to pray before this painting, asking for protection and pledging themselves to the Virgin Mary.

INSIDER TIP:

Try to see Siena from the ramparts of the Museo dell'Opera del Duomo. The views across the medieval rooftops toward the Tuscan hills haven't changed in centuries.

—LARRY PORGES
National Geographic Travel Books editor

Don't miss other paintings in the same room, notably several works by Sano di Pietro (1406–1481): These include "St. Bernardino of Siena Preaching in the Campo" and "St. Bernardino Preaching in Piazza San Francesco"—both interesting for their contemporary views of Siena—and a "Madonna and Child with St. Apollonia," the patron saint of dentists. Rooms beyond this *sala* contain paintings from later periods, among which the works of Domenico Beccafumi stand out. The museum's grand finale is provided by the magnificent views from its exterior ramparts; follow signs for the Panorama. ■

Pinacoteca Nazionale

Siena's artists developed a distinctive style, or school, of painting in the centuries before the Renaissance. Examples of their art are scattered across Tuscany and beyond, but the single best place to study both the range and the development of their work is the city's Pinacoteca Nazionale, or National Art Gallery.

The gallery has been housed in the impressive 14th-century Palazzo Buonsignori since 1932. Be warned, however, that the arrangement of paintings is often altered, and over the next few years various exhibits may be moved to as yet unfinalized locations elsewhere in the city—probably to Santa Maria della Scala (see pp. 208–210). Whatever the collection's final destination, its basic chronological order and its main highlights will remain the same.

The lower of the gallery's two principal floors is often used for temporary exhibitions. The main upper floor, by contrast, traces the roots of Sienese art. It begins with its origins in Byzantine art, whose stylized appearance, austere and formal beauty, and fondness for gold backgrounds continued to infuse the city's paintings long after such attributes had been abandoned by Florence's more forward-thinking artists. Highlights of this early period include a "Crucifix" from the end of the 12th century, removed from the church of San Pietro in Villore, and three scenes from the life of Christ (1280) by Guido da Siena. The latter picture is one of the earliest known works painted on canvas as opposed to wood. Despite

"Prophet" by Sassetta

this hint of innovation, Guido's work still looked for inspiration to Byzantine art, as its jewel-studded surface—a Byzantine device—makes clear.

Duccio & Martini

Successive rooms move on to the work of Duccio di Buonin-segna (1255–1318), who, with Simone Martini, was the most eminent of Siena's plethora of artists. He is also widely considered by art historians as the last of the great medieval painters before the more naturalistic work of pioneers such as Giotto. As a painter he was much respected in his own time, but if the heavy fines imposed on him by the city are anything to go by, he led a far from blameless life. His greatest masterpiece, the "Maestà," is elsewhere in the city (see p. 212), but **Rooms 3** and **4** feature several other preeminent works, including the tiny but lauded "Madonna dei Francesani" and a polyptych, or multipaneled painting, of the "Madonna and Child with St. Agnes, St. John, St. John the Baptist, and Mary Magdalene."

Hard on the heels of these paintings come two diverting pictures by Duccio's pupil, Simone Martini (circa 1284–1344), an artist whose lyrical and courtly style produced some of the most beautiful of all 14th-century Italian paintings. According to the Renaissance critic Giorgio Vasari, the Sienese themselves considered him the finest of all their painters. Look for his "Madonna and Child," removed from the parish church of Lucignano d'Arbia, a village just south of Siena, and the picture depicting "The Miracles of Beato Agostino," removed from the church of Sant'Agostino (see sidebar this page) in Siena. Look for works by Lippo Memmi, Simone Martini's brother-in-law, a leading painter in his own right—although the two often worked in partnership on the same painting.

The Lorenzetti Brothers

The next major artists represented—and note numerous lesser names are interspersed with these highlights—are Pietro and Ambrogio Lorenzetti, brothers who probably perished in the 1348 Black Death (see sidebar p. 216). Like Martini, the pair established a reputation far beyond the walls of their native city; both, however, showed greater concern with naturalistic forms than the more lyrical Martini.

Pinacoteca Nazionale

🄰 193 C2

✉ Via San Pietro 29

☎ 0577 281 161 or 0577 286 143

🕒 Closed p.m. Sun. & Mon.

💲 $$

A Peaceful Refuge

Just a few moments' walk from the Pinacoteca Nazionale is a delightful and peaceful corner of Siena centered on the trees and green spaces around Sant'Agostino (begun 1258). Long closed to the public, this church, one of the city's richest, is now open part of the year (Mon.–Sat. 2 p.m.–5 p.m. mid-March–Oct., $) and well worth visiting. Like most Augustinian churches it was built near the city walls as the Augustinians came late to church building, when space in town centers was no longer available. Inside, the many fine paintings include works by Perugino, Sodoma, Signorelli, and Ambrogio Lorenzetti.

The Plague in Siena

The Black Death of 1348 affected Siena disproportionately badly: Its grandiose new cathedral was abandoned (see pp. 202–203), key painters such as Ambrogio Lorenzetti died, and though the city would know subsequent periods of prosperity, it was never the same again. The pre-1348 population figure has barely been reached today. After the plague, Agnolo di Tura, who lost all five of his children, wrote that "everyone thought himself rich because he had escaped and lived according to his own caprice, seeking only pleasure, eating and drinking, hunting, catching birds, and gaming."

Pietro's outstanding painting here is the "Carmine Altarpiece" (1329), parts of which, like Duccio's "Maestà," have been lost to overseas museums. What remains is still captivating, especially the five little *predella* paintings (small panels below the main painting) describing episodes from the founding of the Carmelite religious order. Ambrogio's single greatest work is the "Allegories of Good and Bad Government" in the Palazzo Pubblico (see p. 198). His most compelling works here are the "Piccolo Maestà" and "Annunciation," the latter poignantly dated 1348, the year of his premature death.

Zenith of Sienese Painting

The Black Death also partly accounts for the lull in Sienese painting in the second half of the 14th century. Late in this same century, however, Sienese art recovered to enter one of its most fertile phases. Henceforth the major names come one after the other, among them Bartolo di Fredi, best known for his paintings in San Gimignano (see pp. 230–239); his pupil, Taddeo di Bartolo (1362–1422); and Sassetta (active 1423–1450). The last was Siena's leading 15th-century painter and one of the first of the city's artists to take on board such Florentine advances as the use of perspective. His paintings include "St. Anthony Beaten by Devils," "Last Supper," and two lovely fragments of landscape—"A Town by the Sea" and "A Castle on the Lake Shore."

While Sassetta and others forged ahead, numerous highly accomplished Sienese painters of the 15th century were happy to plow a more traditional furrow. These included Sano di Pietro, Giovanni di Paolo, and Matteo di Giovanni, whose hidebound paintings, while beautiful, were executed at the same time as more radical pictures were becoming commonplace just a few miles to the north in Florence.

Although Siena reached its artistic zenith in the 14th and 15th centuries, it was not entirely without hallowed names in its 16th-century dotage. Two of the leading artists in this later period were Tuscan-born Domenico Beccafumi (1486–1551) and Giovanni Antonio Bazzi (1477–1549). The latter, from Vercelli in northern Italy, is better known by his nickname Sodoma, probably after an exaggerated account of his life by the Renaissance critic Giorgio Vasari—who hated him. Vasari claimed he was "always surrounded by young men, in whose company he took great pleasure." Paintings by both artists can be seen in the final rooms of the gallery's main upper floor.

Beccafumi spent part of his apprenticeship in Rome, where he came into contact with the late works of Raphael and Michelangelo, both of whom produced paintings that looked forward to a style of painting that would become known as mannerism. On his return to Siena in 1513, Beccafumi began to paint in the same style, employing strong, or exaggerated, perspective; portraying intense displays of emotion; using occasionally lurid colors; and often painting dramatic and unnatural effects of light. Strange perspective provides the dominant note in his painting of "St. Catherine Receiving the Stigmata," while his mastery of light can be seen to good effect in the "Nativity of the Virgin." Don't miss the cartoons, or preparatory sketches, that Beccafumi created as outlines for his pavement panels in Siena's Duomo.

Interspersed with the paintings by Beccafumi and others are works by Sodoma, a hint of whose character can be gleaned from the tax return he filed in 1531: "I have an ape, a talking raven . . . and three beastly she-animals, which are women, and I have also 30 grown up children, which is a real encumbrance . . . and as 12 children exempt a man from taxation I recommend myself to you. Farewell." Sodoma's masterwork is the fresco cycle on the life of St. Benedict at the abbey of Monte Oliveto Maggiore (see pp. 266–267), but he is also well represented in Siena's Pinacoteca Nazionale—watch for his painting of "The Scourging of Christ" (1511–1514)—and church of San Domenico (see p. 222). ■

The PInacoteca Nazionale offers a glorious chronological account of Sienese art over several centuries.

A Loop Walk From the Campo

This short circular walk enables you to visit some of Siena's most impressive churches and monuments, from the cluster of palaces around the Campo to the half-hidden churches in the south and west of the city.

A walk along Via di Stalloreggi allows time for earthly delights like shopping and gelato.

The walk begins as you situate yourself in **Il Campo ❶** (see pp. 194–199) facing the Fonte Gaia and away from the Palazzo Pubblico, take the alley just ahead of you—Vicolo di San Pietro. This leads you to the junction of Via di Città, Via Banchi di Sopra, and Via Banchi di Sotto, an intersection marked by the **Torre di Roccabruna**—one of the city's highest towers until it was truncated in the 16th century—and the **Loggia della Mercanzia ❷** (1428–1444), a three-arched loggia built in Gothic-Renaissance style. Two of its pillar tabernacle statues, St. Peter and St. Paul (1460–1462), are by Vecchietta.

Turn right on Via Banchi di Sotto, passing the **Palazzo Piccolomini ❸** (see p. 221) on the right. Immediately past the palazzo you see the **Logge del Papa ❹** (1462), raised on the orders of Tuscan-born Pope Pius II (Enea Silvio Piccolomini). Bear right here and you come to the baroque church of San Martino and **Via del Porrione,** one of the city's most ancient streets. It takes its name

NOT TO BE MISSED:

Il Campo • Palazzo Piccolomini • Pinacoteca Nazionale • Battistero • Duomo

from the Latin *emporium,* meaning "place of the market," recalling the Roman markets that once stood nearby. If you have time, it's well worth following Via del Porrione and its continuations (Via San Martino and Via San Girolamo) for some good city views and the interesting church of **Santa Maria dei Servi** (see p. 222).

Otherwise, cross Via del Porrione immediately and continue down Vicolo delle Scotte, passing Siena's synagogue on the right. This district was the heart of the city's Jewish ghetto, which was created in 1571 on the orders of Grand Duke Cosimo I de' Medici. Turn left on Via di Salicotto, take the first right, and you come to the large Piazza del Mercato. Cross the square and bear right to pick up Via del Mercato. Then turn left almost immediately to follow Via Giovanni Duprè, named after the 19th-century sculptor who was born on this street at No. 35. At the church of San Giuseppe on your left take Via Sant'Agata straight on to an open grassy area on your left that fronts the 13th-century church of **Sant'Agostino ❺** (see sidebar p. 215), whose interior contains notable paintings by Sodoma ("Epiphany") and Ambrogio Lorenzetti (an appealing fresco of the "Maestà").

At the junction of Via Sant'Agata and Via San Pietro, a left turn takes you to the city's **Orto Botanico ❻**, or Botanical Garden *(Via Pier Andrea Mattioli 4, closed Sat. p.m.*

& *Sun.*). Turn right on Via San Pietro, by contrast, and you come to the church of San Pietro (on your right) and the **Pinacoteca Nazionale** ❼ (see pp. 214–217) beyond. Just before the church, turn left on Via di Castelvecchio and follow it as it bears right to Via di Stalloreggi. If time is short, a right turn on Via di Stalloreggi will take you back to the city center. Alternatively, turn left to the **Arco delle Due Porte,** an arch that formed part of the city's 11th-century walls. En route, you pass the house at Nos. 91–93 where Duccio painted his famous "Maestà" (see p. 212).

Turn right after the arch and follow Via del Fosso di San Ansano as it dips into a quiet corner of the city. At Piazzetta della Selva notice the *contrada* church of San

Sebastiano (see p. 220), and take any of the three alleys leading to the right off the piazza. Via Franciosa or either of its two companions will take you to Piazza San Giovanni, home to the **Battistero** ❽ (see p. 207), with the **Duomo** ❾ (see pp. 202–207) and **Museo dell'Opera del Duomo** (see pp. 211–213) up the steps to your left. Via dei Pellegrini leads from Piazza San Giovanni to Via di Città and thus will take you back to Il Campo.

> ⊠ See also area map pp. 192–193
> ▶ Il Campo
> 🕐 Allow a morning, depending on the sights you wish to visit
> ↔ 1.75 miles (2.8 km) without diversion to Santa Maria dei Servi
> ▶ Il Campo

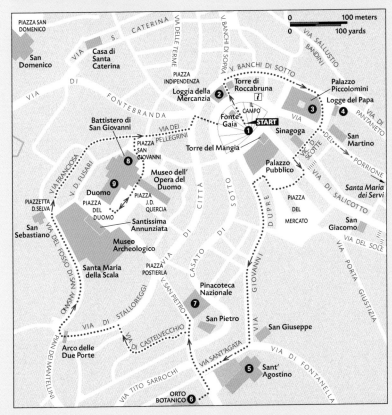

More Places to Visit in Siena

"Madonna della Misericordia" ("Our Lady of the Mercy") at the Museo Archeologico

Contrada Churches

Each of Siena's 17 *contrade,* or parishes, has its own church, social club, heraldic device, fountain, piazza, and museum. Visits to the museums need to be arranged by appointment at least a week in advance, making them beyond the scope of most visitors. The city's visitor center (see p. 194), provides lists of contact numbers. The *contrada* churches and fountains are much easier to see, and you often find them by accident as you wander the streets.

All but two of the contrade are named after birds and other animals—the exceptions are the two largest, **Torre** (Tower) and **Selva** (Forest). The creatures in question invariably feature as figures in the relevant fountains. The Torre's territory lies just east of the Campo, with a museum at Via di Salicotto 76 *(tel 0577 222 555)* and a church nearby in the shape of the 16th-century **Oratorio di San Giacomo.** The Selva domain lies on and around Via dei Fusari just northwest of the cathedral, where a little alley called Vicolo San Girolamo leads to the contrada's spiritual home, the early 16th-century church of **San Sebastiano** in Valle Piatta. Its museum is in Piazzetta della Selva *(tel 0577 45 093).*

Museo Archeologico

Siena's archaeological museum has been moved from pillar to post over the years, but has now found a permanent home inside the Santa Maria della Scala complex (see pp. 208–210). It is worth taking time from Santa Maria's enticing attractions to see this small but sprightly collection of mainly Etruscan artifacts, arranged according to provenance.

Italy's most celebrated Etruscan sites are in Lazio, near Rome, but Tuscany also has a scattering of sites, and there are finds from excavations near Pienza, Casole d'Elsa, and Siena itself. As ever in Etruscan collections, urns and burial items predominate, but there are also some beautiful pieces of jewelry and goldware from a tomb close to Monteriggioni.

🅰 193 C2 ✉ Piazza del Duomo ☎ 0577 49 153 🕐 Closed p.m. 💲 $$

Palazzo Piccolomini

Only a tiny proportion of Siena's visitors bother to step inside the Palazzo Picco-lomini, just off the Campo, one of three palaces in the city commissioned by Pope Pius II (Enea Silvio Piccolomini). Much of the building is given over to council offices, but its upper floors also house the extraordinary **Archivio di Stato,** or Sienese State Archives. Some visitors may be ignorant of this hidden gem, while others are perhaps put off by having to see the archives accompanied by a city employee. In practice, however, visiting this unmissable minor sight could hardly be easier. Enter the palace courtyard and take the stairs to your left. These bring you to a reception area where someone will accompany you to the archives.

The walk is memorable in its own right, as you pass along corridors and rooms lined with enormous bundles of ancient papers and manuscripts—a total of some 60,000 documents pertaining to towns and villages in the old Sienese Republic. Each historical bundle is labeled in ornate medieval script and dated with the year—1387, 1389, 1390, and so on down through the centuries. You may also be able to steal a glance through windows overlooking the Campo, catching a unique and little-seen view of the square.

Eventually, your guide leaves you alone to admire the archive's artistic highlights—the Tavolette di Biccherna (the city's account books), the Gabelle (its tax records), and a series of selected manuscripts and documents dating to earliest days (the first from A.D. 736). Among the documents are ninth-century papal bulls and letters of artistic commission for such famous works as Duccio's "Maestà" and Nicola Pisano's cathedral pulpit. More recent are the Tavolette di Biccherna, which take their name from Blacherne, the name of the imperial treasury in the Byzantine capital of Constantinople (modern-day Istanbul). The Tavolette are painted wooden panels and were commissioned by magistrates and officials in the city's tax and account departments at the end of their six-month terms of office to act as covers for their documents. What lends them significance is that in the period they were created—between 1258 and 1682—they were commissioned from some leading artists of their day (Pietro and Ambrogio Lorenzetti, Sano di Pietro, Vecchietta, Domenico Beccafumi, and others). Initially the scenes were religious but quickly moved to symbolic and secular subjects, providing a documentary record of daily life in Siena over four centuries.

🅰 193 D3 ✉ Banchi di Sotto 52 ☎ 0577 247 145 🕐 Closed Sun. & p.m., guided tours Mon.–Sat. at 9:30, 10:30, & 11:30 a.m.

EXPERIENCE: See Siena by Bike

In April 2014 bicyclists were given the freedom of most of central Siena's traffic-free zones—parts of the Campo are the chief exceptions—for the first time in decades. Bike rental *(noleggio bici)* is still difficult, but you can sign up for two-hour small group tours *(viator.com/tours /Siena)* through the city, with bike and helmet provided. Meet the guide in the center of town, see the main sights, including the **Campo** and **Piazza del Duomo,** but then you'll take advantage of the fact you're cycling to explore farther than most visitors can manage, notably around and beyond the city gates of **Porta San Marco** and **Porta Camollia.**

The basilica church of San Francesco (1228–1255)

San Domenico

San Domenico's gaunt Gothic outline dominates northern Siena. Begun in 1226, the austere, brick-built church is associated with St. Catherine of Siena, patron saint of both Siena and—with St. Francis—of Italy. It was here that she performed several miracles, became a Dominican nun, and received the stigmata (the wounds of Christ). Her links with the church are commemorated in the **Cappella delle Volte**—which contains her portrait—and in the **Cappella di Santa Caterina** (midway down the south aisle), whose 15th-century marble tabernacle contains part of her skull. The latter chapel also has two frescoes by Sodoma of episodes from her life. Chapels on either side of the high altar feature several Sienese paintings, and the altar is adorned with a tabernacle and angels (1465) by Benedetto da Maiano. *basilicacateriniana.com* 🅰 192 B3 ✉ Piazza San Domenico ☎ 0577 246 848 🕐 Closed Sun. a.m.

San Francesco

Fire and heavy-handed restoration have left San Francesco's gloomy interior bereft of character and works of art. Its best remaining artifacts are the 14th-century tombs of the Tolomei at the end of the south aisle, burial places of the city's leading medieval families. Also worth finding are frescoes by Sassetta (right of the main door) and Pietro and Ambrogio Lorenzetti (first and third chapels left of the high altar). More remarkable still is the **Oratorio di San Bernardino,** south of the church, whose lovely wood-paneled salon upstairs contains frescoes (1496–1518) on the life of the Virgin by the painters Sodoma, Beccafumi, and Girolamo del Pacchia. 🅰 193 D5 ✉ Piazza San Francesco ☎ 0577 283 048 or 0577 42 020 (Oratorio) 🕐 Closed Sun. a.m.; Oratorio: closed Nov.– mid-March & a.m. daily mid-March–Oct. 💲 $ or $$$$ for combined Opasi Pass, which covers baptistery, crypt, & Museo dell'Opera del Duomo

Santa Maria dei Servi

Santa Maria dei Servi is worth the ten-minute walk southeast from the city center (take Via di Salicotto from the Campo, then Via dei Servi to Piazza A. Manzoni), both for the church and for the city views along its tree-lined piazza. Its oldest painting (first altar of the south aisle) is the "Madonna di Bordone" by Coppo da Marcovaldo (born 1225), a Florentine artist captured in battle and forced to paint this as part of his ransom. At the end of the same aisle is Matteo di Giovanni's harrowing "Massacre of the Innocents" (1491). Another depiction of the same event by Pietro Lorenzetti graces the right wall of the second chapel to the right of the high altar. Lorenzetti also painted in the second chapel left of the altar, with his follower, Taddeo di Bartolo, whose "Adoration of the Shepherds" (1404) hangs here. 🅰 193 F1 ✉ Piazza A. Manzoni 5 ☎ 0577 222 633 🕐 Closed noon–4 p.m.

Pisa, both medieval and modern; the village of San Gimignano; lovely Lucca; and the vineyards, woods and hills of celebrated Chianti

Northern Tuscany

The Leaning Tower of Pisa

Northern Tuscany

Tuscany is a large area, and to see even its highlights requires careful planning. Most visitors head south to Siena after Florence, but to get the most out of the rest of the region it makes sense first to head north and west from the Tuscan capital. Some places you can see as day trips from Florence, notably Fiesole, Prato, and Pistoia, but these are minor attractions by Tuscan standards.

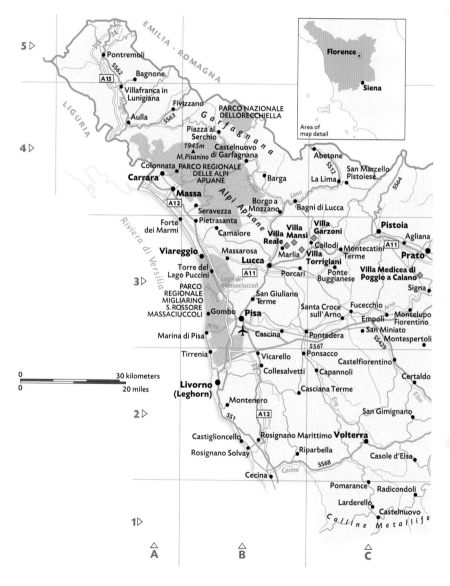

Lovely Lucca can be seen in a day from Florence—a train takes just over an hour—but its pretty streets, superb churches, and many monuments merit an overnight stay. If you have a car, Lucca is a starting point for exploring some of Tuscany's spectacular and little-known landscapes, notably the high mountain scenery of the Alpi Apuane and Orecchiella to the north. This is touring or hiking country, as there are few towns of interest. Nor should you expect too much of the coastline: Viareggio is the best of the area's mediocre resorts. Lucca is also close

to Pisa, whose charms are limited. Much of Pisa was rebuilt after World War II, and its surviving historic buildings—beautiful as they are—should occupy you only for a morning.

More time is needed for the towns and countryside south of Florence. Chianti has high wooded hills interspersed with villas, farmhouses, isolated villages, and large vineyards. This is a relaxing area to stay in if you are renting a house or villa, but it offers little to see or do if you are driving through. One option is to take the specially designated Chiantigiana road, which threads through the best of the region between Florence and Siena, perhaps stopping off to visit one or two of the vineyards to sample some of Tuscany's top wines.

Alternatively, take the fast *superstrada* highway between the two cities, turning off close to Siena for San Gimignano, one of Italy's most celebrated villages, on your way to medieval Monteriggioni and Colle di Val d'Elsa.

San Gimignano boasts a good museum, exceptional fresco cycles, and medieval towers. In high season, stay overnight to enjoy the streets and piazzas without the day-trippers.

From San Gimignano you could travel west to see Volterra, stranded in lonely countryside on the road to Pisa and the coast. ∎

Fiesole

Fiesole is a small town set in the cypress-scattered hills above Florence. A popular excursion from the city, it is a place that can trace its history back to Etruscan times—about 600 B.C. It predates the Tuscan capital by several centuries but in 1150 surrendered its independence to its larger rival. Its leafy surroundings make it a favored place in which to escape Florence's summer heat.

Fiesole offers sublime vistas of Florence and the hills beyond.

Fiesole

- 🗺 225 D3

Visitor Information

- ✉ Via Portigiani 3
- ☎ 055 596 1323, 055 596 1296, or 055 596 1311
- 🕐 Closed p.m. Nov.–Feb.
- 🚌 Bus: No. 7 from Santa Maria Novella railroad station in Florence

museidifiesole.it

There's plenty to see here on a day trip, but in summer the streets are crowded. If your trip's confined to Florence, then by all means come here. If you're headed into Tuscany, then your time can be better spent elsewhere. To reach the town—5 miles (8 km) from Florence—take the No. 7 bus from outside the Santa Maria Novella railroad station (on its eastern side). The city transit's standard 60-minute flat-fare ticket works for the trip (one way). Travel time is about 20 minutes.

The Piazza Mino da Fiesole & Around: The bus drops you in Piazza Mino da Fiesole, named after sculptor Mino da Fiesole (1430–1484). Here you'll find the **Duomo,** founded in 1028, its plain 19th-century facade masking an interior enlivened by Bicci di Lorenzo's altarpiece (1450) and the Cappella Salutati, with an altar frontal and tomb by da Fiesole.

Just behind the Duomo stands the **Museo Bandini** (*Via Duprè 1, tel 055 596 1293, museidifiesole.it, closed Mon.–Thurs., $$ or $$$$ combined ticket with archaeological* zone & Museo Civico Archeologico), a small museum devoted mainly to ivories, ceramics, and Florentine paintings. Walk a little farther east, and on Via Marini you'll find the entrance to Fiesole's **archaeological zone,** a shady spot in which to while away an hour in the afternoon heat. It incorporates the **Museo Civico Archeologico,** devoted to some of the Etruscan and Roman finds excavated on the site. Highlights include a 2,500-year-old tombstone, a large lead *cista,* or urn, from about the third or fourth century, and evocative articles such as pearls and silver hairpins removed from skeletons found in tombs around the site. Also in the area is a 3,000-seat Roman theater dating from the first century B.C. It is still used to stage performances during the Estate Fiesolana, Fiesole's summer arts and music festival (see sidebar this page). Also scattered around the site are the remains of a Roman bath complex, temples, and Etruscan walls.

Walks Around Town: Returning to Piazza Mino da Fiesole, you might want to climb Via San Francesco, a steep lane from the piazza's western edge that leads to the churches of **San Francesco** and **Sant'Alessandro;** Gothic San Francesco probably occupied the site of the Etruscan acropolis. The climb rewards with fine views of Florence, spread out below. Then take the path in front of San Francesco, which winds into a wooded public park with paths that lead back to the town.

For another modest walk of about 1.75 miles (3 km), take Via Vecchia Fiesolana from the southern side of Piazza Mino da Fiesole. Dropping steeply, the lane passes the **Villa Medici** *(inquire at visitor center for current opening times),* built by Michelozzo for Cosimo de' Medici (Cosimo the Elder). It eventually arrives at the church and convent of **San Domenico.** This was the home of painter and monk Fra Angelico, and it holds

his painting of the "Madonna with Saints and Angels" (1425). A five-minute walk down another small lane, Via della Badia, brings you to the **Badia Fiesolana,** the town's cathedral until 1028. Cosimo de' Medici had the church altered in the 1460s but left the sublime old Romanesque facade intact. As a result, the old frontage was left picturesquely enclosed by the later, 15th-century church. ∎

Archaeological Zone & Museo Civico Archeologico

- ✉ Via Marini–Via Portigiani L1
- 🕐 Closed Tues. & p.m. daily Nov.–Feb.
- 💲 $$$, $$$$ (combined ticket with Museo Bandini)

museidifiesole.it

Fiesole's Summer Festival

The Estate Fiesolana is a popular and wide-ranging summer festival of cinema, music, and theater that has been held in various venues in and around Fiesole since 1948. Italian-language events will be beyond most visitors, but the musical performances—with jazz well to the fore—have widespread appeal, especially those held outdoors in the town's Roman theater, which makes for a spectacular setting.

You can obtain tickets for individual events directly from the festival *(estate fiesolana.it)* or through the outlets and website of Italy's Box Office ticket agency *(boxol.it).* Discounted Green, Blue, and Red multievent Fiesole Cards are available for the first or second halves of the festival, or for all events.

A Drive Through the Chianti Countryside

This loop drive through vineyards, olive groves, small towns, and wooded hills allows you to see the best of Chianti, Tuscany's most famous region. En route you can stop in tiny villages or buy wine and olive oil from some of the area's many farms.

Whether you follow the loop or drive from Florence, you'll see the best of the Chianti region. The route from Florence (see below) is a much prettier route than the *superstrada* highway between the two cities.

For the loop, leave Siena on the SS2 road (the Via Cassia) to the west, watching for signs to Castellina in Chianti and the Chiantigiana. All manner of diversions are possible, but note that while roads in Chianti are well made, they're also often full of twists and turns. Distances on the ground and journey times are therefore greater than they appear on the map. The region's towns are often unmemorable, making the countryside Chianti's main attraction. You'll pass dozens of **vineyards,** producers of Chianti's famous wine (see sidebar p. 238). Most of the these are well signposted and open to the public for buying and tasting.

For an introduction to the region's viticulture you could do worse than pause in **Castellina in Chianti ❶**, 16 miles (26 km) from Siena, where local wines and olive oils are sold at the Bottega del Vino Gallo Nero *(Via della Rocca 10)*. The Gallo Nero, or Black Cockerel, is one of the most respected federations of Chianti producers.

From Castellina head east for 7.5 miles (12 km) on the scenic SS429 to **Radda in Chianti ❷**. Radda's modern outskirts are unappealing, though the inner core still retains its medieval aspect. Beyond Radda, continue east another 7.5 miles (12 km) into the heart of the heavily wooded Monti del Chianti, the Chianti Hills, and to **Badia a Coltibuono ❸** *(tel 0577 74 481, restaurant 0577 749 031, www .coltibuono.com, guided tours & tastings 2 p.m.– 5 p.m., April–Oct., $$)*, a beautifully located

NOT TO BE MISSED:

Renowned Vineyards • Badia a Coltibuono • Castello di Brolio

11th-century abbey now given over to a restaurant and wine cellars, and offering B&B accommodations. Just south of the abbey the road joins with the SS408, on which you turn right for 4 miles (6.4 km) toward **Gaiole in Chianti ❹**, another wine town with a quaint old center ringed by modern development.

Ignore the turns to Radda and Castagnoli off the SS408, 4 miles (6.4 km) south of Gaiole. Instead, press on the same distance again to the next main junction. Turn left on the SS484 and follow signs for **Castello di Brolio ❺** *(near San Regolo, tel 0577 747 104 or 0577 747 156, ricasoli .it, restaurant closed Thurs.)*, a vast crenellated castle that has been in the Ricasoli family since the 12th century. The battlements have sweeping views of the Arbia Valley and the Chianti Hills, and in the on-site cantina you can buy the noted wines produced on the estate. There is also a restaurant. Several minor roads, most of them gravel-surfaced *strade bianche* (white roads), lead back to the SS408 via either San Felice or Monti and Cacchiano. Once back on the SS408 it's 12.5 miles (20 km) to Siena.

Alternatively, return from Castello di Brolio to the SS484 and continue 6 miles (10 km) past Villa a Sesta to an intersection at **San Gusme ❻**, one of the region's most picturesque villages. From here the return to Siena is via a minor road for 7 miles (11 km) to Pianella, where you join the SS408 about 7.5 miles (12 km) from Siena.

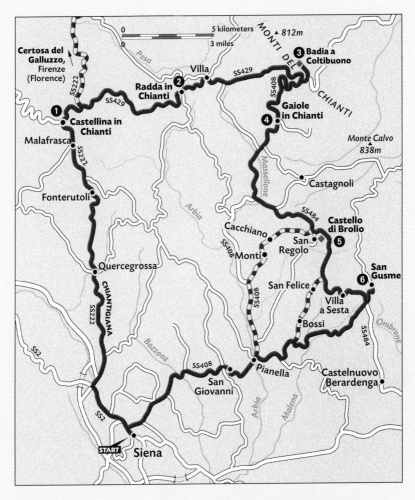

This tour makes a loop from Siena, but you could take much of the route on the SS222 road, a designated, signposted scenic route known as the **Chiantigiana**, which goes from Florence toward Siena. Leave Florence on the Via Sienese south, following signs for Galluzzo, 5 miles (8 km) away, where you can see the **Certosa del Galluzzo,** or Florence Charter-house, a 14th-century monastery (*Via della Certosa, tel 055 204 9226, cistercensi.info, tours hourly Tues.–Sat. & Sun. p.m., donation*). From here, follow signs for 7.5 miles (12 km) to Impruneta, where signed roads lead for 6 miles (10 km), by

way of Strada in Chianti, to the SS222. Follow the SS222 another 10 miles (16 km) south to Greve in Chianti, and then 15 miles (24 km) farther to Castellina in Chianti, where you can pick up the itinerary to Siena described above.

- ⬛ See also area map pp. 224–225
- ▶ Siena
- 🕐 Allow a day
- ↔ Siena loop 62 miles (100 km); Florence–Siena on the Chianti-giana 53 miles (87 km)
- ▶ Siena

San Gimignano

One look at the skyline of San Gimignano and its crop of ancient stone towers is enough to see why the village is often called a "medieval Manhattan." The towers and the village's picture-book prettiness make this a much visited spot, yet it is also a place that retains its charm. It has a fascinating art gallery, a pair of superb fresco-filled churches, and some beautiful and far-reaching views of the Tuscan countryside.

San Gimignano prospered initially thanks to its defensive hilltop position.

San Gimignano's famous **towers** began to appear around 1150. They had a variety of purposes, some practical, some fanciful. At their most basic they provided a readily defended place of retreat during attack or periods of civil strife. Yet they also served as medieval status symbols: A noble's power and wealth could be measured by the height of his tower, especially if it was higher than those of his rivals.

Yet towers and individual power were no defense against plague or constant civil strife, both of which gradually sapped the strength of the village. In 1348, fatally weakened, it placed itself under the protection of the city of Florence. The move undermined the power of the nobles, one reason why so many towers survived; as they posed no threat, so there was no need to tear them down.

Many people visit San Gimignano as a day trip from Siena, often traveling by either bus or train. Bus journeys usually involve a change of bus at Poggibonsi, an undistinguished and largely modern town, but you can buy through-tickets from the TRA-IN bus company office in Siena's Piazza San Domenico. Alternatively, take a train from Siena to

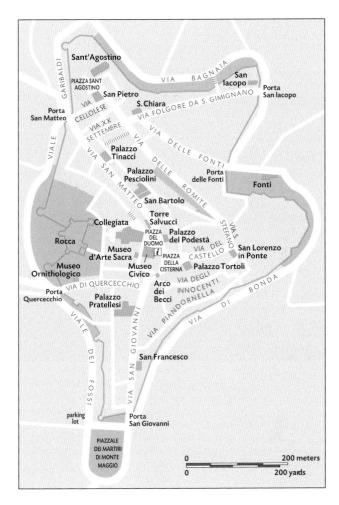

Poggibonsi, and then you can walk the short distance to the TRA-IN bus depot (exit the railroad station and take the right turn in the piazza in front of the station). The total journey time from Siena to San Gimignano is about an hour. The route is straightforward if you're driving, but be sure to stop off en route at Monteriggioni (see p. 262) and perhaps Colle di Val d'Elsa (see pp. 261–262). Parking in San Gimignano can be difficult at busy times. Your best bet is to use the parking lot at the southern edge of the village by Via Roma and walk from there.

Exploring San Gimignano on foot is easy; you can stroll from one end of the village to the other in a matter of minutes. Most of the key things to see lie in or near the central Piazza del Duomo, but this is a place where you should devote plenty of time to casual exploration. Start your tour

San Gimignano

224 C2

Visitor Information

✉ Piazza del Duomo 1

☎ 0577 940 008

🕐 Closed 1 p.m.–3 p.m. March–Oct. & 1 p.m.–2 p.m. Nov.–Feb.

sangimignano.com

Cafés in Piazza della Cisterna, San Gimignano beckon travelers to sit, rest, and reflect on life.

beyond Via Roma and Piazzale dei Martiri di Monte Maggio at the southern gateway, Porta San Giovanni, and then walk north on Via San Giovanni. This street once formed part of the Via Francigena, one of the main medieval pilgrimage roads between Rome and northern Europe. San Gimignano's position on the road was one reason for the town's early growth and prosperity. Make sure you stop at **San Francesco** midway up the street on the right, a deconsecrated 13th-century Romanesque church now given over, like many places around town, to the sale of the local Vernaccia white wine. Its rear terrace has memorable views over the Tuscan hills.

At the top of the street a medieval arch, **Arco dei Becci,** ushers you into Piazza della Cisterna, the first of two linked central squares. The Arco dei Becci formed part of the town's original ring of defensive walls, built before a second set of ramparts was raised in the 13th century to enclose the burgeoning town. **Piazza della Cisterna** is ringed with towers, medieval buildings, and tempting cafés. It takes its name from the *cisterna* (public well) at its heart, built in 1287 but extended in 1346 on the orders of Guccio de' Malavoli, then the town's Podestà, or ruling magistrate, whose coat of arms is emblazoned on its side.

Note the grooves cut into the well by ropes used to pull up pails of water.

Off to the left of Piazza della Cisterna lies the second central square, **Piazza del Duomo,** home to the village's principal sights: the Collegiata and Museo Civico. Here, too, is the **Museo d'Arte Sacra** (tel 0577 940 316, $ or $$ combined ticket with Collegiata, closed Jan. 16–31, Nov. 16–30, & Sun. a.m.), a modest museum of sacred art and archaeological finds. At the top of the steps stands the Collegiata. On your left is the **Palazzo del Popolo** (1288), where the visitor center and Museo Civico (see pp. 235–238) are based, and behind you is the **Palazzo del Podestà** (1239), whose tower, the **Torre della Rognasa,** was cited in a civic statute of 1255 as having the maximum height allowed for any private tower—167 feet (52 m). Many nobles ignored the law, or subtly subverted it, as in the case of the twin **Torre Salvucci** (to the left of the palace as you face it). Here, the Salvucci family built towers that were below the regulation height, but they placed them so close together that it was obvious their combined height would be greater than anything built by the town council or by rival families.

The Collegiata

The Collegiata—also known as Santa Maria Assunta—was at one time San Gimignano's cathedral, or Duomo, but forsook its title when the village lost its status as a bishopric in 1348. Founded about 1056, the church was consecrated in 1148 and enlarged by architect and sculptor Giuliano da Maiano between 1466 and 1468.

INSIDER TIP:

Take a break from sightseeing at a village café, but remember that your drink will cost more if you sit down than if you stand at the bar.

—PETER GWIN
National Geographic writer

First Fresco Cycle: Beyond the Collegiata's blank facade lies an extraordinary interior almost completely covered in frescoes. Three principal cycles adorn the walls, beginning on the rear (entrance) wall with "Last Judgment" (1410) by leading Sienese painter Taddeo di Bartolo. "Inferno" is portrayed on the right, "Paradiso" on the left. Between these two scenes, which are painted on protruding walls, is a fresco by Benozzo Gozzoli of "St. Sebastian" (1465), a saint invoked against infectious diseases and so often painted during or after plague epidemics. One such epidemic had struck San Gimignano a year before the painting was commissioned. Sebastian was chosen as the subject in such paintings for his immense powers of physical recovery. He miraculously survived his ordeal by arrows—the event

Collegiata & Cappella di Santa Fina

- Map p. 231
- Piazza Luigi Recori 1–2
- Closed Jan. 16–31, Nov. 16–30, & Sun. a.m.
- $, $$ (combined ticket with Museo d'Arte Sacra)

traditionally depicted in paintings of the saint—and was eventually martyred by being crushed to death. The two painted wooden statues flanking the fresco, the "Archangel Gabriel" and the "Madonna Annunciate," are the work of 15th-century Sienese master Jacopo della Quercia.

Second Cycle: The church's second fresco cycle fills the north (left) wall and was painted by Bartolo di Fredi (active 1353–1410) with episodes from the Old Testament (main wall) and scenes of the Creation (in the lunettes above). The most celebrated scene, if only because it includes

A stroll down Via San Giovanni

a graphically depicted penis, is the "Drunkenness of Noah" (sixth fresco from the left in the upper of the two main registers as you face the frescoes). Tradition has it that Noah was the first to cultivate the vine, as well as the first to abuse its fruits. Also note the lovely scene portraying the "Creation of Eve" (fourth lunette from the left), in which Eve is shown emerging from Adam's rib. Many of the scenes show the influence of Ambrogio Lorenzetti's "Allegories of Good and Bad Government" (see pp. 198–199) in Siena's Palazzo Pubblico, and in particular the painter's love of incidental detail. Several contemporary fishing scenes, for example, are included in the turbulent fresco of "The Passage across the Red Sea" (lower register, fourth from the left).

New Testament Cycles: The cycle of New Testament scenes on the opposite wall is earlier (from about 1333) and is attributed to one of two Sienese artists, Lippo Memmi or Barna da Siena. Here, the scenes are arranged in three levels, with several damaged frescoes from other eras interspersed. Starting at the top and reading from right to left the scenes depicted are as follows: (top register) "Annunciation," "Nativity," "Epiphany," "Presentation in the Temple," "Massacre of the Innocents," and "Flight to Egypt"; (second tier, eight panels, reading left to right) "Dispute in the Temple," "Baptism of Jesus," "Vocation of Peter," "Marriage of Canaan," "Transfiguration,"

Cappella di Santa Fina

On your visit to the Collegiata be sure to admire the Cappella di San Gimignano (left of the high altar), which contains an altar by Benedetto da Maiano (brother of Giuliano). It's also worth paying the small admission fee to enter the Cappella di Santa Fina off the south (right-hand) aisle. Benedetto was responsible for the altar, marble shrine, and bas-reliefs in this chapel, which is dedicated to one of San Gimignano's patron saints, St. Fina, the subject of lunette frescoes by the 15th-century Florentine painter Domenico Ghirlandaio.

St. Fina was born in San Gimignano in 1238. At the age of ten she developed an incurable illness and for the next five years lay on a plank, aiming to bring herself closer to Christ through her suffering. Her last days are depicted in the fresco in the right lunette, the "Announcement of St. Fina's Death." Its details include St. Gregory, who told Fina of her death

in a vision; a mouse in the gloom to the rear of the picture (Fina was paralyzed in her last days and unable to scare away the mice that tormented her); and the flower-covered board on which she had lain (the flowers appeared miraculously on her death).

The fresco on the left shows the "Funeral of St. Fina," a picture said to have greatly impressed Raphael. It portrays the saint on her deathbed with the towers of her native village in the background. Also shown are three miracles associated with the saint: the ringing of San Gimignano's bells by angels on her death; the restoration of a blind boy's sight; and the curing of her nurse's paralyzed hand. Look, too, for self-portraits of Ghirlandaio (the figure behind the bishop saying Mass) and his assistants—(shown to either side)—Davide (Ghirlandaio's brother) and Sebastiano Mainardi (his brother-in-law).

"Resurrection of Lazarus," "Entry of Jesus Into Jerusalem," and "The Crowd Meeting Jesus"; (lower register, eight panels, from right to left) "Last Supper," "Betrayal of Judas," "Jesus in the Garden," "Kiss of Judas," "Jesus in the Pretorian Palace," "Flagellation," "Crown of Thorns," and "Calvary." Among many graphic frescoes here, few are as dramatic as the "Resurrection of Lazarus," which portrays an awed crowd watching as Lazarus's tomb is opened to reveal the deceased man—wrapped in burial robes—miraculously raised from the dead.

Museo Civico

Leaving the Collegiata, your next port of call should be the

Museo Civico, San Gimignano's civic museum. This is divided in two: One ticket admits you to the museum proper, another to the **Torre Grossa** (begun 1300), the only one of San Gimignano's towers currently open to the public. You enter both via a pretty courtyard, dotted with archaeological fragments and three frescoes (1513) by Sodoma. Steps lead from here to the ticket office.

The museum opens with the **Sala del Consiglio,** dominated by Lippo Memmi's majestic painting of the "Maestà" (1317), or "Madonna Enthroned," a favorite subject among Sienese painters. Memmi's picture was closely modeled on one his

Museo Civico

🅜 Map p. 231

✉ Palazzo del Popolo, Piazza del Duomo 2

☎ 0577 990 348

💲 $$ (museum), $$$ (combined ticket for all civic museums)

The Museo Civico offers visitors their only chance to climb one of San Gimignano's medieval towers.

brother-in-law, Simone Martini, had completed two years earlier in Siena's Palazzo Pubblico. The Sala del Consiglio is also known as the Sala di Dante, for it was in this room that Dante—then a Florentine diplomat—met representatives of San Gimignano's ruling council to seek their support (see pp. 78–79). Several other small rooms on this floor show temporary exhibits. Upstairs are the four main rooms of the gallery, full of masterpieces by a host of Sienese and Florentine painters, most notably Benozzo Gozzoli and Filippino Lippi.

Moving Upstairs: The best paintings hang in the large room that you'll find immediately on the right at the top of the stairs, beginning with a painted 13th-century "Crucifix" by Coppo di Marcovaldo, a Florentine painter

captured by the Sienese at the Battle of Montaperti in 1260. The work was probably executed while he was in captivity and ranks among the great early Tuscan masterpieces. The top of the painting is adorned with small panels portraying the "Assumption of the Virgin" and "Christ Pantocrater" (Christ in the act of blessing). More small figures around Christ's hands depict scenes from the Passion.

Other exceptional paintings include two tondi, or round paintings (1482), on the opposite wall; they are by Filippino Lippi. One shows the "Angel Annunciate," the angel Gabriel announcing to Mary that she is to become the mother of a child. The other is "Virgin Annunciate," or Mary receiving the news, an event that coincided with the Immaculate Conception of Christ. The two episodes are more usually portrayed together in one painting and called the "Annunciation." Nearby are outstanding paintings by Umbrian master Pinturicchio—"Madonna Enthroned with St. Gregory and St. Benedict" (1512)—and two pictures by Benozzo Gozzoli of the "Madonna and Child With Saints" (both 1466).

Main Room: The other, larger room here contains several multi-panel paintings depicting episodes from lives of various saints, all of them fascinating for their incidental narrative detail. If you've visited the Cappella di Santa Fina in the Collegiata (see sidebar p. 235), you'll be familiar with some of the episodes in Lorenzo di Niccolò's (active 1391–1412) double-sided scenes from the life of St. Fina (1402). The same artist executed the similar scenes from the life of St. Bartholomew (1401) in the same room, one macabre panel of which shows attempts to martyr the saint by flaying him alive. Another shows his eventual beheading, his flayed strips of skin hampering his executioners. A third painting, by Taddeo di Bartolo, offers a narrative of the life of San Gimignano (1393), painted when the artist was working on the New Testament frescoes in the Collegiata. The work once stood on the church's high altar.

St. Gimignano was born in the northern Italian town of Modena but became associated with San Gimignano when he helped save the village from Attila the Hun. This episode, in which the saint is shown remonstrating with Attila, is one of several depicted on the left of the painting. The other scenes show the saint preventing his followers from being drenched in a leaky church, and St. Severus officiating at Gimignano's funeral. One extraordinary vignette on the right shows the saint meeting Lucifer as he answers the call of nature and causing the devil to disappear by making the sign of the Cross. The three other episodes here are concerned with the saint's exorcizing of a devil from the daughter of a Byzantine emperor. They show the saint crossing to Constantinople, calming storm-tossed waters on this voyage, and performing the exorcism of the princess.

INSIDER TIP:

In the Museo Civico look out for St. Martha in Benozzo Gozzoli's "Madonna and Child With Saints." She is esteemed in Tuscany as the patron saint of builders and cooks.

—STEFANIA MARTORELLI
National Geographic Italy editor

Other Works: A separate room on this floor contains some of Tuscany's most beguiling pictures (reached by turning left at the top of the stairs). They are the work of a local painter, Memmo di Filipuccio (active 1303–1345), father of the more celebrated Lippo Memmi. The early 14th-century panels portray three wedding scenes, including two vignettes in which the couple share a bath and then a bed. Some have seen these as innocent narratives on the joy of marriage, others as allegorical warnings on the wiles of women.

Sant'Agostino

From the museum and Piazza del Duomo you should take a circuitous route to San Gimignano's third major set piece, the church of Sant'Agostino (*Piazza Sant'Agostino, closed noon–3 p.m.*). This enables you to enjoy some pretty backstreets en route. Head west to explore the remains of the **Rocca** (1353), or castle,

and its peaceful public gardens; then walk east to visit the two churches of **San Lorenzo in Ponte** (1240) and **San Iacopo.** The latter was reputedly founded by the Knights Templar in the 13th century, and the former has a variety of 15th-century fresco fragments. If you take the more direct route north to Sant'Agostino (on Via San Matteo), watch for the lovely 13th-century Romanesque church of **San Bartolo,** just north of Piazza del Duomo (on the right), and the **Palazzo Pesciolini** to its left, a house and tower complex.

EXPERIENCE: Wine Tasting in Chianti

To the east of San Gimignano, many small wineries in the Chianti region between Florence and Siena offer short, informal tours and tastings. The visitor centers in Radda, Greve, and Castellina have details, or just pick a winery with a sign saying *Vendita Diretta* ("direct sales") or *Degustazioni* ("tastings"). For more in-depth tours of larger wineries, it is usually necessary to make an appointment. English will invariably be spoken.

Of Chianti's many wineries open to visitors, **Badia a Coltibuono** (*tel 0577 74 481, www.coltibuono.com, set tours mid-April–Oct. daily 2 p.m.–5 p.m., $$; 90-min. tour with tasting by appt. May–Sept. Tues., Wed., & Fri. 11 a.m., $$$*), where you can also stay overnight (see Travelwise p. 315), is a step above the rest. It sits high in the Chianti hills, with glorious views across the Val di Chiana. The *badia*, or abbey, and its church, date from the 11th century, and for some 800 years the Benedictine monks who lived here made—and drank—wine. The abbey was dissolved at the start of the 19th century,

with the arrival of Napoleon, and later passed to a Florentine banking family.

Inside the abbey is an exquisite small courtyard—note the badia's ancient symbols above the door, the grill of St. Laurence, and the planting stick of the abbey's founder, San Giovanni Gualberto. Wander the delightful rear garden, then start your tour and tasting in the frescoed former rectory. Wine is no longer made at the abbey, but the ancient cellars are a perfect temperature for storing and aging wine made at Badia a Coltibuono's wineries elsewhere in Chianti. The rows of French-oak barrels in the dark, chilly vaults make for a memorable sight.

Other Chianti wineries offering appointment-only tours include **Castello di Volpaia** (*tel 0577 738 066, volpaia.com*) near Radda; **Castello di Verrazzano** (*tel 0577 854 243, verrazzano.com*); **Castello di Brolio** (*tel 0577 730 220, ricasoli.it*); **Villa Vignamaggio** (*tel 055 854 661, vignamaggio.com*), where you can also spend the night; and **Rocca delle Macìe** (*tel 0577 732 236, roccadellemacie.com*).

Cappella di San Bartolo:

On entering Sant'Agostino, the west wall on your left contains the Cappella di San Bartolo, inside which lies the tomb of St. Bartolo, another of San Gimignano's saints. The tomb's reliefs (1495) of three episodes from his life are by Benedetto da Maiano, and in one of them the saint is shown reattaching his leprous toes after they had come off in the hands of a nurse.

Working your way down along the right (south) wall, you pass a painting of the "Madonna and Child With Eight Saints" (1494) by Pier Francesco Fiorentino (beside the first altar) and a nearby figure of "Christ With the Symbols of the Passion" by Bartolo di Fredi. Bartolo worked on the Collegiata's Old Testament frescoes (see p. 234) and was also responsible for the frescoes on the life of the Virgin on the walls of the chapel to the right of Sant'Agostino's high altar. Most people miss these pictures, seduced by the more eye-catching fresco cycle around the high altar itself. The work of Florentine painter Benozzo Gozzoli, a pupil of Fra Angelico, the 17 panels describe episodes from the life of St. Augustine. Like many of Gozzoli's frescoes in Tuscany—you may have seen his paintings in Florence's Palazzo Medici-Riccardi (see pp. 133–135)—these paintings are as charming for their portrayal of 15th-century Italy as for their religious subject.

The eye-catching painting on the high altar is the "Coronation of the Virgin" by Piero del Pollaiuolo (1441–1496), brother

Vineyards around San Gimignano offer spectacular vistas.

of the more famous Florentine painter, jeweler, and engraver Antonio del Pollaiuolo. Toward the entrance of the church, the north (left) wall contains other artistic oddments, most notably five round reliefs by Tino di Camaino (probably removed from a tomb of St. Bartolo that predated the present sepulcher) and a 15th-century fresco of "St. Sebastian" by Benozzo Gozzoli (third altar). ■

Villas & Gardens

It is no surprise to find a wide range of villas and gardens in a place like Tuscany, a region that has been blessed with beautiful countryside, fertile soil, mild climate, and architecturally enlightened patrons with wealth to spare. Many villas are private, some you stumble across by accident, and others are easily accessible from Florence and Lucca.

The formal garden of Villa Garzoni

Villas Around Florence

Rich urban families originally built fortified country houses or castles as refuges from political turmoil in their home cities. Later they commissioned properties as retreats from a city's summer heat. Later still, they turned their houses into showrooms of wealth and taste, or transformed them into rural oases of culture and learning. Many exploited the land for agricultural purposes, particularly as Tuscany's textile and other industries began to decline in the 16th and 17th centuries. Houses—and gardens—were also subject to the vagaries of architectural taste and fashion, and many old houses and their gardens were repeatedly modified.

No family's villas exemplify these changes better than those of the Medici. The family had houses across the region, but many of the most famous lie close to Florence. The **Villa Medicea La Petraia** (*map 225 D3, Via della Petraia 40, tel 055 452 691, polomuseale.firenze .it, closed 2nd & 3rd Mon. of month*) was built as a castle, turned into a country house in the 1570s by Grand Duke Ferdinando I de' Medici, and then remodeled in the 19th century by the House of Savoy, the Italian royal family. Its parkland is delightful, its garden less so—not something you could say of the nearby **Villa Medicea di Castello** (*map 25 D3, Via di Castello 47; details as for La Petraia above*), whose gardens are exquisite. The house (closed to the public) was bought in 1477 by cousins of Lorenzo the Magnificent, shortly before their uncle bought a farmhouse and turned it into the **Villa Medicea di Poggio a Caiano** (*map 225 D3, Piazza de Medici 14, Poggio a Caiano, tel 055 877 012, closed 2nd & 3rd Mon. of month*), 11 miles (18 km) northwest of Florence. This Medici villa offers great insight into how life was lived in a rural retreat of old. The gardens were remodeled in the 18th century to resemble English-style parkland, the horticultural fashion of the day.

Villas Around Lucca

Much as you can make a tour of these and other estates around Florence (contact the visitor center for details), so you can visit a coronet of villas and gardens around Lucca. These villas suffer less from the urban sprawl that has engulfed the Medicean villas. The best is the **Villa Reale** (*map 224 B3, tel 0583 30 108, parcovillareale.it, guided tours Tues.–Sun. March– Nov. on the hour 10 a.m.–noon & 3 p.m.–6 p.m.,*

$$) near the village of Marlia, about 9 miles (14 km) northeast of Lucca. The gardens are charming, as is the 14th-century villa (closed to the public), which Napoleon's sister, Elisa Baciocchi, restored along neoclassical lines in 1806. The environs of the **Villa Torrigiani** *(map 224 C3, tel 0583/928-041, villeepalazzilucchesi.it, closed 1 p.m.–3 p.m. & Nov.–Feb., $$),* about 5 miles (8 km) east of Marlia, are more built up, but the gardens and baroque house are captivating. The 16th-century **Villa Mansi** *(map 224 B3, Via delle Selvette 242, Segromigno in Monte, Capannori, tel 0583 920 234, closed Mon. 1 p.m.–3 p.m.*

April–Sept., & 1 p.m.–2 p.m. Oct.–March, $$$) just a mile away (1.6 km) is also worth a visit, as is the superb formal garden at the **Villa Garzoni** *(map 224 C3, Via delle Cartiere 4, tel 0572 429 590, $$$)* near Collodi, 10 miles (16 km) east of Lucca. Collodi is also home to **Parco di Pinocchio** *(Via San Genaro 3, tel 0572 429 342, pinocchio.it, closed 2nd & 3rd Mon. of month, $$$ or $$$$ combined ticket with Villa Garzoni garden),* a theme park devoted to the storybook character Pinocchio, whose creator, Carlo Lorenzini (1826–1890)—known as Carlo Collodi—was born in the village.

The baroque exuberance of the Villa Torrigiani near Lucca, with its English-style gardens

Volterra

On a gloomy day Volterra can seem a brooding, desolate sort of place, a lonely sentinel set amid volcanic hills that seem a world away from Tuscany's more pastoral countryside. English writer D. H. Lawrence (1885–1930) described it in *Etruscan Places* (1932) as a place that "gets all the winds, and sees all the world, . . . a sort of inland island, still curiously isolated and grim."

Volterra

🔼 224 C2

Visitor Information

✉ Piazza dei Priori 20

☎ 0588 87 257

volterratur.it

This said, Volterra is also a majestic town, perched on a craggy summit behind rings of Etruscan and medieval walls, and filled with churches, parks, Roman remains, stone-flagged streets, and one of the region's leading archaeological museums. Sunny weather turns it into a perfect day's outing from

The "Cemento e Ferro" ("Cement and Steel") sculpture by Mario Staccioli outside Volterra

San Gimignano or elsewhere. Latterly, the town has become known for its role in the popular Twilight series of novels—though the movie version of *New Moon* was actually filmed in Montepulciano.

The town began as an Etruscan outpost, its lofty site and the presence of mineral and alabaster deposits accounting for its early rise (alabaster products are still sold in its shops). It was vital too in medieval times for its alum mines, which provided an essential raw material for the dyeing of cloth.

Monuments & Masterpieces: Volterra's medieval prosperity is reflected in the scope of the monuments in **Piazza dei Priori,** the heart of the old town. Buildings here include the Palazzo dei Priori (1208), one of Tuscany's earliest civic palaces, and the slightly later Palazzo Pretorio, best known for its **Torre del Porcellino** (Piglet's Tower), named for the worn, carved boar that sits alongside an upper-floor window.

Also in the square is the **Duomo,** or cathedral, begun in 1120, but much altered over the centuries. Its main treasure is a "Deposition" (1228) in a chapel off the right transept, a rare work that consists of a group of brightly painted wooden figures. On the

EXPERIENCE: See Tuscany on Two Wheels

Many foreign companies offer cycling vacations, though it is also easy to rent bikes on arrival and travel independently. Locally, **Toscana Adventure Team** (tel 348 791 1215, tateam.it) can organize guided and self-guided day and longer bike tours. Contact the local visitor centers for bike rental outlets in larger towns such as Volterra. The best hiking areas (see sidebar p. 277) are also often the best cycling areas, though Chianti is hilly and wooded, with restricted views. Many backcountry "roads" are often *strade bianche,* or "white" compacted gravel roads that may not offer the best surface for cycling.

high altar is a *ciborio,* or marble altarpiece (1471), by Mino da Fiesole, who was also responsible for the flanking angels. Behind the cathedral stands the 13th-century octagonal **baptistery,** partly decorated in the striped marble bands typical of Pisan-style Romanesque architecture. Its interior highlight is a baptismal font by Andrea Sansovino (1460–1529).

Just south of the baptistery on Via Roma lies the Palazzo Vescovile, or Bishops' Palace. It is now home to the **Museo Diocesano d'Arte Sacra,** a rich little museum filled with paintings, sculptures, and other precious artifacts. Its principal treasures are a terracotta bust of St. Linus, the next pope after St. Peter, by Andrea della Robbia; an anonymous 13th-century painted "Crucifix"; and a painting of the "Madonna Enthroned With Saints" (1521) by mannerist artist Rosso Fiorentino.

Another great work by Fiorentino, "Descent from the Cross"— many consider it a masterpiece of the mannerist tradition—is found in the town's **Pinacoteca e Museo Civico** (art gallery, civic, and alabaster museum), along with excellent paintings by other leading Tuscan artists such as Taddeo di Bartolo and Luca Signorelli (see p. 43).

Another masterpiece from a different era awaits in the **Museo Etrusco Guarnacci** *(Via Don Minzoni 14, tel 0588 86 347, $$$ or $$$$ combined ticket with Pinacoteca e Museo Civico),* one of Italy's best Etruscan museums outside Rome. Etruscan art is not to all tastes, but few people would not be moved by the first-century B.C. statue of "Gli Sposi" ("The Newlyweds"), a vivid sculptural tomb portrait, or by the collection's bronze statuettes, such as the third-century B.C. "Ombra della Sera" ("Shadow of the Evening"), an elongated nude.

Volterra is not just a town of museums, however, and you should try to walk to its eastern margins to see the **Rocca** (a Medici castle) and the **Parco Archeologico,** a lovely area of parkland. Breach the old medieval walls to the north through the Porta Fiorentina and you come to the excavations with an impressive Roman theater, bath complex, and other remains. Leave time to walk to the west of the town to see the famous **Balze,** a series of sheer, eroded cliffs and alabaster mines where the ruins of Volterra's Etruscan walls are still visible. ∎

Museo Diocesano d'Arte Sacra

⊠ Via Roma 13
☎ 0588 86 290
$ $

Pinacoteca e Museo Civico

⊠ Via dei Sarti 1
☎ 0588 87 580
🕐 Alabaster Ecomuseum section closed Mon. p.m. Nov.– mid-March
$ $$, $$$ (combined ticket with Museo Etrusco Guarnacci)

Pisa

Most people know Pisa's famous Leaning Tower. Fewer know that it's just one component in a lovely ensemble of medieval buildings; fewer still know that the rest of the city—sadly—is a largely modern place, the result of heavy bombing during World War II. Allow an hour or so to see the tower and its surroundings, and about the same again to explore Pisa's other medieval sights.

The Leaning Tower and the cathedral dominate Pisa's Campo dei Miracoli.

Pisa

🔼 224 B3

Visitor Information

✉ Piazza Vittorio Emanuele II 16

☎ 050 42 291

🕐 Closed p.m.

✉ Pisa Airport (Arrivals)

☎ 050 502 518

pisaunicaterra.it

Pisa began as an Etruscan and subsequently a Roman colony, and it continued to thrive under Lombard rule in the 7th and 8th centuries. Its glory came in the 11th and 12th centuries, when a thriving port and far-flung trading links turned it into a Mediterranean maritime power. The wealth from this era yielded the Leaning Tower and other key monuments, although the city's golden age was cut short by a naval defeat at the hands of the Genoese in 1284 and by the silting up of the city's harbor. Florence assumed control of the

city in 1406, accelerating Pisa's transformation into a quiet center of science and learning. A university had been established in 1343, among whose alumni was Pisan-born Galileo Galilei. Much of Pisa's heritage was ravaged in a few weeks, however, when the city was shelled in 1944 by both Nazi and Allied forces during World War II.

Campo dei Miracoli

The **Torre Pendente** (Leaning Tower) survived the bombs—a miraculous outcome, especially as other monuments within a few feet were destroyed. The tower is one element of the Campo dei Miracoli, or Field of Miracles, a large, grassy piazza that also contains Pisa's cathedral, baptistery, and Camposanto (cemetery).

The tower was begun in 1173 as the cathedral's campanile, or bell tower, and started to lean almost immediately, the result of the weak, sandy subsoil underpinning its foundations. Attempts to rectify the lean over the next 180 years–the time it took to complete the tower–ended in failure. Galileo famously made use of the overhang when he dropped metal balls from the tower to show that falling bodies of different weight descend at the same rate. The lean intensified during the 20th century, leading to the tower's closure in 1990 and a raft of schemes designed to prevent its collapse (see pp. 248–249).

The tower's drama detracts from the Campo's other monuments, which in any other place would be accounted must-see masterpieces. The **Duomo,** or cathedral–among Italy's finest Romanesque buildings–was begun about a century earlier than the tower, in 1064, well before the start of the present-day cathedrals in rival cities such as Florence (1296) and Siena

Leaning Tower of Pisa

🅜 245 (Torre Pendente)

Visitor Information

✉ Piazza Duomo, 17

☎ 050 83 50 11/12

🕑 Open Mon.– Thurs. 8 a.m.– 1:30 p.m. & 3 p.m.–6 p.m. Fri. 8:30 a.m.–1:30 p.m.

boxoffice.opapisa.it /Turisti

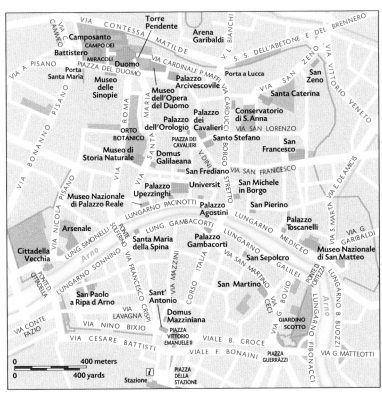

(1179). With its array of pillars, columns, and colored marbles, the Duomo became the model for similar "Pisan-Romanesque" churches across central Italy, many of which borrowed its use of a striped marble exterior and ornate decorative motifs, a style assimilated by Pisa through its trading links with the Arab, Byzantine, and Levantine worlds.

Duomo Treasures: The carving on the exterior predates the appearance of Pisa's finest sculptors, Nicola and Giovanni Pisano in the 13th century. Their inspired and often innovative work is found inside the building instead, as well as in the baptistery and other centers across Italy, such as Lucca and Pistoia. In their absence, the exterior's highlight is the **Portale di San Ranieri** (1180), previously the main entrance—now tucked away behind the right transept facing the Leaning Tower. The work of a local sculptor, Bonanno Pisano, it consists

INSIDER TIP:

If you're unfit, or suffer from vertigo or claustrophobia, or just aren't inclined toward crowds, the Leaning Tower is best admired from the ground.

—NEIL SHEA
National Geographic writer

of 24 bronze panels portraying stories from the New Testament. Don't miss the door's surrounds, or architrave, which incorporate fragments of Roman friezes and sculptures from the second century A.D. The visitors' entrance is normally the side door on the right-hand side of the cathedral as you face it from the baptistery.

Some of the cathedral's earliest treasures were lost in a fire in 1595, meaning that much of the **interior** dates from the ensuing period of restoration (1602–1616). Two items that

Visiting the Leaning Tower & Campo dei Miracoli

There are so many rules, regulations, and restrictions involved in climbing Pisa's Leaning Tower these days that many savvy travelers find good reasons to ponder its mystique from ground level. Visits to the Leaning Tower must be reserved online 12–20 days in advance *(opapisa.it, €18)*. The tower's opening times vary greatly with the seasons, so if you do wish to make the climb, always check online once you've confirmed the dates of your visit *(opapisa .it/en/plan-your-visit)*. Tours are guided and strictly limited to 30 minutes. Tours

do not wait, and slots are forfeited if you are late. Children under 8 are not admitted; and children 8–18 must be accompanied by an adult. And remember: Visits require climbing 300 steps in confined and exposed areas. The other key sights on the Campo dei Miracoli are the Duomo *(free, tokens must be collected at the Campo ticket office)* and the Camposanto, Museo delle Sinopie, Museo dell'Opera del Duomo, and Battistero. You can buy tickets for individual sights *(€5)* or two *(€7)*, three *(€8)*, and four *(€9)* sights combined.

survived were the apse mosaic of "Christ in Majesty" (1302), part of which is by Cimabue, the teacher of Giotto, and Tino di Camaino's tomb (1315) of Holy Roman Emperor Henry VII (*R.*1308–1313), which you will find high on the left wall of the south (right-hand) transept. The tomb was partly damaged by the fire, and several of its statues were moved to the Museo dell'Opera del Duomo (see pp. 250–251) following restoration. Henry died near Siena, having ransacked the city and then, reputedly, eaten a poisoned wafer at Mass. The Pisans, allies of the emperor, bore his body back to their native city.

Far greater than either of these works is Giovanni Pisano's exceptional **pulpit,** which was stored away after the fire and restored to public view only in 1926. It was the last and finest of the series of pulpits created by Nicola and Giovanni Pisano across Tuscany. Note how most of the figures crowding its surface are carved almost "free" of the block of stone—a technically demanding discipline. Note, too, the work's immense narrative skill, particularly the manner in which several scenes depicting Christ's Passion—from Judas's betrayal to Christ's scourging—are compressed into a single panel. The inscription on the cornice, incidentally, states that Giovanni knew the "art of pure sculpture . . . and would not know how to carve base or ugly things, even if he wished to."

An equally staggering pulpit by Nicola Pisano stands in the circular **Battistero** (begun in 1152), a

The interior of the Duomo in the Campo dei Miracoli

building whose plain interior is in marked contrast to its intricately fashioned exterior. The **pulpit** stands on slender pillars bearing the allegorical figures of the "Virtues," while its main narrative scenes describe the "Annunciation," "Nativity," "Announcement to the Shepherds," "Adoration of the Magi," "Presentation in the Temple," "Crucifixion," and "Last Judgment." Between 1270 and 1297, Nicola and Giovanni were also responsible for much of the exquisite carving on the baptistery's exterior, added after a lull in building caused by financial *(continued on p. 250)*

Saving the Leaning Tower

Pisa's Torre Pendente, or Leaning Tower, was in trouble from the start. Begun in 1173, the tower was built on weak, sandy subsoil that had once been covered by the sea. It had already started to sink when work was abandoned at the third of its planned eight levels in 1178. In 1272 engineers attempted to correct the lean—then already 3 feet (1 m) from the vertical—by changing the thickness of the marble as they built. In 1370 the upper belfry was added off-center in another attempt to straighten the tower. The result, in the words of one modern engineer, was a structure that "curved like a banana."

British and French engineers conducted tests on the tower in the 19th century—the lean in 1817 was 12 feet 6 inches (3.8 m)—but the first accurate measurements were made only in 1911. By January 7, 1990, the day the tower was finally closed to visitors, the 196-foot (60 m), 16,000-ton (14,500 metric tons) tower was 17 feet 6 inches (5.4 m) from the vertical—a lean of 5.5 degrees. Worse, the rate of lean was accelerating. Various interventions in 1935 and 1970 had made things worse by disturbing the already unstable subsoil. At the rate of lean current in 1990,

experts foresaw two doomsday scenarios: A gravity-induced collapse would occur within 25 years, or a structural collapse could happen at any time because of the internal pressures exerted on the tower's second story by the imbalance of weight above it.

In 1990 an international panel was convened to ponder the problem. Endless theories and solutions were proposed: The Russians suggested slicing off the base, the Chinese argued for a second "twin" to the tower to pull on its neighbor, and the Japanese proposed pulling the tower down and

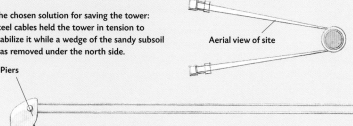

Aerial view of site

The chosen solution for saving the tower: Steel cables held the tower in tension to stabilize it while a wedge of the sandy subsoil was removed under the north side.

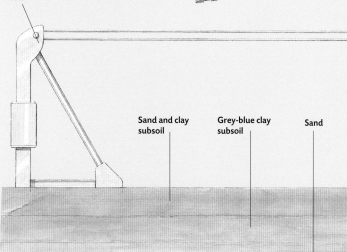

Piers

Sand and clay subsoil

Grey-blue clay subsoil

Sand

rebuilding it straight. Meanwhile, contingency measures were put in place, including fastening 18 steel belts around sections of the tower to prevent buckling and laying a concrete ring around the base. In 1993, 661 tons (600 metric tons) of lead weights were fixed to the tower's north side to counterbalance the southward tilt. In six months the tower had straightened—but by just half an inch (1.25 cm).

The Plan: The chosen solution, budgeted to cost $26.7 million, was begun in 1998. First, vast steel cables were attached to the tower 65 feet (20 m) up and anchored in huge concrete blocks about 100 yards (91 m) away. These were a stabilizing, not a corrective, measure. The real work of correction was to be achieved by the gradual removal of a 26-inch (66 cm) wedge of subsoil from beneath the north side of the tower. This would allow the structure to settle back toward the vertical. After five months of work the results were impressive. The tower had returned to its position of around 110 years ago, a movement back to the vertical of 5 inches (12.5 cm). Work continued

to remove some 14 cubic yards (10 cu m) of soil to arrive at a 10 percent or 17-inch (43 cm) correction by mid-2001. The final stages involved the reinforcement of the foundations and the removal of the cables, concrete anchors, lead weights, and other eyesores. For visitors the difference is not noticeable—the Leaning Tower still leans—but for the tower it should mean salvation for at least another 350 years. Or so the engineers and scientists hope.

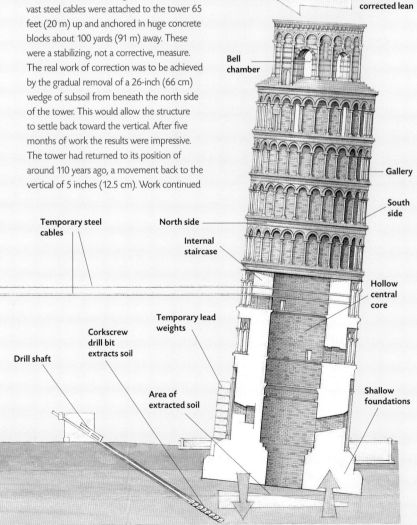

Direction of corrected lean

Bell chamber

Gallery

South side

North side

Internal staircase

Temporary steel cables

Hollow central core

Corkscrew drill bit extracts soil

Temporary lead weights

Drill shaft

Area of extracted soil

Shallow foundations

Age-old refreshment in Pisa's Piazza dei Cavalieri

sarcophagi), and while interesting in their own way, they are a poor substitute for what by all accounts was one of Tuscany's foremost fresco cycles before it succumbed to an Allied incendiary bomb on July 27, 1944. Only a handful of frescoes survived the molten lead that streamed from the burning roof, notably the anonymous "Triumph of Death" in a room opposite the entrance. Painted in the wake of the Black Death in 1348, it shows three huntsmen confronted by three coffins, the noxious contents of which force one of the nobles to pinch his nose. Angels and demons bear the souls of the dead to their fate, which is delineated in a nearby fresco of the "Last Judgment," probably the work of the same artist. Some surviving sketches of other frescoes are in the **Museo delle Sinopie** (Piazza del Duomo).

Artistic treasures from both the cathedral and the baptistery can be seen in the **Museo dell'Opera del Duomo** in the Campo's southeast corner. Some of its most captivating works are sculptural, particularly those of Giovanni Pisano, whose masterpiece here is the "Madonna del Colloquio," a carved group of the Madonna and Child with St. John the Baptist and St. John the Evangelist. Removed from above the baptistery's main door in 1935, it takes its name from the intimate, or colloquial, gaze being exchanged by the Virgin and Child. Giovanni was also responsible for the fine ivory "Madonna and Child" in the museum Treasury, which also contains the noted "Croce dei Pisani," a cross carried by Pisan troops in the First Crusade. Other

shortfalls following loss of trade to Genoa. The interior's lovely inlaid font (1246) is by a sculptor from northern Italy, Guido Bigarelli da Como. Notice the four small fonts inside its main octagonal basin, designed for baptizing infants.

The Campo's last component, the **Camposanto,** is a medieval cemetery (begun 1278) that takes the form of a large Gothic cloister. According to legend it was filled with earth brought back from the Holy Land during the Crusades— the aim being to allow notable Pisans to be buried in sacred ground. The cemetery contains a large range of tombs from different eras (including Roman

INSIDER TIP:

Cross the Arno via the Ponte Solferino to see the spiky exterior of Santa Maria della Spina. This church was built by a 14th-century merchant, inspired by the thorn (spina) he obtained from Christ's crown of thorns.

—TOM O'NEILL
National Geographic writer

notable sculptors represented in the museum include Tino di Camaino, who often collaborated with Giovanni Pisano, and who here was responsible for the statues removed from the tomb of Henry VII in the cathedral.

Other Highlights

Moving away from Campo dei Miracoli, the highlights of the rest of the town begin with **Piazza dei Cavalieri,** a square ringed by medieval buildings. At the end of Via Dini you come to Borgo Stretto, home to many of Pisa's stores. This street reaches the river past San Michele in Borgo, an 11th-century church on the left. Turn left on Lungarno Mediceo and you come to the **Museo Nazionale di San Matteo** *(Piazza San Matteo, tel 050 541 865, closed Sun. p.m. & Mon., $$ or $$$ combined ticket with Museo Nazionale di Palazzo Reale),* which has a wide-ranging collection of paintings, ceramics, sculptures, and other decorative arts, most collected from Pisa's churches. You'll find several gems here, namely paintings of the "Madonna and Child" by Fra Angelico, a superb "Madonna and Child With Saints" by Simone Martini, a "Madonna of Humility" by Gentile da Fabriano, and a bronze bust of "St. Lussorio" by Donatello.

San Matteo is Pisa's principal museum, but you might also visit the **Museo Nazionale di Palazzo Reale** *(Piazza Carrara, Lungarno Pacinotti 46, tel 050 926 539, closed p.m. daily & Tues. & Sun., $ or $$$ combined ticket with Museo Nazionale di San Matteo)* farther west on the banks of the Arno. It houses several private collections left to the city, including a huge range of textiles, ceramics, paintings, prints, sculptures, and other objets d'art. ∎

EXPERIENCE: Escape on Horseback into Tuscany

Tired of the crowds in Pisa? Why not ride off into a Tuscan sunset? Tuscany is perfect for horseback riding, thanks to its ancient mule tracks, quiet country lanes, numerous woodland trails, and the preponderance of rural farm-stay accommodations, or *agriturismi,* where riding is one of many countryside pursuits available. Typically, farm stays offer small self-catering apartments rather than rooms, usually on properties dotted around the farm estate. Prices are often lower than those charged by hotels.

Visitor centers in Pisa, Siena, San Gimignano, and other Tuscan towns carry lists of *agriturismo* accommodations, along with information on riding. Numerous online agencies also offer listings, including *agriturismitaliani.it* and *agriturismo.it.* Many of the properties also offer half- or full-day excursions from cities such as Pisa even if you are not staying on the property.

Lucca

Lucca is one of those hallowed historic places where, in the words of English essayist Hilaire Belloc (1870–1953), "everything . . . is good" (*The Path to Rome*, 1902). Within ancient walls, the town is peaceful and urbane, its medieval heart an attractive mix of piazzas, tiny churches, galleries, and cobbled lanes. You will still find it, in the words of American novelist Henry James (1843–1916), "overflowing with everything that makes for ease, for plenty, for beauty, for interest and good example" (*Italy Revisited*, 1877).

The Piazza San Michele at the heart of Lucca was once the site of the old Roman forum.

Lucca

🄰 224 B3

Visitor Information

✉ Piazzale Giuseppe Verdi

☎ 0583 583 150

**www.luccatourist.it
luccaterre.it**

Lucca is easily reached as a day trip from Florence: Trains take about 70 minutes and arrive at the station in Piazza Ricasoli just south of the city's magnificent walls and a five-minute walk from the center. If you're coming by car, park outside these walls; parking in the old center is difficult and there are strict time limits on how long you can stay. One of the bigger parking lots is on the west edge of the old center by Porta San Donato, just five minutes from the main sights. Everything you want to see lies within the walls, and everything can easily be seen on foot. If you've parked by Porta San Donato, you're also close to the **visitor center** in Piazzale Giuseppe Verdi.

The best plan is to start in the central square, Piazza San Michele, work south toward the cathedral, and then walk through the eastern part of the city to visit the sights in the north—the itinerary followed below. There's plenty to see and you could easily stay overnight, but if time is short be certain to see the church of San Martino in Foro, the Duomo di San Martino, the Casa Guinigi (for the view from its tower), the Museo Nazionale di Villa Guinigi, Piazza dell'Anfiteatro, and the church of San Frediano. Also allow time to walk around part of the city walls.

As you walk, you'll quickly notice the gridiron plan of its city center, a legacy of the Romans' rational approach to town planning. Under the Goths and Lombards the city later served as the Tuscan capital, and it is widely believed to have been the first

center in the region to embrace Christianity. It rose to medieval prominence as a result of a flourishing trade in silk—lingerie is still a major Lucchese money-earner—and during the 14th century the city captured both Pisa and Pistoia. It even came close to conquering Florence. Thereafter, the city declined but maintained an independent status outside the Grand Duchy of Tuscany until the arrival of Napoleon, who presented the city to his sister Elisa Baciocchi. The Bourbons then assumed control until Italian Unification.

Lucca's natural heart is **Piazza San Michele,** the place to start your visit. Few sights are quite as breathtaking as its dazzling centerpiece, the church of **San Michele in Foro** (closed noon–3 p.m.), begun in 1070 on the site of the old

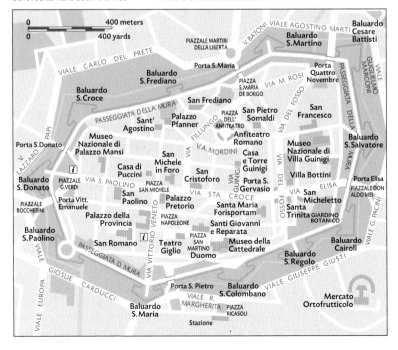

Roman *foro, or* forum. Its stupendous **facade** combines a distinctive marble-striped veneer with an astounding confection of miniature loggias, blind arcades, and inventively twisted columns. This decorative combination, and the striped marble motifs in particular, is typical of the so-called Pisan style of Romanesque architecture, a style developed in the light of

---

Take A Day Trip to Barga

If you are in Lucca, consider driving north to the delightful village of Barga, in a little-visited region known as the Garfagnana. The village sits in the lee of the Orecchiella Hills, nestled on green slopes overlooking the Serchio Valley and the jagged peaks of the distant Alpi Apuane. The highlight of Barga is a captivating tenth-century cathedral, a vision of honey-colored stone fronted by a beautiful panoramic terrace. The facade is adorned with reliefs and other carvings, and inside are a huge tenth-century statue of St. Christopher and a carved pulpit by the 13th-century sculptor Bigarelli da Como.

Pisa's trading links with the Orient and the ornate influence of Byzantine art. In time, the style's influence extended to Siena (the cathedral), Florence (cathedral and baptistery), and beyond. It's an architectural hybrid you'll come across often in Lucca, one of the city's many pleasures being the number of times you round a corner to find yourself confronted with a little jewel of a church.

San Michele's plain **interior** is less arresting than the facade, largely because most of the church's funds were lavished on the exterior. It does have one major work of art, however: Filippino Lippi's late 15th-century painting of "Sts. Jerome, Sebastian, Roch, and Helena" at the end of the south (right) nave. After seeing the interior, walk around the outside of the church to look at the tiny windows sunk low on the apse, part of a ninth-century church on the site.

After inspecting the **Casa di Puccini** (see sidebar p. 257), walk back to Piazza San Michele and turn right on Via Vittorio Veneto to Piazza Napoleone. Here the vast building on your right is the **Palazzo della Provincia** (1578–1728; *occasional opening Mon.–Fri. 9 a.m.–1 p.m.*), formerly the Palazzo della Signoria, the seat of Lucca's ruling council.

Duomo

Bear left across the piazza into the linked and smaller Piazza del Giglio, where an alley on the left leads to Piazza San Giovanni and Lucca's cathedral, the **Duomo** *(Piazza San Martino, closed Sun. 10:45 a.m.–noon & during services).* According to tradition, the first church on the Duomo's site was founded in the sixth century by St. Frediano, an Irish monk, and became the seat of the local bishopric in the eighth century. Anselmo da Baggio, Bishop of Lucca, commissioned the present structure in 1060 and consecrated it ten years later, by which time he had become Pope Alexander II (R.1061–1073).

Another wonderful **facade** (1060–1241) fronts the building, its effect undiminished by its curious asymmetry. This is the result of its having been squeezed next to the campanile, or bell tower, the lower part of which—originally built as a defensive bastion—was already in place when work began. The facade's most important feature is a series of 13th-century relief carvings around the atrium and the entrance doors. Those on and around the left-hand door are almost certainly the work of celebrated Pisan sculptor Nicola Pisano, and they depict the "Annunciation," "Nativity," "Adoration of the Magi," and—in the lunette—the "Deposition." The equally captivating panels between the doors are probably the work of the facade's principal architect, Guidetto da Como, who was active in the early 13th century. Some show episodes from the life of St. Martin (San Martino), to whom the cathedral is dedicated; others, the labors and activities associated with the "Twelve Months of the Year." In the latter scenes you can easily make out the labors concerned—winemaking, threshing, a graphic pig-sticking, fruit-picking, and so on. The right-hand door lunette has a relief showing the "Beheading of St. Regolus," a Christian martyr whose relics were honored inside the church and whose altar (see p. 256) was reached via this door.

Unlike San Michele, San Martino's **interior** is filled with points of artistic interest. Immediately on entering, turn around to admire the 13th-century sculpture of "St. Martin on Horseback with the Beggar" to the left of the main door, by an unknown hand. It shows the fourth-century saint sharing his cloak with a poor man, a figure he later recognized as Christ. Above the left door spreads a late 15th-century fresco describing the story of the Volto Santo. Its meaning becomes clearer midway down the nave on the left when you come to the **Tempietto,** a gaudy octagonal chapel designed by a prolific

INSIDER TIP:

See Lucca from above, along the ramparts circling the city that have now been converted into pretty parkland, ideal for walking.

—BARBARA A. NOE
National Geographic Travel Books senior editor

local sculptor, Matteo Civitali (1435–1511). It was created to house the much venerated Volto Santo (Holy Face), a cedarwood crucifix said to be a true likeness of Christ carved by Nicodemus, an eyewitness to the Crucifixion. In truth it's probably a 13th-century copy of an original 8th-century work. Legend claims the statue miraculously found its way to Lucca of its own accord, journeying by boat and then being carried to the city on oxen guided by Divine Will. Whatever the truth, it attracted countless pilgrims to the city, generating enormous wealth for the church in the process. It is perhaps no coincidence that the statue appeared during the reign of Bishop Anselmo, whose elevation to the papacy was hardly hurt by its miraculous apparition.

Of greater artistic merit is the tomb of Ilaria del Carretto (1408), second wife of Paolo Guinigi, one of Lucca's leading medieval rulers. This masterpiece of Sienese sculptor Jacopo della Quercia is one of the loveliest sculptures in Italy. Especially touching is the little dog, a symbol of Ilaria's faithfulness. The work is housed in the sacristy off the south (right-hand) side; a small fee ($) is payable for admission (see Museo della Cattedrale below). This payment also allows you to admire the "Madonna and Child With Saints" by Florentine artist Domenico Ghirlandaio.

Beyond the entrance to the sacristy turn into the right transept, where on the wall immediately on your right is another good work by Civitali, the tomb of Pietro da Noceto, secretary to Pope Niccolò V. Civitali was also responsible for the fine **Altare di San Regolo,** which contains the tomb of San Regolo (St. Regolus), a martyred early bishop of Lucca. It stands on the wall to the right of the main high altar. The cathedral's final outstanding work of art is Fra Bartolommeo's "Madonna and Child With Saints" (1509), housed in the **Cappella del Santuario,** to the left of the high altar.

Museo della Cattedrale:
A combined ticket for the sacristy also admits you to the Museo della Cattedrale (Piazza

Lucca is almost unique in Tuscany in that its inhabitants choose to use bicycles rather than cars.

Antelminelli, tel 0583 490 530,
www.museocattedralelucca.it, closed
p.m. Mon.–Fri. Nov.–mid-March, $
or $$ combined ticket with cathedral
sacristy & Santi Giovanni e Reparata)
outside the cathedral, which has
a fine collection of paintings,
sculptures, illustrated manuscripts,
and religious ephemera. It also
allows you into the nearby church
of **Santi Giovanni e Reparata**
(Piazza Antelminelli, closed Mon.–Fri.
Nov.–mid-March, $ or $$ combined
ticket with cathedral sacristy &
Museo della Cattedrale), where
excavations have revealed Roman
buildings, the remains of Lucca's
first cathedral, and—to the rear left
of the present church—two early
baptisteries from the fifth and
eighth centuries.

Walking the Walls

From the lanes just south of the
cathedral climb up to Lucca's
magnificent walls (1544–1645),
which offer a broad, tree-lined
2.5-mile (4.2 km) path around
the city that are ideal for walking or biking on. The ramparts
were begun partly in response
to the threat posed by Florence
in the early 16th century and
partly because the old medieval
walls (raised in 1198) were
redundant with recent advances
in weaponry. The resulting
defenses were an impressive
100 feet (30 m) wide at the
base, 40 feet (12 m) high, and
protected by moats 120 feet
(35 m) wide. Although the
effort required to build them
was enormous, the city never
needed to use them in a
conflict; the only siege the

residents ever faced was from
the floodwaters of the Serchio
River in 1812, when the gates
were sealed to prevent the city's
being deluged. Napoleon's sister
Elisa Baciocchi, then the city's
governor, returned to Lucca at
the last minute and had to
be winched over the city walls
by crane.

Giacomo Puccini

Lucca's most famous son, composer
Giacomo Puccini (1858–1924), was born
a stone's throw from San Michele. His
birthplace, the **Casa di Puccini** *(Corte*
San Lorenzo 9, Via di Poggio 30, tel 0583
584 028, puccinimuseum.org, closed Tues.,
$$), now contains a music academy and a
small museum devoted to the composer.
Puccini came from a local family that had
provided organists for the city's cathedral
for four generations, although in early life
he was no more than a chorister at nearby
San Michele. Later he went on to become
one of Italy's foremost opera composers,
responsible for great works such as *Tosca,*
Madama Butterfly, and *La Bohème.*

Beyond the ramparts, a
swathe of grass insulates the old
center from the modern world,
the legacy of a medieval decree
that ordered the removal of
any vegetation that might offer
cover to an enemy lurking
without with schemes of siege
or invasion. One target on your
walk might be Il Caffè della Mura
(Via Vittorio Emanuele II 2, tel
0583 464 552), a fine old café-
restaurant next to the Baluardo
Santa Maria, one of the walls'
11 major bastions, southwest
of the cathedral.

EXPERIENCE: Stay in a Convent or Monastery

Several Tuscan monasteries have been converted into fine accommodations, such as **Badia a Coltibuono** (see sidebar p. 238), for example—but you can also stay in the real thing: working convents or monasteries, often in beautiful locations and at low cost. In some of these you can take some part in the community's religious life; in others you can just enjoy a period of retreat from the rest of the world. **Monastery Stays** (*monasterystays.com*) offers numerous Tuscan options, including the **Casa Diocesana E. Bartoletti** near Lucca, and several in Florence, with lots of information and reservation details, or you can contact the listed monasteries directly.

Walking East: Walk east from here and you soon look down on the **Giardino Botanico** (*Via del Giardino Botanico 14, tel 0583 583 086, open daily mid-March–Nov.*), a peaceful botanical garden entered from just off Via del Fosso.

Green-thumbed visitors might want to explore the beautiful gardens just north of the Giardino Botanico at the **Villa Bottini,** also known as the Villa Buonvisi (*Via Elisa, tel 0583 442 140, closed Sun.*), once owned by Elisa Baciocchi. To reach the villa, you follow Via del Fosso (the street with a canal) north and turn right (east) on Via Elisa. You soon come to **San Micheletto,** an ancient but much altered church. Another, larger church, San Ponziano, lies a little farther down the street. The villa's entrance is close to San Micheletto on the left.

Retracing your steps back down Via Elisa and crossing Via del Fosso, just past the little church of Santa Trìnita on the left, you come to the **Porta San Gervasio** (1260), one of the most impressive of the city's original medieval gateways. Follow Via Santa Croce beyond and you come to a piazza containing **Santa Maria Forisportam** (literally "St. Mary Outside the Walls"), a charming but unfinished 13th-century Pisan-Romanesque church that once lay close to the city's Roman and medieval walls. From here, walk down Via Santa Croce, whose side streets contain a cluster of interesting little churches: 13th-century San Giulio and the Chiesa del Suffragio lie to the north (take the first alley on the right after Via Guinigi), San Benedetto in Gottella and Santa Maria dei Servi to the south.

Walk back to the junction of Via Santa Croce and Via Guinigi; turn left up Via Guinigi and you come to the city's strangest sight, the **Casa Guinigi** (*Via Sant'Andrea 41–Via Guinigi 29, tel 0583 48 524, $$*), a medieval town house built by the Guinigi, Lucca's preeminent noble family. It's best known for its **tower**—which has lovely city views—and the holm oaks sprouting from its roof.

Walking North: From the tower walk north on Via Guinigi and turn right at the top on Via A. Mordini, following the street as it bears left to **San Pietro Somaldi** (*closed noon–3 p.m.*), a tiny gem of a church built in the 12th century over an earlier, 8th-century church. From here you can take Via della

Fratta to see the immense church of **San Francesco** (1228), worth a look for its fresco fragments and fine choir stalls. Beyond it on the right, another former Guinigi palace houses the **Museo Nazionale di Villa Guinigi** (*Via della Quarquonia, tel 0583 496 033, closed Mon. & p.m. Sun., $$$ combined ticket with Museo Nazionale di Palazzo Mansi*), built in 1418 and today given over to a collection of archaeological displays, medieval paintings, sculptures, textiles, and applied arts. The highlights are paintings by Fra Bartolommeo and sculptures by Matteo Civitali, whose work is also in the cathedral.

Piazza dell'Anfiteatro & Beyond: Walk back to San Pietro and go right, and then take the first left, Via del Portico, to Piazza dell'Anfiteatro. The medieval houses of this wonderfully distinctive piazza were built into the oval of Lucca's old Roman amphitheater. Traces of the ancient structure are still visible, woven into the later buildings, although much of the original stone was ransacked during the 12th century for use in Lucca's many Romanesque churches.

A short distance to the northwest, across Via Fillungo, stands **San Frediano** (1112–1147; *closed noon–3 p.m. Mon.–Sat.*), the third of Lucca's great churches. Its exterior is distinguished not by the columns and reliefs of San Martino and San Michele, but by a striking 13th-century facade mosaic of the "Ascension." Inside, the main highlight is the

12th-century **Fontana Lustrale,** a large font close to the entrance on the south (right-hand) side. It is thought three sculptors were responsible for the work. The first, Maestro Roberto, produced the stories of Moses on the outer sections of the main basin (notice the scene of the "Crossing of the Red Sea," in which the Egyptian

The striking facade mosaic of San Frediano

soldiers are portrayed as chivalric medieval knights); the second, an unknown artist, added the figures of the six Apostles and the Good Shepherd; and the third, also unknown, carved the remaining Apostles and the "Months of the Year" labors above the basin.

Behind the font on the wall are terra-cotta sculptures of the "Annunciation" and a figure of "St. Bartholomew" by Matteo and Andrea della Robbia, respectively. Behind these to the left lies the Cappella Fatinelli, which contains the uncorrupted body of St. Zita, a 13th-century Lucca-born maidservant who became the patron saint of domestic servants. According to one story, she habitually took bread from her master's house to give to the poor. When asked one day what she was carrying in her apron, she replied: "Only roses and other flowers." When examined, it transpired that the bread had been miraculously transformed.

Moving on, watch for the 12th-century marble pavement around the high altar, which was raised above the body of St. Frediano. Back toward the church entrance, the first chapel on the right, the **Cappella Trenta** (fourth from the entrance), built

INSIDER TIP:

If you have a car, don't miss visiting the nearby medieval town of Monteriggioni [see p. 262]. It's one of the most beautiful walled villages in the world.

—MICHAEL BROUSE
National Geographic author

in 1413, contains an exceptional carved altarpiece (1422) and the worn pavement tombs of the chapel's patron, Lorenzo Trenta, and his wife. All three are by Sienese sculptor Jacopo della Quercia. Continuing, the **Cappella di Sant'Agostino** features the church's best frescoes (1508–1509), by Amico Aspertini (circa 1474–1552). They portray "St. Frediano Diverting the River Serchio" (thus saving Lucca) and the "Nativity" on the right wall and the "Baptism of St. Augustine" and "Arrival of the Volto Santo in Lucca" on the left.

Southwest of the church lie the formal 18th-century gardens of the **Palazzo Pfanner** *(Via degli Asili 33, tel 0583 491 243, open daily in summer)* and—farther west—the **Museo Nazionale di Palazzo Mansi** *(Via Galli Tassi 43, tel 340 923 3085, closed Sun. p.m. & Mon., $$ or $$$ combined ticket with Museo Nazionale di Villa Guinigi),* whose rococo decoration provides the backdrop for a fine collection of paintings. ∎

Beachlife *all'Italiana:* Join Tuscans on the Beach

The Tuscany shore does not have the deserted beaches of the Greek islands, say, or the glamorous resorts of other Mediterranean regions such as the South of France. What it does have are easygoing and unpretentious resorts where you'll gain an insight into how many Italian families spend their summer vacations *al mare*—at the seaside.

Don't expect quiet or much sand to yourself: Italians are gregarious, and the seaside is about beach games, gossip, teenage canoodling, preening, ice cream, and long, animated lunches.

All Tuscan coastal resorts have stretches of *spiaggia pubblica* (free public beach), and most are lined with *stabilimenti balneari,* or bathing concessions, where you can pay for well-groomed sand, towels, sun-loungers, showers, locker rooms, and changing and refreshment facilities.

More Places to Visit in Northern Tuscany

The beach at Viareggio attracts Italian families for vacations *al mare* (at the seaside).

The Garfagnana

If you take a day trip to Barga (see sidebar p. 254), you should expand your drive into the surrounding Garfagnana region. The Serchio Valley and the **Orecchiella** and **Apuane** mountains that flank Barga are well worth exploring. Both upland areas are crossed by tiny scenic roads, and both have plenty of marked hiking trails. Good maps are available from most local centers, notably **Castelnuovo di Garfagnana,** a town just northwest of Barga. The towns on the west, or seaward, side of the Alpi Apuane, are known for their marble quarries and have been scoured for stone by sculptors from Michelangelo to Henry Moore. **Carrara** *(aptmassacarrara .it)*, has a fine cathedral, an interesting marble museum, the **Museo del Marmo** *(Via XX Settembre, tel 0585 845 746, museodelmarmo.com, closed Sun. & 12:30 p.m.–2:30 p.m.)*, and a pretty square. It's possible to see some of the mines at closer hand *(marmotour.com)*. Follow signs from Carrara for Strada Panoramica per Le Cave.

🅰 224 B4 **Visitor Information** ✉ Comune, Via di Mezzo 45 ☎ 0583 724 743

Colle di Val d'Elsa

Colle di Val d'Elsa is an unfairly neglected town not helped by its new suburbs, which form the lower part of town, known as Colle Basso. The old medieval town on the hill, however—Colle Alto—is a delight and well worth a detour as you travel between Siena and San Gimignano. The town's medieval prosperity was based on abundant supplies of water, which nurtured glass and paper industries, both still mainstays of the local economy. **The Museo del Cristallo** *(Via dei Fossi 8a, tel 0577 924 135, cristallo .org, closed Mon. noon–3:30/4 p.m. & a.m. Tues.–Fri. mid-Oct.–April, $ or $$ combined ticket with museums below)* is devoted to the glass industry. Colle Alto consists of two streets and a web of small lanes on a hilly ridge. Follow the main street, Via del Castello, along the ridge to see the sights and catch the best views. Stop off at the **Duomo** *(Piazza del Duomo)*, notable for a beautiful marble tabernacle in the right transept attributed to Mino da Fiesole; the **Museo**

Archeologico (*Piazza del Duomo 42, tel 0577 922 954, museisenesi.org, closed Tues.–Thurs., $ or $$ combined ticket*) next door, a museum of Etruscan and other finds; and the **Museo Civico e Diocesano d'Arte Sacra** (*Via del Castello 31, tel 0577 923 095, museisenesi.org, closed L & Mon. mid-June–Sept.*). *www.comune .colle-di-val-d-elsa.si.it* 🅰 225 D2

Monteriggioni

Monteriggioni doesn't take long to see, but no village in Tuscany presents as perfect a vision of the Middle Ages. It lies just off the main Siena–Poggibonsi road, 8 miles (13 km) south of Poggibonsi. Founded by the Sienese in 1203 as a defensive citadel, it is enclosed by a perfectly preserved set of walls and towers added in 1213. Dante described its towers, added in 1260, as resembling giants in an abyss, and the relevant passage from the poet's *Inferno* greets you as you enter the walls. *monteriggioniturismo.it* 🅰 225 D2 **Visitor Information** ✉ Piazza Roma 23 ☎ 0577 304 834

INSIDER TIP:

In Pistoia, be certain to visit the church of Sant'Andrea, site of a truly magnificent pulpit that was carved in 1297 by Giovanni Pisano.

—MARINA CONTI
National Geographic Italy editor

Pistoia

Pistoia is a large town located in a seam of unprepossessing countryside between Florence and Lucca. By any standards other than those of Tuscany, however, this would be a town with lots to recommend it.

Start exploring the town in the central **Piazza del Duomo,** ringed by medieval palaces, several small museums, and the baptistery and bell tower. While here, be sure to visit the 12th-century **Duomo,** which contains the famous Dossale di San Jacopo (Altarpiece of St. James), one of Italy's most impressive pieces of silverware, begun in 1287 and completed some 200 years later. It contains 628 sculptured figures, some partially gilded, and weighs close to a ton. Visitors are charged a small fee to see the work. Also, search out the **Ospedale del Ceppo** at the end of Via Pacani, a medieval hospital adorned with a lively terra-cotta frieze (1526–1529). 🅰 224 C3 **Visitor Information** ✉ Piazza del Duomo 4 ☎ 0573 21 622

Tuscan Beach Resorts

Northern Tuscany enjoys much better developed resorts and prettier villages than the south. Much of the northern coast is known as the Riviera di Versilia. Mostly the north has mid-market resorts—Forte del Marmi is the nicest. Most are big and modern, with lots of restaurants, shops, and nightlife. Out of season (July and August) they are largely dead.

Viareggio (*map 224 B3, visitor information, Viale Carducci 10, tel 0584 962 233*) is northern Tuscany's most elegant resort, with big 19th-century hotels, a palm-lined promenade, and a hint of art nouveau architecture. It's the closest resort to Florence (an hour away by train), so it's often crowded in summer. **Forte dei Marmi** farther north is the most chic of the otherwise rather downbeat resorts of the Versilian Riviera, the coastal strip that runs to Massa.

For less developed beaches, look farther south, beyond the coastal *pineta* (pine woodland) near Capalbio or Marina di Alberese.

A beguiling mix of idyllic landscapes, hidden villages, hilltop towns, superb wines, timeless abbeys, and artistic and architectural wonders

Southern Tuscany

History and age-old culture swirl through Arezzo's Giostra del Saracino pageant.

Southern Tuscany

Few areas of Tuscany disappoint, but for sheer variety of landscape, historical interest, and outstanding villages, none quite compare with the area south of Siena. This is quintessential Tuscany, the Tuscany of vineyards, cypress-ringed villas, and olive-cloaked hills. Two of the region's finest abbeys are here, along with many of its loveliest towns. All are linked by a tangle of quiet roads that cross some of Italy's most beautiful countryside.

The best starting point for a tour is Siena, from which you can drive south-east toward Asciano, a route that leads through the so-called Crete, a "badlands" scenery of bare clay hills, sweeping vistas, and summer fields of wheat, flax, and sunflowers. Following scenic minor roads—one of the region's glories—you come to the fresco-filled Monte Oliveto Maggiore,

the first of the area's two major abbeys.

From here it's a short hop to picture-perfect Montalcino, a lofty and unspoiled hill town that makes a perfect base for the region. It's ideal for forays to the area's second major abbey, Sant'Antimo, a Romanesque building in some of the prettiest pastoral scenery imaginable. It is also good for more aimless

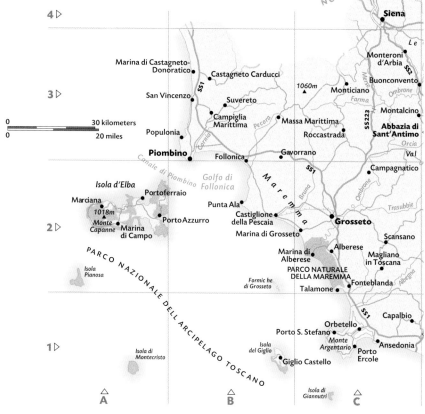

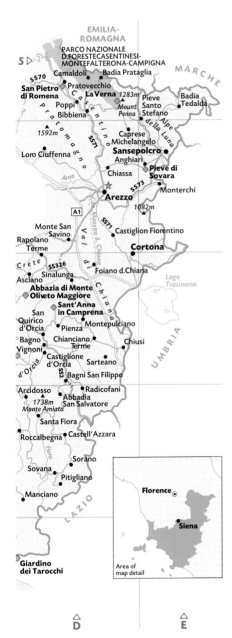

EMILIA-
ROMAGNA

PARCO NAZIONALE
D.FORESTECASENTINESI-
MONTEFALTERONA-CAMPIGNA

5 ▷

MARCHE

SS70
Camaldoli ● Badia Prataglia
San Pietro ● Pratovecchio
di Romena ● La Verna 1283m ▲ Pieve ● Badia
Poppi ● ● Mount Santo ● Tedalda
Bibbiena ● Penna Stefano
Casentino
Pratomagno
1592m ▲
Caprese
Michelangelo
Loro Ciuffenna ● Sansepolcro ●
Anghiari ●
Arno
Chiassa ● Pieve di
Sovara
SS73
● Monterchi
Arezzo ▲
1082m
A1
Val di Chiana
Monte San ● Castiglion Fiorentino
Savino
Rapolano ●
Terme ● Cortona
Crete SS326
Sinalunga ●
Asciano ● Foiano d.Chiana
Lago
Trasimeno
Abbazia di Monte
Oliveto Maggiore ◈
Sant'Anna
San in Camprena
Quirico ● ● Montepulciano
d'Orcia ● Pienza
Bagno ● Chianciano ● Chiusi
Vignoni ● Terme
Castiglione
d'Orcia ● Sarteano
d'Orcia SS2 ● Bagni San Filippo
Arcidosso ● ● Radicofani
1738m ● Abbadia
Monte Amiata San Salvatore
● Santa Fiora
Roccalbegna ● ● Castell'Azzara
Fiora
● Sorano
Sovana ●
● Pitigliano
Manciano ●
LAZIO
Giardino
dei Tarocchi

UMBRIA

Florence ◉

Siena ●

Area of
map detail

△
D

△
E

exploration—roads in most directions have their scenic rewards—and produces one of Italy's most deservedly praised red wines, Brunello di Montalcino, in vineyards around the town.

From Montalcino, move on to the villages of the Val d'Orcia, the verdant valley of the Orcia River, or head farther south to the little-known countryside around Monte Amiata and the villages of Sovana and Pitigliano. If time is short, push on to Pienza, another gem of a place. A few miles to the east is Montepulciano, a town as appealing as Montalcino and Pienza, situated on Tuscany's eastern periphery.

From here you could loop back to Siena, but that would be to miss Cortona to the north, another captivating hill town, and nearby Arezzo, whose modern outskirts conceal a medieval center and one of Italy's most famous fresco cycles. From Arezzo, both Siena and Florence are within range on good roads, but if you've a day to spare, use it to explore the back roads of the Casentino and Pratomagno, two almost unvisited scenic enclaves between Arezzo and the Tuscan capital. ■

Abbazia di Monte Oliveto Maggiore & Around

Monte Oliveto Maggiore is the second of southern Tuscany's great abbeys. Although architecturally less distinguished than Sant'Antimo (see pp. 272–273), its not too distant neighbor, it is just as prettily nestled in timeless countryside and has the considerable artistic bonus of a superb Renaissance fresco cycle.

Cloisters lined with Renaissance frescoes are the major draw for visitors to the abbey.

Abbazia di Monte Oliveto Maggiore

🗺 265 D3
✉ Near Chiusure
☎ 0577 707 611
🕐 Closed noon–3 p.m.

monteoliveto maggiore.it

From whichever direction you approach Monte Oliveto, you find yourself surrounded by lovely countryside. Cypresses, oak woods, and olive groves provide a fine setting for the monastery's cluster of red-stoned buildings. The first retreat here was founded in 1313 by a Sienese aristocrat, Bernardo Tolomei (1272–1348), who abandoned worldly life after being struck blind and experiencing visions of the Virgin. With two companions he lived as a hermit on land owned by his family, land that was then so lonely and inhospitable it

was known as a *deserto,* or desert. Within six years, the Bishop of Arezzo approved the building of a hermitage, and a year later work began on the first abbey building. In 1344 Pope Clement VI recognized the monks as Olivetans, or White Benedictines, an order that sought to return to the simple ways of the first Benedictines. Ironically, the abbey became immensely powerful over the centuries, only losing its influence when monastic houses were suppressed in the 19th century. Today, large areas of the abbey are closed to visitors.

Chiostro Grande

The principal attraction at the abbey is the main cloister, the Chiostro Grande (1426–1443). Around its walls is spread a fresco cycle on the life of St. Benedict by Luca Signorelli (1441–1523), a painter from the Tuscan town of Cortona (see pp. 281–283), and the Milanese artist Giovanni Antonio Bazzi, better known by his naughty nickname, Sodoma (see p. 216). Signorelli finished eight frescoes between 1497 and 1498; Sodoma completed the last 27 panels between 1505 and 1508. The sequence starts on the east wall, to the right of a door that leads to the abbey's rather disappointing church, remodeled to dull effect in the 18th century. Only the amazing **choir stalls** (1503–1505) reward attention; they are some of the most intricately crafted works of their kind in Italy.

The fresco cycle traces the life of the fifth-century Umbrian founder of Western monasticism, St. Benedict, whose monks—laboring, copying, writing, and recording in Benedictine abbeys across Europe—were partly responsible for preserving the continent's culture through the so-called Dark Ages (the centuries following the fall of the Roman Empire). The frescoes detail several events from the saint's life, with a wealth of drama and incidental detail.

Elsewhere in the abbey, it's fun to browse in the monastery shop, full of foodstuffs, potions, soaps, and elixirs, many made by the monks. Also look into the **Refettorio,** or refectory, the room in which the monks ate. Its scale gives some idea of Monte Oliveto's importance in its heyday.

Around Monte Oliveto

Monte Oliveto can be seen from **Buonconvento** *(visitor information, Via Soccini 32, tel 0577 807 181, tur ismobuonconvento.it)*, a small historic town 5 miles (8 km) to the southwest, whose ugly outskirts conceal a pretty medieval center. The main draws here are the **Museo d'Arte Sacra** *(Via Soccini 18, tel 0577 807 181, museisenesi.org, closed Mon. & 1 p.m.–2:30 p.m., $$)*, filled with medieval and Renaissance art

INSIDER TIP:

Listen for the Gregorian chant at Monte Oliveto Maggiore: It is sung at Mass, Vespers, Compline, and Lauds.

—JUSTIN KAVANAGH
*National Geographic
Travel Books editor*

and the **Museo della Mezzadria** *(Piazzale Garibaldi 10, tel 0577 809 075, closed Mon. & 1 p.m.–2:30 p.m.)*, devoted to the region's rural and peasant history. Or you can drive from Asciano, reached from Siena on the SS438 road. Pause in **Asciano** to visit the **Collegiata di Sant'Agata,** a Romanesque-Gothic church, and the medieval Sienese paintings in the **Museo d'Arte Sacra** *(Palazzo Corboli, Corso G. Matteotti 122, tel 0577 719 524, museisenesi.org, closed Mon. & 1 p.m.–2:30 p.m., $$)*. ■

Montalcino

Montalcino from afar is a picture of medieval perfection, its pristine hill almost untouched by the modern sprawl that detracts from many Italian hill towns. Close up, the town is equally alluring, enclosed by walls, crowned by a fairy-tale castle, blessed with magnificent views, and edged by vineyards that produce one of Italy's most magnificent wines.

The hill upon which Montalcino sits has probably been settled since Etruscan times.

Montalcino

🔼 264 C3

Visitor Information

✉ Costa del Municipio 1, off Piazza del Popolo

☎ 0577 849 331

🕐 Closed Mon.

prolocomontalcino .com

There has probably been a settlement on Montalcino's site since Paleolithic or Etruscan times. The present town takes its name from the Latin Mons Ilcinus (Mount of the Holm Oak), hence its coat of arms, a holm oak atop six hills. The first reference to the settlement comes in 814, when it features in a list of lands given to the abbey of Sant'Antimo by Louis the Pious, son of Charlemagne. The spur to its early medieval growth came about 1000, when it was inhabited by refugees fleeing Saracen attacks on the Tuscan coast. The four leading refugee families settled the town's four

contrade, or parishes, creating divisions that survive to this day: The rival Borghetto, Pianello, Ruca, and Travaglio hang their flags in the streets and compete in a twice-yearly archery tournament. The town's moment of glory came in 1555, when, as the last bastion of the Sienese Republic, it held out for four years against the Florentines.

Many people are lured here by one of Italy's greatest red wines, Brunello di Montalcino, which can be bought, along with Rosso di Montalcino, its cheaper cousin, in many local shops (you get the best deals in the local co-op supermarket). If you're driving, park in the lot just outside the walls off Via Aldo Moro below the or **Fortezza,** or Rocca, a glorious 14th-century castle that has a wine shop and bracing views from its battlements.

The next important sight lies just up the street in front of the castle, the **Museo Civico e Diocesano d'Arte Sacra,** full of superbly displayed medieval paintings and sculptures. Watch for Sano di Pietro's "Madonna dell'Umilità" ("Madonna of Humility"), a rare subject in which the Madonna is shown sitting or kneeling on a cushion or carpet rather than a throne. This aspect began to appear in Italian art after new ideas on the importance of humility were promulgated by St. Francis in the early 13th century.

The museum is housed in part of a monastic complex belonging to the church of **Sant'Agostino** (begun 1360), worth seeing for its variety of 14th- and 15th-century Sienese fresco fragments. From the church you could take Via Spagni north to see the 11th-century **Duomo,** or cathedral, and continue on the same street to the **Madonna del Soccorso.** This

17th-century Renaissance church features a magnificent panorama over half of Tuscany from the gardens to the right of the facade. Alternatively, take the lane down the left side of Sant'Agostino as you face it, and follow the steps through the arch in front of you as the lane bears right. This brings you out a few steps from Montalcino's visitor center (turn right) and narrow main square, the **Piazza del Popolo** (turn left), hunched beneath the tower of the Palazzo dei Priori (1292), seat of Montalcino's ruling medieval council. Take a break in the hub of town life, the Fiaschetteria Italiana, a café with a 19th-century interior and plenty of outside tables.

From here walk down the town's main streets—Via Mazzini to the north, Via Matteotti and Via Saloni to the south. Exploring at random, as ever in Tuscany's medieval towns, brings its own rewards, but good targets include the deconsecrated church of **San Francesco** (turn right off Via Mazzini) and the tiny church of **Sant'Egidio** just off Piazza Garibaldi and Via Boldrini between Via Matteotti and the Fortezza. ◾

Fortezza
- ✉ Piazzale della Fortezza
- ☎ 0577 849 211
- 🕐 Closed Mon. Nov.–March
- 💲 $ (battlements), $$ (combined ticket with Museo Civico e Diocesano d'Arte Sacra)

Museo Civico e Diocesano d'Arte Sacra
- ✉ Via Ricasoli
- ☎ 0577 846 014
- 🕐 Closed Mon. & 1 p.m.– 2 p.m.
- 💲 $, $$ (combined ticket with Fortezza)

EXPERIENCE: Yoga Retreats for Body, Mind, & Spirit

The peaceful rural countryside of much of Tuscany lends itself to vacations catering to mind, body, and spirit, and to yoga in particular. Most vacations combine yoga practice (often with the option to be outdoors) with free time, excursions, or other activities such as walking, and most are based in villas rented for the purpose. Before reserving a Tuscan yoga trip, check how close your center is to places you want to visit—some are relatively remote—and how easy it will be to reach them. More rarely, you can find longer established centers with facilities and dedicated practice areas, such as **Ebbio** (tel 338 947 1215, ebbio.com), a beautifully located 14th-century farmhouse, 35 miles (57 km) from Montalcino.

Tuscan Wines: Aging Well

Time was when Tuscan wine meant Chianti, a thin, tannic red once found in Italian restaurants the world over. Those days are gone. Not only has Chianti improved beyond all measure, but as producers have turned to new methods and new grape varieties, the quality—and variety—of Tuscan wines has been transformed across the region.

Vineyards like these at Montepulciano face south and west to soak up the Tuscan sunshine.

Some of the region's wines have always passed muster. There have been good Chiantis for those who knew where to look, and Brunello di Montalcino—produced from a clone of the Sangiovese grape that makes Chianti—has enjoyed an exalted reputation. Vino Nobile di Montepulciano, although less consistent, is another big, bold red that receives plaudits.

Until recently, however, these wines have been known only to the cognoscenti of the outside world. And while Italy always produced a lot of wine, most of it was for home consumption. Methods of production, moreover, had hardly changed for centuries.

Improved Methods & Varieties:
Matters began to change in the 1970s and 1980s, when younger and more adventurous producers began to take on board the lessons being learned in California and Australia. Modern production methods and new grape varieties were introduced, along with a readiness to blend traditional Tuscan grapes with French and other imports. The result was so-called "super Tuscans"—Tignanello, Sassicaia, Solaia, Sammarco, Tavernelle, and others.

Most of these early innovations blended Sangiovese grapes with Cabernet Sauvignon, the mainstay of the great French wines of Bordeaux. As time has gone by, however, other

INSIDER TIP:

Most basic Chiantis usually reach their peak drinking qualities between three and five years after vintage. Ask a local before you choose the year of your bottle.

—LARRY PORGES
National Geographic Travel Books editor

The cellar at the Tenuta San Filippo, one of many wineries in the Montalcino area

varieties such as Merlot and Pinot Noir also have been planted. The improvements of these pioneers has had a ripple effect on quality and variety, so that today you have a broad choice of good—and occasionally exceptional—wine. Price is not always a reliable indicator of quality, however, and there's no doubt that many beautifully packaged and over-marketed Tuscan wines cost more than they should.

Choosing Tuscan Wines: So what should you drink? One of the strengths of basic Tuscan wines is that they go perfectly with simple Italian food, so don't scorn the humble *vino da tavola*, or table wine, and don't pay too much heed to the "D.O.C." and other official gradings on bottles; Italy's system of wine classifications is currently a mess. You can rarely go wrong with Brunello, but prices can be sky-high.

Stick with one of the less exalted producers rather than with the famous names such as Bondi-Santi. Better still, try Brunello's cheaper cousin, Rosso di Montalcino, a wine with many of Brunello's qualities but at a fraction of the price. Chianti can still be very good or very average, and there's huge choice. Wines from the Gallo Nero consortium of producers are usually reliable: Watch for the distinctive Black Cockerel motif on bottles. San Gimignano's ancient white Vernaccia is improving, but much is still cheap, cheerful wine aimed at tourists.

Perhaps the best way to taste and buy wine is to visit a vineyard (see sidebar p. 238). More and more wineries are opening their doors, especially in Chianti. Visitor centers have details.

EXPERIENCE: Live & Work on a Tuscan Farm

Agriculture has been the lifeblood of Tuscany for centuries, and the region has long shared its natural bounty of grapes, olives, and other delights with Italy and with the wider world. To experience life on a farm—harvesting olives, trimming vines, picking grapes—is to experience an age-old element of traditional Tuscan life.

WWOOF, or **World Wide Opportunities on Organic Farms** (*wwoof.org*), links volunteers with organic farms in Tuscany,

offering travelers the chance to learn the traditional, small-scale farming methods that have sustained generations of Tuscan peasant families. You pay a nominal fee for membership in the Italian branch of the organization, which entitles you to a contact list of affiliated farms. You then arrange a stay with one of the host farms directly. In exchange for labor, you will receive basic room and board, which varies from farm to farm.

Abbazia di Sant'Antimo

Sant'Antimo is the most beautiful of Tuscany's medieval abbeys. Isolated in glorious country-side south of Montalcino, it has a matchless rural setting, a history that dates back to the days of Charlemagne, and artistic and architectural riches that place it in the pantheon of Italy's Romanesque buildings.

After some five centuries of lying empty, the abbey of Sant'Antimo is again occupied by monks.

Abbazia di Sant'Antimo

 265 D3

✉ Near Castelnuovo dell'Abate

🕐 Closed 12:30 p.m.–3 p.m. Mon.–Sat. & 10:45 a.m.–3 p.m. Sun.

antimo.it

Tradition claims the abbey was founded by Charlemagne, who was subsequently crowned the first Holy Roman Emperor. He is said to have stopped close to the abbey's present site on his way north from Rome in 781. His army had been crippled by a mysterious disease, leading Charlemagne to promise God a church, should his men be cured. An angel appeared, telling him to grind a local herb (still called *carolina*) and give it to his troops with wine. The remedy worked,

and Charlemagne duly founded Sant'Antimo. More concrete evidence of Charlemagne's involvement comes from the fact that in 781 the pope had also presented him with the relics of St. Antimo, a bishop martyred around A.D. 305—the same relics venerated at the abbey that took his name.

It is also known that the abbey existed in 814, when Louis the Pious, Charlemagne's son, enriched it with lands in a charter of that year. Over the next two centuries it became the second richest abbey in Tuscany, thanks in part to its position astride several vital trade and pilgrimage routes. These included an old sunken Etruscan road between the coast and the Tuscan heartland (traces of which can still be seen in the fields in front of the abbey), the old Roman Via Clodia, the Strada Pecorile (an ancient sheep track), and—most important—the Via Francigena, the main pilgrimage route between Rome and northern Europe.

In 1118 the abbey expanded further after receiving a vast bequest, the terms of which are engraved on the main altar steps. In time, Sant'Antimo's funds began to run dry, partly because benefactors began to bestow their gifts on new religious orders such as the Cistercians, and partly because the growing power of Siena began to strip the abbey of its lands. By 1293 it retained just a fifth of its original territories; in 1439 the abbot was imprisoned for "villainy"; and in 1462 the abbey was suppressed for good.

Visiting the Abbey: The abbey's appeal for visitors is partly its setting: The drive, if you're coming from Montalcino, is delightful. The surroundings are perfect, from the cypress-dotted hills and fields to the great single tree that stands sentinel alongside the church **bell tower.** The abbey's **interior** is similarly impressive, a picture of honey-colored stone and fine medieval carving. Its French-inspired form—a single nave with an ambulatory (a walkway around the high altar)—is unique in Tuscany and found in only a handful of churches elsewhere in Italy.

Among the fine Romanesque **carvings**—many of which are in subtly hued alabaster—the capital on the second pillar on the right side of the nave is well worth a close look. It depicts a graphic representation of "Daniel in the Lions' Den," the work of the Master of Cabestany, a sculptor of French or Spanish origin whose work has been identified in several major Benedictine abbeys across Western Europe. ∎

Discover Hidden Tuscany

If medieval abbeys leave you wanting to escape modernity and see parts of Tuscany still virtually unknown to most foreign visitors, then head for the swathe of countryside south of Montalcino and the Val d'Orcia.

The best of the area is inland; the coastal Maremma is less enticing (see pp. 294–295). Don't expect the cultural riches of the area around Siena, however. Heading south, you reach Monte Amiata (map 265 D2, visitor information, Via Adua 25,

tel 0577 775 811, www.terresiena.it/en /amiata), 5,702 feet (1,738 m) high, the "mother" mountain whose looming peak dominates many southern Tuscan vistas. You can drive almost to the summit through beech woods laced with marked hiking trails; or tour the little-known villages on the mountain's flanks—Santa Fiora, Pescina, Piancastagnaio, and Castel del Piano. Be sure to visit the village of Abbadia San Salvatore, named after its stunning 11th-century abbey church.

Pienza

Pienza was a sleepy hamlet known as Corsignano until 1459, the year Pope Pius II decided to transform his birthplace into a model Renaissance city. Pius died soon afterward, but not before creating a cathedral, a papal residence, and a palace-ringed central piazza. This hint of city still survives, forming the heart of one of Italy's most charming villages.

Piazza Pio II, dominated by the town hall and clock tower

Although there's little specific to see here, you'll remember the flower-hung streets and magnificent vistas—the views extend over some of the region's loveliest countryside—long after other Tuscan memories have faded. Pienza also has a good hotel, Il Chiostro, converted from a 15th-century convent (see Travelwise p. 320), and several fine restaurants, making it a great base for exploring the region.

Roads outside the walls meet in Piazza Dante, from which a single main street, Corso Rossellino, leads to **Piazza Pio II,** the heart of Pius's model "city." The Corso takes its name from Bernardo Rossellino, the architect commissioned by Pius to realize his dream. He began work in 1459, less than a year after his patron became pope. Pius was christened Enea Silvio Piccolomini, and it was to him that another Tuscan highlight, the magnificent library in Siena cathedral, was dedicated (see p. 205).

Pius's coat of arms is enclosed by a large garland of fruit on the facade of the **cathedral,** the piazza's centerpiece. Inside the church, note the tall windows, requested by Pius to let in a flood of light and designed to symbolize humanist enlightenment. Pius also commissioned the interior's five major altarpieces, demanding that the painters should be Sienese rather than the more advanced Florentines. The pictures are still outstanding, the best being Vecchietta's "Assumption with Pius I and Sts. Agatha, Callistus, and Catherine of Siena" (in the fourth chapel as you work around the church from the right). Pius's insistence on having the cathedral built on its cramped site, however, means the future of these paintings and other interior treasures is doubtful, for the building is very obviously slipping down the hillside to the rear—as the ominous cracks and measuring devices on the walls make clear.

The Palaces: To the cathedral's left, as you face it, stand two palaces. The Palazzo Borgia, or Palazzo dei Vescovi, houses the **Museo Diocesano** (*Corso Rossellino 30, tel 0578 749 905, closed Tues., & Mon., Wed., & Fri. Nov.–March, $$*) and its collection of medieval paintings, sculptures, miniatures, illuminated manuscripts, portrait busts, and tapestries. The star turn is a 14th-century *piviale,* or cope, a wondrously embroidered English-made cloak—it bears the words *Opus Anglicanum* ("an English work")—from Pius's papal wardrobe. Equally notable are the paintings, which include an anonymous "Madonna dell'Umilità," a "Madonna della Misericordia" (1364) by Bartolo di Fredi (his first signed and dated work), Vecchietta's "Madonna and Child With Saints" (1462), and—most interesting of all—an anonymous 48-panel work whose miniature paintings

portray scenes from the life of Christ. The last is one of only a handful of surviving "portable" paintings once carried by monks for use as aids when preaching to illiterate congregations.

To the cathedral's right lies the **Palazzo Piccolomini** (*Piazza Pio II, tel 0578 748 503, palazzopiccolo minipienza.it. closed Mon. & Jan.– mid-Feb., $$*), built by Rossellino on the site of a former Piccolomini family house. Rossellino spent five

Pienza
🅰 265 D3
Visitor Information
✉ Corso Rossellino 30
☎ 0577 749 905
🕐 Closed Tues. & 1:30 p.m.– 2:30 p.m. mid-March–Nov. & Mon.–Fri. rest of year

prolocopienza.it
www.comune.pienza .siena.it

EXPERIENCE:
Take a Vespa Tour of the Tuscan Countryside

A great way to reach a remote Tuscan town like Pienza is to rent a Vespa. The Vespa is the classic small Italian motor scooter— Gregory Peck rode one with Audrey Hepburn in the movie *Roman Holiday* (1953). On a sunny day, riding a Vespa on the quiet roads of rural Tuscany is a definitive Italian experience and a great way to see the countryside. **Tuscany Vespa Tours** (*tuscany-vespatours.com*) offers guided group tours of Chianti (*daily 10 a.m.–5 p.m. March–Nov.; driver €110, passenger €90*). Drivers need a driving license but not a special motorcycle license. **Tuscany by Vespa** (*tuscanybyvespa.com*) offers similar tours with a Florence pickup and two daily departures.

---

times his budget on the project, a sum he was liable to repay, but Pius was so pleased he forgave the extravagance. Admire the courtyard and the view from the rear loggia, then join a tour around Pius's former state apartments, where highlights are the papal bedroom and the armory.

After seeing the sights on Piazza Pio II, be sure to walk along the little streets and alleys behind and to the east of the square (to the left as you face the cathedral). They offer remarkable views over the surrounding countryside. Then walk east on the main street, Corso Rossellino, where you come to the church of **San Francesco,** a survivor from pre-Pius Pienza. Inside, it has traces of 14th-century frescoes on the life of St. Francis. Beyond lies Piazza Dante, from which a tempting small lane runs along the old walls for more sensational views. This short stroll is highly recommended, as is the ten-minute walk down the road from the piazza's lower-left (southwest) corner, signposted to **Pieve di Corsignano,** the lovely 10th- to 11th-century parish church. Among the church's rare and precious features are an unusual tower—used to shelter townspeople during bandit raids— and the Romanesque carvings above the main and side doors. The farm next door holds the key to the interior *(leave a tip),* which contains, among other things, the font used to baptize Pius II.

Longer Excursions

Two longer excursions from Pienza are highly worthwhile. One takes you to the little-known abbey of **Sant'Anna in Camprena,** 5 miles (8 km) away, reached by taking the road for San Quirico for a mile (1.6 km) and then going north on a signed secondary road. The abbey's refectory contains frescoes (1502–1503) by Sodoma, whose work you may have seen at Monte Oliveto Maggiore (see pp. 266– 267). The frescoes are open to view daily in summer, afternoons only the rest of the year, but check with the visitor center in Pienza for current details. You can also stay in the abbey complex *(tel 0578 748 037, www.camprena.it).* The country-side en route is ravishing.

The same goes for the scenery elsewhere around Pienza, notably along the *strada bianca,* or white road, toward Montepulciano to the east. After 3 miles (5 km) the road takes you to the sleepy walled village of **Monticchiello,** worth a pause to wander its streets and to admire its fresco-dotted parish church (Santissime Leonardo e Cristoforo). ∎

Pinocchio, the Italian wooden toy and puppet for sale in Pienza

EXPERIENCE: Hiking the Hills & Valleys of Tuscany

Tuscany's perfect mixture of pastoral and higher mountain landscapes, along with quiet rural roads and a network of ancient paths and mule tracks, make the region ideal for hiking. Added to this are a multitude of historic small towns and villages that offer plenty of art and culture on days off, as well as the promise of relaxed surroundings and good food, wine, and lodgings at journey's end. Hikers may need help on the ground with route-finding and moving their luggage between accommodations.

Parts of northern Italy—mostly those with a tradition of Alpine hiking and climbing—are well served by marked trails, well-trodden hikes, and detailed mapping. This is less true in much of Tuscany, where until recently there has been less of an outdoor pursuits culture, and where the ancient tracks that linked communities for centuries have been largely lost and overgrown as people moved from the land and the automobile became king.

The gently rolling hills of the Val d'Orcia are perfect for walkers.

While trails in Southern Tuscany are more scarce, the mountainous areas of the Alpi Apuane and Orecchiella in the northwest are better hiking grounds. Here you'll find trails aplenty, with options such as the nine-day **Garfagnana Trekking** (turismo.garfagnana .eu/en/fare/Garfagnana-Trekking.html) loop walk and 24-stage **Grande Escursione Appenninica** (GEA). Visitor centers and websites offer details and accurate maps, such as the *Edizioni Multigraphic* series, making this part of the region easier for independent hiking.

Improved mapping and some marked but still relatively little-used trails are beginning to appear in the **Casentino, Chianti,** the **Val d'Orcia,** and other lower, more pastoral areas south of Siena. The Internet or bookstores in Siena are the best sources for maps, and visitor centers often carry details of local hikes.

Organized Tours

To get the best out of these most beautiful parts of the region, therefore, it often pays to contact one of the many hiking companies that have sprung up to offer guided or self-guided hikes on routes that have been mapped and plotted for you.

The most popular and least expensive approach is self-guided, with the company providing detailed notes, recommended accommodations (which it will reserve), and moving your luggage between hotels. A pioneer in the field is **ATG-Oxford** (atg-oxford .co.uk). It can tailor Tuscan itineraries to your needs, with options on length and types of accommodations.

When to Go

The best time to hike is May, for glorious wildflowers, reliable weather, and with the countryside at its spring best: Temperatures should also be comfortable. September also usually has reliable weather, but the landscapes, while still striking, will have been burned brown by the summer sun. July and August are too hot.

Montepulciano

Montepulciano is a classic hill town ranged over a narrow volcanic outcrop. It has art and architecture galore, sweeping views over Tuscany and the hills of nearby Umbria, a velvety red wine—Vino Nobile—an easygoing air, and one of Tuscany's most lauded Renaissance churches.

It also makes a good base for much of southern Tuscany and a logical stop-off after Pienza as you journey between Siena, Arezzo, and Florence. Arriving by car can be confusing, however, for the twisting approach roads do their best to keep you from the old town high on the hill. Parking, needless to say, is difficult, but try to leave your car as near to the walls or as high as possible, preferably at the southern end of town by the Fortezza (castle). Failing that, park at the lowest part of town near Piazza Sant'Agnese.

Wherever you start exploring, you're going to have to climb at some point, for Montepulciano effectively consists of a single main street—known as the **Corso**—that ascends from Piazza Sant'Agnese to the Fortezza, passing the town's theatrical main square, Piazza Grande, en route. Unless you take a cab one way, you'll have to follow the street in both directions. The account below assumes you start at the bottom and work up.

Things to watch for include a string of late-Renaissance and baroque palaces, Montepulciano having received a thorough architectural makeover during the 16th century. Before that, the town had oscillated between independence and submission to either Florence or Siena. Florence took permanent control in 1511 and dispatched architect Antonio da Sangallo the Elder (1455–1534) to rebuild the town's defenses. His employers were so pleased with the result that they commissioned him to remodel many of the town's churches and palaces,

When Montepulciano's San Biagio was begun in 1518, the only larger church in Italy was St. Peter's in Rome.

a process continued by Jacopo Vignola (1507–1573), Baldassare Peruzzi (1481–1536), Ippolito Scalza (1532–1617), and others.

Local Highlights

Before starting your climb, enter the 1306 church of **Sant'Agnese** *(Piazza Sant'Agnese),* where the first chapel on the right has a frescoed Madonna attributed to Simone Martini or his school, and the second altar on the left holds a 14th-century painting of the "Madonna del Latte" ("Madonna of the Milk"). The latter shows a breast-feeding Virgin, a common Tuscan subject. The Virgin's milk symbolized the fount of Eternal Life, and many Tuscan churches claimed to possess "drops" of it.

Walking past the **Giardino di Poggiofanti** on your left, gardens laid out in 1866, you enter the old town proper through Sangallo's Porta del Prato gateway. The first square beyond this features the **Colonna del Marzocco,** a column bearing Florence's heraldic lion *(marzocco),* raised after the town fell to the Tuscan capital in 1511. Palaces to watch for thereafter include Palazzo Avignonesi (No. 91) and Palazzo Tartugi (No. 82), both probably designed by Vignola; Sangallo's Palazzo Cocconi (No. 70); and the Palazzo Bucelli (No. 73), the last easily recognizable from the Roman and Etruscan remains built into its base. Pietro Bucelli, its 17th-century owner, was a keen collector of antiquities.

Just beyond these palaces on the right stands the church of **Sant'Agostino,** founded in 1285; its facade was remodeled in the 15th century by Michelozzo, who also carved the delicate terra-cotta "Madonna and Child With Saints" above the door. Inside, the key work is Sangallo's crucifix above the high altar, a work attributed to Donatello. Opposite the church, the **tower house** is a rare survivor of medieval Montepulciano, mounted on which is a clock whose hours are struck by the figure of Pulcinella, the stock clown character of early Italian plays.

Montepulciano
🗺 265 D3
Visitor Information
✉ Piazzale Don Minzoni 1
☎ 0578 757 341
prolocomonte pulciano.it

EXPERIENCE:
Go Truffle Hunting

On a misty fall morning you are walking through woods with a guide and a small dog. Suddenly the dog stops, nose in the air, and starts scrabbling at the undergrowth. The man pulls the dog gently back, produces a small trowel, and then lifts a small, dark nugget from the ground . . . truffle hunting is fun and combines a gentle hike, the fresh morning air, beautiful Tuscan scenery, and insights into this most unusual and prized of foodstuffs. Several locations in Tuscany are known for their truffles, and often hotels or visitor centers can put you in touch with local guides and hunters. Or visit *lebaccanti.com* or *trufflehunter.net* for English-language hunts in Chianti and elsewhere. Visit *www.italyandwine.net/chiantiandtruffles .htm* for hunts in the Montepulciano area.

About 100 yards (91 m) farther up the Corso you come to **Piazza dell' Erbe,** long the site of the town's market, with the distinctive arches of the Loggia del Grano (1570) on your right. Here you should turn right and then dogleg immediately left up Via del Poggiolo: This offers the most

Vino Nobile wine from Montepulciano

direct route to Piazza Grande. Take the lane that strikes off right from the dogleg and you come to a pretty little square fronting the baroque church of **Santa Lucia** (1633). Return to Via del Poggiolo and continue upward. Pass the church of **San Francesco** on the right, which offers a good view of the countryside west of Montepulciano. The street then becomes Via Ricci, passing the **Museo Civico** *(Via Ricci 10, tel 0578 717 300, museociviomontepulciano.it, closed Mon. 1 p.m.–3 p.m. year-round, & Tues.–Fri. Nov.–Feb., $$)*, a modest collection of medieval art.

At the top of the climb you come to **Piazza del Duomo,** a wonderful square ringed by palaces and dominated by the Duomo, or cathedral. The palace on its right (west) flank is the 14th-century **Palazzo Comunale.** Climb its tower for sensational views as far as Siena and Lake Trasimeno in Umbria. At the palace on the left, **Palazzo Contucci** *(Via del Teatro, tel 0578 757 006, contucci.it),* you can sample Vino Nobile di Montepulciano, one of Tuscany's "big three" wines.

Dominating the square is the **Duomo** (rebuilt after 1680), known for Taddeo di Bartolo's astounding high altarpiece of the "Assumption" (1401), perhaps the loveliest rendition of a subject that was a favorite of Sienese artists. The baptistery, the first chapel on the north (left) wall, is filled with fine art: The eye-catching plethora of glazed terra-cotta, known as the "Altar of the Lilies," is by Andrea della Robbia; the marble bas-relief it frames is by Benedetto da Maiano; the niche statues of Sts. Peter and John the Baptist are attributed to Mino da Camaino; and the font and six bas-reliefs are the work of Giovanni d'Agostino.

INSIDER TIP:

A classic Vespa motor-bike is ideal for the hills in Tuscan towns like Montepulciano. You can rent one at Vintage Tours *[tel 393 965 5122, vintagetours.it].*

—TOM O'NEILL
National Geographic writer

Explore the streets beyond Piazza Grande to the east, then backtrack down Via Ricci and follow the signs down Via di San Biagio to **San Biagio,** a Renaissance church begun by Sangallo in 1518. ■

Cortona

Cortona is one of the most ancient of all Tuscan hill towns. Chroniclers in the Middle Ages believed it was as old as Troy, and it was a flourishing center under the Etruscans in the eighth century B.C. Today, its appearance is largely medieval, something that when added to two excellent small museums, a medley of fine churches, and sweeping views from its hilltop ramparts makes it one of Tuscany's most pleasant—and still little-visited—small towns.

The Palazzo Comunale, with its huge flight of steps, commands the Piazza Luca Signorelli.

Most people approach Cortona from the village of Camucia, following a road through olive groves and vineyards that takes them past the area's most celebrated church, **Santa Maria del Calcinaio**, 1.5 miles (2.5 km) from Cortona's walls. An austere creation built on a Greek Cross plan, it was begun in 1485 and is now considered one of the finest of Tuscany's Renaissance churches.

Closer to town, park at one of several lots outside the walls and walk to the main square, **Piazza della Repubblica.** From here it's a short stroll through Piazza Luca Signorelli—named after the Cortona-born Renaissance painter—to a lackluster cathedral and the town's chief attraction, the **Museo Diocesano** *(Piazza del Duomo 1, tel 0575 62 830, closed Mon., $$).* The latter is dominated by two compelling paintings by

Cortona

🔼 265 D3

Visitor Information

✉ Piazza Luca Signorelli 9

☎ 0575 637 221 or 0575 637 223

🕐 Closed Sat.–Sun. p.m. & 1 p.m.–3:15 p.m. daily

turismo.provincia .arezzo.it

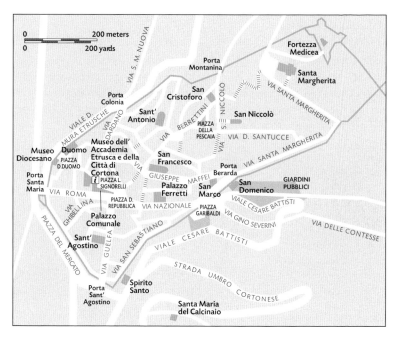

Fra Angelico (see sidebar p. 142), who spent ten years in the town's Dominican convent. His "Annunciation" here is one of Italy's supreme Renaissance masterpieces, although his second work, a "Madonna and Child With Saints," barely suffers by comparison. Other paintings here include several works by Signorelli, an "Assumption" (1470–1475) by Bartolomeo della Gatta, and a fetching "Madonna dell'Umiltà" (1435) by Sienese artist Sassetta. Don't miss the museum's archaeological exhibit, a second-century Roman sarcophagus carved with reliefs showing "Dionysus and the Amazons."

Near the gallery stands Cortona's second major museum, the **Museo dell'Accademia Etruscae della Città di Cortona** (*Piazza Luca Signorelli 9, tel 0575 630 415, www.cortonamaec.org, closed Mon.*

Nov.–March, $$$$). Its collection embraces a variety of paintings, sculptures, and other artifacts, but its most appealing exhibits are those connected with Cortona's Etruscan heritage. Of special note is the "Lampadario Etrusco," an enormous fifth-century B.C. bronze lamp whose design and extravagance would have been striking in any era. The same can be said of the museum's beautiful collection of Etruscan jewelry, but skip its dull collection of urns and vases. More prepossessing are the remains from a local tomb, the Melone II del Sodo, part of which has been reconstructed on the gallery's top floor. Other exhibits include Renaissance medallions, gold and silverware, a modest collection of medieval paintings, and mummies and other ancient Egyptian artifacts.

As in most medieval Italian towns, it's as much fun simply wandering Cortona's streets as it is seeing the museums. Brave the streets' steep grades to reach the town's upper levels and the ruined 1556 **Fortezza Medicea** (Medici Fortress), in particular, where the views are sensational. From here look over the town and out to Lake Trasimeno and the hills of Umbria, Tuscany's neighbor. The sanctuary of **Santa Margherita** just below the fortress (rebuilt in the 19th century) houses the body of Margherita di Cortona, the town's patron saint, but there is little to recommend it save the saint's tomb (1362) housed in a chapel left of the high altar.

Other Sights: Other churches around town more worthy of a visit include **San Cristoforo,** a rough-hewn little Romanesque chapel just off Piazza della Pescaia, and **San Niccolò** off Via San

Summer Festivals

One of the pleasures of summer in Tuscany is the chance to visit small festivals held in small towns and villages such as Cortona. Some, often billed as a *sagra,* are food based and celebrate a local wine or specialty; others honor a town's patron saint. A few offer music and theater, often under the stars. Virtually all are fun, informal affairs, with fireworks, local brass or other bands, and regional food and wine. Consult visitor centers for details or look out for posters advertising a "Festa" or "Sagra."

Niccolò. The latter has an intriguing double-sided altarpiece by Luca Signorelli. Another work by the same painter is found in **San Domenico,** which also has a poetic "Coronation of the Virgin" (1402) by Lorenzo di Niccolò Gerini. The church stands near the **Giardini Pubblici** (public gardens) off Piazza Garibaldi, whose long "Passeggiata in Piano" walkway offers yet more glorious views. ■

A fragment of Signorelli's "Assumption of the Virgin" (1519–1520) in Cortona's Museo Diocesano

Arezzo

Arezzo today is visited mostly for its medieval center and Piero della Francesca's "Legend of the True Cross," one of Tuscany's most celebrated fresco cycles. Art aside, it is also a prosperous town, thanks in large part to its jewelry and gold-working industry—the world's largest—a tradition that developed in Etruscan, Roman, and medieval times, when the ancient settlement flourished as a result of its position on the trade routes across the Apennines.

Reflections on Fraternità dei Laici tower inspire angels and dolls in Arezzo's Piazza Grande.

Arezzo

🗺 265 D4

Visitor Information

✉ Piazza della Repubblica 28

☎ 0575 26 850

🕐 Closed 1 p.m.– 2 p.m. Mon.–Fri.

arezzo.intoscana.it turismo.provincia .arezzo.it

This strategic position also invited bombing in World War II, and as a result the out-skirts are largely modern. Don't be put off, however, for the 20th-century veneer conceals an almost perfect historic core. The town is well connected by road and rail to the rest of Tus-cany: Florence is only an hour away by train.

Most visitors spend a few moments in the excellent visitor center outside the railroad station and then walk straight to the church of **San Francesco** (begun in 1318) in Piazza San Francesco, where Piero della Francesca's (1416–1492) famous frescoes (1453–1466) adorn the walls of the apse. Their theme is the "Legend of the True Cross," a complicated story that follows the story of the wood used to build the Cross on which Christ was crucified.

The source for the story was the *Legenda Aurea (Golden Legend)* of Jacopo da Varagine, a 13th-century tract that had returned

many apocryphal and other stories to the public domain. Piero is less concerned with simple narrative, however—the story is not told sequentially—than with the rigid sense of symmetry and artistic proportion that infused many of his unsettling and almost mystical paintings. For example, the cycle's two battle scenes (5 and 8 on the plan shown on pp. 286–287) are placed facing one another across the apse—not where their position in the narrative demands— while the retinue of the Queen of Sheba is shown twice in a mirror image.

San Francesco

🅰 Map p. 285
✉ Via di San Francesco
☎ 0575 352 727
🕐 Closed Sun a.m.
♿ Tours every half hour Mon.–Sat. & Sun. p.m.; max. 25 people at a time; reservations essential
💲 $$$

pierodellafrancesca .it

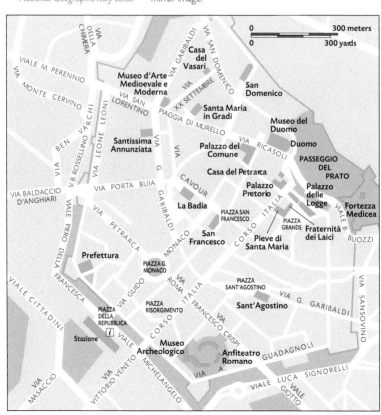

	9	
7		6
8		10

Opposite and above:
"Legend of the True
Cross" by Piero della
Francesca

In this plan above:

1a. Adam foretells his death and asks his son Seth to seek the "oil of mercy" from the Angel of Eden.

1b. Instead, the Angel gives Seth a shoot from the "Tree of Knowledge." Seth plants it in Adam's mouth, from which will grow the tree that will become Christ's Cross.

2a. King Solomon has a bridge built from this tree. The Queen of Sheba, visiting Solomon,

senses the wood's holiness and kneels in prayer.

2b. The queen foresees the wood will be used in a forth-coming crucifixion. She tells Solomon of the vision.

3. Solomon has the wood buried by three men.

4. Constantine, the first Christian Roman emperor, asleep in his tent before battle in A.D. 313, dreams of the Cross and is told by an angel that "under this sign you shall be victorious."

5. Constantine defeats his rival, Maxentius, next morning and is baptized.

6. Under torture, the Levite Jew, Judas, reveals to Helena, Constantine's mother, the burial place of the three crosses of Golgotha, stolen and buried after the Crucifixion.

7. Judas digs up the Cross in front of Helena and her court. Its authenticity is confirmed when it revives a dead man as Helena kneels in wonder.

Arezzo is painted (left) in the place of Jerusalem, the scene's setting.

8. The seventh-century Persian king Chrosroes, who had stolen the Cross and incorporated it into his throne (shown right), is defeated in battle by Emperor Heraclius. He awaits his execution (right).

9. Heraclius returns the Cross to Jerusalem.

10. The Annunciation, or the apparition of an angel, to Helena.

The Giostra del Saracino is a jousting tournament to win the coveted golden lance. Two festivals are held annually, one in June and another on the first Sunday in September.

Most of Arezzo's other highlights lie on or close to the **Piazza Grande,** the town's sloping main square. At the top of its incline stands the **Palazzo delle Logge** (1573), fronted by a Renaissance loggia designed by Giorgio Vasari. Facing uphill, in the square's top left-hand corner stands the **Fraternità dei Laici,** a Gothic palace renowned for its doorway and beautiful lunette sculptures (1434)—the work of Bernardo Rossellino.

Lower down the square is the rear apse of **Pieve di Santa Maria,** a magical 12th-century Romanesque church whose entrance lies on Corso Italia. Its ornate Pisan-Romanesque style, with its distinctive tiny columns and arcades, is rarely found in eastern Tuscany. Note the lovely carvings around the doors, especially the four little panels containing allegories of the months. Step inside to admire Pietro Lorenzetti's altarpiece painting of the "Madonna and Saints" (1320). The saint on the painting's far left is St. Donatus (San Donato), Arezzo's patron saint, who was martyred in the fifth century and whose relics lie in the gold reliquary (1346) on the altar, a consummate example of Arezzo's superb gold-working tradition.

As you leave the church, notice the carved "Epiphany" to the right of the main door on the rear wall, a lovely 11th- or 12th-century sculpture that probably once formed part of a pulpit.

North of the square stretches the **Passeggio del Prato,** a pleasant public park flanked by the Duomo and the remnants of the **Fortezza Medicea,** a 16th-century castle built by Florence's Medici rulers (Florence captured Arezzo in 1384). The **Duomo** with gothic columns and pointed arches warrants a visit for its lovely stained-glass windows (1523) by French artist Guglielmo di Marcillat, who settled in Arezzo, and a fresco of "Mary Magdalene" by Piero della Francesca in the north (left-hand) aisle beyond the organ. Another treasure is the tomb (1330) of Guido Tarlati (next to Piero's fresco), the 14th-century Bishop of Arezzo who commissioned Lorenzetti's painting in Santa Maria. Also worth seeking out is the Cappella di Ciuccio Tarlati, the last chapel on the south (right) wall before the high altar, which has an eye-catching sculpture (1334) and a series of mid-15th-century frescoes, both by unknown hands.

Literary pilgrims may want to see the house of Arezzo-born architect and art historian Giorgio Vasari, **Casa dei Vasari** (*Via XX Settembre 55, tel 0575 409 040, closed Tues. & Sun. p.m., $*), and the **Casa dei Petrarca** (*Via dell'Orto 28, tel 0575 24 700, closed Wed., $*), reputed to have been the birthplace of poet Petrarch in 1304. ∎

Giostra del Saracino: Arezzo's Jubilant Jousts

Thanks to their scope, vivid color, and authenticity, the jousting tournaments of Arezzo—which still maintain the rules of knights made centuries ago—stand out among the many medieval pageants and other events staged in Tuscany.

The Joust of the Saracen (Giostra del Saracino) dates back to the Middle Ages and involves four districts of the town, each represented by a knight wearing its colors: The districts are Porta Crucifera (known as *culcitrone*), represented by its green and red colors; Porta del Foro (known as Porta San Lorentino), represented in yellow and crimson; Porta Sant'Andrea with its white and green; and Porta del Borgo, today called Porta Santo Spirito, wearing yellow and blue colors. These reenactments take place every year in Arezzo on the second to last Saturday of June, by night (the so-called Joust of San Donato, dedicated to the town's patron saint), and on the afternoon of the first Sunday of September (the September Joust).

The September event begins with a procession of 350 costumed characters and 27 horses parading through the streets of the town, followed by a blessing on the steps of the Duomo. The jousting begins in the afternoon after the procession enters Piazza Grande. The winning district receives the coveted golden lance, and at the end of the joust, mortar shots hail the victors. *Pappardelle all'aretina* (ribbon-shaped pasta served with a thin meat sauce) is a famous local dish, so grab a bite when there's a break in the action.

A Drive Through the Casentino

This loop from Arezzo takes you through some of Tuscany's least-traveled, most picturesque countryside: a scenic alternative to the A1 highway between Arezzo and Florence.

Parco Nazionale delle Foreste Casentinesi

NOT TO BE MISSED:

Parco Nazionale delle Foreste Casentinesi • La Verna • Camaldoli

Many Tuscan visitors explore the landscapes of southern Tuscany. Few see two of the region's other areas of outstanding country-side—the Casentino and Pratomagno, two linked enclaves of wild hills, high mountains, remote abbeys, and ancient forests.

The area's scenic highlight is **Parco Nazio-nale delle Foreste Casentinesi** (parcoforeste casentinesi.it). Visit Arezzo's visitor center (see p. 284) for park details (including marked hiking trails). Shorten the drive if necessary by traveling directly to Poppi or Pratovecchio, gateways to the park.

From Arezzo take the SS71 road 4 miles (7 km) north to Ponte alla Chiassa and turn right, following signs to Chiassa and **Anghiari**, 12.5 miles (20 km). About a mile (2 km) before Anghiari, watch for a minor road signposted

to the **Pieve di Sovara ❶**, a ninth-century Romanesque church. Pause in Anghiari to see its tiny medieval center and the art of the **Museo di Palazzo Taglieschi** (Piazza Mameli 16, tel 0575 788 001, closed Sun. p.m. & winter).

From Anghiari take the road north for 11 miles (18 km) to **Caprese Michelangelo ❷**, the birthplace of Michelangelo. The cliff-top village is pretty, but the sculptor's former home has only a modest museum (Casa del Podestà). From Caprese take the mountain road via Chiusi della Verna to the junction with the SS208, 8 miles (13 km) northwest of Caprese. Signs here lead you 2.5 miles (4 km) to **La Verna ❸** (tel 0575 5341, santuariolaverna.org), one of Italy's most important Franciscan abbeys. Here St. Francis received the stigmata, the wounds of Christ. Pilgrims flock to the shrine but do not spoil its charm. The mountain setting is superb, and above the sanctuary you can take a trail to the summit of Mount Penna, 4,209 feet (1,283 m) high, for superlative views.

Return to the SS208 and turn right for Bibbiena, 16 miles (24 km) west. Here, pick up the SS71 then SS70 and head north for 2 miles (5 km) to **Poppi ❹**, where you should see the **Catello dei Conti Guidi** (off Piazza della Repub-blica 1, tel 0575 520 516, castellodipoppi.it, closed Mon.–Wed. Nov.–mid-March, $$) a large fortress, and the 12th-century church of San Fedele. Just before Poppi is a signed turning to the right for **Camaldoli ❺**, 10 miles (16 km), which is the Eremo monastery and at the heart of Parco Nazionale delle Foreste Casentinesi.

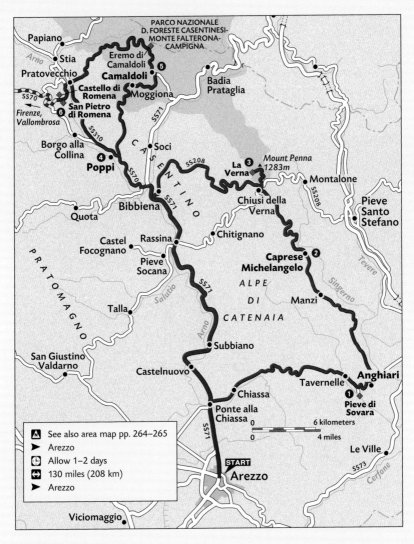

Papiano

Arno

Stia
Pratovecchio

SS70

Firenze,
Vallombrosa

PARCO NAZIONALE
D. FORESTE CASENTINESI-
MONTE FALTERONA-
CAMPIGNA

Eremo di
Camaldoli **5**

Camaldoli

**Castello di
Romena** Moggiona

**San Pietro
di Romena** **6**

SS310

Borgo alla
Collina

4 Soci
Poppi

SS70

Badia
Prataglia

SS71

C
A
S
E
N
T
I
N
O

SS208

La **3**
Verna

Mount Penna
▲ 1283m

Montalone

SS208

Pieve
Santo
Stefano

Bibbiena

Quota

SS71

Castel
Focognano

Rassina

Pieve
Socana

Chitignano

Chiusi della
Verna

**Caprese
Michelangelo** **2**

ALPE

DI

CATENAIA

Manzi

Tevere

Singerno

P R A T O M A G N O

Talla

Salutio

SS71

Arno

Subbiano

San Giustino
Valdarno

Castelnuovo

Chiassa

Ponte alla
Chiassa

SS71

Tavernelle

Anghiari

1
**Pieve di
Sovara**

0   6 kilometers
0   4 miles

Le Ville

SS73

Cerfone

N See also area map pp. 264–265
► Arezzo
🕐 Allow 1–2 days
↔ 130 miles (208 km)
► Arezzo

START
Arezzo

Viciomaggio

From near the monastery, take the only road west to Pratovecchio, from where you will drive 1.5 miles (3 km) on the minor road to the southwest signed to Firenze and see **San Pietro di Romena** **6** *(tel 0575 582 060, romena.it),* a beautiful eighth-century church set in lovely countryside. A road from the church leads to the **Castello di Romena,** a castle that offers magnificent views. From Pratovecchio you can drive the 28 miles (46 km) to Arezzo

on the SS310/SS70/SS71. Alternatively, you could continue to Florence by driving beyond San Pietro to the SS70 road and going west for 20 miles (32 km) toward Pontassieve. If you have time, turn left after 5 miles (8 km) for **Vallombrosa,** 11 miles (18 km) farther on, another celebrated monastery. Return to the SS70 via Tosi and Pelago, a more scenic route. From Pontassieve the SS69 road follows the Arno Valley for 11 miles (18 km) to Florence.

Elba

The Isola d'Elba is a world unto itself, an island that many European visitors treat as a vacation destination in its own right. Most people come here for the beaches and sapphire seas; the resorts teem with over a million visitors in summer. But the island also has its picturesque and historical side, not least its associations with Napoleon, the French emperor exiled here in 1814.

Sun, sea, and sand are the reasons most people visit Elba.

Elba

⚑ 264 A2

Visitor Information

✉ Viale Elba 4, Portoferraio

☎ 0565 914 671

turismo-elba.it
isoleditoscana.it
infoelba.it

Elba is the largest of several offshore islands making up the so-called Tuscan Archipelago. It measures just 17 by 11 miles (27 by 18 km), and it is about 9 miles (14 km) from the mainland port of Piombino (which offers regular car and passenger ferries). Most boats dock at **Portoferraio,** the island's capital, whose modern docks give way to the more alluring old town, rebuilt by the Medici Grand Duke Cosimo I in 1548.

Island legend has it that Napoleon was attracted here, after being forced to renounce the thrones of France and Italy, by "the gentleness of the climate and its people." In fact,

the victorious forces chose his place of exile, while allowing that the tiny domain would be a "separate principality for his lifetime, held by him in complete sovereignty."

Napoleon remained on the island for just nine months in 1814 and 1815, during which time he is remembered for improving roads, clearing land, repairing defenses, and improving education and the legal system. Intrigue and unrest in France enabled him to escape, whereupon he embarked on the 100-day adventure that led to his final defeat at Waterloo.

In Portoferraio you can visit the emperor's former home, the **Villa dei Mulini** *(Via Garibaldi, tel 0565 915 846, currently closed for restoration).* You can also visit his less appealing summer home—the **Villa di San Martino** *(tel 0565 914 688, closed Sun. p.m. & Mon., $$)*—4 miles (6 km) out of town, south of the road to Marciana.

If you've come to Elba for the beaches then it's best to reserve a place well in advance. In summer most hotels are filled with visitors on packaged vacations, and hotels often accept other tourists for stays of more than one night. Perhaps the best approach if you want to see Elba as part of a Tuscan itinerary is to

INSIDER TIP:

If you're too tired to hike up Monte Capanne, take the cable car from the village of Marciana.

—TOM O'NEILL
*National Geographic
writer*

3,308 feet (1,018 m) from several points, notably the village of Poggio on its northeast flanks. Hiking maps showing paths across the island marked for walkers by the Italian Alpine Club (C.A.I.) are available from most visitor centers.

The west end of the island also has some of the best coastal scenery and some of its quieter beaches and resorts. The settlements of **Chiessi** and **Pomonte** have stony beaches, little development, and crystal-clear waters; **Fetovaia** to the south has good sand but more people, as does **Cavoli,** farther east.

cross over for the day. If you want a swim, you'll find lots of beaches as you drive. **Marina di Campo** has the largest stretch of sand but is also the most developed town after Portoferraio, with bars, hotels, restaurants, and lively nightlife.

The island's most attractive region is the western interior and the forest and scrub-covered countryside around the main peak, **Monte Capanne.** You can hike to the mountain's summit at

Don't overlook the eastern part of the island: **Porto Azzurro** is a fashionable retreat overlooking a pretty bay; **Capoliveri,** in the hills, is a relatively unspoiled village; and tiny upland roads near Bagnaia, 6 miles (10 km) east of Portoferraio, or Ottone and Rio nell'Elba, offer the best of the scenery. ■

More Places to Visit in Southern Tuscany

Il Giardino dei Tarocchi, or the Garden of Tarot, in the village of Pescia Fiorentina.

Bagno Vignoni

Bagno Vignoni is a slip of a village, but one with a special attraction that shouldn't be missed. It can be incorporated into a tour of the area around Montalcino, Sant'Antimo, and the Val d'Orcia. The village is famous for its main square, which is not a square at all, but a large open *piscina,* or pool, which bubbles with waters from sulphurous hot springs below. If you can, try to be here first thing on a cool morning, when the steaming square provides one of Tuscany's most magical sights. The Romans bathed here, as did the Medici. The latter built the pretty Renaissance arcade that surrounds the springs. The pool is now out of bounds, but you can bathe in waters from the same source in the Posta Marcucci Hotel for a fee. 🔼 265 D3 **Visitor Information** ✉ Piazza Chigi 2 ☎ 0577 897 211 🕐 Closed Wed. & 1 p.m.–1:30 p.m.

The Maremma

The Maremma is a region that embraces Tuscany's southerly coastal margins, encompassing the dismal town of Grosseto and the more enticing medieval charms of **Massa Marittima** *(map 264 B3, visitor information, Via Parenti 22, tel 0566 902 456),* the one town in the region worth a special visit (the cathedral is magnificent). Once an area of wetland and coastal flats, the region was drained by the Etruscans and Romans, but in later centuries it slipped back to its original marshy state.

The landscape of coastal lowlands and occasional hills has a melancholy character. If you do come, it'll be for the coastline, which is dotted with a variety of small resorts and beaches. The best of these are the undeveloped sands at **Marina di Alberese** (southwest of Grosseto), the pretty fishing village of **Castiglione della Pescaia,** and the chic resorts of **Porto Ercole** and **Porto Santo Stefano** on Monte Argentario, a spectacular rocky promontory. The nicest reachable beach is the one at Marina di Alberese, where the views to Monte Argentario are memorable and the trees come down to the sand in the manner of a tropical island.

The best of the coastal scenery is protected by the glorious **Parco Naturale della Maremma** *(visitor information, Centro Visite, Via del Bersagliere 7–9, Alberese, tel 0564 407 098, parco-maremma.it).* Visit it from **Talamone** *(visitor information, Via Nizza 12, tel 0564 887 173, closed noon–3:30 p.m.),* another pretty

EXPERIENCE: Join an Archaeological Dig

Become one of the paying volunteers at Poggio del Molino, on the Tuscan coast, 68 miles (110 km) southwest of Siena, and you can help excavate the remains of a Roman villa and maritime settlement. The work includes uncovering, cleaning, and documenting finds; collecting organic samples with a paleobotanist, and surveying the area around the site. You will search for mosaics, frescoes, coins, metal, and pottery. Accommodation is near Populonia, 2.5 miles (5 km) from the site. You'll work with local senior high school students, as well as a technical team and trained students from U.S. and European universities. You can join the project for between 6 and 13 days from about mid-March to mid-October.

Several organizations can provide placements, including the **Archaeological Institute of America** *(archaeological .org)*, which has a minimum placement of one week, and the Italian-based **Archeodig** field school *(archeodig.com)*. The latter also has places on a dig at the nearby Etruscan necropolis of San Cerbone.

resort village, or by special shuttle bus from Alberese south of Grosseto *(park closed to automobiles; check bus schedules with the park visitor center, $$$)*. The bus drops you on one of Italy's finest tracts of virgin coastline. You can walk on the beach, stroll at will through the beautiful *pineta* (pine wood), or follow one or more of the four easy marked trails through the park's wide variety of natural habitats, including the typical Mediterranean *macchia* of myrtle and juniper bushes.

The isolated inland village of **Capalbio,** with its hilltop maze of old streets, is also worth a detour, as is the extraordinary **Giardino dei Tarocchi** *(Garavicchio, near Pescia Fiorentina, tel 0564 895 700, nikidesaintphalle .com, closed a.m. & mid-Oct.–March except 1st Sat. a.m. of month Nov.–March)* southeast of the village. It is a monumental sculpture garden based on the cards of the Tarot created by modern sculptor Niki de Saint Phalle. Opening times may vary. *turismoinmaremma.it, altamaremmaturismo.it* ⚑ 264 B2–C2, C1 & 265 D1

Pitigliano & Sovana

Well south of Monte Amiata, close to Tuscany's neighboring region of Lazio, lie two exceptional villages, Pitigliano and Sovana. Pitigliano is a village of Etruscan vintage superbly located on a narrow rocky ridge, its old castle and medieval houses perched precariously above the encircling ravine. There are a couple of modest museums here, but the beautiful setting is the real attraction.

Tiny nearby Sovana, by contrast, has two major artistic lures: The parish church of **Santa Maria,** in the tiny main square (the village has just a couple of streets), has a rare and beautiful stone altar canopy; the venerable **cathedral** is well worth viewing, boasting walls and a main door that are graced with some of Tuscany's finest Lombard-Romanesque carvings. All around the village lie well-signed Etruscan tombs; the most important is the **Tomba Ildebranda.** Other tombs can be seen en route for Saturnia to the west or the neighboring village of **Sorano** to the east, whose ancient approach road is lined with niche tombs cut deep into the soft volcanic stone. ⚑ 265 D2 **Visitor Information** ✉ Piazza Garibaldi 51, Pitigliano ☎ 0564 617 111 🕐 Closed Mon. 12:30 p.m.–3:30 p.m. & Sun. p.m. Nov.–May

San Quirico d'Orcia

Some 3.5 miles (6 km) north of Bagno Vignoni lies the village of San Quirico d'Orcia, a curious mixture of the medieval and modern known primarily for the **Collegiata,** an outstanding Romanesque church just off Piazza Chigi. Built in the 12th century, this ancient church

The Piero Trail

Art lovers and devotees of Piero della Francesca (1416–1492), an influential and enigmatic Renaissance painter (see p. 43), may wish to visit the village of Monterchi, 20 miles (33 km) east of Arezzo, where the old school building contains his strange painting of the pregnant Madonna, "Madonna del Parto." The town museum in nearby Sansepolcro (11 miles/18 km, northeast) contains two more paintings by the artist: "Resurrection" and "Madonna della Misericordia."

is renowned for its earlier main portal (1080), considered the region's finest work of its kind. The interior is almost as admirable; be sure to see Sano di Pietro's 15th-century Sienese painting of the "Madonna and Saints" in the north transept. Also worth visiting is the **Palazzo Chigi,** now the seat of the city government for San Quirico. The palace stands to the side and back of the Collegiata. You should also stop into the **Horti Leonini** by the Porta Nuova, a simple Renaissance garden, and the little 11th-century church of **Santa Maria Assunta** in Via Dante Alighieri. *comunesanquirico.it* 🄰 265 D3 **Visitor Information** ✉ Piazza Chigi 2 ☎ 0577 897 211 🕐 Closed Wed. & 1 p.m.–1:30 p.m.

Val d'Orcia

The Val d'Orcia is a picturesque valley south of Montalcino and Sant'Antimo. Make a big effort to incorporate its lonely roads and little villages into a tour, for its quintessential pastoral landscapes are some of Tuscany's finest. Assuming you're coming from the north, drive on the country road from the abbey of Sant'Antimo southeast to **Castiglione d'Orcia** *(map 265 D3, visitor information, Via San Giovanni, tel 0577 8840, closed Mon. 12:30 p.m.–2:30 p.m. & Tues.–Fri. Nov.–Easter)* 12 miles (19 km) away, a village huddled around an imposing fortress. From here meander on country roads through hamlets to the south—Campiglia d'Orcia, Vivo d'Orcia, Bagni San Filippo, and the imposing fortress village of **Radicofani** *(map 265 D2, visitor information, Via Roma 49, tel 0578 55-684, closed Sun. p.m., lunch, & Oct.–May)*. Most routes and signposts eventually bring you to the main SS2 highway, the old Roman Via Cassia road to Siena. Take this road north (toward Siena), visiting Bagno Vignoni and San Quirico d'Orcia en route. From the latter you can return to Montalcino or go on to Pienza and Montepulciano to the east. 🄰 264–265 C3–D3

Palazzo Chigi, San Quirico d'Orcia

Travelwise

The classic Vespa: A fun way to go

TRAVELWISE

PLANNING YOUR TRIP

When to Go

Deciding when to visit Florence and Tuscany depends on your chosen vacation. The countryside is at its best from April to June, which is also a good time for sightseeing. In fall, try late September through October when the countryside has been parched by the sun, but the weather is still good enough for sightseeing. July and August are extremely busy and hot in the towns and cities. From January through March, there are fewer lines and lower prices. Easter, however, is always busy. Many festivals take place in summer, but others are scattered throughout the year (see p. 326).

For help planning your trip, contact the Italian State Tourist Offices outside Italy (see p. 304). Some organizations also have useful websites.

alitalia.it (routes and schedules for Italy's national airline)

beniculturali.it (website for Italy's Ministry of Art and Culture)

firenzeturismo.it (Florence's official tourism site)

italia.it (Italy's official tourism site)

terresiena.it (official tourism site for Siena and southern Tuscany)

trenitalia.com (Italian State Railroads)

uffizi.firenze.it (the Uffizi's official site)

Climate

As a general rule, Tuscany has mild winters and hot summers, but its varied topography produces a wide range of climactic conditions. Winters in the Apennines and mountainous areas can be severe, with snow and temperatures below freezing. Winter across the rest of the region is comparable to the colder climate of northern Europe. Spring tends to be short, and fall is more drawn out.

Winter daytime temperatures in Tuscany range from around 15° to 59°F (-10° to +14°C), and summer temperatures from 65° to 90°F (18° to 33°C), although temperatures may often exceed these extremes. Italy uses degree Celsius (°C) as its unit of temperature.

What to Take

You should be able to buy anything you need in Florence and Tuscany except in the smallest towns. Pharmacies offer a wide range of drugs, medical supplies, and toiletries, along with expert advice, but you should bring any prescription drugs you might need. Many brand-name drugs are different in Italy. A pharmacy (una farmacia) is shown by a green cross outside the store. It is sensible to bring a second pair of glasses or contact lenses if you wear them. Don't forget sunscreen and mosquito repellents in summer.

Clothing depends on when you travel and what you plan to do. You only need to dress up for the grandest restaurants. Don't be too casual, though, because Italians generally dress better than most U.S., Canadian, and northern European visitors. Make some effort for any meal out, and always dress appropriately in churches (no bare shoulders or shorts for women). Note, too, that dress codes are more conservative in rural areas. Bring a sweater, even in summer, as nights can be chilly. Be prepared for some rain and cool temperatures any time except high summer. Hiking, camping, and sports equipment is easily bought or rented; bring more personalized equipment such as hiking boots.

Lastly, don't forget the essentials: passport, driver's license, tickets, credit cards or travelers' checks, and insurance documentation.

Insurance

Make sure you have adequate travel and medical coverage for treatment and expenses. Keep all receipts for expenses. Report losses or thefts to the police and get a signed statement (una denuncia) from police stations to help with insurance claims.

Entry Formalities

U.S. and Canadian citizens need passports for stays of up to 90 days. No visa is required. U.K. citizens need passports.

Further Reading

Florence and Tuscany have spawned much poetry, fiction, and nonfiction from native and foreign writers. One essential read is The Italians, by Luigi Barzini (Simon & Schuster, 1996). It was first published in 1964, but no one before or since has produced a better written analysis of Italy and the Italians.

HOW TO GET TO FLORENCE & TUSCANY

Airlines

Most major airlines have flights to Italy, and many arrange package tours or offer budget-price flights. Alitalia, the main Italian carrier, has reservation offices abroad in most major cities. Direct flights from North America fly either to Milan or Rome, with some direct flights to Pisa, Naples, Palermo, and some other centers in summer. Rome is the most convenient hub for Florence and Tuscany. It is worth considering flights to London's Heathrow Airport, where you can connect with British Airways and several low-cost airlines that fly into Pisa or Florence. This airport is convenient for most of Tuscany and is an easy 60-mile (95 km) drive to Florence. Florence also has a small airport, Peretola, that is serviced by two daily flights with Meridiana (see below) from London's Gatwick Airport.

Flying time to Rome is about 8–9 hours from New York, 10–11 hours from Chicago, and 12–13 hours from Los Angeles. Flying time from London to Pisa or Florence is about 2 hours.

You can fly to Rome, Pisa, Florence, or Bologna from the United Kingdom on British Airways, Alitalia, Meridiana and a host of cut-price carriers from Heathrow, Gatwick, Stansted, Luton, Manchester, and other regional airports.

Driving to Italy from the United Kingdom takes up to 24 hours. Routes go through France or Germany and Switzerland.

Useful Numbers
Italy:
Alitalia, tel 89 20 10 (inside Italy), tel 003 9066 5649 (from outside Italy), alitalia.it
Rome Fiumicino Airport, tel 06 65951, adr.it
Milan Malpensa Airport, tel 02 23 23 23, sea-aeroport ofmilano.it
U.S. and Canada:
Alitalia (U.S.), tel 800/223-5730, alitalia.com; (Canada), tel 800/361-8336, alitalia.ca
American Airlines, tel 800/433-7300, aa.com

Continental, tel 800/525-0280, continental.com
Delta, tel 800/221-1212, delta.com
United, tel 800/231-0856, ual.com
U.K.:
Alitalia, tel 0871 781 3713, alitalia.co.uk
British Airways, tel 0844 493 0787, ba.com
Meridiana, tel 0871 222 9319, meridiana.it
Ryanair, tel 0871 246 0000, ryanair.com

GETTING AROUND
Airports
You will arrive in Italy from the United States and Canada at Rome's Leonardo da Vinci Airport (better known by its local name of Fiumicino). If you fly from London, you will land at Pisa's Galileo Galilei Airport or Florence's Peretola (or Amerigo Vespucci) Airport.

Fiumicino-Leonardo da Vinci
Fiumicino is 19 miles (30 km) west of Rome's city center. If you are renting a car to drive to Tuscany, the rental desks are across the raised walkway from above the main international departure terminal (follow signs) for the railroad station. Driving from the airport, follow signs for "Roma" and "Centro" and then watch for the "Firenze" turnoff after about 6 miles (10 km); the turn comes suddenly. This takes you onto the Rome ring road, Grande Raccordo Anulare (G.R.A.). Follow the ring road for about 11 miles (18 km), looking out for the Firenze–A1 turnoff (intersection 10). Then follow the A1, Italy's main highway, north to Florence (about 150 miles/ 240 km). Road tolls are payable on the A1.

The best way into Rome if you

wish to catch a train to Florence or other parts of Tuscany (see p. 300) is on the special airport express rail service, which leaves the airport hourly between 6:30 a.m. and midnight, taking 30 minutes to reach Stazione Termini, Rome's main train station. Connections to Florence (2 hours), Pisa (3 hours), and other parts of the country leave from Termini. Train tickets can be bought online at trenitalia.com, from automated machines in the airport arrivals (Arrivi) terminal, or from a small ticket office (biglietteria) on the right as you face the railroad station platforms. The same office also sells tickets for the state (FS) network: Buying tickets here saves waiting in long lines at Termini.

Galileo Galilei Airport
Most scheduled and charter flights fly to Pisa's airport (tel 050 849 111 for switchboard, 050 849 400 for lost luggage, and 050 849 300 for visitor information, pisa-airport.com), 60 miles (95 km) west of Florence. Direct trains for the city leave every hour from a platform at the left-hand end of the airport concourse as you face the exit, 150 yards (140 m) from arrivals. The trip takes about an hour. Tickets can be bought at an office midway down the concourse on the right. You must validate your ticket in the machines on the platform before boarding.

When returning, there's a check-in desk for most airlines by platform 5 at Santa Maria Novella, Florence's main railroad station. Bags have to be checked in at least 30 minutes before the departure of the train, which must arrive at the Pisa airport at least 30 minutes before the departure of the flight. When catching the train, be sure that it runs through to Pisa Aeroporto; some do not go beyond Pisa's central station, Pisa Centrale.

Peretola-Amerigo Vespucci
A limited number of international carriers use Florence's Peretola Airport, also called Amerigo Vespucci *(tel 055 306 1300, aeroporto.firenze.it),* 3 miles (6 km) northwest of the city center. There is a small arrivals hall, with a foreign exchange machine, several car rental desks, a lost baggage counter, and a visitor center *(tel 055 306 1302, open 8:30 a.m.–10:30 p.m.).*

ATAF-SITA "Vola in bus" shuttles *(tel 800 425400 free phone in Italy or 800 373360, ataf.net, sitabus.it)* run shuttles about every half hour to and from the airport from outside the arrivals area. Tickets can be bought on board the bus. In Florence, buses arrive and leave from the main terminal on Via di Santa Caterina da Siena, a few steps west of Santa Maria Novella railroad station. Cabs are also available. The trip takes 15 to 30 minutes depending on the traffic.

TRAVELING IN FLORENCE & TUSCANY
By Bus
Most of central Florence is easily explored on foot. If you need public transportation, the city's ATAF company *(ataf.net)* runs orange city buses. Florence has no subway. Tickets *(biglietti)* are valid for any number of journeys for 90 minutes. They must be bought before boarding a bus (or on board for a premium) from shops and bars displaying an ATAF sticker, from the automatic machines situated around the city, or from the main ATAF ticket and information office in the bus bays immediately east of the Santa Maria Novella railroad station. Four 90-minute tickets bought in a block *(un biglietto multiplo)* and 24-hour passes offer

savings on the basic rate tickets. Two-, three-, seven-day, and family passes are also available. All tickets must be stamped on board buses in the machines provided at the beginning of your first journey; spot fines are levied by roving inspectors if you travel without a ticket or with an unvalidated ticket.

Around Tuscany, trains are usually quicker and cheaper than inter-town buses (pullman or *corriere*), but in more remote areas such buses (usually blue in color) may be the only viable means of public transportation. Services are operated by many different companies, but usually depart from a town's major square, outside the railroad station, or a bus depot.

In Florence, the main SITA bus *(sitabus.it)* company depot for most Tuscan connections (including the Peretola airport bus) is just west of Santa Maria Novella railroad station at Via Santa Caterina da Siena 17. Other companies operate from Piazza Stazione *(LAZZI & CLAP buses to Lucca, Pisa, Pistoia, Prato, Viareggio, & Lucca province, both lazzi .it).* Tickets in Florence and other towns must generally be bought before boarding the bus, usually from the depot, or the nearest bar or station kiosk. Ask at local visitor centers for precise details.

By Train
Trains are a great way of traveling in Tuscany. Fares on the state-run railroad network *(trenitalia.com)* are reasonable, and service and comfort are improving. Key lines run from Florence, a major railroad hub, to Siena (direct services or change at Empoli), Pisa, Lucca (via Prato and Pistoia), Viareggio, and Arezzo. Smaller scenic lines run from Siena to Grosseto, Lucca to Aulla (via the Garfagnana), and Arezzo to Stia (in the Casentino).

Tickets can be bought online, at stations and from some travel

agents, and are issued in first *(prima)* or second class *(seconda classe).* On fast Frecciarossa, Frecciabianca, and InteCity (I.C.) trains, an extra supplement *(supplemento)* must be paid when you buy your ticket or (for a higher fee) on the train. On the superfast Frecciarossa services between Florence and Rome, or Florence and Bologna, you must pay a supplement and make seat reservations in advance. Seats can often be reserved until a few minutes before departure.

Trenitalia offers three- to ten-day passes with a two-month validity for nonresident visitors to Italy, but they're not a good value if you are only traveling within Tuscany. Before traveling, you must validate all tickets in the special machines (small gold or yellow boxes) on platforms and station ticket halls; a heavy fine is payable if you travel with a non-validated ticket.

By Cab
Florentine taxies are white with yellow trim. It's easier to pick up cabs at a taxi stand than to hail them on the street. Central stands can be found at the railroad station, Piazza della Repubblica, Piazza del Duomo, Piazza Santa Maria Novella, Piazza San Marco, Piazza Santa Croce, and Piazza Santa Trìnita. When you get a cab, be sure the meter is set at zero. When you set off it will jump to the current minimum fare for the first 220 yards (200 m) and then rise quickly. Supplements are charged on Sundays, public holidays, for fares between 10 p.m. and 7 a.m., and for each piece of luggage placed in the trunk. All current supplements should be posted on a list inside the cab. Take a cab driver's name and number if you suspect that he has been dishonest. Making clear to the driver that you are doing this is often enough to set matters right. Report any complaint to a

visitor center or, in serious cases, to the police (see p. 305).

The best to way to be sure of a cab is to call ahead. Most operators speak a little English. Otherwise, ask your hotel to call for you. When you call, give the address of where you wish to be picked up. The operator will then give you a taxi-code number (always a geographical location followed by a number), plus how much time you will have to wait: for example, *"Firenze dodici in cinque minuti"* (Florence 12 in five minutes). Meters run from the moment a taxi sets off to pick you up. Cabs can be called on the following numbers and sites: tel 055 4798, 055 4242 *(socata.it),* 055 4499, or 055 4390 *(4390.it).*

By Car

Tuscany's urban centers may be congested, but the rest of the region has an excellent network of well-marked roads, from the ordinary highway—known as a Nazionale (N) or Strade Statale (S or SS)—to the fast four- or six-lane expressways known as *autostrade.* There are tolls on autostrade. Sometimes you pay a fixed rate, but usually you take a card from automated machines when you get on the road and then pay at a manned booth (Alt Stazione) on exiting. Prepaid Viacards *(autostrada.it),* available from autostrada 24-hour gas and food stops, at toll gates, and tobacco stores, make payment quicker, especially at busy times.

Gravel-surface roads known as *strade bianche* (white roads) are common in rural areas but are intended for automobiles and are usually marked on maps. You may have to drive slowly on them, but they are passable and often very attractive. Maps are widely available in bookstores. The best motoring map is the Touring Club of Italy (T.C.I.) Toscana 1:200,000 sheet.

Renting a Car

It's easy to rent a car in Florence or larger Tuscan towns such as Siena, Pisa, Lucca, and Arezzo. Leading international companies also have offices in some railroad stations and Pisa and Peretola airports. Costs are high by North American and U.K. standards, and it can be worth arranging car rental through a travel agent before leaving home.

You can often get a better deal through smaller local companies. Contact visitor centers or see under "Autonoleggio" in the *Yellow Pages (Pagine Gialle; paginegialle.it).* Drivers must be over 21 and have a license to rent a car. Rental companies in Florence include the following:

Avis, Borgo Ognissanti 128r *(tel 055 213 629)* and Peretola Airport *(tel 055 315 588, avisautonoleggio.it)*
Hertz, Via Borgo Ognissanti 137r *(tel 055 239 8205, airport 055 307 370, hertz.it)*
Europcar, Borgo Ognissanti 53r–55r *(tel 055 290 0438, airport 055 318 609, europcar.it)*

Driving Information

Accidents See p. 305.

Breakdowns Put on hazard lights and place a warning triangle behind the car. Call the Automobile Club d'Italia (A.C.I.) emergency number *(tel 803 116 in Florence, aci.it),* giving your location, car make, and registration. The car will be towed to the nearest A.C.I.-approved garage. Car rental firms often have their own arrangements for breakdowns and accidents; ask when renting.

Busy Periods Tuscan and most other Italian roads are busy on Friday and Sunday nights, and before and after holidays. The first and last weekends of August, when many Italians begin

and end their vacations, are also busy. In cities, traffic is bad early in the morning, before lunch, and at night.

Distances All distances on signposts in Italy are shown in kilometers (1 km = 0.62 mile).

Gas In Italy gas *(benzina)* is expensive and priced by the liter (0.26 U.S. gallon). Gas stations on autostrade are open 24 hours and generally accept credit cards. Other gas stations may close from around 1 p.m. to 4 p.m., after 7 p.m., and all day Sunday. Smaller stations may accept cash only. Be sure all pump meters are set to zero before the attendant starts filling your tank. Some gas stations have automatic dispensers that take a range of large-denomination euro notes when there are no attendants.

Headlights It is obligatory to drive with headlights on main roads even during daylight.

Licenses U.S., Canadian, and U.K. drivers in Italy must have a valid driver's license *(patente)* or International Driver's License (permit). They are also legally bound to carry a translation of the license to help police, but this is rarely enforced. For details of current regulations and how to obtain translations and an International Driver's License, contact the American Automobile Association, Canadian Automobile Association, or A.A., in the U.K.

Parking Parking is often very difficult in Florence and in Tuscany's major towns. Most spots on the streets and in parking lots *(parcheggi)* are filled by locals. Many historic centers, such as Florence and Siena, have blue zones *(zona blu)* or similar areas that are closed to traffic: Some towns have restrictions in place for busy times of day. Metered parking (parcometro) is being introduced in some cities. Try to park your car in a supervised lot, and never leave valuables or luggage in a parked vehicle. Illegally parked cars, especially those left in a removal zone (zona rimozione), may be towed away or police may issue tickets.

Rules of the Road Most regulations in Italy are similar to those in the United States, notably the fact that you drive on the right and can pass only on the left. Seat belts are mandatory in the front and back seats. Drivers must carry licenses, insurance, and other documentation at all times. Drunken driving penalties are severe, with heavy fines and the possibility of six months' imprisonment. A red warning triangle for use during breakdowns or accidents must be carried by law.

Speed Limits The limit in cities and built-up areas is 50 kph (31 mph). Outside such places the limit is 110 kph (70 mph) unless marked at 90 kph (56 mph). Autostrade limits are 130 kph (80 mph) and 110 kph (70 mph) for vehicles with engine capacity of less than 1100 cc. Speed cameras are installed on autostrada and are able to calculate if you have exceeded the speed limit between the fixed points of your entry and exit from the autostrada. A spot fine is levied at the exit toll booth if you have exceeded the limit.

PRACTICAL ADVICE
Communications
Post Offices
Stamps (francobolli) can be bought from a post office (ufficio postale, poste.it) or most tobacconists (tabacchi), the latter indicated by a blue sign with a white "T." Most offices are generally open from about 8 or 9 a.m. to 2 p.m., Monday through Friday, 8 a.m. to noon on Saturday. Main post offices in larger towns and cities usually open from 8 or 9 a.m. to 7 or 8 p.m., Monday through Saturday. The Italian mail system can be slow: Allow 15 days for letters between Italy and North America, longer for postcards. Use fax or e-mail for hotel reservations.

Mailboxes Small red mailboxes are found outside post offices or on walls in towns and cities. They are marked "Poste" and usually have two slots: One marked "Per La Città" (City Mail), the other "Per Tutte Le Altre Destinazioni" (Other Destinations). An express service (posta priorita) is available for slightly higher postage rates. Posta priorita boxes are blue.

Receiving Mail You can arrange to have mail sent to you in Italy poste restante (fermo posta in Italian). Mail must carry your name and be addressed to the "Ufficio Postale Centrale, Fermo Posta" plus the name of the town or city. Collect it from the town's main post office. You will need to present a passport or photo ID and pay a small fee.

Florence's main central post offices are at Via Pellicceria 3 (tel 055 273 6481, poste.it, open Mon.–Fri. 8:20 a.m.–7:05 p.m. & Sat. 8:20 a.m.–12:35 p.m.) near Piazza della Repubblica, and Via Pietrapiana 53 (tel 055 267 4231, open Mon.–Fri. 8:20 a.m.–7:05 p.m. & Sat 8:20 a.m.–12:35 p.m.).

Telephones
Italy's telephone network is operated mainly by Telecom Italia (TI; telecomitalia.com). Public phones are found on the streets and in bars, restaurants, and TI offices in larger towns. Look for red or yellow signs showing a telephone receiver or receiver and dial. Most take coins and cards (schede telefoniche), the latter available from tabacchi and newsstands in a variety of euro denominations. Cards have a small perforated corner that must be removed before use.

To make a call, pick up the phone, insert money or card, and dial the number. Most call boxes have instructions in English. All calls can be made direct, without operator (call 10 if you do need the operator) or long-distance connections. Telephone numbers may have anything between seven and eleven digits. Call 1254 or visit 1254.it for all telephone inquiries and information. Hotels always add a significant surcharge to calls made from rooms.

To call an Italian number within Italy, use the full number, including the town or city code (for example, 055 in Florence). The code must also be used when calling within a city. Thus in Florence you still add the 055 code when calling another number in the city. To call an Italian number from abroad, dial the international code (011 from the United States and Canada, 00 from the U.K.) then the code for Italy (39), followed by the city code (including the initial 0) and number.

CONVERSIONS
1 kilo = 2.2 lbs
1 liter = 0.2642 U.S. gallon
1.6 km = 1 mile

Women's clothing

U.S.	8	10	12	14	16	18
Italian	40	42	44	46	48	50

Men's clothing

U.S.	36	38	40	42	44	46
Italian	46	48	50	52	54	56

Women's shoes

U.S.	6-6½	7-7½	8-8½	9-9½
Italian	38	39	40–41	42

Men's shoes

U.S.	8	8½	9½	10½	11½	12
Italian	41	42	43	44	45	46

Electricity

Electricity in Italy is 220 volts, 50 Hz, and most plugs have two (sometimes three) round pins. If you bring electrical equipment, you will need a plug adapter plus a transformer for appliances.

Holidays

Stores, banks, offices, and schools close on these national holidays:

January 1 (New Year's Day)
January 6 (Epiphany)
Easter Sunday
Easter Monday
April 25 (Liberation Day)
May 1 (Labor Day or May Day)
August 15 (Ferragosto or Assumption)
November 1 (All Saints' Day)
December 8 (Immaculate Conception)
December 25 (Christmas)
December 26 (St. Stephen's Day)

Some cities have special holidays when businesses may close. In Florence the main city holiday is June 24 (St. John's Day).

Liquor Laws

Liquor laws are far more relaxed in Italy than in North America—most bars stay open all day and late into the night—but restrictions on drunken driving are strict and transgressions are punished.

Media
Useful Publications

Most Italian newspapers are sold from a street newsstand (edicola), many of which in larger cities and tourist centers also stock American, British, and other foreign language newspapers and periodicals. The International Herald Tribune, USA Today, and most U.K. papers are available on the day of issue after about 2 p.m. Airports and railroad stations often have the largest selection of foreign publications.

Italy has a buoyant newspaper market. Among national papers, Corriere della Sera is one of the most authoritative publications, while the more populist La Repubblica is also widely read. The best-selling papers of all are sports publications such as the pink Corriere dello Sport. Many papers have strong city or regional links. Florence and Tuscany's paper is La Nazione. People often read a regional or city paper in preference to a national one. Local newspapers are a good source of information on forthcoming events and museum opening times.

Television

Italian television has three main state channels—RAI 1, 2, and 3—three prominent privately owned channels (Rete Quattro, Canale 5, and Italia Uno), and many cable, local, and other private channels. In most parts of the country you can get at least 15 channels. Foreign movies and shows are almost always dubbed into Italian, never with English subtitles. Better hotels get CNN, Sky, BBC World, and other foreign stations via cable and satellite. The main RAI 1 news bulletin is at 8 p.m.

Radio

Italian radio is generally poor, although the number of stations, particularly FM music stations, is huge. The only English broadcasts are those of the BBC World Service and similar organizations.

Money Matters

On January 1, 1999, the euro became the official currency of Italy. One euro (€) is made up of 100 cents. Euro coins are issued in denominations of 1, 2, 5, 20, and 50 cents, and 1 and 2 euros. Euro notes are issued in denominations of 5, 10, 50, 100, and 500 euros.

Most major banks, airports, and railroad stations have ATMs (bancomat in Italian) for money cards and international credit cards (carta di credito) with instructions in a choice of languages. Arrange the four-digit "PIN" number needed to access these ATMs with your credit card company before leaving home. Currency and travelers' checks—best bought in euros before you leave—can be exchanged in most banks and Bureaux de Change (cambio), but lines are often long and the procedures slow. ATMs and cambio facilities are rarer—sometimes nonexistent—in rural areas and small towns.

Credit cards are accepted in hotels and restaurants in most major towns and cities. Look for Visa, MasterCard, or American Express stickers (Diners Club is less well known), or the Italian "Carta Si" (Yes to Cards) sign. Many businesses still prefer cash, however, and smaller stores, hotels, and so forth, especially in rural areas, may not take cards. Always check before eating a meal or reserving a room.

Opening Times

Opening times are problematic in Florence and Tuscany. There are few hard and fast rules, and opening times of museums and churches, in particular, can change without notice. Stores, banks, and other institutions in big cities are also increasingly moving to northern European hours—that is, with no lunch and afternoon closing: Look for the words orario continuato. Treat the following times as a general guide only:

Banks 8:30 a.m.–1:30 p.m. Mon.–Fri. Major banks may also open for an hour in the afternoon and Saturday morning. Hours are becoming longer and more flexible.

Churches 8 a.m. or 9 a.m.–noon and 3 p.m. or 4 p.m.–6 p.m. or 8 p.m. excluding services; many churches close on Sunday afternoons.

Gas stations 24 hours on auto-strade; store hours elsewhere (see below).

Post offices 8 a.m. or 9 a.m.– 2 p.m., Mon.–Fri./Sat., but larger offices 8 a.m. or 9 a.m.–6 p.m. or 8 p.m. Mon.–Sat.

Museums State-run national museums usually close Sunday afternoon and all day Monday. Most close for lunch (1 p.m.– 3 p.m. or 4 p.m.), although major museums are increasingly open 9 a.m.–7:00 p.m. or 7:30 p.m. Winter hours are usually shorter.

Restaurants Many bars and restaurants close on Sunday evening and all day Monday or one other statutory closing day a week (*la chiusura settimanale*). Many close in January and periods in July or August.

Stores Generally 8:30 a.m. or 9 a.m.–1 p.m. and 3:30 p.m. or 4 p.m.–8 p.m. Mon.–Sat. Many stores close Monday morning and another half-day a week. A few department stores and major city stores may stay open seven days a week from 9 a.m. to 8 p.m. or later (10 p.m.).

Restrooms

Few Italian public buildings have restrooms. Generally you need to use the facilities available in bars, railroad stations, and gas stations, where standards are generally low. Ask for *il bagno*, take a few tissues in with you to be sure, and don't confuse *Signori* (Men) with *Signore* (Women). Tip any attendants about 50 cents.

Time Differences

Italy runs on CET (central European time), one hour ahead of Greenwich mean time and six hours ahead of eastern standard time. Noon in Italy is 6 a.m. in New York. Clocks change for daylight saving in May (1 hour forward) and late September or October (1 hour back). Italy uses the 24-hour clock.

Tipping

In restaurants where a service charge *(servizio)* is not levied, leave 10–15 percent: Even where it is, you may wish to leave 5–10 percent for the waiter. In bars tip 20–50 cents for drinks consumed standing up, and €1–€1.50 for waiter service. In hotel bars be slightly more generous. Cab drivers merit around 10 percent. Service is included in hotel rates, but tip chambermaids €2–€3 and doormen about €1–€3 for calling a cab, the bellhop €1 for carrying your bags, and the concierge-porter *(portiere)* about €5–€15 if he has been helpful. Double these figures in the most expensive hotels. Tip restroom and checkroom attendants up to 50 cents. Porters at airports and railroad stations generally work to fixed tariffs, but tip €2–€4 extra at your discretion. Barbers merit around €3–€5, a hairdresser's assistant €3–€8 depending on the level of establishment. Tip church or other custodians €2–€4.

Visitor Centers

Every Tuscan city and town—plus many villages—has a visitor center. These usually provide maps, lists of accommodations (but no reservation service), leaflets on local sights, and lists of festivals and local cultural and other events.

The main Florence visitor center is just north of the cathedral (Duomo) at Via Cavour 1r *(tel 055 290 832 or 055 290 833, closed Sunday).* There are centers on the east side of Santa Maria Novella railroad station in Piazza della Stazione 4 *(tel 055 212 245, closed Sunday p.m.)* and in front of the Duomo at Piazza San Giovanni 1 *(tel 055 288 496, closed Sun. p.m.).* Florence's official tourism website is *firenzeturismo.it.* Details of local visitor centers are given in the main text of this guide.

Italian State Tourist Offices

UNITED STATES
New York
630 Fifth Avenue, Suite 1965, New York, NY 10111, tel 212/245-5618, fax 212/586-9249, enit.it
Chicago
500 North Michigan Avenue, Suite 506, Chicago, Il 60611, tel 312/644-0990 or 312/644-0996, fax 312/644-3109
Los Angeles
10850 Wilshire Boulevard, Suite 575, Los Angeles, CA 90024, tel 310/820-1898 or 310/820-9807, fax 310/470-7788

CANADA
Toronto
110 Yonge Street, Suite 503, Toronto, Ontario M5C 1T4, tel 416/925-4882, fax 416/925-4799

UNITED KINGDOM
London
1 Princes Street, London W1R 8AY, tel 020 7408-1254, fax 020 7399-3567, italia.it

Travelers With Disabilities

Museums, galleries, and public buildings across Italy are making great strides in providing wheelchair access, but much remains to be done. Few buses or trains have dedicated facilities, and virtually no cabs. Historic cities with narrow streets and old buildings present special problems. Only hotels in higher star categories provide dedicated rooms, but hotels and restaurants will usually provide help if you call ahead. Consult your nearest Italian embassy or consulate for details of the procedures required to bring an assistance dog into Italy.

Useful contacts in North America include SATH (tel 212/ 447-7284 or 447-0027, sath.org) and Mobility International (miusa.org).

EMERGENCIES
Embassies in Italy

U.S. Embassy, Via Vittorio Veneto 121, Rome, tel 06 46 741, italyusembassy.gov

U.S. Consulate, Lungarno Vespucci 38, Florence, tel 055 266 951, florence.usconsulate.gov

U.S. Consulate, Via Principe Amadeo 2/10, Milan, tel 02 290 351, milan.usconsulate.gov

Canadian Embassy, Via Salaria 243 (visa and consular section at Via Zara 30), tel 06 854 441, canadainternational.gc.ca

U.K. Embassy, Via XX Settembre 80/A, Rome, tel 06 4220 0001, gov.co.uk

Emergency Phone Numbers

112 Police
112 Emergency Services
803 116 Car breakdown
112 Ambulance

For legal assistance in an emergency, contact your embassy or consulate (see above) for a list of English-speaking lawyers.

What to Do in a Traffic Accident

Put on hazard lights and place a warning triangle 165 feet (50 m) behind the car. Call the police (tel 112) from a public phone box (see above): Autostrade have emergency telephones at regular intervals. At the scene, don't admit liability or make potentially incriminating statements to police or onlookers. Ask any witnesses to remain, make a police statement, and exchange insurance and other relevant details with the other driver(s). Call the car rental agency, if necessary, to inform them of the incident.

Lost Property & Crime

If you lose anything, go first to the local visitor center and ask for help. Bus, tram, train, and subway systems in cities usually have special offices to deal with lost property, but they can be hard to find and usually only open a few hours a day. Ask for directions at visitor centers, and try bus depots and railroad stations. Hotels should also provide assistance.

To report a more serious loss or theft, go to the local police station or Questura. In Florence this is at Via Zara 2 (tel 055 49 771) and in Siena in Via del Castoro, east of the cathedral.

Many police stations have special English-speaking staff to deal with visitors' problems. You will be asked to help fill in and sign a form (una denuncia) reporting any crime: Keep your copy for any possible insurance claims.

Report the loss or theft of a passport to the police and then notify your embassy.

Health

Be sure that your health insurance covers visits to Italy and that any travel insurance also includes sufficient medical coverage. For minor complaints go to a pharmacy (una farmacia), indicated by a green cross outside. Staff are well trained and can help in finding a doctor (un medico) or dentist (un dentista), if necessary. Or consult your hotel, the Yellow Pages (Pagine Gialle; paginegialle .it), or visitor centers. The private Tourist Medical Service (tel 055 475 411) has doctors on call 24 hours a day.

Bring enough prescription medicine (medicina) for the duration, because brand names may be different in Italy. If you need a prescription, pharmacies will direct you to a doctor.

For more serious complaints go to a hospital (un ospedale). Immediate treatment is provided at the Pronto Soccorso. Italian hospitals often look rundown, but the standards of treatment are generally good.

Consider contacting the International Association for Medical Assistance to Travelers (iamat.org), a nonprofit organization that anyone can join for free. Members get a directory of English-speaking IAMAT doctors and are entitled to services at set rates (tel 716/754-4883 in the U.S. & 416/652-0137 or 519/836-0102 in Canada).

The most common minor complaints in Italy are likely to be too much sun, stomachaches, and insect bites. There are poisonous snakes (viperes), but bites are fatal only if you have an allergic reaction. Tap water is safe unless marked "acqua non potabile." Milk is pasteurized.

Hospital

Florence Santa Maria Nuova, Piazza Santa Maria Nuova 1 (tel 055 69 381, asf.toscana.it).

Hotels & Restaurants

When it comes to travel, where you sleep and eat can make all the difference. Florence offers a wide range of hotel and restaurant selections in all price categories and styles. In Tuscany, especially the more rural parts, the choice can be more limited.

HOTELS
Grading System
Italian hotels are officially graded from one star, the simplest accommodations, to five stars (luxury). Grading criteria are complex, but in a three-star establishment and above, all rooms should have private baths, a phone, and a TV. Most two-star hotels also have private bathrooms. Note that in even the smartest hotels, bathrooms may only have a shower *(una doccia)* and no tub *(una vasca)*. Always ask to see a selection of rooms—you may be shown the worst first. Rooms are often small by U.S. standards, even in smart hotels. All-day room service and air-conditioning are also comparatively rare.

Recommended hotels have a restaurant unless stated otherwise. A restaurant symbol is given where the restaurant is outstanding in its own right. Note that the term *pensione,* referring to private rooms or the simplest hotels, is still seen, but is no longer in use as an official designation.

Location
Hotels have been selected to provide the best centrally placed accommodations within a town or city. Noise can be a problem in many urban areas, however, and a quiet, out-of-town option is therefore often provided.

Hotels are also chosen where possible for the character, charm, and historical associations. In country areas the emphasis is on period villas and restored historic properties with pools, grounds, and gardens. Choice and quality of accommodations are generally poorer in the more remote rural areas of Italy.

Reservations
It is advisable to reserve all hotels in advance, especially in the major towns, and particularly in high season (June–Aug.). Note that in Florence "high season" often means Christmas, New Year, and Easter through October.

Reservations should be made by phone and confirmed by e-mail. It is also a good idea to reconfirm reservations a couple of days before arrival. Hoteliers are obliged to register every guest, so on checking in you have to hand in your passport. Usually it is returned within a few hours or on the day of departure.

Check-out times range from around 10 a.m. to noon, but you'll be able to leave luggage at reception for collection later in the day.

Prices
All prices are officially set, and room rates must be displayed by law at reception and in each room. Prices for different rooms can vary within a hotel, but all taxes and services should be included in the rate.

Hotels often levy additional charges for air-conditioning and garage facilities, while laundry, drinks from minibars, and phone calls made from rooms invariably carry large surcharges. Price categories are for double *(una matrimoniale)* or twin *(una camera doppia)* rooms, and are given for guidance only. Seasonal variations often apply, especially in coastal resorts, where high-season (summer) rates are usually higher.

At busy times there may also be a two- or three-day minimum stay policy, and you may be obliged to take full- or half-board packages. Half-board *(mezza pensione)* includes breakfast and lunch; full-board *(pensione completa)* includes all meals. Such packages are usually priced on a per person basis. Prices usually include breakfast *(colazione),* but where breakfast is optional (see rate cards in rooms), it always costs less to eat at the nearest coffee shop. Breakfasts in better hotels are improving—U.S.-style buffets are now more common—but for the most part colazione means a "continental" breakfast—a coffee, a roll, and jelly.

Credit Cards
Many large hotels accept all major credit cards. Smaller ones may only accept some, as shown in their entry. Abbreviations used are AE (American Express), DC (Diners Club), MC (MasterCard), V (Visa). Look for individual card symbols outside establishments or the Italian "Carta Sì" (Yes to Cards) sign. As a general rule, AE and DC are less widely accepted than V and MC.

RESTAURANTS
Tuscany enjoys a great cuisine, and the pleasures of Italian food and wine are as much a part of a visit to the region as museums and galleries. Restaurants of different type and quality are found in every town or village, from the humble pizzeria to the venerable classics of Florence.

Our selection includes restaurants that reflect the best regional cooking available, but don't be afraid to experiment, especially in small towns. If in doubt, look for somewhere where local people are eating.

Types of Restaurant
Categories of restaurants in Italy are increasingly blurred. Once an *osteria* was a simple inn, a *trattoria* was a neighborhood eating place, and a *ristorante* was a smart establishment with culinary pretensions. Now some of the best places to eat can be *osterie*, increasingly being revamped as informal restaurants with an innovative approach to cooking. Old-fashioned trattorias with checked tablecloths are also largely things of the past—except in smaller towns off the beaten path—while ristorante is a term now applied to just about any eating place. A pizzeria *(una pizzeria)* remains the one constant—a simple place that often serves basic pastas, main courses, and desserts as well as pizzas. Wherever you eat, remember that neither price nor a restaurant's smartness necessarily reflect the quality of the food. A pizza in a boisterous pizzeria may be every bit as good—and as memorable—as a five-course feast in a sleek Florentine hotel restaurant full of people in business attire.

Dining Hours
Breakfast *(colazione)* is usually a cappuccino and a roll or pastry *(una brioche)* taken standing up in a bar between 7 a.m. and 9 a.m. Lunch *(pranzo)* starts around 12:30 p.m. and finishes about 2 p.m.; the long lunch is becoming a thing of the past. Dinner *(cena)* begins about 8 p.m., with last orders around 10 p.m., although dinner hours may be earlier in rural areas and smaller towns.

Pizzerias often open only in the evenings, especially those with wood-fuel ovens *(forno a*

legno). Most eateries close one day a week *(la chiusura settimanale)*, and many take long vacations *(ferie)* in July or August.

Meals
Italian meals traditionally start with appetizers *(antipasti*—literally "before the meal"), a first course *(il primo)* of soup, pasta, or rice, and a main course *(il secondo)* of meat or fish. Vegetables *(contorni)* or salads *(insalata)* are often served separately, with or after the secondo. Desserts *(dolci)* may include, or be followed by, fruit *(frutta)* and cheese *(formaggio)*. You needn't indulge in every stage—a primo and salad is acceptable in all but the smartest restaurants. Many Italians choose to go on an after-dinner stroll to an ice-cream parlor *(gelateria)* for dessert.

Meals are usually accompanied by bread and mineral water, for which you pay extra.

Set Menus
The menu in Italian is *il menù* or *la lista*. Set-price menus are available in many restaurants in tourist areas. The *menù turistico* usually includes two courses, a simple dessert, and half a bottle of wine and water per person. Quantities and quality of food are invariably poor. Of better value in more upscale restaurants is the *menù gastronomico*, where you pay a set price to sample a selection of the restaurant's special dishes.

Bars, Cafés, & Snacks
Bars and cafés are perfect for breakfast and often provide snacks such as filled rolls *(panini)* or sandwiches *(tramezzini)* through the day. A few may offer a light meal at lunch. Kiosks or small stores selling slices of pizza are common.

It always costs less to stand at the bar. Specify what you want

and pay at the separate cash desk *(la cassa)*, then take your chit *(lo scontrino)* to the bar and repeat your order. A small coin as a tip placed on the bar often helps secure prompt service. Where a bar has a waiter and tables, especially outside tables, you pay more to sit and give your order to the waiter. Only in small rural bars can you pay at the bar and then sit down.

Wine bars *(enoteche)* are becoming more common. All serve wine by the glass or bottle, often in informal surroundings, and most provide bread, cheeses, other snacks, and light meals. A *birreria*, or beer cellar, is similar, but aims at a younger generation.

Paying
The check *(il conto)* must be presented to you by law as a formal receipt. A price scrawled on a piece of paper is illegal, and you can demand an itemized *ricevuta*. Bills once included a cover charge *(pane e coperto)*, a practice the authorities are trying to outlaw. Many restaurants attempt to get around the law by charging for bread brought to your table whether you want it or not. Smaller and rural restaurants are less likely to accept credit cards, and it can be worth checking if your card is acceptable, even in places with card signs outside.

Tipping & Dress
Tip between 10 and 15 percent where service has been good and where a service charge *(servizio)* is not included. As a rule, Italians dress well but informally to eat out, especially in better restaurants. A relaxed casual style is a good rule of thumb: Jacket and tie for men are rarely necessary, but often the better dressed you are, the better service you can expect.

Smoking
Smoking is banned in cafés, bars, restaurants and all other enclosed public spaces.

Organization
Hotels and restaurants are listed by chapter area, then by price category, then alphabetically. Hotel restaurants of note have been bolded in the hotel entries and indicated by a restaurant icon beneath the hotel icon (if they're unusually special, they are treated in a separate entry within the restaurant section).

FLORENCE

◼ PIAZZA DEL DUOMO

HOTELS

🏨 BRUNELLESCHI
$$$$–$$$$$ ✪✪✪✪
PIAZZA SANTA ELISABETTA 3
TEL 055 27370
hotelbrunelleschi.it
The location of this fascinating hotel, just off the main Via dei Calzaiuoli, could hardly be more central. Designed by leading Italian architect Italo Gamberini, it has been stylishly converted from a Byzantine chapel and fifth-century tower (the latter is one of the city's oldest surviving structures). Old brick and stone have been preserved in the public areas and complemented by the tasteful use of wood, while the recently renovated rooms are bright, airy, and comfortable.
🛈 88 + 8 suites; 30 non-smoking rooms 🅿 🚌 23, A
🛗 🚭 💳 All major cards

🏨 CASCI
$$ ✪✪
VIA CAVOUR 13
TEL 055 211 686
hotelcasci.it
This excellent two-star hotel is the best in its class and enjoys a perfect position just two minutes' walk north of the cathedral. Rooms are modest in size, but immaculate and modern, and the courtesy and welcome of the multilingual family owners are faultless. Buffet breakfast but no restaurant.
🛈 24 🚌 1, 6, 7, 14, 23 🛗
🚭 💳 All major cards

🏨 LA DIMORA DEGLI ANGELI
$$
VIA DE BRUNELLESCHI 4
TEL 055 288 478 OR
340 988 7988
ladimoradegliangeli.com
This boutique B&B on the third and fourth floors of a historic palazzo has few hotel services and facilities, but it offers good value for money, cheerful rooms, a warm welcome from owner Claudio Cherubini, and an excellent location moments from the Duomo. The Tea Room is open to guests 24 hours a day, and a voucher entitles you to a simple breakfast in a choice of nearby bars.
🛈 15 🛗 🚭 💳 All major cards

RESTAURANTS

🍴 PAOLI
$$$
VIA DEI TAVOLINI 12R
TEL 055 216 215
casatrattoria.com
A tempting place to eat in the very heart of the city (just off Via dei Calzaiuoli), although the attraction is not so much the food—a mixture of Tuscan grilled meats, pastas, and soups—as the frescoed dining room—one of the oldest and most beautiful in the city.
🛈 85 🚌 A 🕐 Closed Tues. & Aug. 💳 All major cards

🍴 CAFFÈ GILLI
$
PIAZZA DELLA REPUBBLICA 36–39R, CNR. OF VIA ROMA
TEL 055 213 896
gilli.it
Piazza della Repubblica is a vast, characterless square distinguished only by its four historic cafés, of which Gilli is the best. Founded in 1733, it moved to its present corner site in 1910, the date of its magnificent belle epoque interior. Its large terrace is a fine place for an aperitif (food is unexceptional and expensive) as you watch the Florentines on early evening parade.
🚌 A 🕐 Closed Tues. 💳 All major cards

🍴 CANTINETTA DEI VERRAZZANO
$
VIA DEI TAVOLINI 18–20R
TEL 055 268 590
verrazzano.com

A hard-to-miss place just off the main Via dei Calzaiuoli for takeout snacks, cakes, and slices of pizza, or a more leisurely lunch and glass of wine at the tables to the rear. Choose from the array of food under the huge glass-fronted display. The Cantinetta is owned by a notable Chianti vineyard, so the wines are as good as the food.

🍽 A 🕐 Closed Sun. & Aug.
🗝 All major cards

■ **EASTERN FLORENCE**

HOTELS

SOMETHING SPECIAL

🏨 FOUR SEASONS HOTEL FLORENCE
$$$$$ ✪✪✪✪✪
BORGO PINTI 99
TEL 055 26 261
fourseasons.com/florence
Four Seasons' Florence hotel is the most luxurious in the city, a sumptuously restored palace and former convent set in glorious gardens and with rooms and public spaces that feature a wealth of frescoes, fine art, antiques, and other period details. Removed from the bustle of the historic center, it is calmer than some accommodations, but also less convenient for sightseeing.

🛈 25 + 24 suites 🅿 🔄 🔆
🗝 🔆 🗝 All major cards

🏨 J & J
$$$$ ✪✪✪✪
VIA DI MEZZO 20
TEL 055 26312
jandjhotel.com
This converted 15th-century convent appears bland from the outside, but within reveals itself as a beautifully romantic little hotel. Patches of old fresco and vaulted ceilings distinguish the public areas, while

the rooms—which vary in size and decor—combine fine fabrics, modern fittings, and an array of antiques. Located away from the throng in the Sant'Ambrogio district, but still within easy walking distance of all the sights. No restaurant.

🛈 21 🅿 🔆 🗝 All major cards

🏨 MONNA LISA
$$$$ ✪✪✪✪
BORGO PINTI 27
TEL 055 247 9751
monnalisa.it
A somber facade conceals a marvelous 14th-century palazzo complete with sweeping staircase, frescoed ceilings, and terra-cotta floors. Rooms vary in size but have an aristocratic, old-world feel, with oil paintings and antiques. Some overlook a quiet rear garden, others an inner courtyard.

🛈 45 🍽 14, 23, A 🅿 🔆
🗝 All major cards

RESTAURANTS

SOMETHING SPECIAL

🍽 ENOTECA PINCHIORRI
$$$$$
VIA GHIBELLINA 87
TEL 055 242 777
enotecapinchiorri.com
Florence's most expensive restaurant has three Michelin stars and—at more than 80,000 bottles—one of Europe's finest wine cellars. The setting—a Renaissance palazzo with lofty frescoed ceilings—and Tuscan/international cuisine are chic and sophisticated, although the formality and ceremony may not be to all tastes. Food is exquisite but comes in tiny portions. Jacket and tie recommended for men.

🍽 80 🍽 14 🕐 Closed Sun.–Mon., Wed. L, & Aug. 🔆
🗝 All major cards

🍽 ALLE MURATE
$$$$
VIA DEL PROCONSOLO 1BR
TEL 055 240 618
allemurate.it
Don't be put off by an initial reception that can border on the brusque, for once inside this intimate restaurant you are treated to some of the city's most innovative cooking. Standards can vary—eat à la carte or opt for one of two set "gastronomic menus." Desserts are especially good (so leave room). So is the wine list, which contains some 150 mainly Tuscan vintages.

🍽 65 🍽 14 🕐 Closed Mon.
🔆 🗝 All major cards

🍽 ORA D'ARIA
$$$$
VIA DEI GEORGOFILI 11–13R
TEL 055 200 1699
www.oradariaristorante.com
Young chef Marco Stabile is one of Florence's new culinary stars. In a cool, contemporary dining room close to Piazza della Signoria he offers light, imaginative, and beautifully presented modern Tuscan and Italian cooking.

🍽 40 🔆 🕐 Closed Sun., Mon. L, & Aug. 🗝 AE, MC, V

🍽 CIBREO
$$$–$$$$
VIA DE' MACCI 122R
TEL 055 234 1100
Cibreo is the choice of most Florentine gastronomes and the best place in the city to enjoy creative interpretations of traditional Tuscan dishes. The dining room is plain, with simple wooden tables and painted walls, and the service and atmosphere are relaxed and informal. Prices are set for each course; try a mouthwatering dessert. Reserve several days in advance.

🍽 70 🍽 14, A 🅿 🕐 Closed Mon. & a period in Jan. & Aug.
🔆 🗝 All major cards

🍴 BALDOVINO
$$–$$$
VIA DI SAN GIUSEPPE 22R
TEL 055 241 773
This chic restaurant just behind
Santa Croce offers pizzas
made in traditional Neapolitan
style in wood-fired ovens or a
choice of good Tuscan pasta
and meat dishes. Its success
is remarkable given that it is
run by a Scottish couple who
opened a wine bar and food
store across the street.
🪑 130 🚌 14, 23 🕐 Closed
Mon. 🏧 All major cards

🍴 CAFFÈ ITALIANO
$$–$$$
VIA ISOLA DELLE STINCHE 11–13R
TEL 055 289 368
caffeitaliano.it
This restaurant consists of a
formal restaurant, a wine bar
for snacks and lighter meals,
and a simple trattoria for
lunches and less formal dining.
All serve well-priced Tuscan
food and have a fine medieval
setting, with vast beams, brick
vaults, terra-cotta floors, and
pretty wooden cabinets.
🪑 50–120 🚌 23 🕐 Closed
Mon. 🏧 All major cards

🍴 OSTERIA DE' BENCI
$$
VIA DE' BENCI 13R
TEL 055 234 4923
osteriadeibenci.it
A busy dining room painted
in pastel colors that give a
fresh, modern air. The staff is
young, energetic, and informal,
and the food offers Tuscan
staples such as *zuppa di verdura*
(vegetable soup) and *agnello
scottaditto* (grilled lamb).
🪑 50–80 🚌 13, 23, B
🕐 Closed some of Aug.
🏧 All major cards

🍴 DEL FAGIOLI
$
CORSO TINTORI 47R
TEL 055 244 285

The same family has run
this trattoria close to Santa
Croce for more than 40 years,
perfecting both traditional
Florentine standards such
as *ribollita* (bean and cabbage
soup) and house specialties
like *involtini alla Gigi* (rolled
and filled meat)
🪑 50 🔌 🕐 Closed Sat.–Sun.,
& Aug. 🏧 No credit cards

🍴 RUGGINI
$
VIA DEI NERI 76R
TEL 055 214 521
A bar and *pasticceria* (pastry
shop) with a sensational selec-
tion of chocolates, cakes, and
other goodies. At the bar
(no seating) you can buy
bowls of pasta at lunch.
🚌 B 🕐 Closed Sun. p.m. &
Mon.

🍴 VIVOLI
$
VIA ISOLA DELLE STINCHE 7R
TEL 055 292 334
vivoli.it
A visit to this *gelateria* is as
essential as a visit to the Uffizi.
Many claim its ice cream is the
best in Italy. It is on a hard-to-
find street off Via Ghibellina
west of Piazza Santa Croce.
🚌 23 🕐 Closed Mon.

■ NORTHERN FLORENCE

HOTELS

🏨 LOGGIATO DEI SERVITI
$$$ ✪✪✪
PIAZZA DELLE SS ANNUNZIATA 3
TEL 055 289 592
loggiatodeiservitihotel.it
This hotel occupies a former
convent in a distinguished
square designed by leading
Renaissance architect Filippo
Brunelleschi. Rooms vary in
style, but all have tasteful,
understated lines and decor

that recalls the simplicity of
the original structure. Some
have vaulted ceilings and
canopy beds, and all are enlivened by rich fabrics and pieces
of period furniture.
🛏 25 + 4 suites 🚌 6, 31, 32
🅿 🚫 🔌 🏧 All major cards

🏨 MORANDI ALLA CROCETTA
$$$ ✪✪✪
VIA LAURA 50
TEL 055 234 4747
hotelmorandi.it
A quiet and intimate hotel—
part of a former monas-
tery—near Piazza delle SS
Annunziata. This is a gem,
thanks to both the charm and
friendly welcome of the owner
and the considerable style
with which she has decorated
individual rooms and public
spaces. Colorful rugs cover
polished wooden floors, and
old prints and antiques deco-
rate the walls. No restaurant.
Reserve well in advance.
🛏 10 🚌 6, 31, 32 🔌 🏧 All
major cards

🏨 HOTEL BELLETTINI
$$ ✪✪
VIA DEI CONTI 7
TEL 055 213 561
More than a hint of the 19th
century pervades this central
hotel, with the type of terra-
cotta floors and wood-beamed
ceilings you would expect to
find in a period Florentine
town house. Rooms can be a
little spartan but are spotless;
the two on the top floor have
fabulous views. The staff is
unfailingly helpful.
🛏 27 🚌 11, 12 🅿 🚫 🔌
🏧 All major cards

RESTAURANTS

🍴 ZÀ-ZÀ
$$
PIAZZA DEL MERCATO
CENTRALE 26R

TEL 055 215 411
trattoriazaza.it
This former market-traders retreat, founded in 1977, has gone from strength to strength, increasing in size and popularity without sacrificing its reasonable prices and reliable Florentine food. Forgo the outside tables on the square for the cheerful, informal, and pleasing old-style trattoria atmosphere inside.
🍴 150 inside, 100 outside
💳 🅰 All major cards

🍴 CASA DEL VINO
$
VIA DELL'ARIENTO 16R
TEL 055 215 609
casadelvino.it
Although close to busy San Lorenzo market and the Mercato Centrale, few foreigners frequent this lively wine bar. But the locals are friendly, so come here for a glass of wine with a selection of rustic snacks (breads, ham, sandwiches, and cheeses).
🚌 7, 10, 11, 12, 25, 32, 33 to Via Nazionale ⊕ Closed Sat. p.m. & Sun.

🍴 NERBONE
$
MERCATO CENTRALE
TEL 055 219 949
There's nowhere better than Nerbone for a taste of local color and robust Florentine food. This little place is a combination of food stall and diner, and has been in business in a corner of the Mercato Centrale, the city's main covered market, since 1872. It's always full of market traders and shoppers.
🚌 7, 10, 11, 12, 25, 32, 33 to Via Nazionale ⊕ Closed Sun. & p.m. Mon.–Sat.

🍴 ZANOBINI
$
VIA SANT'ANTONINO 47R
TEL 055 239 6850
Like the nearby Casa del Vino

(see above), this is an old wood-paneled wine bar that sees few foreign visitors. Sip a glass of wine with a rough and ready hunk of bread and cheese, or buy a bottle at the rear of the bar.
🚌 7, 10, 11, 12, 25, 32, 33 to Via Nazionale ⊕ Closed Sun. & a period in Aug.
💳 No credit cards

▧ WESTERN FLORENCE

HOTELS

🏨 HELVETIA & BRISTOL
$$$$$ ⭑⭑⭑⭑⭑
VIA DEI PESCIONI 2
TEL 055 26 651
royaldemeure.com
First choice in Florence if money is no object. Luxurious and exclusive, this superb hotel has been in business since the 18th century. Facilities and bathrooms are state of the art, but rooms are in a more sober, traditional style with antiques and old paintings. Some rooms are relatively small.
🛏 52 + 15 suites 🚌 🅰 🅿 🔄 💳 🅰 All major cards

🏨 WESTIN EXCELSIOR
$$$$$ ⭑⭑⭑⭑⭑
PIAZZA OGNISSANTI 3
TEL 055 27 151
starwoodhotels.com
Florence's second grandest hotel is undermined only by its position on one of the city's less attractive piazzas. Otherwise the antique-filled rooms are visions of traditional elegance, while the public areas are sumptuous with marble columns and ornate ceilings. More regal than the St. Regis Grand, the rival hotel right across the square.
🛏 171, including 50 non-smoking suites 🅿 🚌 12, B 🔄 💳 🅰 All major cards

🏨 HERMITAGE
$$$ ⭑⭑⭑
VICOLO MARZIO 1
PIAZZA DEL PESCE
TEL 055 287 216
hermitagehotel.com
This is one of Florence's most popular small hotels, thanks largely to its position close to the Ponte Vecchio, friendly service, and good facilities. Rooms are cozy, adorned with the occasional antique. Some rooms have river views but can be noisy, despite double-glazing. The roof terrace where you can take breakfast in summer is a major plus.
🛏 27 🚌 B 🅿 🔄 💳 🅰 All major cards

🏨 PORTA ROSSA
$$–$$$ ⭑⭑⭑⭑
VIA PORTA ROSSA 19
TEL 055 271 0911 OR
0039 848 390 227 (reservations)
nh-hotels.it
One of Italy's oldest inns, this dates from 1386 and has played host to the likes of poet Lord Byron and French writer Stendhal. Long rather dated and plain, it has been extensively renovated, and now bright, contemporary rooms and chic interiors, plus an excellent location, make this a good midrange choice.
🛏 72 🅿 🚌 B 🔄 💳 All major cards

RESTAURANTS

🍴 CANTINETTA ANTINORI
$$$
PIAZZA ANTINORI 3 (CNR. OF VIA DE' PECORI & VIA DE' TORNABUONI)
TEL 055 292 234
cantinetta-antinori.com
Antinori is one of Tuscany's most prestigious wine producers, but its Florentine restaurant is a simple, faux-rustic

trattoria, with shared wooden tables and excellent traditional Florentine staples such as *ribollita* soup and *tagliata* (sliced, grilled steak).

🔲 60 🔲 🕐 Closed Sat.–Sun. 🔲 All major cards

🍴 CAFFÈ AMERINI
$
VIA DELLA VIGNA NUOVA 63R
TEL 055 284 941
The interior at Amerini combines modern splashes of color and design with art deco mirrors and medieval brick ceilings. Customers tend to be elderly locals, shoppers, and students, attracted by the excellent lunch salads, snacks, and sandwiches.

🚌 6, 11, 12, 36, 37 🕐 Closed Sun.

🍴 CAFFÈ GIACOSA
$
VIA DE' TORNABUONI 83R
TEL 055 239 6226
caffegiacosa.it
Take a break from shopping in Giacosa, once the favored retreat of Florence's 19th-century beau monde, and now extravagantly updated by designer Roberto Cavalli. It serves excellent chocolate and cakes, but it is best known for its Negroni cocktail.

🚌 6, 11, 12, 36, 37 🕐 Closed Sun.

🍴 CAFFÈ MEGARA
$
VIA DELLA SPADA 15–17R
TEL 055 211 837
The Megara is similar to the Amerini (see above) in that it attracts a local crowd at lunch. Breakfast is good here, as are the snacks and happy hour cocktails (5 p.m.–8 p.m.), but the main attractions are the light lunches. Open until 2 a.m.

🚌 6, 11, 12, 36, 37

🍴 CAPOCACCIA
$
LUNGARNO CORSINI 12–14R
TEL 055 210 751
A smart combination of café, bistro, and bar—and a haunt for stylish and cosmopolitan locals by day and night—it's been voted the Florentines' favorite nighttime rendezvous. Don't be put off by the busy roadside position. Coffee, drinks, snacks, and light meals are available in the pretty wood and blue-tiled interior.

🚌 B

🏨 OLTRARNO

HOTEL

🏨 LUNGARNO
$$$$ ✪✪✪✪
BORGO SAN JACOPO 14
TEL 055 27 261
lungarnocollection.com
The Lungarno is on the banks of the Arno in the Oltrarno district, but not all rooms have river views (request these when you reserve). The bar, restaurant, and sitting area overlook the water. Bedrooms aren't large but are tastefully decorated; those in the hotel's medieval tower have stone walls. Visit the website for other local, tasteful hotels in this Ferragamo-owned group.

🛈 57 + 14 suites 🚌 11, 36, 37 🅿 🔲 🔲 🔲 All major cards

RESTAURANTS

🍴 ALLE VECCHIA BETTOLA
$$–$$$
VIALE LUDOVICO ARIOSTO 32–34R
TEL 055 224 158
Historically, a *bettola* was a simple Florentine eating place. Opened in 1979, this family-run restaurant continues the

tradition, with plain Tuscan cuisine—hearty soups, pastas, and grilled meat—in rustic surroundings (tiled walls and lots of hanging fruits and hams). You sit on benches, eat off marble tables, and pay for wine from the flask by the amount you drink. The menu changes daily, but among the regulars the cured hams and carpaccio (sliced beef) are outstanding. Ice cream comes from Vivoli (see p. 310).

🔲 50–85 🚌 6, D 🕐 Closed Sun.–Mon. & 3 weeks in Aug. 🔲 All major cards

🍴 ANGIOLINO
$$–$$$
VIA SANTO SPIRITO 36R
TEL 055 239 8976
casatrattoria.com
Angiolino is an old-school trattoria. Cooking is good and Florentine in flavor, with appetizers such as crostini (small toasts with liver or olive paste) and hearty soups

---

PRICES

HOTELS
An indication of the cost of a double room in the high season is given by $ signs.

$$$$$	Over $300
$$$$	$200–$300
$$$	$130–$200
$$	$100–$130
$	Under $100

RESTAURANTS
An indication of the cost of a three-course meal without drinks is given by $ signs.

$$$$$	Over $80
$$$$	$50–$80
$$$	$35–$50
$$	$20–$35
$	Under $20

such as *ribollita* and *pappa al
pomodoro*.

🍽 95 🚗 11, 36, 37 🅰 🅰 All
major cards

🍽 IL SANTO BEVITORE
$$

VIA SANTO SPIRITO 64–66R
TEL 055 211 264
ilsantobevitore.com
The "Saintly Drinker" is just
across the Carraia bridge, in
the Oltrarno district, home to
many of the city's better value
and more traditional eating
places. The atmosphere
is young and welcoming,
and the Tuscan food has a
creative edge.

🍽 100 🚗 6, D 🕐 Closed Mon.
& L 🅰 🅰 All major cards

🍽 FUORI PORTA
$

VIA DEL MONTE ALLE CROCI 10R
TEL 055 234 2483
This celebrated wine bar—Flor-
ence's most famous—is per-
fectly situated in the Oltrarno
as a refreshment stop on the
walk up to the church of San
Miniato al Monte. It's always
busy, thanks to more than 600
wines by the bottle, 40 by the
glass (the selection changes
regularly), and the excellent
range of snacks and Tuscan
bread laden with a variety of
savory toppings.

🚗 12, 13 🕐 Closed part of
Aug.

🍽 HEMINGWAY
$

PIAZZA PIATTELLINA 9R
(OFF PIAZZA DEL CARMINE)
TEL 055 284 781
This café in the Oltrarno
breaks the Florentine mold
with its modern, stylish decor.
It specializes in all forms of
chocolate, plus more than
20 coffees and many teas,
including cream teas and
tea cocktails such as Victoria
Tea (milk, vanilla tea, and
Southern Comfort.)

🍽 60 🚗 D 🕐 Evenings only.
Closed Sun. 🅰 MC, V

🍽 LE VOLPI E L'UVA
$

PIAZZA DEI ROSSI 1R
TEL 055 239 8132
levolpieluva.com
A discreet wine bar tucked
away just off Piazza di Santa
Felicita a little south of the
Ponte Vecchio. It offers a
well-chosen and interesting
selection of wines that
regularly change, as well
as a first-rate selection of
cheese and snacks as an
accompaniment.

🚗 B, D 🕐 Closed Sun. &
1 week in Aug. 🅰 AE, MC, V

OUTER FLORENCE

🏨 GRAND HOTEL VILLA CORA
$$$$$ ⭕⭕⭕⭕⭕

VIALE NICCOLÒ MACHIAVELLI 18
TEL 055 228 790
villacora.it
This is a luxury hotel in the
grand old style and was
once home to Napoleon III's
wife, Empress Eugénie. Its
modest size, 19th-century villa
interior—full of rich stucco
and glass chandeliers from
Murano—and pretty gardens
enable it to preserve the feel
of a private country house. It
lies close to the Porta Romana
to the south of the city. A
courtesy car service to the
center is provided. Rooms vary
in style from lavish and ornate,
with richly draped beds, to the
more classical and restrained.

🛈 40 + 6 suites 🚗 12, 13 🅿
🔄 🅰 🏊 🅰 All major cards

🏨 TORRE DI BELLOSGUARDO
$$$–$$$$$ ⭕⭕⭕⭕

VIA ROTI MICHELOZZI 2
TEL 055 229 8145
torrebellosguardo.it
Florence's finest hotel if you

wish to be away from the city
center. This Renaissance villa
hotel lies among hilltop gardens
with lovely views, a five-minute
drive south of the Oltrarno. The
lofty public spaces have vaulted
and frescoed ceilings and vast
stone fireplaces, creating a
historic atmosphere, while
the spacious rooms are individually decorated in a suitably
old-fashioned manner. Breakfast
and light meals served, but
there is no restaurant.

🛈 10 + 6 suites 🅿 🔄 🅰 3
rooms 🏊 🅰 All major cards

TUSCANY

🏙 SIENA

SOMETHING SPECIAL

🏨 CERTOSA DI MAGGIANO
$$$$$ ⭕⭕⭕⭕

STRADA DI CERTOSA 82/86
TEL 0577 288 180
certosadimaggiano.com
Favored by honeymoon and
anniversary couples, this
magnificent converted 14th-
century abbey on fine grounds
2 miles (3 km) east of Siena
is one of central Italy's finest
and most romantic hotels.
Antiques and paintings grace
the elegant rooms, and the
atmosphere is relaxing.

🛈 6 rooms + 11 suites
(9 nonsmoking) 🅿 🅰
🏊 🅰 All major cards

🏨 GRAND HOTEL CONTINENTAL
$$$$$ ⭕⭕⭕⭕

VIA BANCHI DI SOPRA 85
TEL 0577 56 011
grandhotelcontinentalsiena
.com
For years, Siena lacked a
sublime luxury hotel. No
longer: This converted 17th-
century palace is a delight with
modern facilities and period

features, including a glorious frescoed main salon.

(i) 51 **P** ⊟ **⟨⟩**
⟨⟩ All major cards

🏨 VILLA SCACCIAPENSIERI
$$$$ ✪✪✪✪
VIA SCACCIAPENSIERI 10
TEL 0577 41 441
villascacciapensieri.it
This peaceful hotel occupies a
19th-century hilltop villa about
2 miles (3 km) north of the
city. Facilities include tennis
courts and swimming pool,
and there are lovely gardens.

(i) 27 + 4 suites **P** ⊟ **⟨⟩**
⟨⟩ ⟨⟩ All major cards

🏨 ANTICA TORRE
$$–$$$ ✪✪✪
VIA FIERAVECCHIA 7
TEL 0577 222 255
anticatorresiena.it
An appealing small hotel
with just eight small rooms
squeezed into an old medieval
tower (torre) a few minutes'
walk southeast of the historic
center. No restaurant.

(i) 8 **⟨⟩** All major cards

🏨 DUOMO
$$–$$$ ✪✪✪
VIA STALLOREGGI 38
TEL 0577 289 088
hotelduomo.it
Siena has few good central
hotels in the upper and
mid-range. Rooms here are
unexceptional, but the location
is perfect. No restaurant.

(i) 23 ⊟ **⟨⟩ ⟨⟩** All major cards

🏨 PALAZZO RAVIZZA
$$–$$$ ✪✪✪✪
PIAN DEI MANTELLINI 34
TEL 0577 280 462
palazzoravizza.it
Siena's most charming mid-
range hotel occupies an 18th-
century palace on the edge
of the center. It retains old
features and original antiques.

(i) 38 **P** ⊟ **⟨⟩ ⟨⟩** All major
cards

🍴 ANTICA TRATTORIA BOTTEGANOVA
$$$$
VIA CHIANTIGIANA 29
TEL 0577 284 230
anticatrattoriabotteganova.it
A formal restaurant located
just beyond the city walls. Its
sublime food has earned a
Michelin star. Signature dishes
include tortelli di pecorino con
fonduta di parmigiano e tartufo,
cheese-filled pasta topped
with truffle-scented sauce.
Less expensive at lunch.

🍴 50 **P** 🕐 Closed Sun. & part
of Jan. & July–Aug. **⟨⟩ ⟨⟩** All
major cards

🍴 AL MANGIA
$$$
PIAZZA DEL CAMPO 42
TEL 0577 281 121
almangia.it
The best of the mostly over-
priced restaurants on Italy's
greatest piazza. The setting
here takes precedence over all
culinary concerns. Locals also
favor Bar Il Palio at Piazza del
Campo 47.

🍴 60 inside, 90 outside
⟨⟩ All major cards

🍴 ANTICA TRATTORIA PAPEI
$$–$$$
PIAZZA DEL MERCATO 6
TEL 0577 280 894
Good food at reasonable
prices is served at this simple
little trattoria in the market
square behind the Campo.

🍴 100 inside, 100 outside
🕐 Closed Mon. **⟨⟩** All major
cards

🍴 LE LOGGE
$$–$$$
VIA DEL PORRIONE 33
TEL 0577 48 013
giannibrunelli.it
No Sienese restaurant is
prettier than this former
medieval pharmacy just off
the Campo, complete with

PRICES

HOTELS
An indication of the cost of
a double room in the high
season is given by **$** signs.

$$$$$	Over $300
$$$$	$200–$300
$$$	$130–$200
$$	$100–$130
$	Under $100

RESTAURANTS
An indication of the cost of
a three-course meal without
drinks is given by **$** signs.

$$$$$	Over $80
$$$$	$50–$80
$$$	$35–$50
$$	$20–$35
$	Under $20

period furniture. Innovative
but occasionally hit-and-miss
Sienese cuisine. Avoid the
upstairs dining room.

🍴 60 inside, 40 outside
🕐 Closed Sun., plus some of
June & Nov. **⟨⟩ ⟨⟩** AE, DC

🍴 LA TAVERNA DI SAN GIUSEPPE
$$–$$$
VIA GIOVANNI DUPRÈ 132
TEL 0577 42 286
tavernasangiuseppe.it
Candlelight and simple
wooden tables and chairs lend
San Giuseppe's remarkable
12th-century brick-vaulted
and bare-rock dining room a
romantic air. Traditional Tuscan
food and friendly service.

🍴 50 🕐 Closed Sun.
& periods in Jan. & July
⟨⟩ ⟨⟩ All major cards

🍴 IL CARROCCIO
$$
CASATO DI SOTTO 32

🏨 Hotel 🍴 Restaurant (i) No. of Guest Rooms 🍴 No. of Seats **P** Parking 🚌 Bus 🕐 Closed ⊟ Elevator

A tiny and discreet one-room trattoria two minutes from the Campo. Simple Sienese dishes (excellent antipasti) plus pleasant and easygoing service. Eat indoors—outside tables are on a busy street.

🛏 35 inside, 20 outside 🕐 Closed Wed. & periods in Feb. & Nov. No credit cards

NORTHERN TUSCANY

CHIANTI

VILLA BORDONI
$$$$ ○○○○
VIA SAN CRESCI 31–32
MEZZUOLA
TEL 055 854 7453
villabordoni.com
Scotsman David Gardner cut his teeth with the successful Baldovino restaurant in Florence and has now opened this comfortable, unpretentious, and romantic hotel in a restored 16th-century villa in the Chianti hills near Greve. The rooms are elegant and the pool, garden, and the Villa Bordoni Restaurant is first-rate. The hotel also hosts a residential and nonresidential cooking school.

🚪 10 🛏 65–110 🅿 ❄ ☼ All major cards

CASTELLO DI SPALTENNA
$$$–$$$$ ○○○○
VIA SPALTENNA 18
PIEVE DI SPALTENNA, GAIOLE IN CHIANTI
TEL 0577 749 483
spaltenna.it
A fine former castle-monastery on the outskirts of Gaiole. Buildings and rooms retain many medieval features. There are two good restaurants, one open lunch only, the other, Il Pievano, for dinner only.

🚪 30 + 8 suites 🅿 🕐 Closed

Jan.–mid-March, restaurant closed Mon. L ❄ ☼ All major cards

TENUTA DI RICAVO
$$$–$$$$ ○○○○
LOCALITÀ RICAVO 4
CASTELLINA IN CHIANTI
TEL 0577 740 221
ricavo.com
In the country 2 miles (3 km) outside Castellina, this converted medieval hamlet is a perfect place to relax. The Pecora Nera restaurant serves refined Tuscan cuisine.

🚪 23 🅿 🕐 Closed Oct.–April, restaurant closed Tues.–Wed. ☼ All major cards

BADIA A COLTIBUONO
$$$
BADIA A COLTIBUONO
(3 MILES/5 KM NE OF GAIOLE)
TEL 0577 744 81 (hotel);
0577 749 031 (restaurant)
www.coltibuono.com
Eight delightful B&B rooms in this isolated, peaceful and beautifully situated 11th-century abbey. Also a restaurant in the former stables nearby, Ristorante Coltibuono, is open to non-guests; both form part of a prominent Chianti winery.

🚪 8 🛏 65–110 🅿 🕐 Closed mid-Nov.–mid-Feb. & Mon. mid-Feb.–April ❄ ☼ All major cards

COLLE DI VAL D'ELSA

ARNOLFO
$$$
VIA XX SETTEMBRE 50–52
TEL 0577 920 549
arnolfo.com
The cooking here has earned two Michelin stars. In summer eat the sophisticated Italian food on the terrace with lovely views of the surrounding hills. Rooms are also available.

🚪 4 🛏 30 inside, 24 terrace 🅿 🕐 Closed Tues.–Wed. &

some of Jan., Feb., & Nov. 🔄 ❄ ☼ All major cards

FIESOLE

SOMETHING SPECIAL

VILLA SAN MICHELE
$$$$$ ○○○○○
VIA DOCCIA 4
TEL 055 567 8200 OR
0039 01 8526 7803 (reservations)
villasanmichele.com
One of Tuscany's finest hotels, this is a good alternative to staying in Florence. The villa was supposedly designed by Michelangelo, and most of the antiques are 17th-century originals. Lovely parks and gardens, and sweeping views of the countryside.

🚪 25 + 15 suites 🅿 🕐 Closed Nov.–mid-March 🔄 ❄ ☼ All major cards

LUCCA

NOBLESSE
$$$$ ○○○○○
VIA SANT'ANASTASIO 23
TEL 0583 440 275
hotelnoblesse.it
Part of a historic city palazzo, the Noblesse has addressed Lucca's long lack of a central, high-quality hotel. Rich fabrics and precious antiques add considerable period style to the calm, sumptuous rooms.

🚪 10 + 5 suites 🅿 🔄 ❄ ☼ All major cards

LA LUNA
$$ ○○○
VIA FILLUNGO-CORTE
COMPAGNI 12
TEL 0583 493 634
hotellaluna.com
A family-run hotel with simple, clean rooms in a sleepy courtyard just off old Lucca's main street. No restaurant.

🚪 29 🅿 🕐 Closed some of Jan. ☼ All major cards

PICCOLO HOTEL PUCCINI
$$ ❍❍❍
VIA DI POGGIO 9
TEL 0583 55 421
hotelpuccini.com
Bright, tasteful rooms in a Renaissance palace at the heart of the old city. Private parking must be requested in advance. No restaurant.
🛏 14 🅿 All major cards

BUCA DI SANT'ANTONIO
$$
VIA DELLA CERVIA 3
TEL 0583 55881
bucadisantantonio.it
Established in 1787, this is the best of Lucca's city-center restaurants. Cooking is based on old Lucchese traditions but is unafraid of innovation. Try the celebrated *semifreddo buccellatto*, a mix of chilled cream and wild berries.
🍴 90 🕐 Closed Sun. D, Mon., & some of July All major cards

OSTERIA BARALLA
$$
VIA ANFITEATRO 59
TEL 0583 440 240
osteriabaralla.it
Lighter cooking here than in some Lucchese restaurants: The *antipasti* (appetizers) are good, as are the grilled meats and chocolate tart (*crostata*).
🍴 80 🕐 Closed Sun. All major cards

OSTERIA DEL NENI
$$
VIA PESCHERIA 3
TEL 0583 492 681
This traditional trattoria is moments from San Michele in Foro, but easily missed down a narrow side street. While service can be slow and a little grumpy at busy times, this is a locals' favorite, thanks to the fair prices and decent, unpre-tentious Lucchese food.
🍴 45 inside, 25 outside
All major cards

CAFFÈ DI SIMO
$
VIA FILLUNGO 58
TEL 0583 496 234
Lucca's loveliest café has a fine belle epoque interior that has played host to many famous names, among them Puccini. Wonderful for cakes, pastries, coffee, and light snacks and sandwiches.
🕐 Closed Mon. All major cards

PISA

HOTEL RELAIS DELL'OROLOGIO
$$$$ ❍❍❍❍❍
VIA DELLA FAGGIOLA 12–14
TEL 050 830 361
hotelrelaisorologio.com
Pisa's leading hotel occupies a palazzo built around a 14th-century tower and has been beautifully and elegantly restored to retain key period features. Centrally located between the Leaning Tower and Piazza dell'Orologio
🛏 21 🅿 All major cards

ROYAL VICTORIA
$$–$$$ ❍❍❍
LUNGARNO PACINOTTI 12
TEL 050 940 111
royalvictoria.it
The Royal stands out among Pisa's mostly modern hotels. Beside the Arno, ten minutes' walk from the Leaning Tower, it has been in the same family for five generations. Service is courteous and attentive, and the atmosphere and fine rooms recall times past.
🛏 48 🅿 All major cards

HOTEL AMALFITANA
$$ ❍❍❍
VIA ROMA 44
TEL 050 29 000
hotelamalfitana.it
A good midrange choice on a street just south of the famous Leaning Tower. Rooms are modern and well equipped.
🛏 21 🅿 All major cards

OSTERIA DEI CAVALIERI
$$
VIA SAN FREDIANO 16
TEL 050 580 858
A plain but welcoming trattoria. The well-priced Tuscan dishes include wild boar (*cinghiale*).
🍴 60 🕐 Closed Sat. L, Sun., & Aug. All major cards

LA MESCITA
$–$$
VIA CAVALCA 2
TEL 050 957 019
An attractive trattoria in the Vettovaglie market.
🍴 35 🕐 Closed Mon. & Aug.

PRICES
HOTELS
An indication of the cost of a double room in the high season is given by $ signs.

$$$$$	Over $300
$$$$	$200–$300
$$$	$130–$200
$$	$100–$130
$	Under $100

RESTAURANTS
An indication of the cost of a three-course meal without drinks is given by $ signs.

$$$$$	Over $80
$$$$	$50–$80
$$$	$35–$50
$$	$20–$35
$	Under $20

🏨 Hotel 🍴 Restaurant 🛏 No. of Guest Rooms 🪑 No. of Seats 🅿 Parking 🚌 Bus 🕐 Closed ⬍ Elevator

PASTICCERIA SALZA
$

BORGO STRETTO 46
TEL 050 580 144
salza.it
The most celebrated of Pisa's cafés. Ideal for coffee, cakes, snacks, or an evening aperitif.
Closed Mon.

PISTOIA

TRATTORIA DELL'ABBONDANZA
$$

VIA DELL'ABBONDANZA 1014
TEL 0573 368 037
Prices here are a bargain, given the quality of the fine regional cooking. Be sure to reserve for evening.
35 inside, 35 outside
Closed Wed., Thurs. L, & periods in May & Oct.

SAN GIMIGNANO

LA COLLEGIATA
$$$$$ ✪✪✪✪

LOCALITÀ STRADA 27
TEL 0577 943 201
lacollegiata.it
A dazzlingly stylish hotel with an excellent restaurant—**Ristorante L'Eco Divino**—housed in a converted 16th-century convent 1 mile (2 km) from the town walls. Fine views of San Gimignano and its towers.
20 + 1 suite ☐ ☐ ☐
☐ All major cards

LA CISTERNA
$$ ✪✪✪✪

PIAZZA DELLA CISTERNA 23
TEL 0577 940 328
www.hotelcisterna.it
The village's oldest established hotel has a central location on the main piazza. Rooms with a view command higher prices.
49 ☐ Closed early Jan.–Feb. or mid-March
☐ All major cards

LEON BIANCO
$$ ✪✪✪

PIAZZA DELLA CISTERNA 13
TEL 0577 941 294
leonbianco.com
Housed in a restored 11th-century palace, this hotel shares the Cisterna's perfect location but is smaller and more intimate. There is a Jacuzzi on the terrace for a post-sightseeing soak.
24 ☐ Closed mid-Jan.–Feb. ☐ ☐ All major cards

DORANDÒ
$$$–$$$$

VICOLO DELL'ORO 2
TEL 0577 941 862
ristorantedorando.it
An intimate restaurant in a medieval setting but with a modern ambience. The chefs are famous for re-creating ancient recipes from the Etruscan and Medici periods.
35 ☐ Closed mid-Jan.–mid-March & Mon. Nov.–Easter
☐ ☐ All major cards

LE VECCHIE MURA
$–$$

VIA PIANDORNELLA 15
TEL 0577 940 270
vecchiemura.it
Tasty pizzas and honest, fairly priced food. Set in converted stables that were built into the city's walls.
65–120 ☐ Closed Tues.
☐ All major cards

GELATERIA DI PIAZZA
$

PIAZZA DELLA CISTERNA 4
TEL 0577 942 244
gelateriadipiazza.com
San Gimignano's best ice-cream parlor.
Closed Nov.–Feb.

VOLTERRA

SAN LINO
$$ ✪✪✪✪

VIA SAN LINO 26

TEL 0588 85 250
hotelsanlino.net
A converted 15th-century convent is Volterra's best central option, but it is not as polished as some four-star Italian hotels. Simply furnished to reflect the building's monastic past, the rooms face the streets or garden.
43 ☐ ☐ ☐ ☐
☐ All major cards

LA VECCHIA LIRA
$$$ ✪✪✪

VIA MATTEOTTI
TEL 0588 86 180
vecchialira.com
The self-service lunch here is quick and excellent value and eaten at communal tables under bright, airy medieval vaults. Dinner is far more expensive, and the setting less than intimate; the fare includes fish and seafood options plus a menu devoted almost entirely to Chianina beef.
100 ☐ Closed Thurs.
☐ All major cards.

LA CARABACCIA
$

PIAZZA XX SETTEMBRE 4–5
TEL 0588 86 239
lacarabaccia.net
Menus at this simple osteria change regularly but always champion traditional recipes and feature the vegetable soup—reputedly Leonardo da Vinci's favorite dish—after which the restaurant is named.
38 inside, 25 outside
Closed periods in Nov. & Feb., & Mon. except in summer
☐ All major cards.

■ SOUTHERN TUSCANY

AREZZO

GRAZIELLA PATIO HOTEL
$$$ ✪✪✪✪

Air-conditioning ☐ Indoor Pool ☐ Outdoor Pool ☐ Health Club ☐ Credit Cards

VIA CAVOUR 23
TEL 0575 401 962
hotelpatio.it
This hotel's bold combination of period features and contemporary styling and color may not be to all tastes, but the centrally located 16th-century palazzo makes a striking addition to Arezzo's hitherto limited range of accommodations. Rooms are spacious, comfortable, and individually designed. Parking is available for a fee, and bikes can be rented.
🛏 10 🅿 🔣 🞗 All major cards

🏨 CASTELLO DI
🍴 GARGONZA
$$–$$$ ✪✪✪
CASTELLO DI GARGONZA, MONTE SANTO SAVINO
TEL 0575 847 021
gargonza.it
ristorantelatorredigargonza.it
A converted medieval hamlet in a peaceful, rural location 4 miles (6 km) west of Monte San Savino, a village 10 miles (16 km) southwest of Arezzo. Rooms must be taken for a minimum of three nights. Flats and cottages in the hamlet are available for weekly rental. **La Torre di Gargonza Restaurant** offers splendid fare.
🛏 45 🅿 🕓 Closed Nov. & some of Jan. 🈲
🞗 All major cards

🍴 TRE BICCHIERI
$$$
PIAZZETTA SOPRA IL PONTE 3–5A
TEL 0575 26 557
ristoranteitrebicchieri.com
Fish, seafood, and the flavors of the Amalfi coast offer a change from the usual Tuscan staples at this small central restaurant which, behind a bland, modern exterior, conceals a more pleasing and intimate dining area.
🪑 80 🕓 Closed Sun. & some of Aug. 🞗 All major cards

🍴 BUCA DI SAN
FRANCESCO
$$–$$$
VIA SAN FRANCESCO 1
TEL 0575 23 271
bucadisanfrancesco.it
The Buca has been serving Tuscan staples such as thick *ribollita* (bean and cabbage) soup and roast lamb *(agnello)* since 1929. The dining room has medieval paintings.
🪑 60 🕓 Closed Mon. D, Tues., & July 🞗 All major cards

🍴 ANTICA OSTERIA
L'AGANIA
$$
VIA MAZZINI 10
TEL 0575 295 381
agania.it
A simple, busy *osteria*, with a small, separate wine bar close by at Via Mazzini 14 *(tel 0575 300 205)*. Centrally located.
🪑 80 🕓 Closed Mon. & some of June 🞗 All major cards

🍴 IL GELATO
$
VIA DEI CENCI 24
TEL 0575 23 240
The best ice cream for miles—handmade, using only fresh ingredients and real fruit.
🕓 Closed Wed. & some of Nov. or Feb.

CASENTINO

🍴 IL TIRABUSCIÒ
$$$
VIA SCOTI 12, BIBBIONA
TEL 0575 595 474
tirabuscio.it
Simple and elegant dining rooms, with white walls and contemporary paintings under beamed ceilings, are matched by unpretentious and well-presented dishes that make good use of fine ingredients. Menus change but might include ravioli filled with bread and Pecorino and *robiola* cheese or *piccione* (pigeon) and

other game dishes. Excellent Tuscan wine list and a good choice of regional cheeses.
🪑 35 🕓 Closed Mon. D & Tues. 🞗 All major cards

CORTONA

🏨 IL FALCONIERE
🍴 **$$$–$$$$ ✪✪✪✪**
LOCALITÀ SAN MARTINO A BOCENA 370
TEL 0575 612 679
ilfalconiere.com
A beautifully restored 17th-century villa about 2 miles (3 km) off the SS71 road for Arezzo. Rooms are furnished in period style; some retain original frescoes. The restaurant offers fine meat and fish, and a good wine list.
🛏 22 🪑 55 inside, 40 outside 🅿 🕓 Restaurant closed Tues. L & Mon. Nov.–March
🔣 🈲 🞗 All major cards

 🏨 Hotel   🍴 Restaurant 🛏 No. of Guest Rooms   🪑 No. of Seats   🅿 Parking   🚌 Bus   🕓 Closed   🛗 Elevator

SAN MICHELE
$$–$$$ ●●●●
VIA GUELFA 15
TEL 0575 604 348
hotelsanmichele.net
Converted Renaissance palace
in the town's historic heart.
The building retains many
original features. The room
in the tower is a gem.
① 43 **P** ⊕ Closed mid-Jan.–
Feb. ⊟ ⑤ ⑥ All major cards

LA BUCCACCIA
$$$
VIA GHIBELLINA 17
TEL 0575 606 039
A much lauded restaurant
where a reservation is advis-
able. The two dining areas, in
the stone-walled cellars of a
13th-century town house, are
delightful. Everything is home-
made and every ingredient
possible in the classic Tuscan
dishes is locally sourced.
Cooking and cheesemaking
courses are available.
🍴 30 ⊕ Closed Mon. & some
of Jan. ⑥ All major cards

OSTERIA DEL TEATRO
$$
VIA MAFFEI 2
TEL 0575 630 556
osteria-del-teatro.it
A restaurant that serves honest regional fare. Pictures of
the actors who have appeared
at the nearby Signorelli Theater hang on the walls.
🍴 70 inside, 14 outside
⊕ Closed Wed. & some of Nov.
⑥ All major cards

ELBA

VILLA OTTONE
$$$–$$$$ ●●●●●
OTTONE, PORTOFERRAIO
TEL 0565 933 042
villaottone.com
An elegant hotel built around
an 18th-century villa, about
6 miles (10 km) southeast of
Portoferraio, Elba's main town.

It is a good base from which to
explore the island.
① 75 + 2 suites **P** ⊕ Closed
Nov.–April ⊟ ⑤ ⊠ ⑦
⑥ All major cards

HOTEL ILIO
$$$ ●●●
VIA SANT'ANDREA 5, CAPO
SANT'ANDREA, NEAR MARCIANO
TEL 0565 908 018
hotelilio.com
A delightful boutique hotel
overlooking a small, pretty
bay, with excellent food in
the **HI** restaurant. The rooms
are relatively plain, modern,
and comfortable; most have
balconies, and views come in
a variety of settings around a
verdant, landscaped site.
① 20 **P** ⑤ ⑥ All major cards

PUBLIUS
$$–$$$
PIAZZA DEL CASTAGNETO 11
TEL 0565 99 208
ristorantepublius.it
Family-run Publius lies up in
the hills above Marciana, on
the west side of Elba. Its outdoor terrace offers exceptional
sea views. Fish and seafood
dominate the menu.
🍴 45 inside, 45 outside
⊕ Closed Nov.–late March
& Mon. except July– Aug.
⑤ ⑥ All major cards

MONTALCINO

CASTELLO DI VELONA
$$$$ ●●●●●
LOCALITÀ VERONA, NEAR
CASTELNUOVO DELL'ABATE
TEL 0577 835 553
castellodivelona.it
A superbly restored hilltop
castle with wonderful views
over the fine countryside
south of Montalcino, with
46 rooms divided between
the castle and the more
recently added "spa" annex.
Modern facilities and technol-
ogy complement the period
features, and there is a fine

pool, distinctive glass-covered
courtyard, a taverna for
wine tasting, and the formal
L'Abbazia restaurant.
① 46 **P** ⑤ ⊕ Closed
Nov.–mid-March or April
⊠ ⑦ ⑥ All major cards

DEI CAPITANI
$$ ●●●
VIA LAPINI 6
TEL 0577 847 227
deicapitani.it
A modern hotel in an old
town house with a terrace, bar
area, and swimming pool.
① 29 **P** ⊟ ⊠ ⑤
⑥ All major cards

GRAPPOLO BLU
$$
VIA SCALE DI MOGLIO 1
TEL 0577 847 150
grappoloblu.it
In an alley off the main Via
Mazzini, the cool, stone walls
of the medieval interior house
two small dining rooms. The
pasta dishes are all good.
🍴 35 ⑥ All major cards

MONTE AMIATA

SOMETHING SPECIAL

SILENE
$$–$$$ ●●●
SIGNED FROM PESCINA, 2 MILES
(4 KM) EAST OF SEGGIANO
TEL 0564 950 805
ilsilene.it
People travel for miles to eat
in this restaurant near one of
the tiny villages ringing Monte
Amiata. Many dishes use
produce from local woods—
wild mushrooms, truffles, and
snails. But there's nothing
rustic about the cooking.
Reservations are wise and
rooms are also available.
① 7 🍴 80 ⊕ Closed Mon.
& Nov. ⑥ AE, MC, V

---

 ⑤ Air-conditioning ⊟ Indoor Pool ⊠ Outdoor Pool ⑦ Health Club ⑥ Credit Cards

MONTEPULCIANO

🏨 DUOMO
$$ ✪✪✪
VIA SAN DONATO 14
TEL 0578 757 473
albergoduomomonte
pulciano.it
A few steps from the town's cathedral and main piazza, this hotel is a family-run place with bright, straightforward rooms.
🛏 13 ⬆ 🅐 All major cards

🍴 OSTERIA ACQUACHETA
$$-$$$
VIA DEL TEATRO 22
TEL 0578 717 086
acquacheta.eu
Reserve well ahead in this small and popular *osteria*. The setting is simple and traditional, with wooden beams and terra-cotta floors, shared tables, and paper tablecloths. The Tuscan food might include dishes such as *pici pasta* with a wild boar sauce, roast guinea fowl (*faraona arrosto*), and truffles in season: The steaks are recommended.
🪑 35 🅿 🕐 Closed Tues. & mid-Jan.–mid-March 🅐 All major cards

🍴 LA GROTTA
$$
LOCALITÀ SAN BIAGIO
TEL 0578 757 607
lagrottamontepulciano.it
La Grotta is a convenient place for lunch, thanks largely to its location directly opposite the noted church of San Biagio.
🪑 50 inside, 30 outside 🅿 🕐 Closed Wed. & Jan.–Feb. 🅐 All major cards

PIENZA

🏨 IL CHIOSTRO
$$$ ✪✪✪✪
CORSO ROSSELLINO 26
TEL 0578 748 400
relaisilchiostrodipienza.com
The central Chiostro takes its name from the cloister

(chiostro) of the 15th-century convent from which it was tastefully converted.
🛏 28 🅿 ⬆ 🏊 🅐 All major cards

🏨 DAL FALCO
🍴 $$
$-$$
PIAZZA DANTE 3
TEL 0578748 551
www.ristorantedalfalco.it
A trattoria with a medieval interior and robust country fare, frequented by locals as well as visitors. Try the famed local Pecorino cheese melted and wrapped in prosciutto. Also has six inexpensive rooms.
🛏 6 🪑 80 🅿 🕐 Closed Fri. 🅐 All major cards

🍴 LATTE DI LUNA
$$
VIA SAN CARLO 2–4
TEL 0578 748 606
A family-run trattoria just inside the walls. Try the local *pici all'aglione*, pasta in a garlicky tomato sauce.
🪑 35 inside, 20 outside 🕐 Closed Tues. & some of Feb. & July 🅐 MC, V

SOVANA

🏨 SOVANA HOTEL &
🍴 RESORT
$$$ ✪✪✪✪
VIA DEL DUOMO 66
TEL 0564 617 030
A bucolic base from which to explore Sovana, set amid olive groves dotted with modern sculpture, and with lovely views of the hills. The separate nearby restaurant is first-rate, with dining outdoors in good weather and a beautiful interior that dates from 1241.
🛏 18 🅿 🅓 🅐 All major cards

VAL D'ORCIA

🏨 CASTELLO DI RIPA
D'ORCIA

$$$ ✪✪✪
VIA DELLA CONTEA 116, RIPA DORCIA, 4 MILES (7 KM) SW OF SAN QUIRICO D'ORCIA
TEL 0577 897 376
castelloripadorcia.com
Stay at this hotel, built around a *borgo*, or fortified village from the 13th century, and you can make easy hikes into the country. Rooms and apartments are spacious.
🛏 6 + 8 suites 🅿 🅐 All major cards

🍴 CISTERNA NEL BORGO
🏨 $$
BORGO MAESTRO 37, ROCCA D'ORCIA
TEL 0577 887 280
cisternanelborgo.com
Rocca d'Orcia has about 50 residents. The restaurant menu revolves around Tuscan staples Three rooms are available.
🛏 3 🪑 45 inside, 16 outside 🕐 Closed Mon. & Jan.–Feb. 🅐 AE, MC, V

Shopping

Shopping is one of the great pleasures of visiting Florence and Tuscany. From the smallest town to the grandest city street, stores offer arrays of food and wine, wonderful clothes, inspired design, beautiful fabrics, precious jewelry, exquisite shoes, leatherware and accessories, precious antiques, objets d'art, and a host of craft items.

Stores

Most Tuscan stores are small, family-run affairs. Many neighbor-hoods still have a baker (*panificio*), pastry store (*pasticce-ria*), butcher (*macellaio*), and food shop (*alimentari*). Department stores and supermarkets are gradually gaining ground, but malls are still almost unknown.

Markets

Large towns have at least one street market (*mercato*). Most open daily except Sunday, from dawn until early afternoon. Times are the same in smaller towns, but markets are usually held just once a week. Many larger towns also hold antique fairs, usually once monthly or on a weekend, or special events devoted to local food or a craft product. These are the only places you might try to bargain: Haggling in food markets or other stores is not appropriate.

What to Buy

Many Tuscan products are unique to one part of the year. Fruit and vegetables appear in stores when they're in season, so don't expect to find grapes in spring or cherries in fall. Some towns have their own food and wine specialties, such as the spicy *panforte* cake of Siena, or handicraft specialties such as leatherware in Florence or alabaster in Volterra.

Food delicacies are obvious purchases, but check import restrictions of meat and other products into North America. Lingerie, silks, lace, linens, soaps,

shoes, bags, wallets, marbled paper products, and jewelry are all easily transportable items. Also leave space for wine, clothes, and every kind of design objects, particularly kitchenware, in which Italian designers excel. Many stores should be able to arrange shipping for larger items such as ceramics, furniture, and antiques.

Opening Hours

Most small stores open Tuesday through Saturday from about 8 a.m. to 1 p.m. and 3:30 p.m. to 8 p.m., and close on Monday morning or one other half day a week. Hours often alter slightly in summer, with a later afternoon opening to avoid the heat of the day. In Florence and larger towns, especially in clothes and depart-ment stores, there's a move toward full-time opening (*orario continuato*) from 9 a.m. to 7:30/8 p.m., Monday through Saturday (and occasionally Sunday).

Payment

Supermarkets and department stores usually accept credit cards and traveler's checks, as do clothes and shoe stores. Cash is required for transactions in small food and other stores.

Exports

Most Italian luxury items and clothing purchases include a value-added goods and services tax of 19 percent (known as IVA in Italy). Non-European Union residents can claim an IVA refund for purchases over $155 (before tax) made in one store. Shop with your passport and ask for

invoices to be made out clearly, showing individual articles and tax components of prices. Department stores often have special counters for this purpose. Keep all receipts and invoices and have them stamped at the customs office at your departure airport, or the last exit from the EU if you are traveling beyond Italy. Then mail the invoice to the store within 90 days of arriv-ing home for your rebate. Many stores are members of the Tax-Free Shopping System and issue a "tax-free check" for the rebate, which can be cashed at special tax-free counters at airports or rebated to your bank or credit card account.

■ FLORENCE

Florence is a great city for luxury goods. Leather, clothes, jewelry, and antiques are top buys, but less expensive gift possibilities include marbled paper and goods from the city's thriving markets. Most clothes and other luxury goods stores are found on and around Via de' Tornabuoni. Antique stores group together in the Oltrarno on and around Via Maggio. Jewelers congregate on the Ponte Vecchio.

To ship large goods home, contact either Fracassi, Via Santo Spirito 11 *(tel 055 283 597)*, or Gondrand, Via Baldanzese 198 *(tel 055 882 6376)*. Neither accepts credit cards.

Artists' Materials

Zecchi Via dello Studio 19r, tel 055 211 470, zecchi.it. It's no surprise that a city with Florence's artistic pedigree has a store of this quality: Zecchi is an Aladdin's cave of pens, paints, pencils, oils, gold leaf, and other items.

Books

Feltrinelli Internazionale Via Cavour 12–20r, tel 055 219 524, lafeltrinelli.it. A modern bookstore just north of Piazza del Duomo with a large selection of English-language titles, including guides.

Camera & Film

Bongi Via Por Santa Maria 82–84r, tel 055 239 8811, otticabongi.it. Try well-stocked Bongi if you need a camera or related photographic equipment. For film processing, try **Fontani,** Viale Strozzi 22, tel 055 463 3661, otticafontani.com.

Coffee

Piansa Borgo Pinti 18r, tel 055 234 2362. Piansa is Florence's main coffee roaster, and bars across the city use its products. This is its city-center outlet and sells different coffees as well as operating as a normal bar, with light meals also available.

Department Stores

COIN Via dei Calzaiuoli 56r, tel 055 280 531, coin.it. Florentines crowd this central midrange store, which sells a wide variety of quality goods.
Rinascente Piazza della Repubblica 3–5, tel 055 219 113, rinascente.it. Of generally higher quality than COIN, but with less stock and a less inviting atmosphere.

Fabrics

Mazzoni Via Don Minzoni 15r, tel 055 570 702, mazzonicasa.it. Mazzoni has been in business for more than a century, selling fabrics, towels, and linens. There are two other outlets in the city.

Fashion

Most of the big-name designers have stores on Via de' Tornabuoni or the nearby Via della Vigna Nuova. Here are some:
Armani Via de' Tornabuoni 45r, tel 055 219 041, armani.com
Bulgari (jewelry & accessories), Via de' Tornabuoni 61–63r, tel 055 239 6786, bulgari.com
Emporio Armani Piazza Strozzi 14–17r, tel 055 284 315
Gucci Via de' Tornabuoni 73r, tel 055 264 011, gucci.com. The famous "double G" label, like Ferragamo (see p. 323), originated in Florence. Sells clothes, shoes, and accessories.
Max Mara Via dei Pecori 23r and Via de' Tornabuoni 66–70r, tel 055 214 133 or 055 287 761, maxmara.com Classic clothes at affordable prices.
Prada Via de' Tornabuoni 53r and 167r, tel 055 267 471, prada.com
Pucci Via de' Tornabuoni 20–22r, tel 055 265 8082, emiliopucci.com. With Ferragamo and Gucci, Emilio Pucci is one of the city's top design names, having made his name with signature silks and prints in the 1960s.

Food & Wine

Dolce e Dolcezze Piazza Beccaria 8r, tel 055 234 5458. This store was started by cake and chocolate enthusiasts with no formal training. The results are superb; the cakes, pastries, and candies are the city's finest.
Enoteca Murgia Via dei Banchi 45r, tel 055 215 686. Choice

and excellent service are the watchwords of this wine store. Also sells olive oils, grappas, and other spirits and liquor.
Pegna Via dello Studio 8r, tel 055 282 701/2, pegnafirenze .com. This shop south of the Duomo has been selling superb cheese, salami, coffee, tea, and other gastronomic delights since 1860.
Pitti Gola & Cantina Piazza de' Pitti 16, tel 055 212 704, pittigolaecantina.com. An inviting store with a selection of Tuscany's best chocolate, wines, oils, and artisan-made food. Also cooking and wine books.
Robiglio Via dei Servi 112r, tel 055 214 501. This *pasticceria* rivals Dolce e Dolcezze with its superb cakes and pastries and a rich hot chocolate drink. Four other Florentine outlets.

Gloves

Madova Via de' Guicciardini 1r, tel 055 239 6526, madova.com. Look no further for leather gloves; this store has every size, style, and color imaginable.

Herbal Products

De Herbore Via del Proconsolo 43r, tel 055 211 706, deherbore .com. Dried herbs, vitamins, soaps, health foods, silk flowers, and natural cosmetics. Come here for the extravagant product displays, even if you don't intend to purchase anything.

Kitchenware

Bartolini Via dei Servi 72r, tel 055 2901 497, bartolini firenze.it. One of Tuscany's best kitchenware stores. Everything from pots, pans, espresso machines, and Alessi designer products to knives, corks, china, glassware, and much more.

Leather

Cellerini Via del Sole 37r,
tel 055 282 533. Wallets,
suitcases, shoes, belts, but
most of all, more than
600 types of bags.
Desmo Piazza de' Rucellai 10r,
tel 055 292 395, desmo.it.
A huge choice of leather
goods under one roof.

Linens

Lorretta Caponi Via de'
Tornabuoni 7r, tel 055 211 074,
lorrettacaponi.com. Embroidery,
linens, and lingerie.

Markets

Cascine Parco del Cascine.
A weekly flea market held in a
park west of the city center—
buses 1, 9, 17 (Tues. 8 a.m.–
2 p.m.).
Mercato Centrale Piazza del
Mercato Centrale. Europe's
largest indoor food market
is a must-see, even if you
don't want to buy anything
(Mon.–Fri. 7 a.m.–2 p.m., Sat.
4 p.m.–7 p.m.).
Mercato delle Pulci Piazza dei
Ciompi. Florence's flea *(pulci)*
market has a predictable but still
fascinating collection of junk,
clothes, and inexpensive goods.
San Lorenzo Piazza San Lorenzo.
Stalls selling clothes and other
general goods cram the square
and its surrounding streets
(daily 9 a.m.–7 p.m., closed Sun.
in winter).
Sant'Ambrogio Piazza Lorenzo
Ghiberti. Smaller than the
Mercato Centrale, this market
has lots of small specialist food
stalls (Mon.–Sat. 7 a.m.–2 p.m.).
Santo Spirito Piazza Santo
Spirito. A flea market (second
Sun. of each month) with used
clothes, pictures, books, handmade jewelry, and other crafts,
plus plenty of unsalable junk.

Paper & Pens

Giulio Giannini & Figlio
Piazza de' Pitti 37r, tel 055
212 621, giuliogiannini.com.
Founded in 1856, this company
still makes marbled paper,
books, leather desk accessories,
and other fine stationery from
its workshop at this address.
Pineider Piazza de' Rucellai
4–7r, tel 055 284 656, pineider
.com. Pineider has branches
around the world but was
founded in Florence in 1774. It
sells pens, paper, and writing
accessories.
Il Torchio Via dei Bardi 17,
tel 055 234 2862, legatoriail
torchio.com. Sells an enormous
variety of marbled and other
paper, plus boxes, books, and
other stationery. Watch book-
binders in the workshop.

Shoes

Salvatore Ferragamo Via de'
Tornabuoni 14r, tel 055 292
123, ferragamo.com. Fer-
ragamo made his name in the
United States, but his home
base was Florence. In addition
to the famous shoes, the shop
sells a good range of clothing
and accessories.
Tod's Via de' Tornabuoni 60r,
tel 055 219 423, tods.com.
Prices for shoes and bags
at this fashionable store are
lower than you'll find in North
America.

Soaps & Perfumes

**Farmaceutica di Santa Maria
Novella** Via della Scala 16r,
tel 055 216 276, smnovella
.com. A beautiful store selling
soaps, perfumes, and cosmetics, many made to ancient
recipes created in monasteries
and convents.
Farmacia del Cinghiale Piazza
del Mercato Nuovo 4r, tel 055
212 128, farmaciadelcinghiale.it.

A store that has sold natural
cosmetics and other toiletries
since the 18th century.

■ SIENA

Siena's main shopping streets
are Via di Città and its neighbors Banchi di Sopra and Banchi
di Sotto. Food and wine are
good buys, especially olive oils
and *panforte*, a rich, dark cake
flavored with cinnamon and
other spices, made in the city
since the Middle Ages.

Books

Libreria Senese Via di Città
62–66, tel 0577 280 845,
libreriasenese.com. Siena has
bigger bookstores, but this
family-run store has a good
selection of guides, maps, art
books, foreign newspapers, and
English-language titles.

Food & Wine

**Antica Drogheria Manganelli
1879** Via di Città 71–73, tel
0577 280 002 (closed Sun.).
A treasury of the finest foods,
wines, and spirits imaginable—
all displayed in old wooden
cabinets. Don't miss.
Consorzio Agrario Siena Via
Pianigiani 5, tel 0577 222 368,
capsi.it. The local Consorzio
Agrario (a farmer's coopera-
tive) sells the goods of its 4,000
members at this market. Good
for olive oils, cheese, honey, and
wine, sold at reasonable prices.
Enoteca Italiana Fortezza
Medicea, Piazza Libertà 1, tel
0577 228 811, enoteca-italiana
.it (closed Sun. a.m.). Vaulted
cellars in Siena's Medici castle
hold about 750 of the best
Italian wines to buy. Choose
from 800 wines by the glass in
the bar.
Gastronomia Morbidi 1925
Via Banchi di Sopra 73–75,

tel 0577 280 268, morbidi.com. The second of Siena's fabulous food shops, this is a superb delicatessen, in business since 1925. Ready-to-eat food is also available to take out, and there's a wine cellar downstairs, so it's great for picnic provisions.

Market

La Lizza Siena's main market is held every Wednesday morning at La Lizza, a large open area in the north of the city beyond Piazza Matteotti and Piazza Gramsci.

NORTHERN TUSCANY

As well as those described below, there are markets at the following northern Tuscany towns: **Barga** General market Fri. a.m. plus flea market second Sun. of the month; **Carrara** Mon. a.m.; **Castelnuovo di Garfagnana** Thurs. a.m.; **Colle di Val d'Elsa** Fri. a.m.; **Pistoia** Wed. & Sat. a.m.; **Prato** Mon. a.m.; **Viareggio** Mon.–Sat.

LUCCA

Food & Wine

Antica Bottega di Prospero Via Santa Lucia 13, bottegadi prospero.it. This extraordinary shop sells every dried good imaginable, from pulses and dried herbs to daffodil bulbs and seeds for Italian staples, such as fennel.
Caniparoli Via San Paolino 96, tel 0583 53 456, caniparoli cioccolateria.it. Sensational handmade chocolates.
Taddeucci Piazza San Michele 34, Lucca, tel 0583 494 933, buccellatotaddeucci.com. A beautiful, wood-paneled bakery: Try specialties such

as *buccellato,* an old-fashioned bread flavored with aniseed and raisins, and *torta di erbe,* spiced vegetable pie.

Markets

Mercato del Carmine Piazza del Carmine (daily except Wed. a.m. & Sun.). There is a similar market in the east of the city in Via dei Bacchettoni (Wed. & Sat.). An antique fair is held in the squares around the Duomo on the third weekend of every month. A craft market takes place in Piazza San Giusto over the last weekend of the month.

PISA

Markets

Mercato Vettovaglie Piazza delle Vettovaglie (Mon.–Sat. a.m.). A general food market, held just north of the river.
Mercatino Antiquario Junction of Borgo Stretto and Ponte di Mezzo (second weekend of every month). This is Pisa's main antiques market.

SAN GIMIGNANO

Crafts & Gifts

Bottega d'Arte Povera Via San Matteo 83, tel 0577 941 951. *Arte povera* means "poor art," or the craft of peasant tradition: Olive wood bowls and boards, chestnut baskets, baskets for drying figs, and terra-cotta ware.

Markets

A large market for clothes, food, and crafts runs Thursday morning in Piazza della Cisterna and Piazza del Duomo; there's a smaller one on Saturday.

SOUTHERN TUSCANY

Regular markets are held at the following towns in southern Tuscany: **Arezzo** Sat. a.m.; **Bibbiena** Thurs. a.m.; **Buonconvento** Sat. a.m.; **Castellina in Chianti** Sat. a.m.; **Cortona** Sat. a.m.; **Gaiole in Chianti** second Tues. p.m. of the month; **Massa Marittima** Wed. a.m.; **Montalcino** Fri. a.m.; **Montepulciano** Thurs. a.m.; **Pienza** Fri. a.m.; **Pitigliano** Wed. a.m.; **Poppi** Tues. a.m.; **Portoferraio** Fri. a.m.; **Radda in Chianti** fourth Mon. p.m. of the month.

ABBADIA SAN SALVATORE

Food

Pinzi Pinzuti Via Cavour 8, tel 0577 778 040, pinzipinzuti.it. This place is crammed with wines, grappas, olive oils, honey, jam, pasta, herbs, and other Tuscan gastronomic treats.

AREZZO

Jewelry

L'Artigiano Via XXV Aprile 22, tel 0575 351 278. A fine example of Arezzo's gold-working and jewelry tradition.

Fabrics

Busatti Corso Italia 48, tel 0575 355 295, busatti.com. Sublime cotton, linen, wool, and other fabrics, many of them handmade. Also in Cortona at Piazza della Repubblica 21, tel 0575 601 640.

Kitchenware

Morini Via Pietro Calamandrei, tel 0575 24666. This may be Tuscany's best kitchenware shop. It stocks the shelves with pans, knives, and other essentials, but also fine china, crystal, and pieces by some of the country's leading designers.

CAMALDOLI

Crafts & Gifts

Antica Farmacia Eremo di Camaldoli, tel 0575 556 143. An old pharmacy that still has its original 1543 walnut paneling and sells herbal products, toiletries, honeys, and jams, many made by the monks of the Camaldoli Eremo, or monastery.

CHIANTI

Wine

Enoteca del Chianti Classico Piazzetta Santa Croce 8, Greve in Chianti, tel 055 853 297, www .chianticlassico.it. A useful store that stocks wines by the Chianti Classico Gallo Nero consortium. Also other wines, olive oils, and vinegar.

CORTONA

Crafts & Gifts

L'Etruria Piazza Luca Signorelli 21, tel 0575 62575. The best place in Cortona for terra-cotta tableware and other ceramics.

Food

Enoteca Enotria Via Nazionale 81, tel 0575 603595, closed Tues., cortonawineshop.com. Drink or buy wine, along with meats, hams, and cheese. **Ristori** Via Santa Margherita 9, tel 0575 159 6212. Top-quality produce from around Cortona.

MONTALCINO

Wine

Fattoria dei Barbi Fattoria del Barbi del Casato, La Croce, 5 miles (8 km) southeast of Montalcino, tel 0577 841 111,

fattoriadeibarbi.com. Most small Brunello vineyards are open by appointment only (details from the visitor center, see p. 268), but not this lovely *fattoria* (estate). You can tour the cellars and buy products made on the estate (tours at noon & 3 p.m. daily, Mon.–Fri.; sales & tasting 10 a.m.–1 p.m. Mon.–Fri.; also 2:30 p.m.–5:30 p.m. Sat.–Sun. April–mid-Nov.).
Fiaschetteria Italiana Piazza del Popolo 6, tel 0577 849 043, caffefiaschetteriaitaliana.com. The co-op supermarket off Via Sant'Antonio has a good selection of Brunello and Rosso di Montal-cino wines at the best prices, but this bar is a far prettier place to sample and buy wine.

MONTEPULCIANO

Food

Cugusi Via della Boccia 8, tel 0578 757 558, caseificiocugusi.it. Local cheeses made on this farm just outside Montepulciano by Silvana Cugusi.
Il Frantoio Via di Martiena 2, tel 0578 758 732, madeinmonte pulciano.it. This is the olive mill for a co-operative of 650 local growers. Oils can be bought direct from the mill or with other local products from the store in the town at Piazza Grande 7.

Wine

Contucci Via del Teatro 1, tel 0578 757 006, contucci.it. This is the most central of several direct-sale single estate outlets for Montepulciano's esteemed Vino Nobile red wine. Also try the estate store outlets of **Avignonesi** (*tel 0578 724 304, avignonesi.it),* **Fattoria del Cerro** (*tel 0578 767 700, saiagricola.it),* and **Poliziano** (*tel 0578 738 171, carlettipoliziano.com).*

Enoteca del Consorzio del Vino Mobile di Monteulciano Piazza Grande 7, tel 0578 757 812, open Mon.–Sat. 1 p.m.–5 p.m., April–Nov. The wine store of the local producers' association. It sells wine by most leading Vino Nobile producers, as well as Chi-anti, Brunello, and other superior Tuscan vintages.

PIENZA

Food

La Cornucopia Piazza Martiri della Libertà 2–3, tel 0578 748 491. Pienza is renowned for its Pecorino, or sheep's cheese, and the village is full of stores selling this and other local foods. Much of the cheese is brought in from elsewhere, however, so be sure to read labels carefully. Buy from this excellent store, or visit small local producers.

Entertainment & Activities

Florence and Tuscany offer a wide range of cultural and other entertainment, from world-class orchestras, opera performances, and music festivals to horseback riding, hiking, and art history or Italian language courses. Local visitor centers carry full details of forthcoming festivals and cultural events, plus contact information for other activities, such as rural horseback riding. They will also help with currently hot nightclubs and live music venues.

▓ FLORENCE

For information contact visitor centers in Florence (see p. 58), or consult the listings section of the local *La Nazione* newspaper *(lanazione.com)* and monthly *Firenze Spettacolo (firenzespettacolo.it)*, available from bookstores such as Feltrinelli (see p. 322).

Tickets for events can be obtained from individual box offices or through Box Office *(boxofficetoscana.it)*.

Art & Language Courses

British Institute Piazza Strozzi 2, tel 055 267 781, britishinstitute .it. The long-established British Institute has short courses in Italian, art history, drawing, and cooking.

Dante Alighieri Piazza della Repubblica 5, tel 055 210 808. Offers Italian language courses for varying levels of expertise. Also opera and literature courses. See sidebar p. 20.

Florence Academy of Art Via delle Casine 21r, tel 055 245 444, florenceacademyofart.com. Summer art classes and life-drawing classes.

L'Instituto per L'Arte e Il Restauro Palazzo Spinelli, Borgo Santa Croce 10, tel 055 246 001, palazzospinelli.org. One of Italy's leading restoration schools, with courses on the restoration of frescoes, paper, furniture, ceramics, paintings, and glass. Courses last 1–3 years, but you can also take monthlong courses in summer.

Cinema

Florence has no shortage of cinemas, but most show movies dubbed into Italian. The **Odeon Cinehall** *(Piazza Strozzi, tel 055 214 068, cinehall.it)* and **Fulgor** *(Via Maso Finiguerra 24r, tel 055 2381 881)* occasionally show original language *(lingua originale)* movies.

Festivals & Events

Sfilata dei Canottieri Regatta of traditional boats on the River Arno on New Year's Day. *(Jan. 1)*

Diladdarno Music, exhibitions, and street events celebrating the history of the Oltrarno. *(events throughout the year, diladdarno.it)*

Scoppio del Carro The "Explosion of the Cart" ends Florence's Easter Sunday ceremonies. A cart of flowers and fireworks is ignited at noon by a mechanical dove that "flies" along a wire from the Duomo's altar out to the piazza.

Mostra Mercato dell'Artigianato A huge fair of crafts and artisan goods such as ceramics, held at the Fortezza di Basso. *(April or May, mostraartigianato.it)*

Maggio Musicale Tuscany's musical festival *(May–June; see sidebar p. 151)*.

Festa di San Giovanni The feast of St. John the Baptist *(June 24)*, one of Florence's patron saints, is marked by a holiday and "I Fochi di San Giovanni" parade and fireworks in Piazzale Michelangelo.

Calcio Storico Three fast and violent games are played in this famous soccer match, the first on the day after the feast of St. John. Huge teams play in 16th-century dress. Piazza Santa Croce or Piazza della Signoria. *(Last week of June; see sidebar p. 17 & p. 21)*

Festa delle Rificolone The Virgin's birthday is celebrated by a procession of children bearing lanterns to Piazza della Santissima Annunziata *(Sept. 7)*.

Performing Arts

Amici della Musica Tel 055 609 012, amicimusica.fi.it. Organizes a season of chamber concerts *(Jan.– April & Oct.–Dec.)*, mostly in 17th-century auditorium of Teatro della Pergola *(Via della Pergola 18, tel 055 22641, box office 055 076 3333, teatrodellapergola.com)*.

Estate Fiesolana Venues around Fiesole *(box office Via Portigianni 3, Fiesole, tel 055 596 1293, estatefiesolana.it)*. A major classical music and performing arts music festival held in Fiesole, usually June–Sept.

Maggio Musicale Fiorentino Venues around Florence. Maggio Musicale *(late April–early July; tel 055 277 9350, maggiofiorentino .com)* is one of Italy's leading music festivals. It has its own orchestra and ballet, but also has concerts by international performers. Tickets from the Teatro Comunale (see below).

Orchestra Regionale Toscana Via Verdi 5, tel 055 234 0710 or 2722, orchestradellatoscana.it. Tuscany's main regional orchestra is based in Florence, where it gives one or two concerts monthly in the season (Dec.– May). Performances are usually in Teatro Verdi *(Via Ghibellina 99–101, box office tel 055 212 320, teatroverdionline.it)*.

Teatro Comunale Corso Italia 16, tel 055 27 791 or 055 277 9236, maggiofiorentino.it. This is the main city theater. It has its own chorus, orchestra (L'Orchestra del Maggio Musicale Fiorentino), and ballet (Maggio Danza).

Nightlife

L'Art Bar Via del Moro 4r, tel 055 287 661. A cozy bar that makes a good place for cocktails or nightcaps.

Dolce Vita Piazza del Carmine, tel 055 284 595, dolcevitaflorence .com. The Dolce Vita bar has been a fixture of Florentine nightlife for years, retaining its appeal through frequent decorative makeovers.

Jazz Club Via Nuova de Cacciani 3, tel 339 498 0752. Florence's foremost jazz club has a sophisticated audience that takes music seriously. Live music in a variety of jazz styles most nights. Closed Sun.–Mon.

Rex Via Fiesolana 25r, tel 055 248 0331. Rex is a friendly bar north of Santa Croce, which comes into its own at night.

Space Electronic Via Palazzuolo 37, tel 055 293 082, spaceclub firenze.com. Space Electronic has been around for years, but that hasn't dulled its appeal as a club and dance venue. Big and brash. Closed Mon. in winter.

Sports & Activities

Golf

The nearest course to Florence is south of the city at Grassina. **Circuito Golf Ugolino** Strada Chiantigiana 3, tel 055 230 1009, golfugolino.it, federgolf.it.

Gyms

These Florence gyms offer day rates: **Gymnasium Asd** Palestra, Via Palazzuolo 49r, tel 055 265 4213; **Ricciardi** Borgo Pinti 75, tel 055 247 8444, palestraricciardi.it; **Gym and Tonic** Via del Leone 10r, tel 055 280 524.

Soccer

Fiorentina, Florence's soccer team, plays at Stadio Artemio Franchi (en.violachannel.tv) during the season (Aug.–May). Tickets sell out fast (see sidebar p. 36).

Swimming

Public pools in Florence include **Il Poggetto** (outdoor, June–Sept.; Via Michele Mercati 24b, tel 055 477 978, flog.it) and **I Piscina di Bellariva** (Nov.–March; Lungarno Aldo Moro 6, tel 055 677 521, fiorentinanuoto.net).

▉ TUSCANY

Activities

Hiking

Visitor centers in Arezzo (for Casentino National Park) and elsewhere often have pamphlets detailing marked trails and hiking itineraries.

Many companies organize hiking vacations, either guided group or self-guided hikes. A long-established company for both types is the Oxford, U.K.–based ATG (tel 0044 1865 315 678 from North America, atg-oxford.co.uk).

Horseback Riding

For horseback riding holidays in Tuscany contact **In the Saddle** (tel 0044 1299 272 997 from North America, inthesaddle.com) or **Equitour** (tel 800/545-0019 in North America, equitours.com).

Festivals

You may wish to plan your trip around some of Tuscany's larger events, but tickets and hotels sell out early. Virtually every village finds an excuse to put on a show. Most smaller events follow a similar pattern: a procession, often in traditional costume, followed by a special church service, fireworks, marching bands, and lots of eating and drinking. Watch for fliers advertising a festa or sagra. Check

visitor centers for details.

The selection of major events below is listed chronologically.
Carnivale Viareggio holds Italy's most lavish Carnevale (Carnival) celebrations outside Venice. Most towns have some sort of Carnivale festival or procession. (Feb. or early March)
Festa di San Ranieri Pisa. Candlelit processions, followed the next day by a rowing regatta in medieval dress (June 16–17).
Gioco del Ponte Pisa. The "Game of the Bridge" is a tug-of-war in medieval costume held on Pisa's Ponte di Mezzo. (last Sun. in June)
Festival di San Gimignano Opera, classical music, and arts festival. (late June–Oct., tel 0577 940 008, sangimignano.com)
Il Palio Siena (July 2 & Aug. 16; see pp. 200–201)
Puccini Opera Festival Torre del Lago. Well-known festival of Puccini operas held near Viareggio. (Aug., tel 0584 359 322 or 0584 350 567, puccinifestival.it)
Accademia Musicale Chigiana Siena. The town's leading musical association (tel 0577 22 091, chigiana.it) organizes concerts throughout much of the year.
Barga Opera Festival A concert series (tel 0583 723 250, operabarga.it) held in a pretty town north of Lucca. The Barga jazz festival (bargajazzfestival.wix .com) is popular. (July–mid-Aug.)
Bravio delle Botti Montepulciano. A barrel-rolling contest, medieval drumming, and flag throwing (last Sun. of Aug., braviodellebotti.com).
Giostra del Saracino Arezzo. Jousting knights and other events in medieval costume. Twice yearly. (Sun. in mid-June & first Sun. of Sept., giostradelsaracino.arezzo.it)
Luminara di Santa Croce Lucca. Torchlit procession bearing the Volto Santo around the streets. (Sept. 14., comune.lucca.it).

Language Guide & Menu Reader

Italians respond well to foreigners who make an effort to speak their language. Many Italians speak at least some English, and most upscale hotels and restaurants have multilingual staff. All Italian words are pronounced as written, with each vowel and consonant sounded. The letter c is hard, as in the English "cat," except when followed by i or e, when it becomes the soft ch of "children." The same applies to g when followed by i or e—soft in giardino (as in the English "giant"); hard in gatto, as in "gate."

yes *sì*
no *no*
OK *d'accordo*
OK/that's fine/sure *Va bene*
I don't understand *Non capisco*
Do you speak English? *Parla inglese?*
I don't know *Non lo so*
I would like *Vorrei*
Do you have ...? *Avete ...?*
How much is it? *Quant'è?*
What is it? *Che cos'è?*
Who? *Chi?*
What? *Quale?*
Why? *Perchè?*
When? *Quando?*
Where? *Dove?*
Where is/where are? *Dov'è/dove sono?*
Where is the restroom? *Dovè il bagno?*
left/right *sinistra/destra*
straight on *sempre dritto*

Good morning *Buon giorno*
Good afternoon/good evening *Buona sera*
Good night *Buona notte*
Hello/goodbye (informal) *Ciao*
Hello (answering the telephone) *Pronto*
Goodbye *Arrivederci*
please *per favore*
thank you (very much) *grazie (mille)*
You're welcome *Prego*
What's your name? *Come si chiama?*
My name is... *Mi chiamo...*
I'm American (man) *Sono Americano*
I'm American (woman) *Sono Americana*
Mr./Sir *Signore*
Mrs./Ma'am *Signora*
Miss *Signorina*

How are you? *Come sta?*
Fine, thanks *Bene, grazie*
And you? *E lei?*
I'm sorry *Mi dispiace*
Excuse me/I beg your pardon *Mi scusi*
Excuse me (in a crowd) *Permesso*
Have a good day *Buona giornata*
No problem *Non c'è problema*

good/bad *buono/cattivo*
big/small *grande/piccolo*
with/without *con/senza*
more/less *più/meno*
enough *basta*
near/far *vicino/lontano*
hot/cold *caldo/freddo*
early/late *presto/ritardo*
straight away *subito*
here/there *qui/là*
now/later *adesso/più tardi*
today/tomorrow *oggi/domani*
yesterday *Ieri*
morning *la mattina*
afternoon *il pomeriggio*
evening *la sera*
entrance/exit *entrata/uscita*
open/closed *aperto/chiuso*
free (of charge) *gratuito*
free (unoccupied) *libero*
bathroom/toilet *il bagno/il gabinetto*
stamp *un francobollo*
postcard *una cartolina*
visitor center *l'uffico di turismo*

Help! *Aiuto!*
Stop! *Alt!/fermate!*
Look out! *Attenzione!*
Can you help me? *Mi puo aiutare?*
I'm not well *Sto male*
doctor *un medico*
Where is the police station? *Dov'è la polizia/la questura?*
hospital *l'ospedale*

road map *una carta stradale*
ticket *un biglietto*
train *un treno*
Let's go *Andiamo*

Menu Reader

Pasta & Sauces
agnolotti large filled pasta parcels
al pomodoro tomato sauce
amatriciana with tomato and bacon
arrabbiata spicy chili tomato sauce
bolognese veal or beef sauce
burro with butter
burro e salvia with sage and butter
cannelloni filled pasta tubes
carbonara with cream, ham, and egg
farfalle butterfly-shaped pasta
gnocchi potato dough dumplings
pasta e fagioli pasta and beans
peperoncino with oil, garlic, and chili
puttanesca with tomato, anchovy, oil, and oregano
ragù any meat sauce
vongole with wine, clams, and parsley

Meats
agnello lamb
anatra duck
bistecca beef steak
carpaccio thin slices of raw beef
cinghiale wild boar
coniglio rabbit
fagiano pheasant
fegatini chicken liver
fegato liver
fritto misto mixed grill
involtini rolled and stuffed meat slices
lepre hare
maiale pork

manzo beef
pancetta pork belly/bacon
pollo chicken
polpette meatballs
salsiccia sausage
tacchino turkey
vitello veal

Fish & Seafood
acciughe anchovies
calamari squid
capesante scallops
cozze mussels
gamberetti shrimps
gamberi prawns
granchio crab
merluzzo cod
ostriche oysters
pesce spada swordfish
polpo octopus
salmone salmon
sarde sardines
seppie cuttlefish
sgombro mackerel
sogliola sole
tonno tuna
vongole clams

Vegetables & Herbs
aglio garlic
carciofi artichokes
cavolo cabbage
cetriolo cucumber
cipolle onions
fagioli beans
finocchio fennel
funghi mushrooms
insalata salad
melanzane egg plant
patate fritte french fries
piselli peas
pomodoro tomato
rucolo/rughetta rocket

Fruit
albicocca apricot
ananas pineapple
arancia orange
ciliegie cherries
cocomero watermelon
ficchi figs
fragole strawberries
mela apple

melone melon
pera pear
pesca peach
pompelmo grapefruit
prugna plum
uva grapes

Drinks
acqua water
acqua minerale mineral water
una birra beer
una bottiglia bottle
caffè coffee
caffè Hag/caffè decaffeinato decaffeinated coffee
cioccolata calda hot chocolate
ghiaccio ice
latte milk
mezza bottiglia half-bottle
secco/dolce dry/sweet
una spremuta fresh fruit juice
spumante sparkling wine
un succo di frutta bottled juice
tè tea
vino della casa house wine

Useful Words & Phrases
breakfast la colazione
lunch il pranzo
dinner la cena
waiter il cameriere
menu il menù/la lista
tourist menu menù turistico
tasting menu menù degustazione
wine list la lista dei vini
knife un coltello
fork una forchetta
spoon un cucchiaio
bread pane (brown: integrale)
bread roll panino
butter burro
oil olio
vinegar aceto
cream panna
meat/fish carne/pesce
seafood frutti di mare
rice riso
eggs uova
salt/pepper sale/pepe
sugar zucchero
appetizers antipasti
first courses primi
soup zuppa/minestra

main courses secondi
vegetables contorni
cheeses formaggi
puddings dolci
without meat senza carne
rare/medium (steaks) al sangue/al punto
well done ben cotto
raw/cooked crudo/cotto
cover charge coperto
service charge servizio
I'd like to reserve a table Vorrei prenotare una tavola
Have you a table for two? Avete una tavola per due?
I'd like to order Vorrei ordinare
I'm a vegetarian Sono vegetariano/a
It's good È buono
The check, please Il conto, per favore
Is service included? Il servizio è incluso?
At a hotel a room una camera
with private bathroom con bagno
Do you have rooms free? Avete camere libere?
I have a reservation Ho una prenotazione
elevator ascensore
key la chiave

INDEX

Bold page numbers indicate illustrations.
CAPS indicates thematic categories.

ILLUSTRATIONS CREDITS

Abbreviations for terms appearing below: (t) top; (b) bottom; (l) left; (r) right; (c) center.

All photographs by Tino Soriano, unless otherwise noted:

Cover, SIME/eStock Photo; 11, Matt Propert/National Geographic Creative; 25, Bill McBee; 26-7, kasta2008/iStockphoto; 28, Gold florin (obverse) with a fleur de lys, Florentine, 1252 (for reverse see 83494), Italian School, (13th century) / Museo Nazionale del Bargello, Florence, Italy / The Bridgeman Art Library; 30-1, Scala/Art Resource, NY; 32, *The Journey of the Magi to Bethlehem*, the right hand wall of the chapel, c.1460 (fresco), Gozzoli, Benozzo di Lese di Sandro (1420-97)/Palazzo Medici-Riccardi, Florence, Italy / Bridgeman Images; 35, US Army Signal Corps; 36-7, Aflo Co. Ltd./Alamy; 60-1, Maltings Partnership, Derby, England; 66, Scala/Art Resource, NY; 67, Maltings Partnership, Derby, England; 83, David, c.1440 (bronze), Donatello, (c.1386-1466)/Museo Nazionale del Bargello, Florence, Italy/The Bridgeman Art Library; 96, Scala/Art Resource, NY; 99, Scala/Art Resource, NY; 110-1, Maltings Partnership, Derby,

England; 131, Scala/Art Resource, NY; 133, Scala/Art Resource, NY; 134, John Kernick/ National Geographic Creative; 137, Maltings Partnership, Derby, England; 141, Scala/Art Resource, NY; 152-3, Maltings Partnership, Derby, England; 160, Alinari Archives/Corbis; 161, Holly LaPratt/National Geographic Society; 165, Matt Propert/National Geographic Creative; 171, Scala/Art Resource, NY; 172, Scala/Art Resource, NY; 174-5 Maltings Partnership, Derby, England; 176, Scala/Art Resource, NY; 178 (UPLE), *Adam and Eve banished from Paradise*, c.1427 (fresco) (post restoration) (see also 200134 & 428037), Masaccio, Tommaso (1401-28)/ Brancacci Chapel, Santa Maria del Carmine, Florence, Italy/Bridgeman Images; 178 (UP CTR & UPRT), Scala/Art Resource, NY; 178 (All LO), Scala/ Art Resource, NY; 179 (All), Scala/Art Resource, NY; 206, gallimaufry/Shutterstock; 208, Renata Sedmakova/Shutterstock.com; 212, Scala/Art Resource, NY; 214, Scala/Art Resource, NY; 217, Combusken/Wikipedia; 248-9, Maltings Partnership, Derby, England; 266, CuboImages srl/Alamy; 274, Leadinglights/iStockphoto.com; 286 (All), Scala/Art Resource, NY; 287 (All), Scala/Art Resource, NY.

National Geographic
TRAVELER
Florence & Tuscany
Tim Jepson

Published by the National Geographic Society
Gary E. Knell, *President and Chief Executive Officer*
John M. Fahey, *Chairman of the Board*
Declan Moore, *Chief Media Officer*
Chris Johns, *Chief Content Officer*
Keith Bellows, *Senior Vice President and Editor in Chief,
 National Geographic Travel Media*

Prepared by the Book Division
Hector Sierra, *Senior Vice President and General Manager*
Janet Goldstein, *Senior Vice President and
 Editorial Director*
Jonathan Halling, *Creative Director*
Marianne R. Koszorus, *Design Director*
Barbara A. Noe, *Senior Editor*
R. Gary Colbert, *Production Director*
Jennifer A. Thornton, *Director of Managing Editorial*
Susan S. Blair, *Director of Photography*
Meredith C. Wilcox, *Director, Administration and
 Rights Clearance*

Staff for This Book
Justin Kavanagh, *Project Editor*
Elisa Gibson, *Art Director*
Kay Kobor Hankins, *Designer and Photo Editor*
Carl Mehler, *Director of Maps*
Mike McNey & Mapping Specialists, *Map Production*
Marshall Kiker, *Associate Managing Editor*
Michael O'Connor, *Production Editor*
Galen Young, *Rights Clearance Specialist*
Katie Olsen, *Design Production Specialist*
Nicole Miller, *Design Production Assistant*
Robert L. Barr, *Manager, Production Services*
Marlena Serviss, *Contributor*

Map illustrations drawn by Chris Orr Associates,
 Southampton, England.
Cutaway illustrations drawn by Maltings Partnership,
 Derby, England.

The information in this book has been carefully
checked and to the best of our knowledge is
accurate. However, details are subject to change,
and the National Geographic Society cannot be
responsible for such changes, or for errors or omissions.
Assessments of sites, hotels, and restaurants are based
on the author's subjective opinions, which do not
necessarily reflect the publisher's opinion.

The National Geographic Society is one of the
world's largest nonprofit scientific and educational
organizations. Founded in 1888 to "increase and dif-
fuse geographic knowledge," the member-supported
Society works to inspire people to care about the planet.
Through its online community, members can get closer
to explorers and photographers, connect with other
members around the world, and help make a difference.
National Geographic reflects the world through its
magazines, television programs, films, music and radio,
books, DVDs, maps, exhibitions, live events, school
publishing programs, interactive media, and merchandise.
National Geographic magazine, the Society's official
journal, published in English and 38 local-language
editions, is read by more than 60 million people each
month. The National Geographic Channel reaches
440 million households in 171 countries in 38 languages.
National Geographic Digital Media receives more than
25 million visitors a month. National Geographic has
funded more than 10,000 scientific research, conservation, and exploration projects and supports an education
program promoting geography literacy. For more
information, visit nationalgeographic.com.

For more information, please call 1-800-NGS LINE
(647-5463) or write to the following address:

National Geographic Society
1145 17th Street N.W.
Washington, D.C. 20036-4688 U.S.A.

For information about special discounts for bulk
purchases, please contact National Geographic Books
Special Sales: ngspecsales@ngs.org

For rights or permissions inquiries, please contact
National Geographic Books Subsidiary Rights:
ngbookrights@ngs.org

National Geographic Traveler: Florence & Tuscany
(Third Edition)
ISBN: 978-1-4262-1462-2

Printed in Hong Kong
14/THK/1

NATIONAL GEOGRAPHIC TRAVELER

brazil

amsterdam

alaska

EXPLORE OUR COLLECTION

EXPEDITIONS   MAGAZINE   APPS

Like us on Facebook: Nat Geo Books

Follow us on Twitter: @NatGeoBooks

© 2014 National Geographic Society